I0763115

Sargent
THE MASTERWORKS

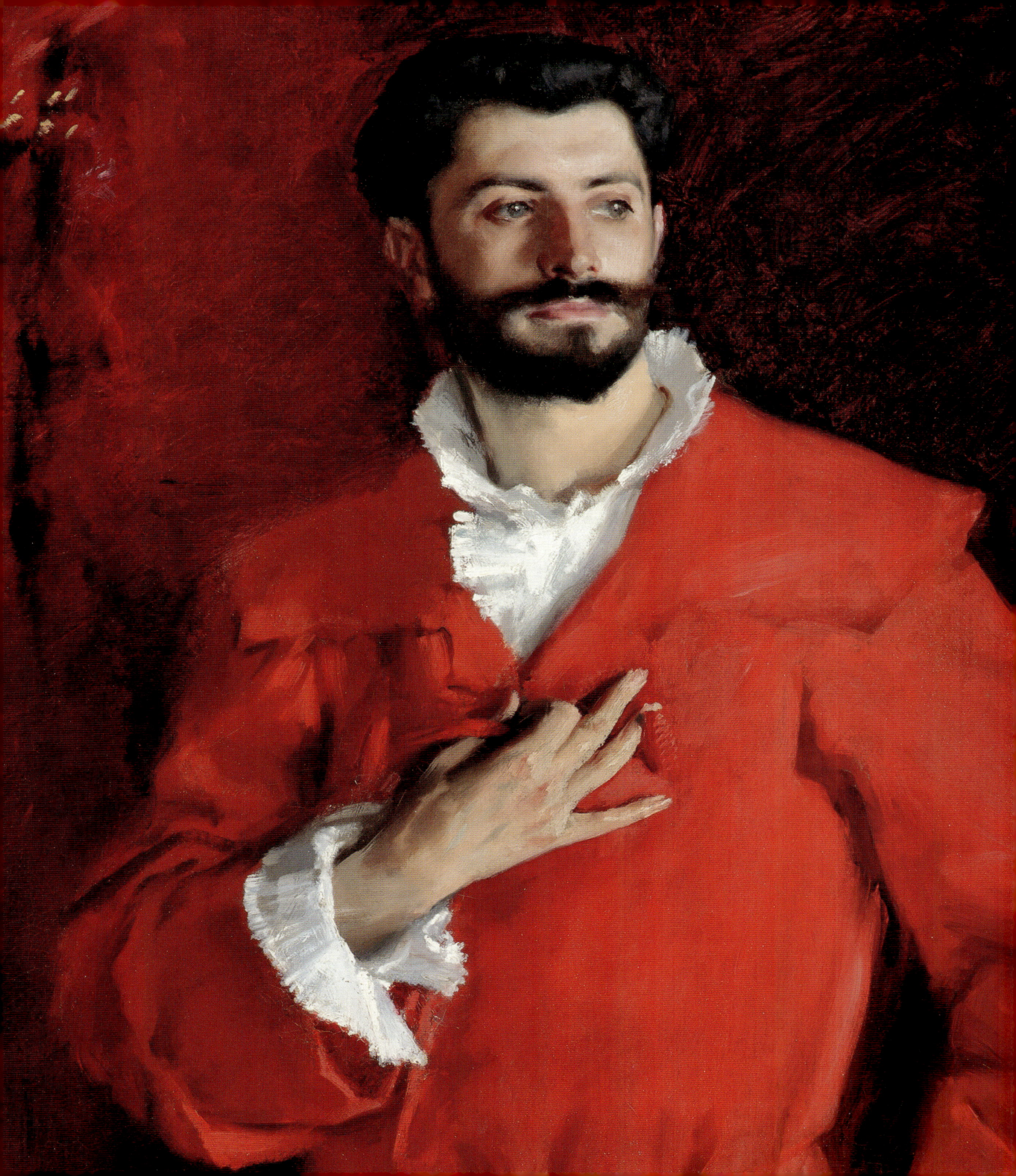

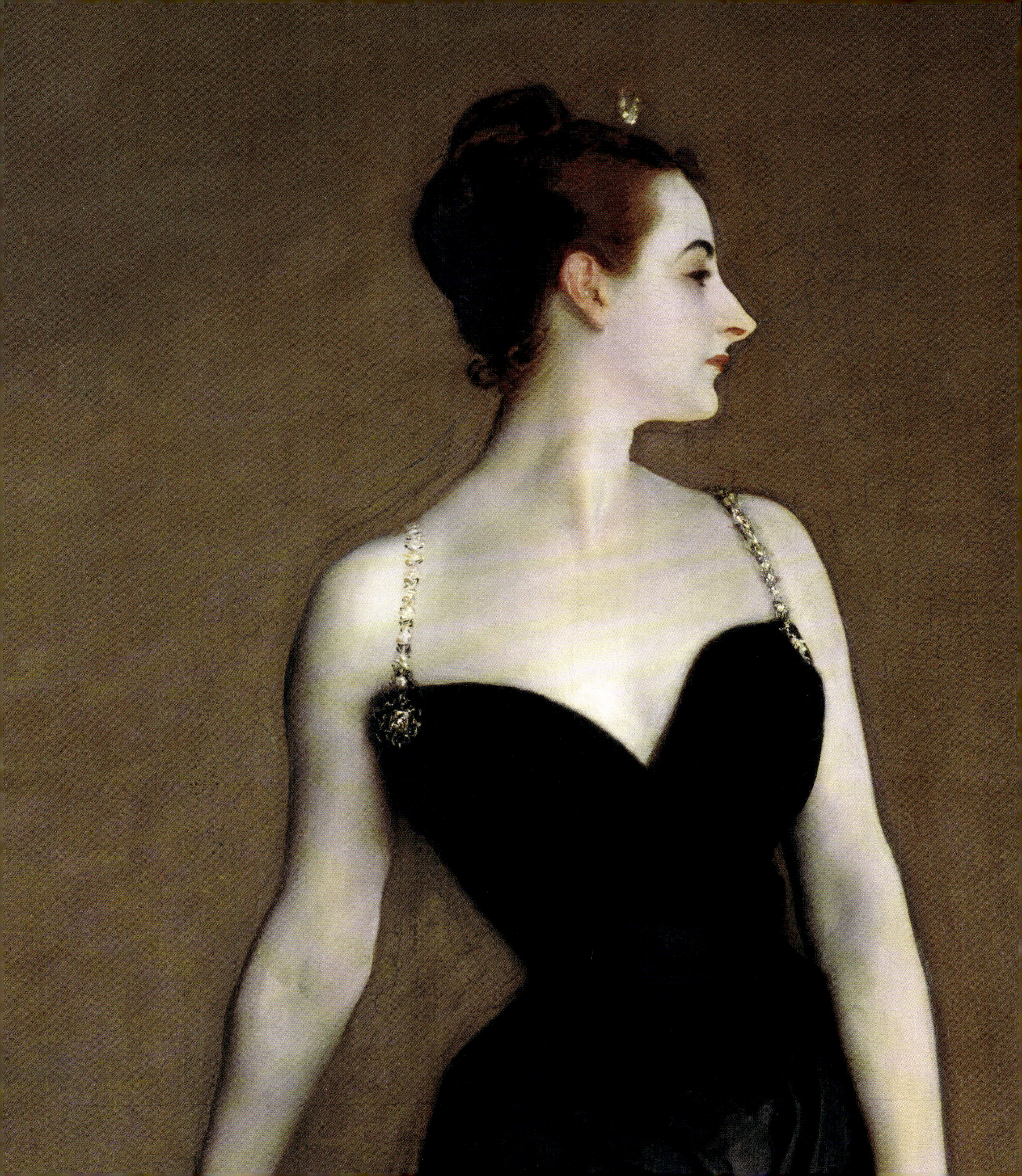

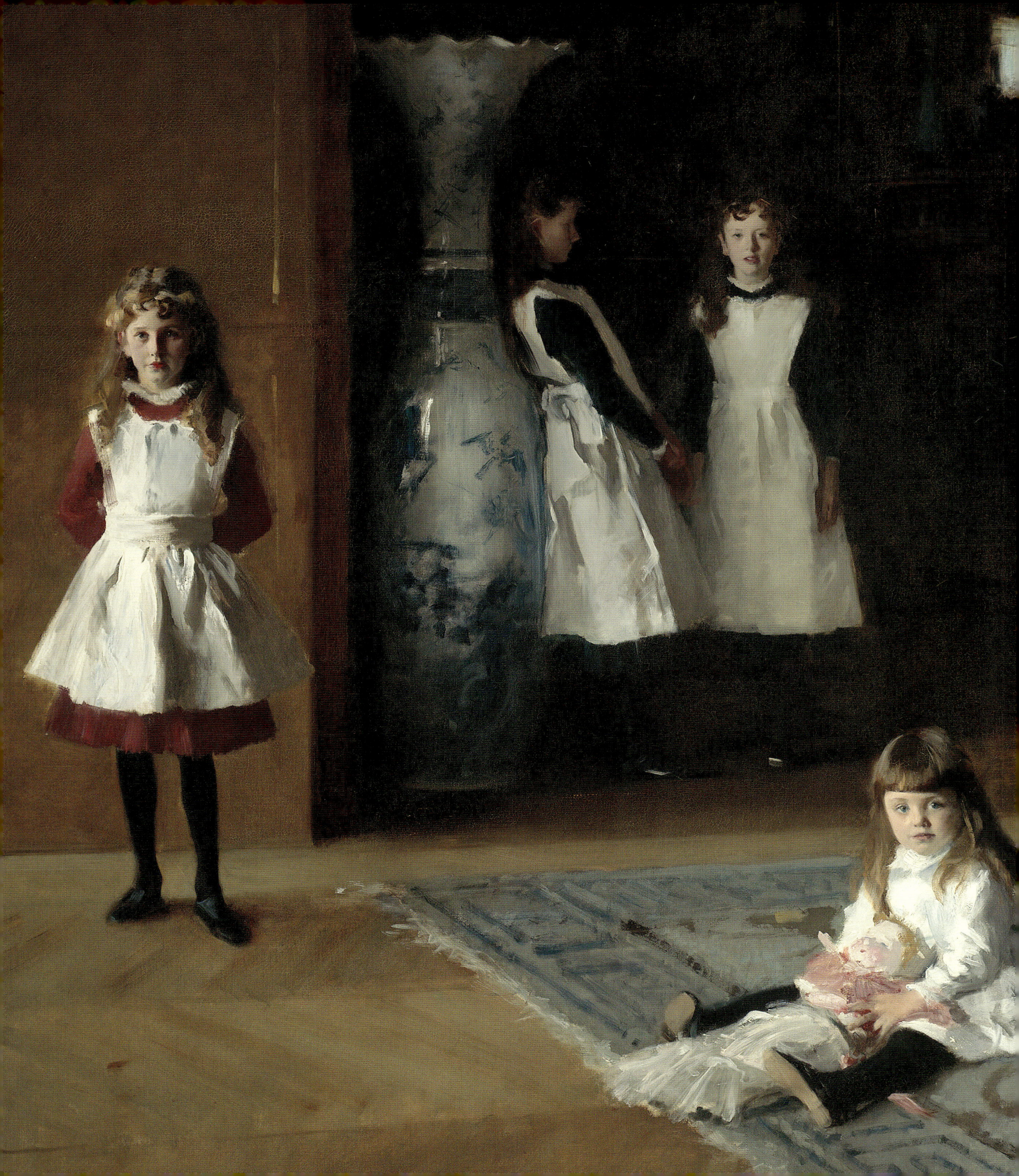

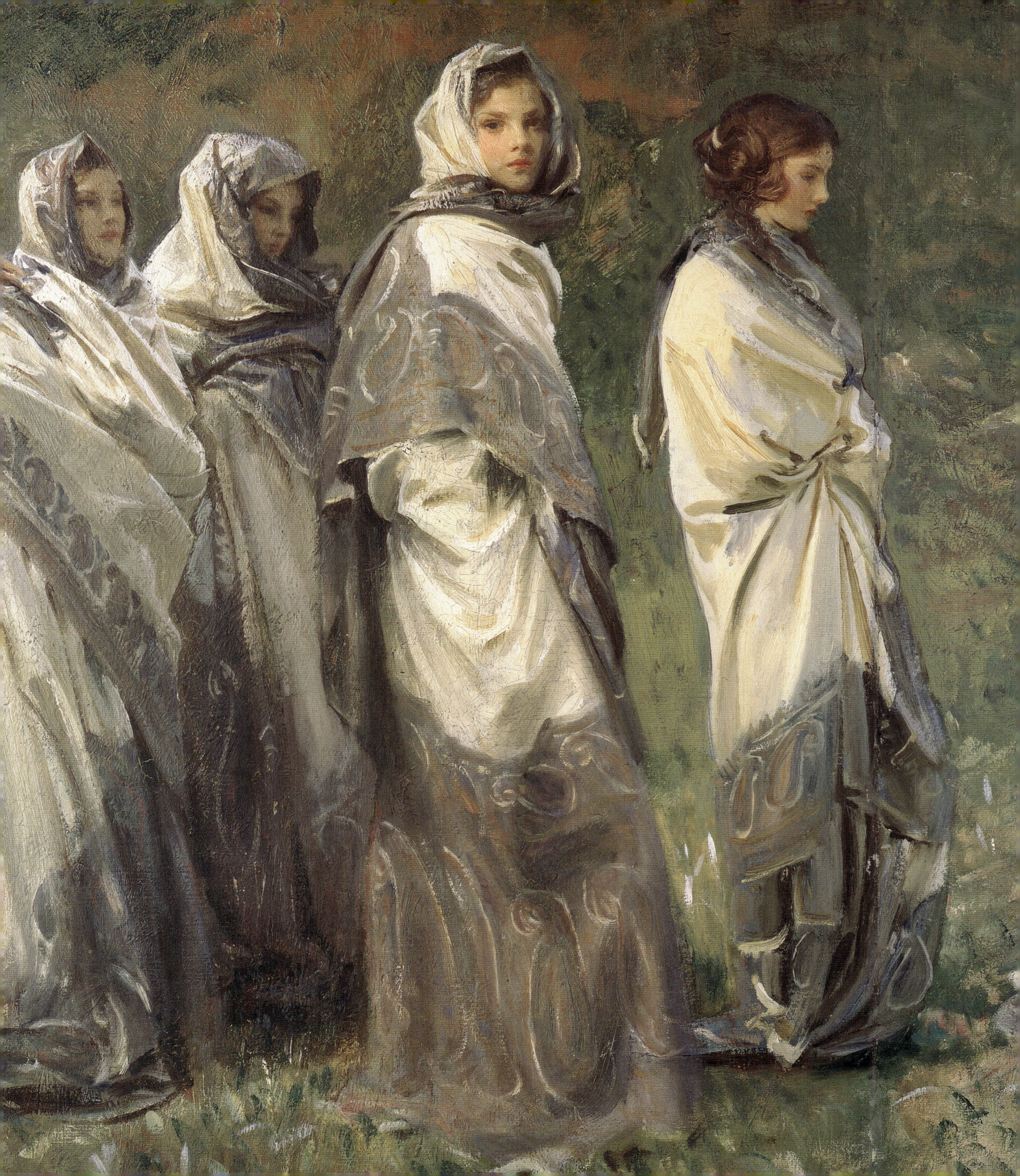

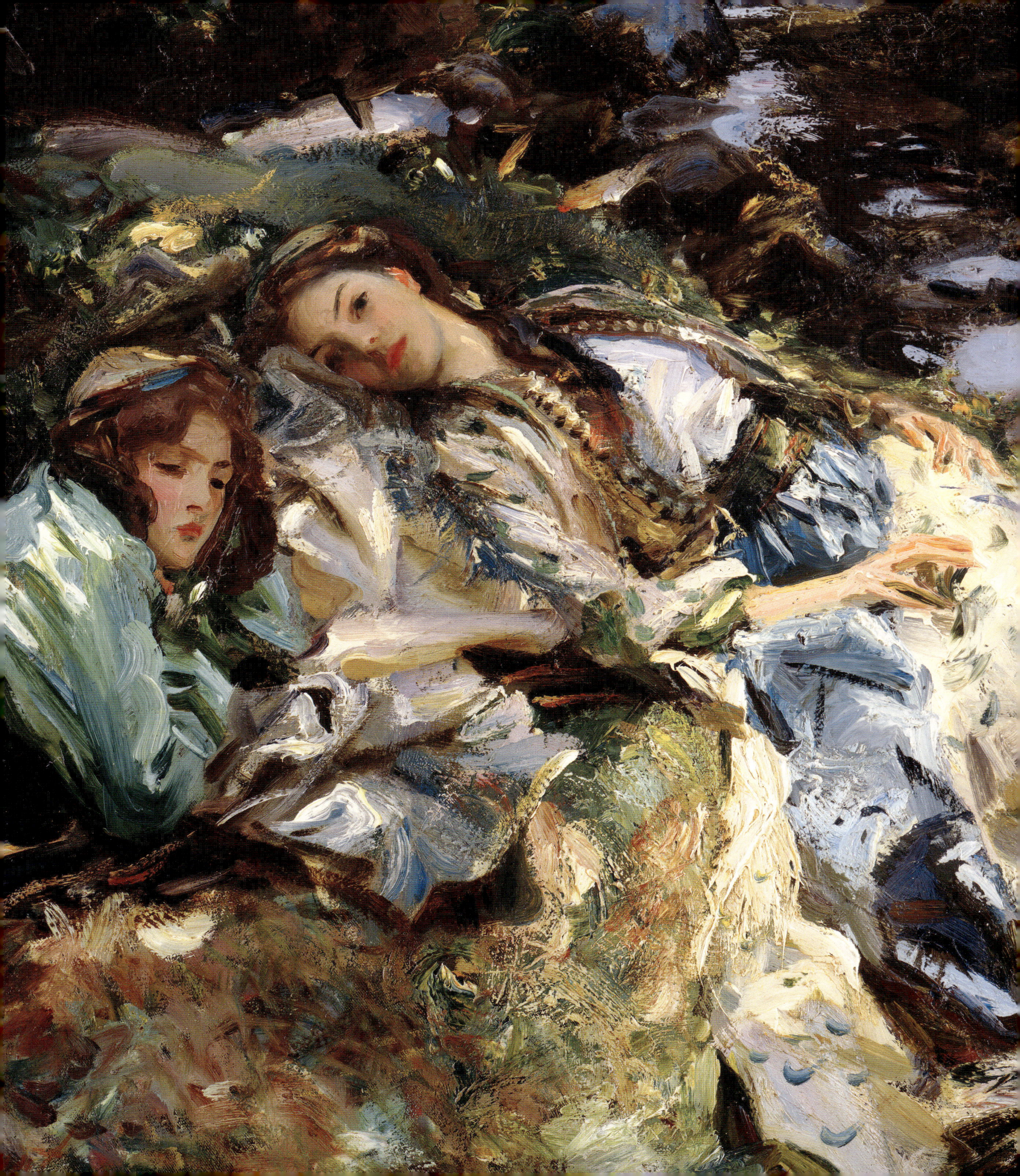

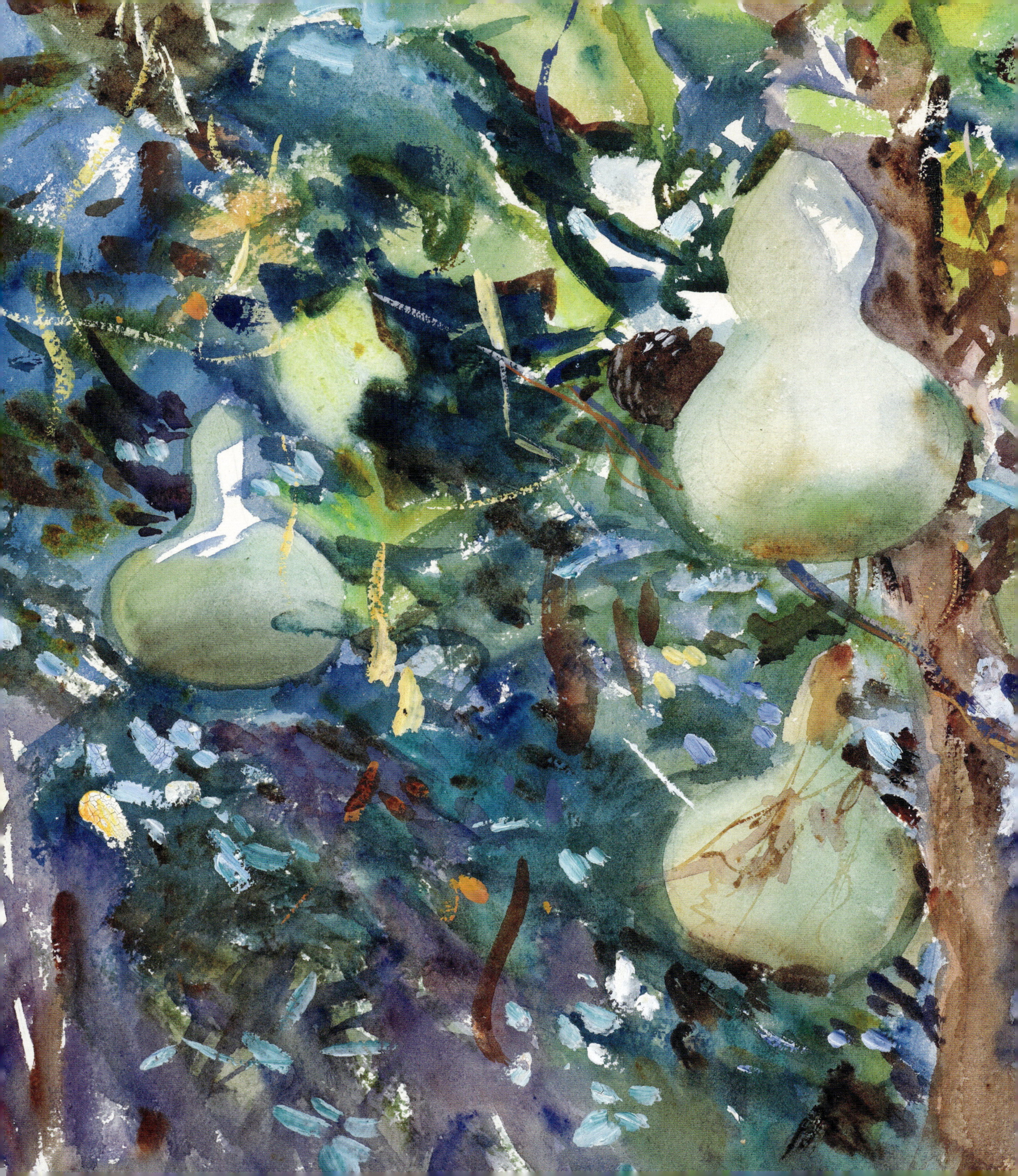

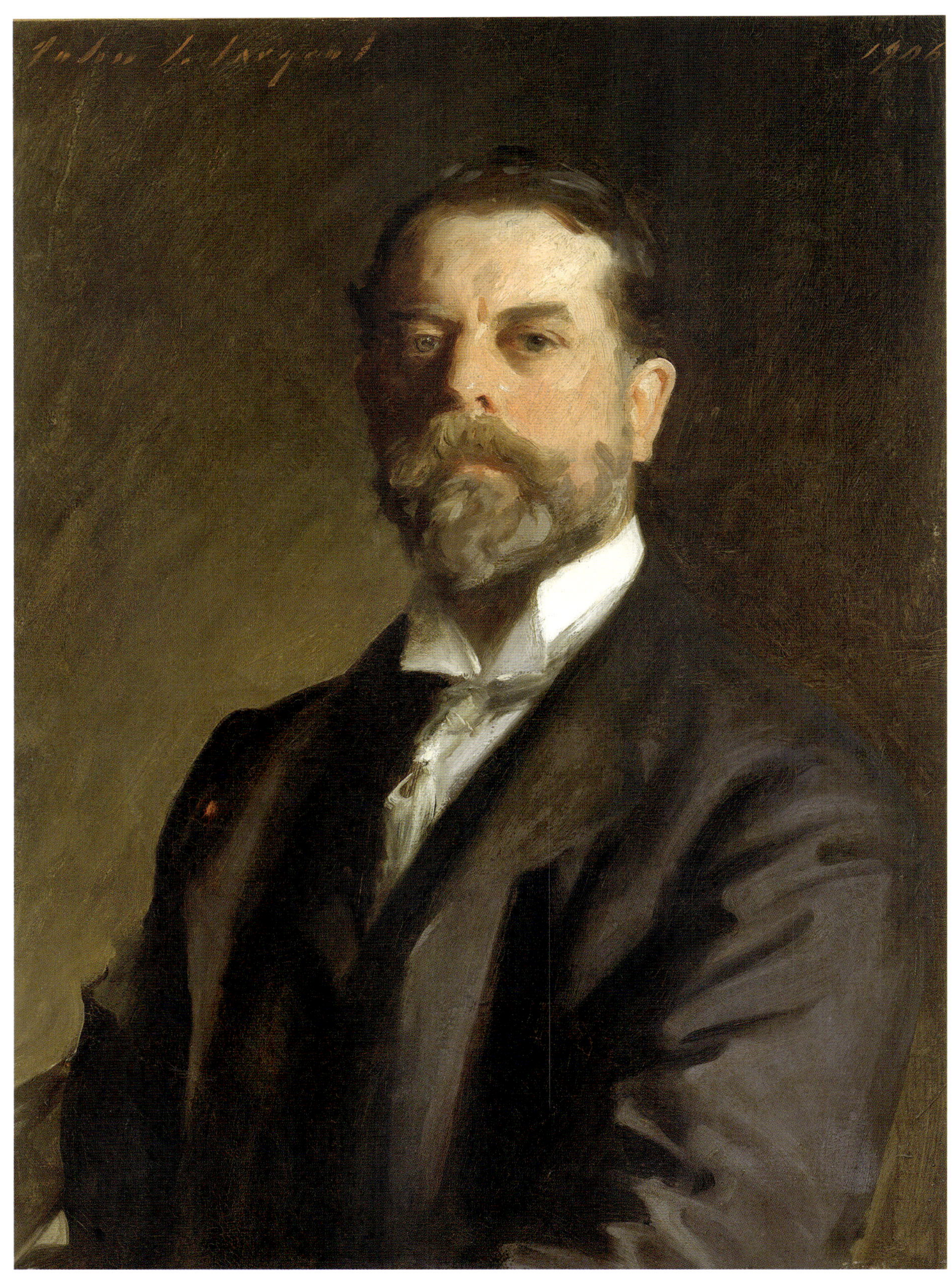

Sargent
THE MASTERWORKS

Stephanie L. Herdrich

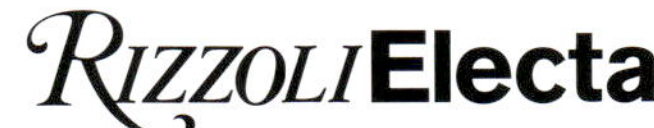

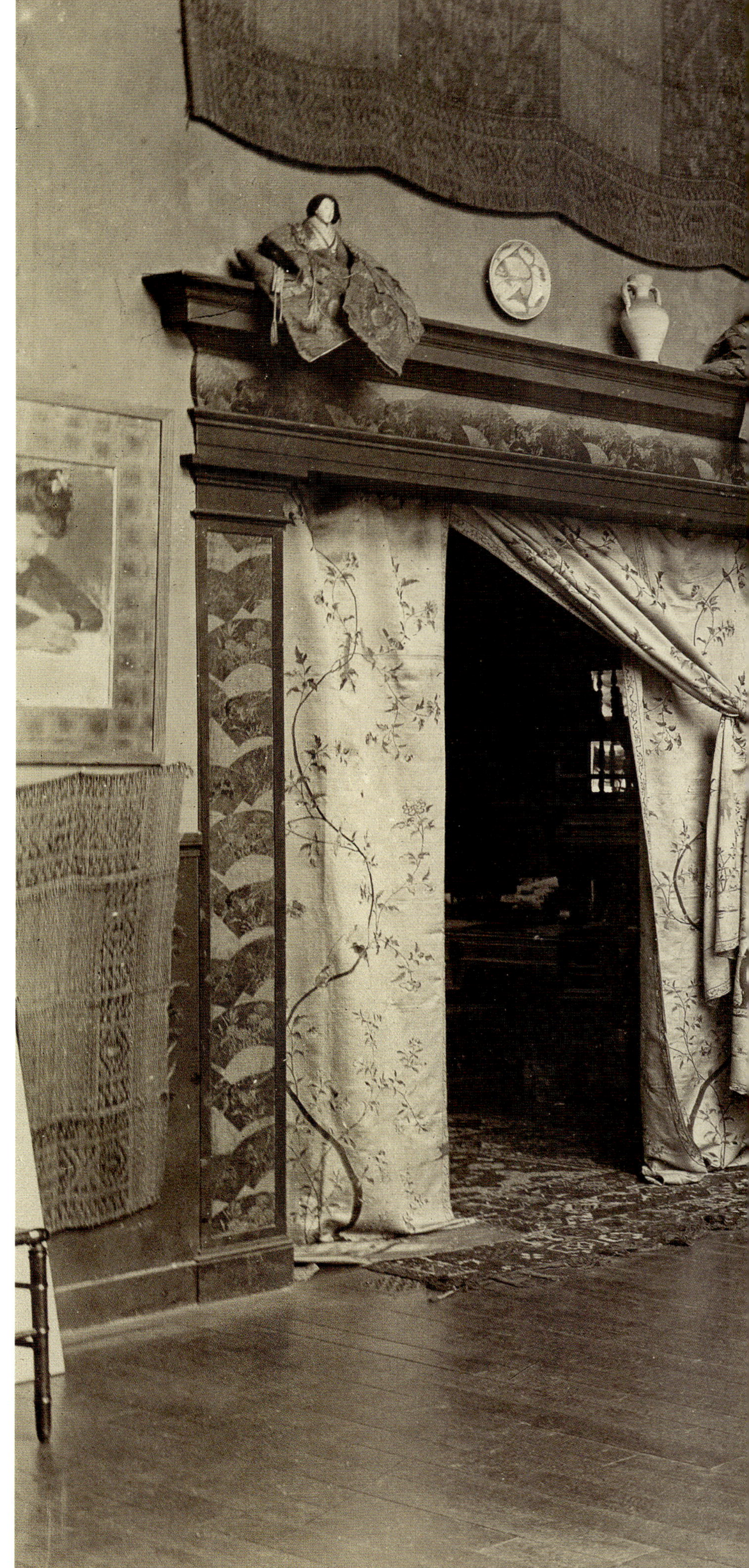

John Singer Sargent in his studio, ca. 1884. Smithsonian Institution, Archives of American Art, Washington, D.C., Photographs of artists in their Paris studios, 1880–90.

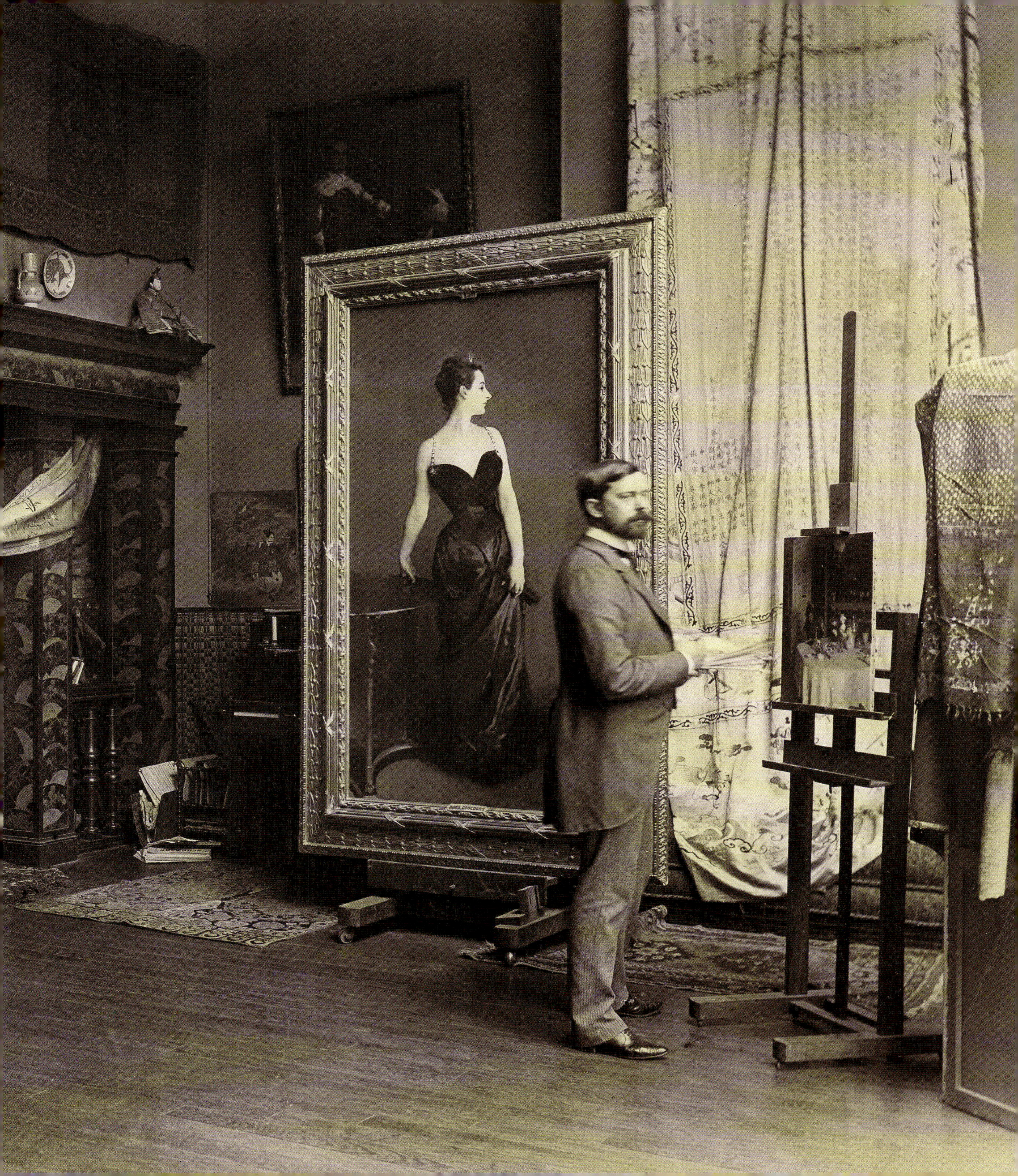

CONTENTS

Introduction

In his lifetime, John Singer Sargent (1856–1925) was celebrated as "the greatest contemporary portrait painter" of his era.[1] Critic Roger Fry noted, in 1900, that Sargent's paintings are "perfect records of the style and manners of a particular period."[2] Nearly a century after his death, his dazzling portraits remain compelling records of their time, celebrated for their skillful characterization and technical brilliance. But Sargent's extraordinarily prolific career went beyond portraiture. At the height of his celebrity—and demand—as a portraitist, he shunned commissions in favor of painting landscapes and subject pictures, in oil and watercolor, of people and places that were dear to him. These personal works were again widely celebrated by critics and sought after by public and private collectors. He devoted half of his life—from 1890 until his death—to creating monumental and ambitious murals for public institutions in the United States. When critics hailed his decorations for the Boston Public Library as an "American Sistine Chapel," Sargent earned a position in the pantheon of great artists alongside the revered Michelangelo (1475–1564). At his death in 1925, critics mourned the passing of a "Modern 'Old Master.'"[3] His obituary in the *New York Times* acknowledged the range of his oeuvre, explaining, "Although portraiture may turn out to be Mr. Sargent's most public monument, other sides of his art have at least as much to say of the nature of his gift and of his mental wealth."[4]

In his portraits, Sargent challenged traditional ideas about the genre, provoking viewers with unconventional choices of subject and style. Many of his greatest portraits, which seem so familiar to us today, were seen as progressive and deemed "eccentric" in their day. Perhaps none more so than the iconic *Madame X* (*Madame Pierre Gautreau*) [fig. 25]:

Sargent's portrayal of her scandalous character and self-fashioning still captivates the millions of visitors who come to gaze at her mysterious beauty each year at The Metropolitan Museum of Art in New York. Like many of Sargent's portraits, *Madame X* transcends individual likeness to embody the dramatically changing society in which it was painted. As early as 1887, Henry James gave a glowing appraisal of Sargent's "gift," writing:

> There is no greater work of art than a great portrait—a truth to be constantly taken to heart by a painter holding in his hands the weapon that Mr. Sargent wields. The gift that he possesses he possesses completely—the immediate perception of the end and of the means. . . . [T]he highest result is achieved when to this element of quick perception a certain faculty of lingering reflection is added.[5]

In addition to his ability for characterization, Sargent astutely responded to his patrons' aspirations in opulent portraits such as *Mrs. Carl Meyer and Her Children* [fig. 50] or *The Wyndham Sisters: Lady Elcho, Mrs. Adeane, and Mrs. Tennant* [fig. 51]. These works secured Sargent's artistic legacy and the social status of his patrons. As Sargent's friend the painter Edwin Howland Blashfield (1848–1936) declared, "[T]o have been painted by [Sargent] added distinction to the most distinguished."[6] *The New York Times* added, "No Briton or American could be regarded as quite assured of regular standing in the Hall of Fame unless he was included in Sargent's gallery of portraits."[7]

After 1900 Sargent grew weary of the demands of the portrait studio, particularly the sustained effort of pleasing difficult patrons. (He once humorously lamented, "Every time I paint a portrait, I lose a friend."[8]) In 1907 he formally declared that he would no longer accept commissions, essentially ending this successful chapter of his career. In a 1923 interview he explained:

> Years and years ago. . . . I painted portraits. I don't do them anymore; and for a long time I've been working on these [mural] panels. It is so much better. It is an artist's work. You can study on and on, and crowd your life into it. The portrait means an attack that lasts a week or a month and then it's over.[9]

Sargent devoted himself to his mural work and approached the creation of art with an eye to art history—firmly rooted in the belief that the study of the great art of the past and present was an essential component to creating a modern, personal art with, as one contemporary critic described it, "his own intense and vigorous individuality."[10] He would incorporate his passion for art history into all aspects of his work, especially his murals.

He increasingly applied his great technical virtuosity to diverse subjects that captivated him as he traveled ceaselessly to picturesque locales throughout Europe and the United States, always in search of new subjects and inspiration. He often returned to places he had traveled with his family as a child—including Venice, the Alps, and Spain—producing personal meditations about his life and the creation of art. Late in his career, he summarized his artistic philosophy when he urged students to "cultivate an ever continuous power of observation. . . . Store up in the mind without ceasing a continuous stream of observations from which to make selections later. Above all things get abroad, see the sunlight, and everything that is to be seen."[11]

Throughout his work, Sargent cultivated a fluid and bravura painting style. His technique often provokes wonder, especially among artists, for its apparent facility. His work—in watercolor and oil—epitomizes what the Italians describe as *sprezzatura*, a studied nonchalance. Sargent's expressive brushwork often belies the conscious planning and effort that he invested in his compositions. In his oil paintings, Sargent tended to avoid painting over an awkward passage or a mistake: instead, he preferred to remove the paint and begin again. According to one eyewitness, Sargent reportedly painted (and scraped away) the head of *Mrs. Hugh Hammersley* [fig. 49] sixteen times before he achieved exactly the vivacious effect he desired.

The surfaces of his oil paintings, in particular, are characterized by his expressive and sensuous brushwork. Up close, quick dabs, calligraphic swirls, and bold dashes of pigment appear almost abstract but seem to materialize into whatever Sargent was painting: the pattern of a brocade fabric on a settee, a string of pearls, or a silver teapot. Painter Julie Heyneman (1866–1942) described the seemingly contradictory characteristics of fluidity and precision in his technique:

> He put out enough paint so it seemed for a dozen pictures. . . . "The thicker you paint, the more your colour flows" he explained. . . . From the moment that he began really to paint, he worked with a kind of concentrated deliberation, a slow haste so to speak holding his brush poised in the air for an instant and then putting it just where and how he intended it to fall.[12]

After 1900, Sargent embraced watercolor, which he had used since his early childhood, becoming one of the greatest masters of the art form, admired for his ability to transform even the most commonplace subject into studies of sparkling light, color, and shadow with little apparent effort. His early biographer and friend Evan Charteris would famously characterize Sargent's talent for recording light: "To live with Sargent's water-colours is to live with sunshine captured and held."[13] His watercolors are also carefully designed and executed to preserve the impression of spontaneity. In *Escutcheon of Charles the V of Spain* [fig. 98], a masterpiece of the possibilities of watercolor, Sargent carefully constructed a precise preparatory underdrawing using a ruler and compass. He then painted in the dazzling effect of Mediterranean light and shadow on pale stone to obliterate the evidence of his effort.

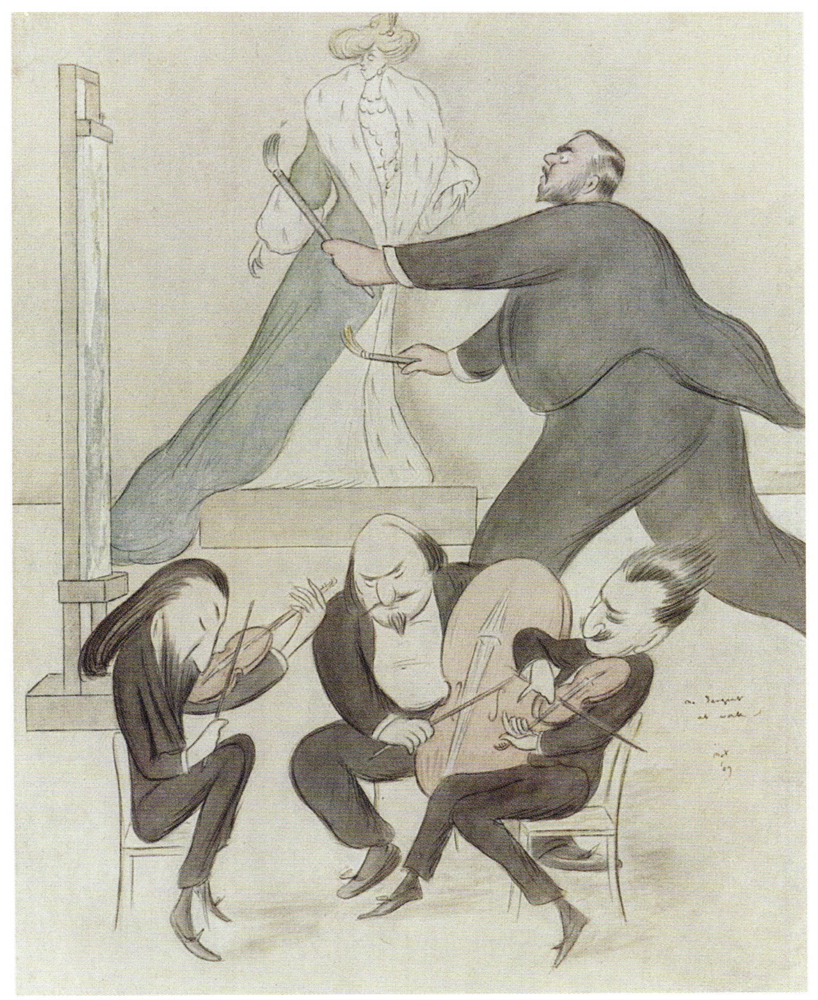

Max Beerbohm (1872–1956), *Sargent at Work*, 1907. Offset lithograph; 8 × 6⅛ in. (20.3 × 15.6 cm). Museum of Fine Arts, Boston. The John Singer Sargent Archive–Gift of Jan and Warren Adelson (2014.2248)

Max Beerbohm's caricature of Sargent at work satirizes the creation of a portrait by representing it as an expressive performance but also suggests the focused resolve and energy that Sargent brought to the task. As he rushes frenetically toward his canvas, arms outstretched, paintbrushes in hand, a drop of paint seems to fly off his brush. His eyeballs bulge with a look of determination. Meanwhile a trio of musicians in the foreground accompanies him, and in the background, his posing society client supervises the scene.

The descriptions of Sargent's method and Beerbohm's cartoon underscore the performative aspect of Sargent's process. Heyneman likened Sargent's painting technique to a musical performance: "each accent was studied with an intensity that kept his brush poised in the mid-air till eye and hand had steadied to one purpose, and then . . . bling! The stroke resounded almost like a note of music."[14] It's not a coincidence that Sargent was a talented musician who often performed for his friends and clients. One acquaintance remarked on "Sargent's wonderful proficiency as a pianist, saying that he might have had a career. This is probable, for he did everything easily and well."[15]

Sargent's exuberant painting style has provoked curiosity about his personality, which was described variously as shy, nervous, awkward, reticent, and reserved.[16] He was particularly private, and his papers were not preserved. Sargent never married or had a family of his own and left no trace of romantic involvements with men or women.[17] Even his stoic self-portrait [fig. 2], painted for the Galleria degli Uffizi in Florence seems to reveal very little about his personality. His peripatetic background confounded some who hoped to understand him in terms of culture or nationality. In 1925, one writer characterized him as "[a]n American, born in Italy, educated in France, who looks like a German, speaks like an Englishman, paints like a Spaniard."[18] Above all else, Sargent considered himself American, writing to James McNeill Whistler (1834–1903), he denied rumors that he had become a British citizen: "As for the question of nationality, I have not been invited to retouch it and I keep my twang. If you should hear anything to the contrary, please state that there was no such transaction and that I am an American."[19]

Sargent formed long-lasting relationships with a broad circle of creative and progressive types, including writers Henry James and Robert Louis Stevenson, artists Claude Monet (1840–1926) and Auguste Rodin (1840–1917), and composer Gabriel Fauré, among others. He cultivated and maintained friendships that were essential to his art—they nourished his creativity, provided inspiration, and were crucial to his career. Sargent constantly expanded his circle of associates while remaining devoted to lifelong friends. It was not uncommon for him to maintain a social relationship with a patron years after he had completed a portrait. (See *Mrs. Hugh Hammersley* [fig. 49] or *Asher Wertheimer* [fig. 53] and other portraits of the Wertheimer family.) His network of friends made it possible for him to achieve success on both sides of the Atlantic and furnished him with travel companions who often served as his models

Sargent's social calendar revolved around the arts. He frequently attended concerts and performances and socialized with a broad array of society—portrait patrons who became dear friends as well as artists, actors, musicians, writers, among others. The artist-illustrator W. Graham Robertson (1866–1948) [fig. 1], who posed for Sargent in 1894, wrote about the painter in his memoirs, reflecting on the dichotomy of a shy person with an active social life: "Sargent talked little and with an effort; why he 'went everywhere' night after night often puzzled me." Robertson added, "[Sargent] had not the gift of tongues, but that mattered little; he was so well able to express himself otherwise."[20] Robertson, who knew that Sargent spoke multiple languages, made the essential point that Sargent expressed himself through his art.[21]

Despite his reputation for being shy or retiring, he tended to be attracted to bold personalities and often sought them out as the subjects for his most innovative portraits.

He seemed fascinated, in particular, by performers of all types: the actor Ellen Terry, the Spanish dancer La Carmencita, the London dandy W. Graham Robertson, and even Virginie Gautreau (Madame X), whose provocative dress and dramatic cosmetics seemed a type of performance to Sargent.

Those who knew Sargent well presented a more nuanced assessment of his character. As one friend wrote after his death,

> Too much stress is laid upon Mr. Sargent's shyness, his capacity for silence. He was the most amusing of companions, the most engaging of hosts. When he was interested in a subject under discussion he spoke freely, vehemently even, with great felicity of phrase, often with a witty and clear decisiveness.[22]

This observation seems essential to his success as a portraitist; and tales of his apparent charm and warmth were often recounted by those who sat for him. After posing for him in 1881, his longtime friend the writer Vernon Lee [fig. 22] described the atmosphere of the single, three-hour session during which he painted her candid portrait: "I enjoyed it very much. John talking the whole time and strumming the piano between whiles."[23] Years later, Mrs. Hammersley [fig. 49] recalled the pleasure of spending extended time with Sargent while posing in the spring of 1892: "Sargent gave [the portrait] his best work and his best energy (and) they are both great! . . . Some days he wld [*sic*] work the whole time without ceasing, as one possessed, whilst others were spent playing the piano, which he did charmingly!"[24] Henry James [fig. 62] lamented the completion of his portrait in 1913: "I am sorry to have ceased to sit, in spite of the repeated holes it made in my precious mornings: J.S.S. being so genial and so delightful."[25]

Sargent's masterworks convey his powerful and intense interest in his subject. The painter was as likely to be mesmerized by the effect of light shimmering off a Venetian canal, an architectural detail of a Spanish fountain, a humble bunch of flowers, a vivid velvet dress as he was with a fascinating "creature" as he often described those to whom he was drawn—like the brilliant writer Robert Louis Stevenson [fig. 32], the sensuous surgeon Dr. Pozzi [fig. 19], or the striking Spanish dancer La Carmencita [fig. 37]. Sargent translated his enthusiasm for his subjects into his expressive painting technique and sensual admiration for textures and surfaces.

Though Sargent painted images of his friends and acquaintances throughout his life, the personal portraits from the early twentieth century are some of the most revealing and intimate works of his career.[26] *An Artist in His Studio* [fig. 3] shows Sargent's dear friend the Italian painter Ambrogio Raffele (1845–1928) at work on a landscape in the cramped conditions of his room at Purtud in northern Italy. Raffele becomes a surrogate for Sargent. The title is playful—it's immediately obvious that the studio is, in fact, the artist's bedroom, possibly a hotel room. The artist's large canvas is propped haphazardly next to the bed. Ironically the plein air painter has his back to the window, facing away from nature. He creates his composition from the preliminary studies, which are scattered about the room.

Sargent's painting is about the creation of his art—inspired by nature but originating with the artist's intellect. Light, from the window at left, illuminates the dome of his head, as if to signify the source of his idea for the painting. He peers through the fingers of his right hand at a small sketch held as he holds a fistful of brushes. Sargent cleverly describes the process of painting—from the artist's head, to his hands, to the small sketches, to the larger studies to the painting, in progression. In between Raffele's head and hand and the final canvas are his tools—his palette and brushes, splayed in his hand and pointing toward the sketches and painting. Sunlight enters the room from behind him, and nearly half of the canvas is filled with Sargent's brilliant rendering of light on the rumpled sheets and his friend's nightshirt draped at the foot of the unmade bed. The composition is tight and intimate, and Sargent is an unseen presence in the crowded room. Sargent is revealing information about his own life, how he lived, and how he created his art. As Sargent makes these personal paintings public by exhibiting them, he's giving us a glimpse of his private life and artistic philosophy.

In her posthumous tribute to Sargent, Vernon Lee described her friend's pleasure in translating his enjoyment of the world into his art:

> More and more it has seemed to me that Sargent's life was absorbed in his painting; and the summing up of a would-be biographer must, I think, be: *he painted.* To some of us he seemed occasionally to paint to the exclusion of living. In later years he seemed to be painting from morning till night, an easel, more than metaphorically, in every corner, a picture under way for every effect of changing weather. But looking over the portfolios of sketches, thinking of all the more elaborated landscapes. . . . I recognize that his life was not merely in painting, but in the more and the more intimate understanding and enjoying the world around him, and which the work of his incomparable hand enables some of us, also to understand and enjoy, if only in part.[27]

1 Charles H. Caffin, "John S. Sargent: The Greatest Contemporary Portrait Painter," *World's Work* 7 (November 1903): 4099–4116.
2 Roger Fry, "Royal Academy," *Pilot* 1 (May 12, 1900): 321.
3 H. I. Brock, "John Sargent, Man and Painter: Death of Modern 'Old Master' Releases Flood of Anecdote Regarding One of the Most Debated Figures in the Art World." *New York Times* (April 19, 1925), section 10: 5.
4 "John Sargent," *New York Times* (April 16, 1925): 20.
5 Henry James, "John S. Sargent," *Harper's New Monthly Magazine* 75 (October 1887): 691.
6 Edwin H. Blashfield, "John Singer Sargent: Recollections," *North American Review* 221 (June–August 1925): 641–53.
7 Brock 1925, 5.
8 Evan Charteris, *John Sargent* (New York: Charles Scribner's Sons, 1927), 123.
9 Gutzon Borglum, "John Singer Sargent—Artist. The Greatest of American Portrait-Painters." *Delineator* [no volume] (February 1923), 15, 106.
10 Charles H. Caffin, "John S. Sargent: His Portraits, Sketches and Studies Exhibited in Boston," *New York Times* (February 25, 1899), 13.
11 Quoted in Charteris 1927, 188.
12 Quoted in Charteris 1927, 182–83.
13 Charteris 1927, 225.
14 Quoted in Charteris 1927, 183.
15 Blashfield 1925, 645.
16 As Trevor Fairbrother perfectly stated, "[Sargent's] life's work celebrated the pleasure of the world by excitedly translating them into audacious passages of paint. . . .Exuberance and showiness are essential qualities of his art." Trevor J. Fairbrother, *John Singer Sargent: The Sensualist* (Seattle: Seattle Art Museum and New Haven: Yale University Press, 2000), 19.
17 It seems likely that Sargent was gay yet he chose to live most of his life in England where homosexuality was illegal until 1967.
18 William Starkweather, "John Singer Sargent Master Portrait Painter," *Mentor* (October 1924), p. 4. Sargent sometimes benefited from his position as outsider: in Paris and London, he was often considered American (which helped him secure portrait commissions from Americans abroad); in the United States, he seemed European (this helped him secure the mural commissions).
19 Sargent to Whistler, no date, Glasgow University Library, quoted in Stanley Olson, *John Singer Sargent: His Portrait* (New York: St. Martin's Press, 1986), 247.
20 Walford Graham Robertson, *Time Was: The Reminiscences of W. Graham Robertson* (London: H. Hamilton, Ltd., 1933), 235.
21 Sargent spoke English, French, Spanish, Italian, and German.
22 "Memories of Sargent by a Friend," *Living Age* 325 (May 30, 1925): 448.
23 Vernon Lee, letter to her mother, June 25, 1881 in Richard Ormond, "John Singer Sargent and Vernon Lee," *Colby Library Quarterly* 9, no. 3 (September 1970): 166.
24 Memorandum from Mrs. Hugh Hammersley, March 30, 1893, The Metropolitan Museum of Art, New York.
25 Henry James, letter to Rhoda Broughton, June 25, 1913, in Percy Lubbock, ed., *The Letters of Henry James*, vol. II (London: Macmillan, 1920), 330.
26 This discussion first appeared as "'No More Paughtraits': Final Thoughts on *Sargent: Portraits of Artists and Friends*." Metmuseum.org. *Sargent: Portraits of Artists and Friends Exhibition Blog*. October 6, 2015.
27 Vernon Lee, "J.S.S. In Memoriam," in Charteris 1927, 254–55.

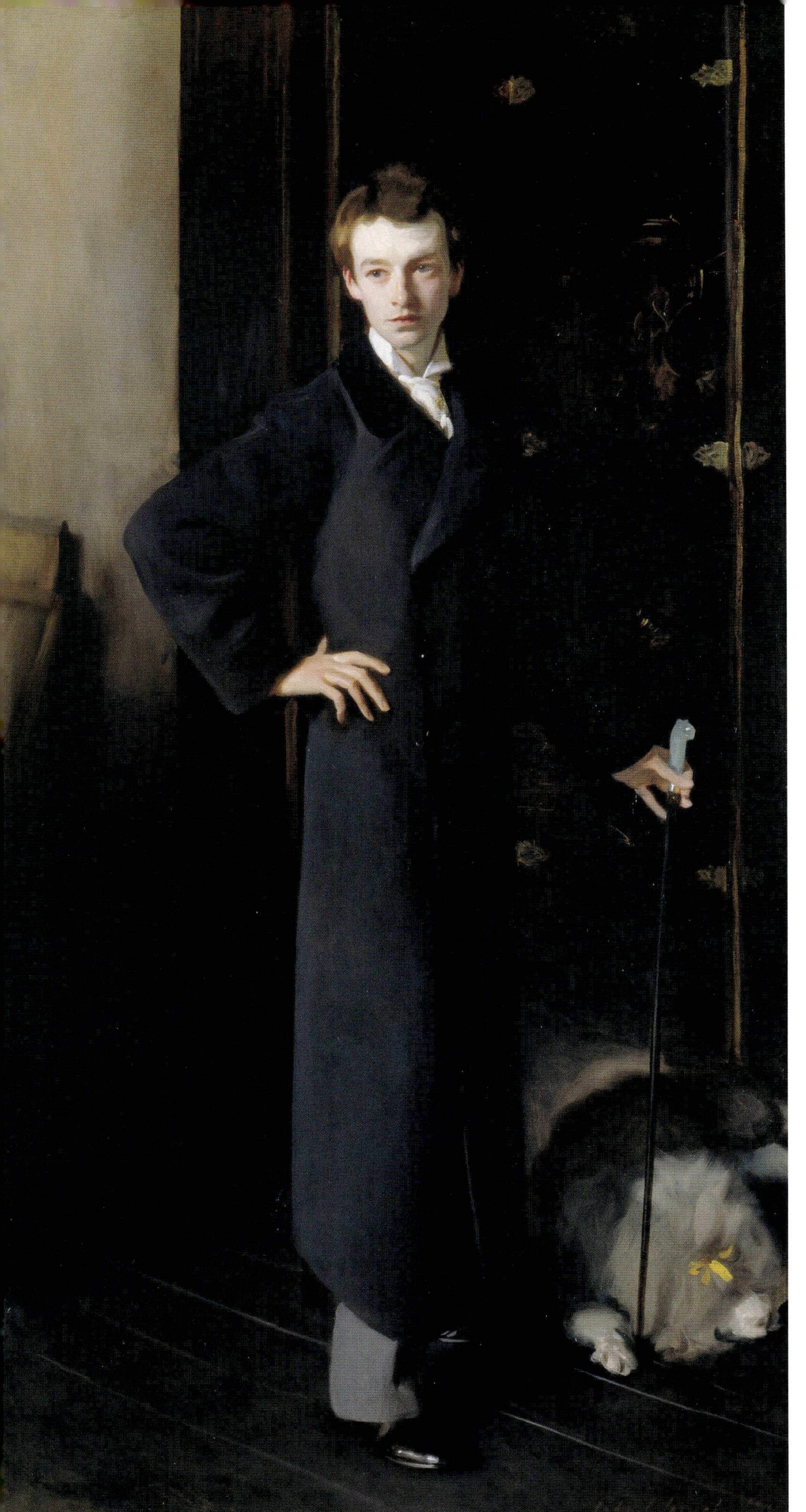

1

W. Graham Robertson

1894
Oil on canvas, 90¾ × 46¾ in.
(230.5 × 118.7 cm)
Signed: "John S. Sargent 1894"
London, Tate, Presented
by W. Graham Robertson 1940
[N05066]

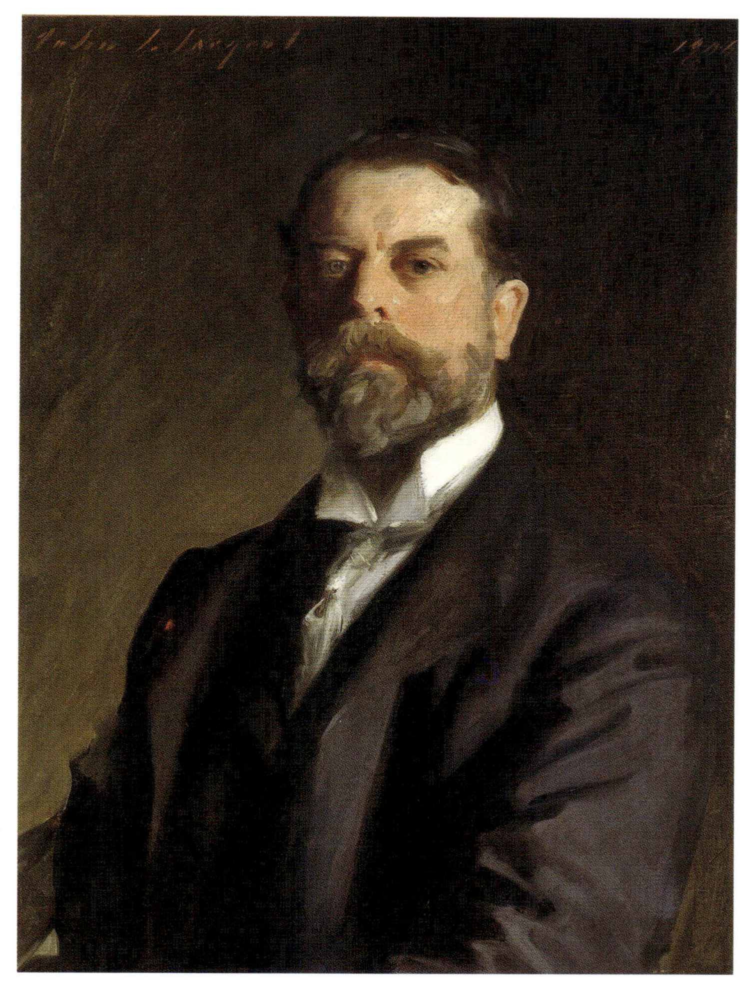

2

Self-Portrait

1906
Oil on canvas, 27 ½ × 20⅞ in. (69.8 × 53 cm)
Signed: "John S. Sargent"
Dated: "1906"
Florence, Galleria degli Uffizi [inv. 1890 n. 3351]

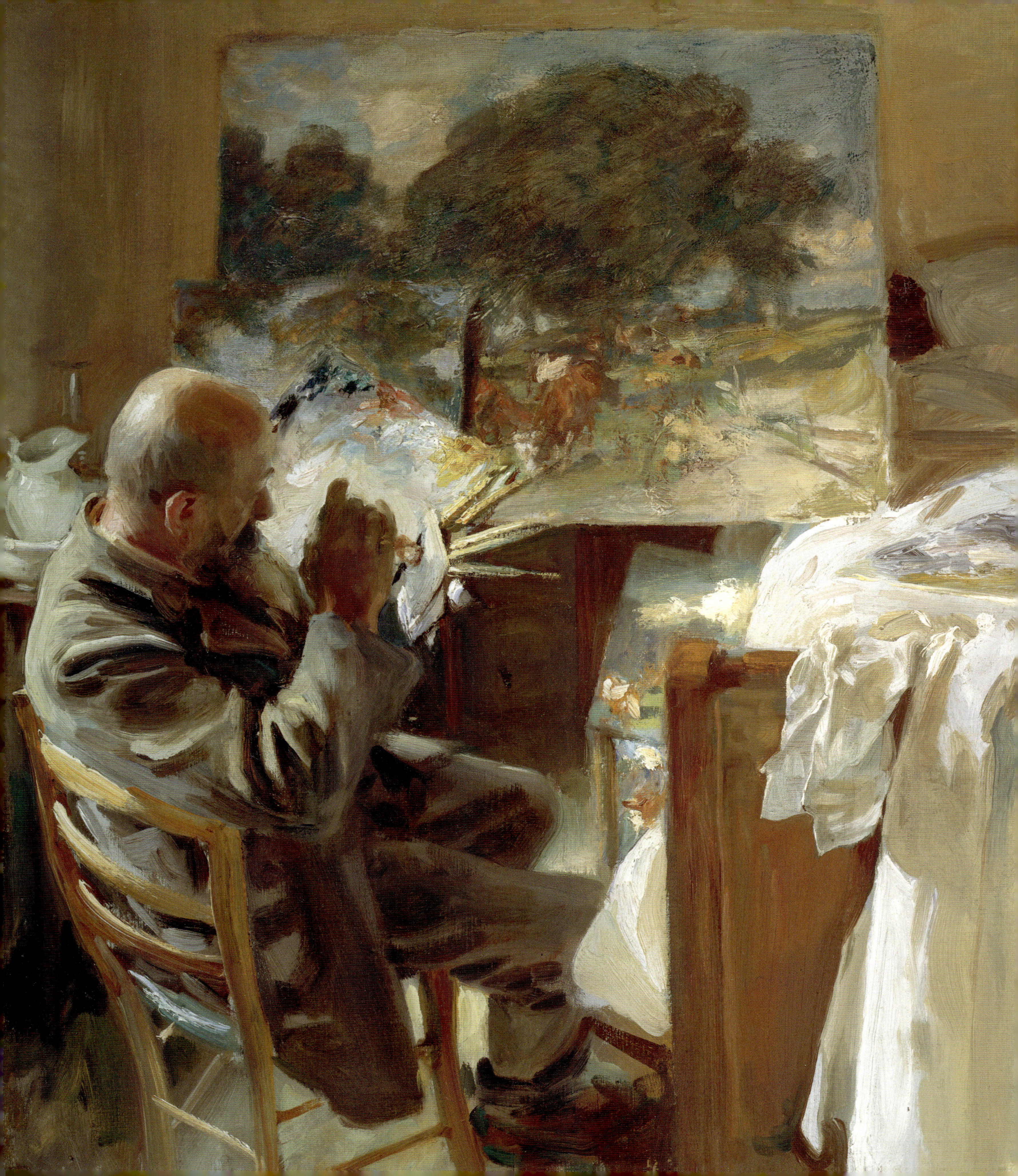

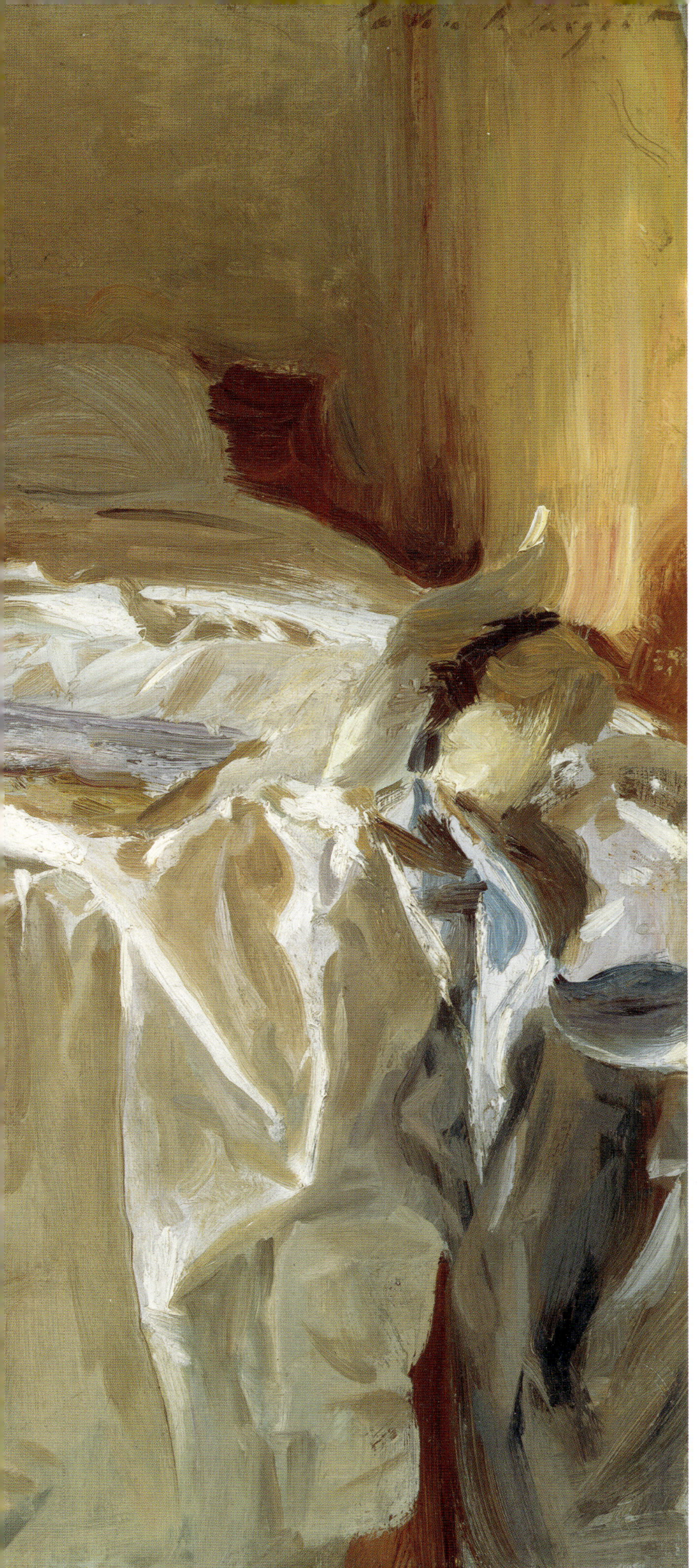

3

An Artist in His Studio

ca. 1904
Oil on canvas, 22⅛ × 28⅜ in.
(56.2 × 72.1 cm)
Signed: "John S. Sargent"
Boston, Museum of Fine Arts,
The Hayden Collection–Charles
Henry Hayden Fund [05.56]

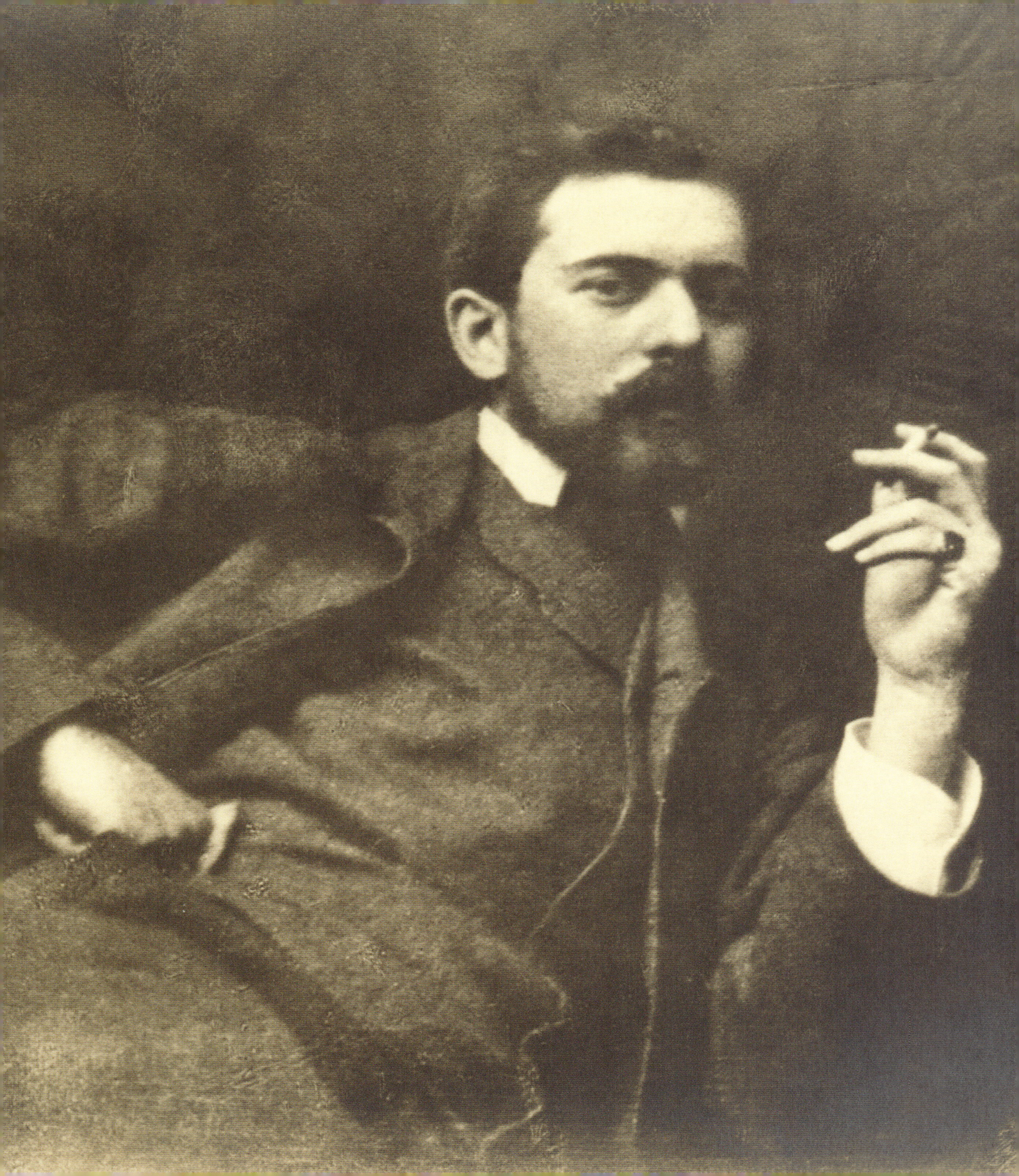

Sargent in Paris, ca. 1884. Museum of Fine Arts, Boston. The John Singer Sargent Archive–Gift of Richard and Leonée Ormond.

Sargent in Paris and Beyond

Early Career to 1887

When John Singer Sargent's parents left Philadelphia for Europe in 1854, they intended their stay to be temporary. Fitzwilliam Sargent (1820–1889), a surgeon, and Mary Newbold Singer (1826–1906) had been married for four years and were devastated by the untimely death of their firstborn child, who was just two years old. Accompanied by Mary's mother (also Mary Newbold Singer, d. 1859), they set out, seeking a healthy climate for Mary, who was suffering from an unknown ailment—physical or psychological—after the loss. Despite their ties to the United States, they repeatedly prolonged their stay and never returned permanently. They were drawn to Europe, in part, because of Mary's youthful memories. Sargent's early biographer Evan Charteris suggests that the lure was sentimental, restorative, and palliative, he explained: "As a girl she had travelled to Italy. The magic of that country never ceased to exercise its spell, and within four years of her marriage she persuaded her husband to give up his [medical] practice, and in 1854 to sail for Europe and take up their residence in Florence," where John Singer Sargent was born in January 1856.[1]

The family established a pattern of traveling with the seasons continuously in search of a temperate climate; they spent their winters in milder southern locales around the Mediterranean such as Nice, Rome, or Florence and their summers in more northern regions, often the Alps. In 1857, Fitzwilliam resigned from his surgical position at Wills Hospital in Philadelphia, and the family lived off income from a modest annuity that Mary received from her father's estate. After her son's birth in 1856, Mary would deliver four more children, only two of whom survived to adulthood. They were also born in Italy: Emily (1857–1936) in Rome, and Violet (1870–1955) in Florence.

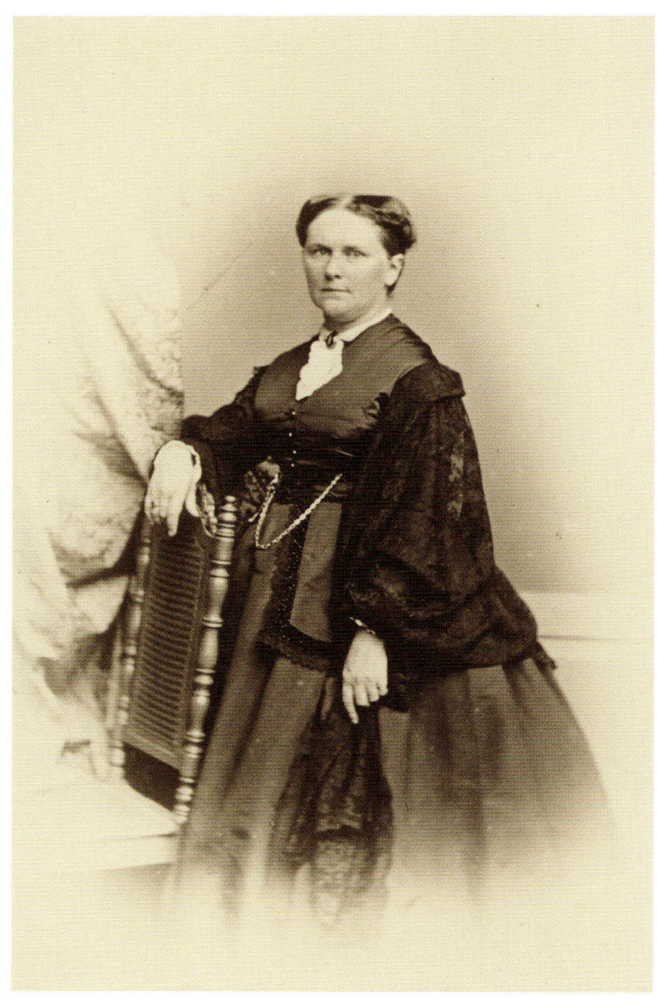

Mary Newbold Singer Sargent, ca. 1865. Museum of Fine Arts, Boston. The John Singer Sargent Archive–Gift of Richard and Leonée Ormond

In his letters to family members in the United States, Fitzwilliam continuously provided a rationale for extending their stay abroad including the pregnancies, confinements, and caring for delicate newborns. As the children grew older, he often described the diverse ailments of various family members. His prescribed treatment almost always involved travel—a change of scenery, taking the waters at a spa town in the Alps, and so on. As a physician, his authoritative voice gave each diagnosis a gravitas that precluded return to the United States. Over time, his endless litany of illnesses, however, begins to seem like a pretext rather than a valid explanation. In a letter to his mother written in 1870, Fitzwilliam lamented the family's lifestyle:

> I am tired of this nomadic sort of life: —the Spring comes, and we strike our tents and migrate for the Summer: the Autumn returns, and we must again pack up our duds and off to some milder region in which Emily and Mary can thrive. I wish there were some prospect of our going home and settling down among our own people and taking permanent root.[2]

While Fitzwilliam regretted this lifestyle, his wife seems to have been the guiding force behind it and embraced it wholeheartedly. The writer Vernon Lee, who was a young child when she first met "Mrs. Sargent" and the family in Nice in the early 1860s, described her as representative of "a breed of Sentimental Travellers, insatiate, indefatigable."[3] Using the vocabulary of religious devotion, Lee anointed Mary "the high priestess of them all, the most favoured and inspired votary of the spirit of Localities, she who averred that the happiest moment in life was in a hotel bus."[4] Her passion for exploration and her curiosity about the world were positive forces in Sargent's life that were manifested in his enduring enthusiasm for travel and discovery and a deep and sentimental attachment to Italy that would inspire him to return to that country and its art throughout his life.

Biographer Evan Charteris described Sargent's mother as

> a woman of culture and an excellent musician. She also painted in water-colour. She was vivacious and restless in disposition. . . . In her family she was a dominating influence. She was one of the first to recognize the genius of her son, and in a large measure responsible for his dedication to art.[5]

Like many of the women of her social standing and class, she was an amateur artist and saw these skills as essential to her children's education. She encouraged all of her children to sketch at an early age, insisting that they finish at least one drawing every day. Sargent avidly recorded the world around him in a series of sketchbooks. Anecdotes of his precocious talent were chronicled in his parents' letters to relatives in the United States. As early as 1861, when Sargent was five years old, his father described his son's enthusiasm in a letter to his mother: "Johnny is well and as fond as ever of drawing."[6]

In his correspondence with childhood friend Ben del Castillo, nine-year-old Sargent revealed his zest for sightseeing, and his eclectic and sophisticated interests, from the natural world, architecture, fine art, and history—often telling his friend that he made drawings after the things that interested him the most. He enthusiastically describes the myriad sites he visited and sketched, from the Zoological Gardens and Crystal Palace in London to the museums of Naples.[7] From this early age, Sargent seems to have almost obsessively recorded his impressions of the people,

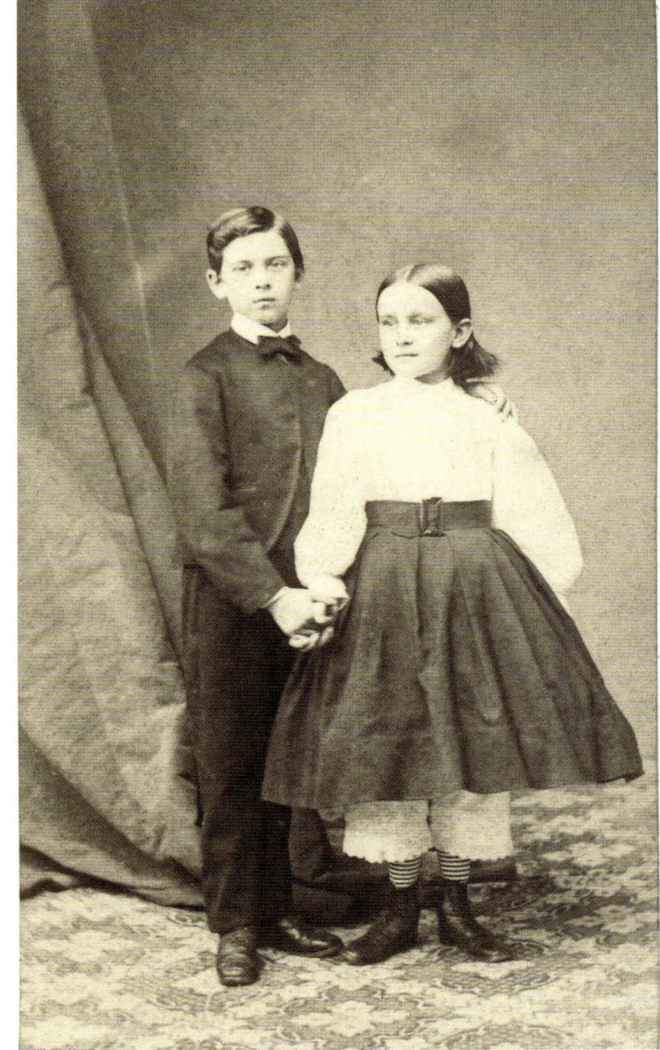

Sargent with his sister Emily, ca. 1867. Photograph by L. Subercaze. Museum of Fine Arts, Boston. The John Singer Sargent Archive–Gift of Richard and Leonée Ormond.

places, art, architecture, and sculpture that captured his attention. As Sargent used drawing to train his eye, hand, and memory, it became an important way for him to process the world. The exploration of each new site and the sense of constant movement became a family tradition—one that Sargent would embrace throughout his life.

Sargent had almost no formal schooling. For a short period in autumn 1868, he enrolled at a school run by an English clergyman in Nice. During the winter of 1869–70 he attended classes at a small school run by a French political refugee in Florence.[8] After these failed attempts, his parents determined to educate their children themselves. Fitzwilliam was responsible for math, science, and history. Mary furnished her children with what biographer Stanley Olson described as an "education by Baedeker and Murray's," referring to the popular series of guidebooks.[9] As they traveled, she made sure that her children saw the major museums and monuments of each locale. Sargent's peripatetic childhood in Europe and his family's circle of refined and cosmopolitan friends provided an eclectic and sophisticated education that helped him develop his fluency in multiple languages while honing his aesthetic preferences at a young age. Sargent developed a fervent appreciation for music and became an accomplished pianist.

Sargent's aptitude for art became increasingly apparent to his family and friends. In October 1867, when Sargent was eleven, Mary wrote to her mother-in-law:

> Johnnie is growing to be such a nice boy, and is getting old enough to enjoy and appreciate the beauties of nature and art, which are lavishly displayed in these old lands. He sketches quite nicely, & has a remarkably quick and correct eye. If we could afford to give him really good lessons, he would soon be quite a little artist. Thus far he has never had any instruction, but artists say that his touch is remarkable.[10]

In Rome, during the winter of 1868–69 Sargent's parents could no longer ignore his talent and determination. In her posthumous tribute to Sargent, Vernon Lee described this particularly memorable winter, when her family and the Sargents lived in the Eternal City. Together the children explored Rome's antiquities, churches, and gardens, and were enthralled by the papal pageantry. There were sketching excursions "through icy miles of Vatican galleries to make hurried forbidden sketches of statues selected for easy portrayal" and sojourns to the Roman *campagna* during which Sargent would record picturesque vistas using his mother's paint box.[11] The Sargents' apartment near the Spanish Steps became an occasional gathering spot for members of the American expatriate community of artists in Rome, particularly the American sculptors Harriet Goodhue Hosmer (1830–1908), Randolph Rogers (1825–1892), and William Wetmore Story (1819–1895), who were drawn to the city's antiquities.[12]

Since her earliest encounters with Sargent in Nice in the 1860s, Lee believed that her friend was destined to be an artist. While he was already "a painter in spirit and in fact," his father was determined that his only son would have a career in the United States Navy.[13] "But," Lee explained, "Rome willed things otherwise."[14] In autumn 1870 Sargent's father acknowledged his son's career goals in a letter to his own mother: "John seems to have a strong desire to be an Artist by profession, a painter, he shows so much evidence of talent in that direction, and takes so much pleasure in cultivating it, that we have concluded to gratify him and to keep that plan in view in his studies."[15]

In 1873, Sargent enrolled at the Accademia di Belle Arti in Florence, for his first formal art instruction. The Accademia had a distinguished heritage dating back to the Renaissance but was then at a low point in its history. Sargent was disappointed and described it as "the most unsatisfactory institution imaginable." After a long winter break during which the Accademia was restructured, Sargent and his classmates lost their teacher. Sargent grew increasingly determined to seek more serious opportunities to further his training. After consulting members of the expatriate community in Florence, he decided that Paris, then the center of the art world, was the best place to continue his studies. As he explained to a friend, "the Academy in Paris is probably better than the one here and we hear that the French artists undoubtedly the best now-a-days, are willing to take pupils in their studios."[16]

Sargent arrived in Paris in May 1874 and immediately sought entrance in the teaching studio of the celebrated French portraitist Charles Auguste-Émile Durand, known as Carolus-Duran (1837-1917), whose paintings he had admired at the Salon shortly after his arrival. Sargent described Duran as "a young and rising artist whose reputation is continuously increasing. He is chiefly a portrait painter and has a very broad, powerful and realistic style."[17] Sargent was probably attracted to Carolus-Duran's cosmopolitan training in Paris, Italy, and Madrid and his connection to many prominent, progressive painters, including Gustave Courbet (1819–1877) and Édouard Manet (1832–1883). Duran promoted the fluid painterly tradition of the seventeenth-century Spanish master Diego Velázquez (1599–1660) above all others and encouraged his students to paint directly on the canvas and preserve the immediacy of the sketch in their finished works. Sargent embraced these methods and adopted his fluid painting technique, quickly becoming his star pupil.

Sargent also gained admittance to the prestigious French academy, the École des Beaux-Arts, where he attended the drawing classes of Adolphe Yvon (1817–1893) and additional painting lessons in the studio of Léon Bonnat (1833–1922), an academic painter with progressive tendencies. He befriended many of his European and American classmates and forged lasting relationships with important innovative artists, including, as early as 1876, Impressionist Claude Monet (1840–1926) and, in the early 1880s, sculptor Auguste Rodin (1840–1917) among others.[18]

Carolus-Duran also urged his students to select their own artistic role models from art history past and present. Sargent fashioned his personal style based on his appreciation of painterly Old Masters such as Diego Velázquez, Anthony van Dyck (1599–1641), and Jacopo Tintoretto (1519–1594) and contemporary artists such as Manet and Monet and his teachers.

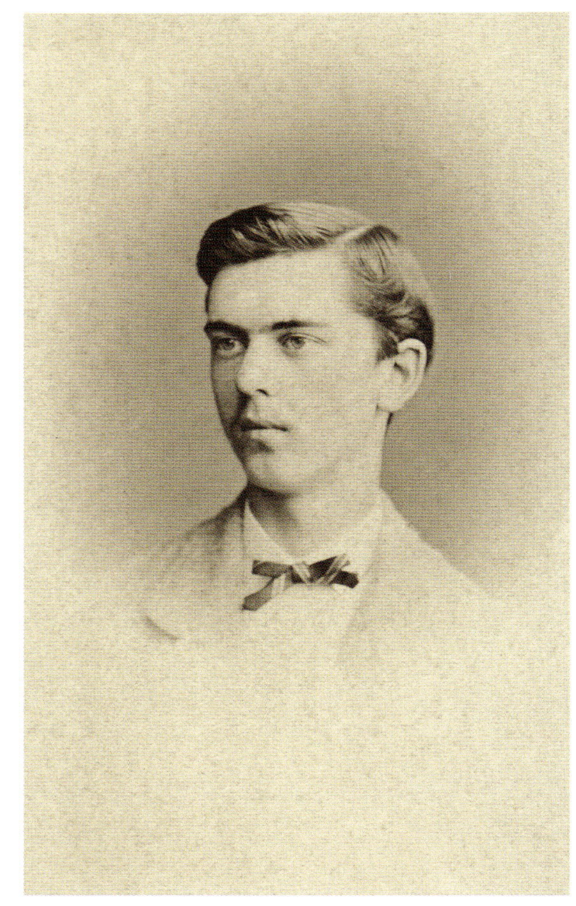

Sargent, Venice, ca. 1874. Photograph by Giuseppe and Luigi Vianelli. Museum of Fine Arts, Boston. The John Singer Sargent Archive–Gift of Richard and Leonée Ormond.

He searched broadly for subjects—painting alpine landscapes in Switzerland, dramatic seascapes as he made his first transatlantic crossing to the United States in 1876, and portraits of family and friends. He built his reputation by exhibiting his paintings first in Paris at the annual Salon, and then more widely at diverse venues in France and England, elsewhere in Europe, and the United States. In the early years, he represented his broad interests and talent by displaying portraits and genre scenes.

Sargent continued the practice, established in his childhood, of traveling with the seasons and spent his summer holidays from the École exploring picturesque locations in Europe. A summer trip to the coast of Brittany in France in 1877 would inspire his submission to the Paris Salon for the annual exhibition of 1878—*En route pour la pêche* (*Setting Out to Fish*) [fig. 4], a sparkling sunlit scene of local fisherfolk preparing to gather oysters at low tide set at Cancale, the region's oyster capital. Sargent's deft handling of the bright, cloud-filled sky, pale sand, and reflective tidal pools preserves the immediacy of plein air execution but was the result of meticulous academic preparation, including many careful figure studies in graphite and oil.

He headed south from Paris for the summer of 1878, visiting Naples and Capri on the Italian coast, lured there by his childhood memories and famously picturesque scenery. In a letter to his friend Ben del Castillo, Sargent complained about the heat and the mosquitoes but acknowledged that "Italy is all that one can dream for beauty and charm."[19] In *Neapolitan Children Bathing* [fig. 5], a delightful and candid study of four naked children on an Italian beach, Sargent masterfully conveys the sizzling Mediterranean sunlight. Broadly painted bands of color define the sky, water, and sand while cool blue shadows and golden highlights accentuate the figures in various poses. At the center of the composition, the young boy with his back to the viewer wears a pair of water wings for flotation (probably made from animal bladders filled with air), causing one reviewer to remark that the group resembled "young cupids" when the painting was shown in New York in 1879.[20] Sargent masterfully suggests the transparency and reflective qualities of the organic material.

Capri, a popular tourist destination, was celebrated in the era for its unspoiled beauty, which Sargent sought to convey in the idyllic painting *A Capriote* [fig. 6]. It features a favorite local model, Rosina Ferrara, whom Sargent painted on several occasions during his stay. He was likely attracted to her olive skin and her "exotic" beauty. He contrived a difficult pose for Rosina, who is shown with her back to the picture plane as she twists to the right, accentuating her distinctive profile as she leans against a gnarled olive branch.[21]

Determined to promote his broad abilities across the genres to potential patrons in the French capital, Sargent sent two paintings to the Paris Salon in 1879: *Dans les oliviers, à Capri* (a version of *A Capriote*) and his most ambitious portrait to date, *Carolus-Duran* [fig. 7]. The portrait is, at once, a devoted homage to his master and a rendering of a stylish type in Parisian society—the gentleman-artist. Sargent had developed a particularly close relationship with his teacher, who recognized the extraordinary talent of his young protégé and agreed to pose for him. Made five years after his arrival in Paris, when Sargent was only twenty-three years old, it is an unofficial diploma picture signifying the end of his formal training. By aligning himself with his elegant and successful teacher in a prominent public forum, Sargent revealed his appreciation for Carolus-Duran (and his astute talent for self-promotion) with a prominent inscription with his signature in the upper right corner: "à mon cher maître M. Carolus Duran, son élève affectioné / John S. Sargent, 1879."

In the portrait, Sargent proudly displays the lessons learned from his teacher: the relatively smooth and broadly painted surfaces, the soft-focus realism, and the subtle, nearly monochromatic palette inspired by Velázquez remind viewers of Carolus-Duran's—and Sargent's—veneration of the Spanish master. Sargent sets off Carolus-Duran's face and hands with the bright white of his collar and flamboyant pleated cuffs. On his lapel at the center of the composition, a dot of red represents his Légion d'honneur pin, prominently signifying his position in the artistic establishment (a distinction that Sargent would receive in 1889). The sitter's pose is informal yet candid—he appears solidly anchored on the bench as he leans forward, gazing directly at the viewer, a formidable presence. The portrait was a striking success; it received an honorable mention at the Salon and helped Sargent earn several portrait commissions.

One of the more prominent commissions came from the rising playwright Édouard Pailleron, who was drawn to the young painter's bold technique and original approach to portraiture. Within two years, Sargent painted portraits of Pailleron [fig. 8], his wife, Marie [fig. 9], and their children [fig. 10]. He traveled to the family's country estate in southeastern France to paint the portrait of Marie, his first full-length portrait at life scale. In choosing to depict his subject *en plein air*, Sargent associated himself with innovative contemporary art. He unites the narrow, vertical format with a high vantage point, practically eliminating the horizon. By placing the elegantly dressed Marie against a verdant lawn punctuated by falling leaves and blossoming autumn crocus he created the effect of a decorative tapestry. Sargent finely painted the details of her face and brilliantly described the lavish details of her sophisticated and refined costume—the sparkle of her dangling earrings, the transparency of her tulle neck scarf, and the ornate bead and lace details of her sleeves—all against the broadly painted background.

Sargent's portrait of her children, Édouard and Marie-Louise Pailleron, is his first formal double portrait. In this unusual composition, the younger Marie-Louise is the dominant presence, with her frontal pose and intense fixed gaze. Her brother Édouard seems almost secondary as he turns his body away from the picture plane. The children are dressed traditionally in black and white against a dramatic red drapery on a patterned Persian carpet. Sargent and Marie-Louise reportedly clashed during the lengthy sittings, disagreeing over details of her dress and her hairstyle. Sargent captured Marie-Louise's fierce intensity in her facial expression and clenched fist, setting aside conventional, sometimes saccharine Victorian pictorial traditions.

Sargent immersed himself in the artistic and cultural life in Paris. A talented pianist and ardent musicologist, he often attended performances. In the mid-1870s, he frequented the *concerts populaires* of the orchestra conducted by the influential Jules-Étienne Pasdeloup at the Cirque d'Hiver, a 5,000-seat amphitheater in Paris's 11th arrondissement. Sargent was drawn to the concerts by the affordable tickets and the progressive musical programs, which often included the work of Richard Wagner, his favorite composer. In his painting of a concert [fig. 11], Sargent records the scene from a high vantage point. Using a limited tonal palette, he creates a blurred effect for the background in order to focus attention on the performance. He carefully delineated the musical instruments to evoke the aural experience of the concert. The composition is punctuated by the repetitive rectangles of the white sheet music and the glint of light on the instruments.

For *In the Luxembourg Gardens* [fig. 12], Sargent presents a quintessentially modern late nineteenth-century subject—a fashionable couple promenading through the public gardens of Paris. The couple is very much on display despite their quiet isolation in the stillness of the evening. Sargent chose a fleeting moment at dusk, as the setting sun hovers over the trees on the horizon at right. The evening light gives the entire composition a tonal harmony as pale light seems to shimmer off the woman's pink dress and creates a remarkable glowing reflection across the pool of water at right.

In late summer 1879, Sargent made an artistic pilgrimage to Madrid where he immersed himself in the study of the great masterpieces by Velázquez (copying at least nine works) at the Museo del Prado.[22] From there, he traveled to southern Spain before crossing to Morocco around the New Year. As always, Sargent sketched and painted throughout the trip, recording scenes that captured his attention in anticipation of creating substantial subject pictures for exhibition. In the architectural vignette *Alhambra, Patio de los Leones* [fig. 13], painted in Granada, Sargent conveys the delicate grace and ornament of the

Moorish architecture with a somber palette. In contrast, the small panel *Courtyard, Tetuan, Morocco* [fig. 14] is a study of light and shadow across the pale architecture. In this brief sketch, the subject is nearly monochromatic but Sargent diversifies his palette to contrast the cool shadows with the saturated sunlight on the white walls. Sargent delighted in rendering the effect of light and shadow on white surfaces throughout his life and frequently sought such colorless expanses. Here, he demonstrates the spontaneity of the sketch with a bravura technique that suggests his facility.

His preoccupation with painting white is manifested in his major Moroccan composition, *Fumée d'Ambre Gris* [fig. 15], which was conceived and begun in Tangier but finished in his Paris studio. The subject is mysterious and obscure, a woman perfuming herself with the essence of amber gris (a waxy substance from the intestines of the sperm whale) that, when burned, emits a distinctive, sweet, musky scent. Sargent re-created the ritual with a model and constructed the composition from studies made on-site to create a fantasy of exotic Orientalist imagery for his Paris audience. His depiction of her white dress and veil against the whitewashed wall is a tour de force of painting, articulated by the decorative tiles and rug and the brilliant rendering of the reflective details of the silver censer.

Sargent's enthusiasm for Spain and its music and culture finds expression in the massive *El Jaleo* [fig. 16], a panoramic, nearly life-size depiction of a nighttime flamenco performance. Painted just four years after Georges Bizet's controversial opera *Carmen* debuted in Paris at the Opéra-Comique, Sargent's *El Jaleo* was also touching on a broader societal interest in Spain. Dramatically lit from below to evoke a stage set, Sargent captured the expressive gestures of the dancer and musicians. Sargent obsessively studied aspects of the dance for authenticity. The dancer's mannered pose captures the intensity of her performance, and the setting evokes the sensory experience. Critics celebrated the painting's novelty and theatricality, praising it as "audacious," "bizarre," "fantastic."[23] The picture was purchased from the Salon by a Boston diplomat, who took it to the United States and later gave it to Isabella Stewart Gardner, who built a specially designed alcove for the painting in her home (now a museum), where it can still be seen today.

At the outset of his training in Paris in 1874, Sargent expressed his desire to return to Italy in a letter to Vernon Lee: "I am persuaded that Paris is the place to learn painting in. When I can paint, *then* away for Venice!" True to his word, Sargent returned to Venice at the first opportunity visiting La Serenissima in 1878, 1880–81 (for about four months), and again in 1882 (for about three months). During these later visits, Sargent pursued two types of subjects in series: mysterious encounters between men and women in the characteristic back alleys of the city (*Street in Venice* [fig. 17]) and darkened interiors showing groups of Venetian women—sometimes engaged in the crafts of Venetian glassworking, bead stringing and glass caning. In *A Venetian Interior* [fig. 18], Sargent uses the palazzo architecture as a stage set for the figures. The space is articulated by the glow of light from the windows in the background—particularly brilliant is the flash of light cutting across the floor in the middle background, painted with a

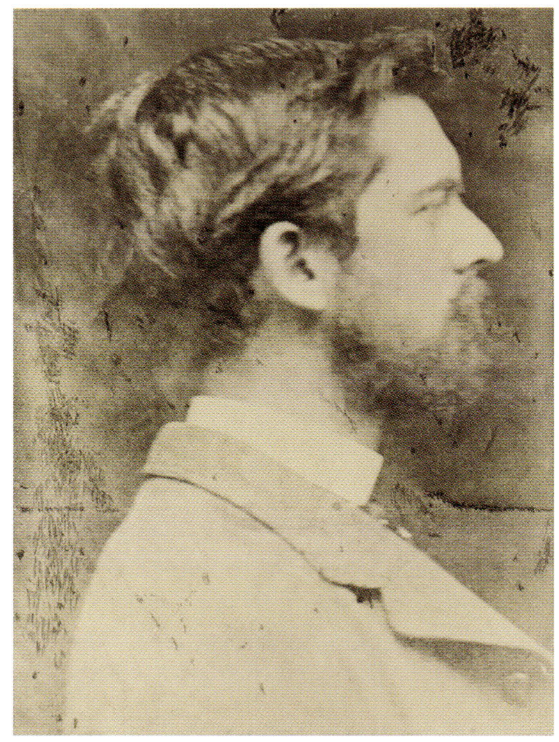

Sargent, ca. 1880. Museum of Fine Arts, Boston. The John Singer Sargent Archive–Gift of Richard and Leonée Ormond

brief, confident brushstroke. These Venetian paintings are the most experimental of his student years and the few in which Sargent depicted scenes of everyday life.

In the early 1880s Sargent continued to build his reputation by showing portraits and subject paintings at select venues in Paris and the United States. As his reputation grew, he began sending works to exhibitions throughout Europe and England.[24] He demonstrated his ability to please and flatter patrons in his commissioned portraits, while creating ambitious subject pictures and innovative, noncommissioned portraits that reveal his professional and personal ambitions.

Many of Sargent's early commissions came from members of the artistic community in Paris. Samuel-Jean Pozzi was a pioneer of modern gynecology in France who is recognized for his role in advancing the reproductive safety of women. He was also an aesthete and an art collector whom Sargent probably met through Carolus-Duran. One grateful patient, the actor Sarah Bernhardt, famously called him "Dr. God." Sargent characterized Pozzi as a "very brilliant creature," and his admiration for his charismatic sitter is evident in his daring portrait [fig. 19]. The gracious and slightly mannered pose, the costume, and the shocking crimson palette reference Old Master images of popes and cardinals. Sargent likely saw the vivid red interior and costume as an appealing artistic challenge. He surpassed the boundaries of traditional portraiture by depicting his progressive patron at home, in his dressing gown, in the sumptuous velvet interior. Sargent blurs the distinction between public and private. Pozzi's long fingers and elegant hands suggest his surgical prowess but also hint at his sensuality, which is further evoked by his intimate attire and the lush setting. He exudes a powerful self-confidence that Sargent celebrates in the portrait.

Whereas Sargent's portrait of Dr. Pozzi startled viewers with its unconventionality, his likeness of family friend Charlotte Louise Burckhardt, known as *Lady with the Rose* [fig. 20], was celebrated as an ideal representation of a young woman. Henry James admired the portrait's simplicity, rapturously declaring that it "overflows with perfection."[25] Like many of Sargent's works from this period, the tonal palette and presentation evoke timeless works by Old Masters such as Velázquez. (James observed that her dress resembled one that "had been worn by some demure princess who might have sat for Velasquez."[26]) Her tilted head, slightly parted lips, and coy gesture—offering a rose—appealed to contemporary viewers. One critic predicted that the idealized presentation would inspire a "rush of commissions from the fairer sex."[27]

Sargent's portrait of *The Daughters of Edward Darley Boit* [fig. 21] departs from traditional group portraits in its innovative composition. Edward Boit (1840–1915) was an expatriate painter from Boston, with whom Sargent would develop a lasting friendship. In the large, square painting, Sargent positioned Boit's four daughters in the hall of their Paris apartment. The palette and arrangement have echoes of Sargent's darkened Venetian interiors from this period but also display evidence of his careful study of Velázquez's paintings in the Prado, particularly *Las Meninas*. Like his depiction of the Pailleron children, the portrait conveys a psychological intensity to his young sitters. Sargent is as concerned with rendering their individual likenesses as constructing a complex array of forms within the asymmetrical composition. The four children emerge from the darkened interior of the apartment, which reveals very little about its inhabitants, and each girl seems absorbed in her own personal world. The most distinctive detail of the decor is the pair of larger-than-life Japanese vases—treasured family heirlooms—which dwarf the children and add an unsettling sense of ambiguity to the scale and composition.

Sargent often created candid portrait studies of friends, which convey the intimacy of friendship in their informality. Since these paintings weren't necessarily created for public display, Sargent could be less conventional and take risks in his depictions. His childhood friend Violet Paget, who assumed the pen name Vernon Lee, was an ardent feminist lesbian, who dressed à la *garçonne*. Sargent admired and respected her brilliant mind: she was an expert on the Italian Renaissance and published work across genres, including supernatural fiction, aesthetics, psychology, literary criticism, nonfiction, and plays. In 1881, Sargent painted her portrait in a single three-hour sitting [fig. 22]. Lee described the spontaneous quality of the picture in a letter to her mother: "The sketch is by everyone's admission extraordinarily clever and characteristic. It is, of course, mere dabs and blurs and considerably caricatured, but certainly more like me than I expected anything could. Rather fierce and cantankerous."[28] Sargent inscribed a dedication "to my friend Violet" in the wet pigment at the upper right and presented the portrait to her as a token of their friendship, leaving the lower left corner of the canvas unpainted.

In some instances, Sargent kept the images he painted of his cherished friends for his personal collection. The casual watercolor portrait of the painter Paul-César Helleu (1859–1927) [fig. 23] hung for many years in Sargent's dining room in Paris. He records Helleu's lanky body and long legs reclining in a relaxed pose in front of a fireplace as he smokes a cigarette. Sargent magnificently combines the specificity of portrait details using a limited palette with a broad, fluid technique in which Helleu's legs fade into pale pigment and the back of the chair dissolves into a pool of shadow.

Violet Sargent (*The Breakfast Table*) [fig. 24] depicts Sargent's youngest sister reading as she eats her morning meal, seemingly unaware of the artist and the viewer. Sargent relishes in painting the carefully studied still-life details on the table: glassware, silver, flowers. Sargent excels at rendering the essence of the object with calligraphic, precise brushstrokes that appear effortless. His dabs of pigment appear spontaneous but are calculated to convey the maximum information. With quick touches of his brush, he creates the lush pink roses, the reflected light on the silver bowl, or the transparency of a glass bottle. This canvas was gifted to his friend, the painter Paul-Albert Besnard (1849–1934) [see fig. 31]. Sargent seems to revel in the pleasure of painting in these decidedly less formal sketches.

At key moments throughout the first decades of his career, Sargent built his public reputation, in part, by convincing friends and notable members of fashionable society to pose for major compositions. He strategically exhibited these works at prominent venues. This is the case for his most famous portrait—the well-known *Madame X* [fig. 25]. Sargent had become fascinated by Virginie Avegno Gautreau, an expatriate from Louisiana who was married to a French banker. She was known in Parisian society for her artful appearance, which she accentuated with dramatic cosmetics and couture gowns. Sargent was drawn to Gautreau's careful self-fashioning. The ambitious painter arranged an introduction through a mutual acquaintance and convinced her to pose for him without a commission. He made more studies in preparation for this portrait than for any other he ever created, including multiple drawings, a watercolor, and a bravura oil study of her drinking a toast [fig. 26]. He harnessed his knowledge of art history and drew inspiration from such diverse sources as antique sculpture and Renaissance portraits. He was particularly preoccupied with Gautreau's distinctive profile, which he carefully delineated in many of the studies and the final portrait. The unusual twisted standing pose that he contrived for Gautreau conveys a sense of torsion and tension.

The portrait was a scandalous success at the Paris Salon in 1884. Even though Sargent had protected his sitter's identity by using an anonymous title (in keeping with tradition), many who saw the portrait immediately identified Gautreau.

Ralph Wormeley Curtis (1854–1922), Sargent's friend (and a distant cousin) who was also a painter, described the "great fuss" that surrounded the picture on the opening day of the Salon: "There was a *grande* [*sic*] *tapage* before it all day. . . . I was disappointed in the colour. She looks decomposed. All the women jeer. Ah voilà 'la belle!' 'Oh quel horreur!' etc."[29]

Gautreau had been complicit in the choice of dress and pose and had even written a mutual friend before the painting was exhibited, "Mr Sargent made a masterpiece of the portrait."[30] She, like Sargent, was devastated by the initial response. Gautreau and her mother rushed to the artist's studio later that day in tears. Her mother begged him to remove the portrait from the exhibition, exclaiming, "My daughter is lost—all Paris mocks her. She will be forced to flee. She will die of chagrin, etc."[31]

Critics recognized the portrait as a description of a new type of woman who used her appearance to acquire celebrity and social standing in breaking with time-honored

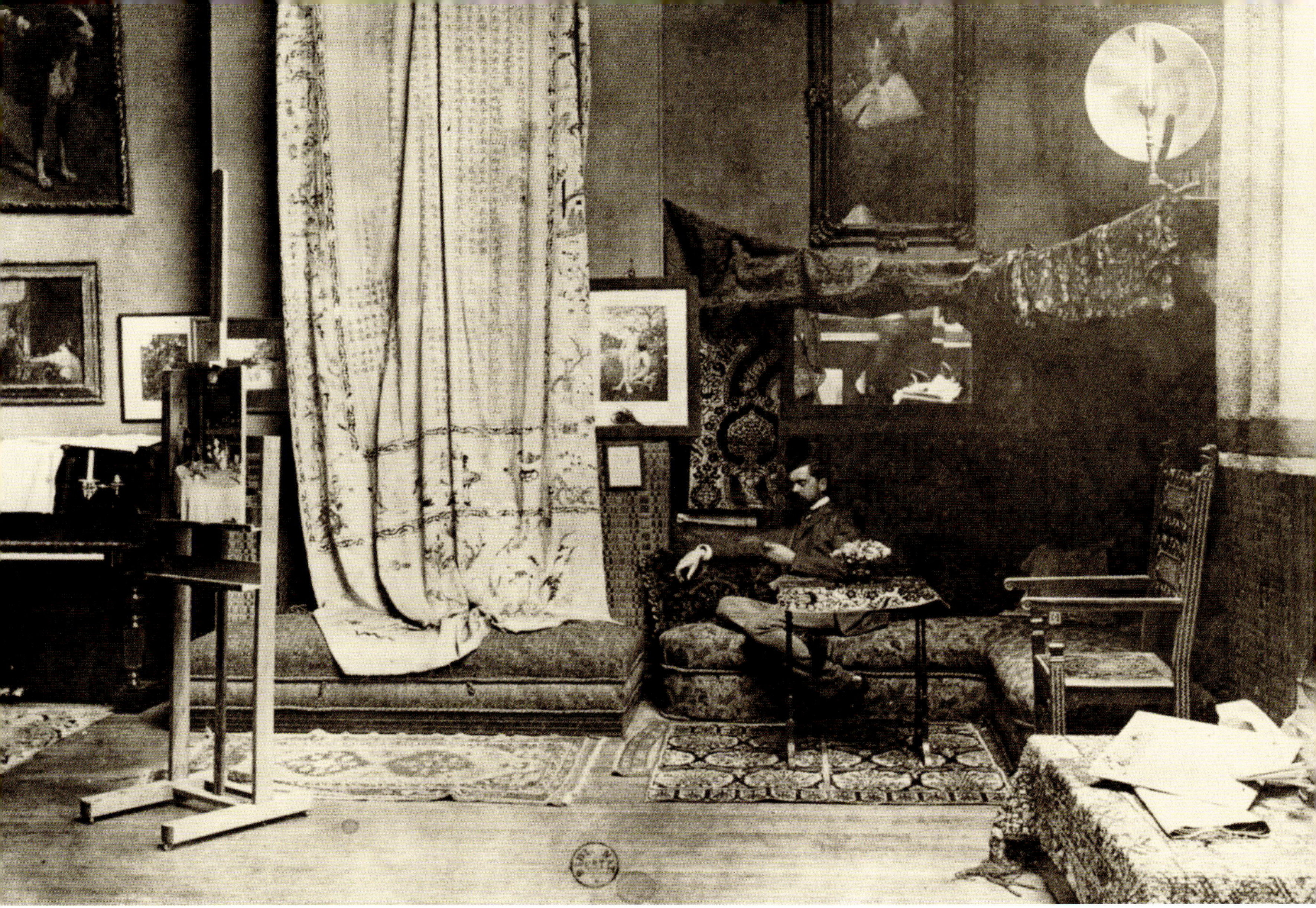

Sargent in his Paris studio, ca. 1884. Smithsonian Institution, Archives of American Art, Washington, D.C. Miscellaneous photographs collection.

hierarchies. Like an artist or an actor, the so-called "professional beauty" enacted a role in Parisian society, which Sargent sought to record in this portrait.[32] Other viewers found Sargent's stylized depiction highly unflattering, offensive, ugly, and eccentric. Her profile pose, which averted her gaze, was seen as haughty by some. Many were shocked that he depicted the right jeweled strap of her daring, low-cut gown slipping from her shoulder.

After the exhibition, Sargent repainted the shoulder strap in the upright position—as we see it today—and since it was not a commissioned work, kept the picture for himself in his studio. Though he was devastated, he defended the portrait, declaring that he had only painted Gautreau as she appeared. When he sold the painting to The Metropolitan Museum of Art after Gautreau's death in 1916, he maintained it was "the best thing I have done."[33]

Author Vernon Lee, Sargent's friend since childhood, explained the effect the portrait had on potential patrons, "[W]omen are afraid of [Sargent] lest he should make them too eccentric looking."[34] The scandal plunged Sargent's career into crisis. As commissions grew scarce in Paris, Sargent began spending more time in England. Reportedly, he had considered moving there as early as 1882—well before the debacle of *Madame X*—encouraged by his friend, the great writer Henry James, whom he had met in Paris about this time. As cosmopolitan expatriates and artistic recorders of the transatlantic social scene, Sargent and James became lifelong friends. James was a staunch supporter of Sargent and used his writing to promote the painter's work on both sides of the Atlantic.

For Sargent, the mid-1880s was a time of turmoil that yielded great experimentation. Between Paris and London, he became acquainted, mainly through James, with a group of American and British artists and writers who gathered in the picturesque Cotswold village of Broadway in Worcestershire. Sargent spent several productive summers at Broadway, where he found solace in his friendships and work at the colony, which included the American artists Edwin Austin Abbey (1852–1911) and Frank Millet (1846–1912), the English illustrator Frederick Barnard (1846–1896), and the writer Edmund Gosse. Lacking portrait commissions, Sargent focused on painting landscapes—both informal sketches and formal exhibition pieces—and also created a series of moody interior scenes as well as candid, informal portraits of friends. The works made during this period are some of the most interesting of his career and show him grappling with new directions as he struggled to gain his reputation in a new country.

Sargent may have met the great Impressionist painter Claude Monet as early as 1876 in Paris. The two artists formed a close friendship that lasted into the twentieth century. They painted alongside one another on multiple occasions during this period, and their long correspondence reveals that Sargent, on occasion, asked Monet for technical advice on pigments and colors. Sargent paid tribute to his mentor and their friendship in his iconic canvas *Claude Monet Painting by the Edge of a Wood* [fig. 28], which demonstrates his full understanding of, and debt to, the Impressionist tradition. Sargent experimented with his open brushwork, Impressionist palette, and attention to recording the optical experience of light and nature. The painting records Monet in his element—working *en plein air*—and had a special and personal significance for Sargent, as it commemorates his relationship with Monet.

Although Sargent usually presented the sketches he made of friends and fellow artists to them as gifts, as was the tradition in artistic circles, he cherished this image of his friend. This painting, along with several works by Monet, was in Sargent's studio when he died. Upon learning of Sargent's death in 1925, Monet wrote their mutual friend, the painter Paul Helleu, that "we [have] lost an old friend. It is very sad."[35]

From the 1880s, Sargent would assimilate aspects of Impressionist practice into his oeuvre. In *The Old Chair* (ca. 1886, private collection), painted at Broadway about this time,

Sargent seems to have created a simple-still life composition as a spontaneous study of light and shadow, pattern and texture. Sargent takes a high vantage point, to study a small glass vase with a few pale pink flowers resting on the seat of a woven rush chair. He eliminates the horizon to create a broad green backdrop. The animated brushwork of the grass contrasts with the rhythmic patterns of the woven chair in dappled sunlight

Sargent also experimented with plein air compositions in watercolor. His painting of Henriette Roger-Jourdain [fig. 27] anticipates a theme that would preoccupy him later in his career when he made a series of images of friends and family lounging out of doors. Madame Roger-Jourdain was a wealthy, engaging society hostess who was involved in the art world. She was Sargent's neighbor on the boulevard Berthier in Paris where he lived after 1883. Sargent eliminates the horizon to set her against a broadly painted sun-dappled lawn. Her overturned parasol and pale, pastel-hued dress become a vehicle for exploration of light and shadow. Sargent maintains a portraitist's specificity in his representation of her facial features and her carefully articulated hand gestures.

Carnation, Lily, Lily, Rose [fig. 29], a charming picture of two young girls lighting Japanese paper lanterns at dusk, set in a luscious garden of flowers, is indebted to Sargent's interest in Impressionism. Sargent delighted in the artistic challenge of capturing a specific, fleeting moment, just at dusk, when the soft, glowing light of the lanterns coalesces with the fading daylight. He lamented, "Fearful difficult subject. Impossible brilliant colours of flowers, and lamps and brightest green lawn background. Paints are not bright enough & then the effect only lasts ten minutes."[36] But it's not an Impressionist picture. He based the composition on a scene he witnessed while boating on the Thames in 1885 that he described as "a paradisiac sight [that] makes one rave with pleasure."[37] He carefully re-created the effect in the garden at Broadway. He made numerous drawings and oil sketches in preparation for the composition, using a friend's daughters for models. Painted over the course of two summers, the deliberately contrived final work synthesizes Sargent's astute study of various impulses, from Impressionism to the Pre-Raphaelites and Aestheticism; his understanding of the character of British art of the period; and his desire to produce a painting that would be acclaimed in London. The association between children and lilies, a symbol of innocence and purity, places the image in a Victorian context, and the title refers to a popular British song.[38] The subject is intentionally pretty, almost self-consciously so, in the Aesthetic tradition. Sargent flattened his composition and created a highly decorative effect with a tapestry of flowers that seems to float on the verdant field and recalls Renaissance tapestries or early Sienese paintings. He references the art of the past and present, merges realist observation with Impressionist brushwork to create a unique work, an aspect that many critics recognized, including one who celebrated the painting's "audacious originality."[39] *Carnation, Lily, Lily, Rose* was exhibited at the Royal Academy in London in 1886 and immediately purchased for the British nation.

Two Women Asleep under the Willows [fig. 30] belongs to a series of paintings made on the river Thames during the summers of 1887 at Henley, and 1888 and 1889 at Calcot.

Sargent was certainly thinking of his friend Monet who had set up a floating studio on the river Seine in the early 1870s. *Two Women Asleep under the Willows* maintains the spontaneity of a plein air painting. Sargent records an idyllic scene, framed by willow branches, two women doze in a punt along the banks of the river. The play of light and shadow across the women's white dresses and the glistening surface of the water conjure shimmering sunlight. The vibrant red cushion beneath their heads focuses attention on the figures.

In contrast to these saturated, sun-filled Impressionist experiments, Sargent produced a series of moody interior scenes at this same moment. *Fête Familiale* (*The Birthday Party*) [fig. 31] captures his friends, the painter Albert Besnard and his wife, the sculptor Charlotte Dubray (1854–1931), as they celebrate their oldest son's birthday. Sargent's unusual composition places the celebration to the right edge of the composition where the birthday boy's face is washed out in the glow of the celebratory candles. Dubray's robust figure, in a striking red dress, occupies the center of the composition. She appears in sharp profile against her husband's dark clothing as she cuts her son's cake. Meanwhile, Besnard, hovers over his family, a faceless but strong presence. The participants seem unaware that they're being painted or watched, and Sargent captures just a brief moment in their celebration. He suggests the family's refined, cosmopolitan tastes in the details of their surroundings: the crimson walls, the Asian-inspired blue curtains, and in the top right corner—the blue-and-white details of the Asian lampshade. Sargent paints the objects on the table, gleaming under the light, with exquisite attention—especially the transparency and reflective qualities of the glassware—to create a dazzling still life.

During this period, Sargent made several excursions to Bournemouth, England—to paint three portraits of writer Robert Louis Stevenson. Sargent had known Stevenson since his early years in Paris. The second of the portraits [fig. 32], which also included Stevenson's wife, Fanny, was painted shortly after *Treasure Island* was published in 1882. Sargent captures Stevenson's nervous energy, showing him in his characteristic manner pacing and talking. He is caught midstride, playing with his mustache, as he moves away from his wife, who, draped in exotic garb, is the peripheral figure at the extreme right edge of the painting. Sargent exploits the distance between them by creating a void at the center of the eccentric composition beyond the open door and depicting her gazing away from her husband. Stevenson admired the portrait, noting that it had "that witty touch of Sargent's; but of course it looks dam [*sic*] queer as a whole."[40] Fanny was also pleased, writing, "Anybody may have a 'portrait of a gentleman,' but nobody ever had one like this. It is an open box of jewels."[41]

1 Evan Charteris, *John Sargent* (New York: Charles Scribner's Sons, 1927), 3. The family did not arrive in Florence until 1855.

2 Fitzwilliam Sargent to Emily Haskell Sargent, October 10, 1870, Florence; quoted in Stephanie L. Herdrich and H. Barbara Weinberg, *American Drawings and Watercolors in The Metropolitan Museum of Art: John Singer Sargent* (New York: The Metropolitan Museum of Art; and New Haven: Yale University Press) V, 2000, 40.

3 Vernon Lee, *The Sentimental Traveller: Notes on Places* (London and New York: J. Lane, 1928), 5.

4 Ibid., 10–11.

5 Charteris 1927, 3.

6 Fitzwilliam Sargent to Emily Haskell Sargent, September 21, 1861; quoted in Herdrich and Weinberg 2000, 40.

7 Sargent met Ben del Castillo about 1862, when both of their families were living in Nice. Several letters from Sargent to Ben del Castillo are reprinted in Charteris 1927. One particularly charming letter (October 14, 1865) begins with an apology, "We have often thought of writing to you . . ., but we have been so busy sightseeing that we have not had time." (Charteris 1927, 9).

8 In 1871 the family moved to Dresden to find a school for John but abandoned the plan after a few months.

9 Stanley Olson, *John Singer Sargent: His Portrait* (New York: St. Martin's Press, 1986), 18.

10 Mary Singer Sargent to Emily Haskell Sargent, October 20, 1967; quoted in Stephen D. Rubin, *John Singer Sargent's Alpine Sketchbooks: A Young Artist's Perspective*, exh. cat. (New York: The Metropolitan Museum of Art, 1991), 12.

11 Vernon Lee, "J.S.S.: In Memoriam," in Charteris 1927, 242–43.

12 Ibid., 243. During this winter, Sargent may have had his first informal lessons in watercolor painting from a German American landscape artist about whom little is known, Karl Welsch (or Charles Feodor Welsch, d. 1904). Charteris claims that "Sargent used to spend the mornings in copying the watercolours of Welsch." (Charteris 1927, 10.) While Sargent once explained that his lessons from Welsch were limited and that he "was kept busy fetching and carrying beer and wine from the nearest wine shops." Olson 1986, 21–22. Olson also asserts that Sargent and Welsch didn't meet until later.

13 Vernon Lee, "J.S.S.: In Memoriam," in Charteris 1927, 240.

14 Ibid., 240–41.

15 Fitzwilliam Sargent to Emily Haskell Sargent, October 10, 1870, Florence; quoted in Rubin 1991, 9.

16 Sargent to Mrs. Austin, Florence, April 25, 1874; quoted in Charteris 1927, 19.

17 Letter, Sargent to Charles Heath Wilson, 11 rue Montaigne, Paris, 12 June 1874. Excerpt transcribed by William H. Allen Bookseller from a now lost letter.

18 For Sargent's relationship with Monet and Rodin, see Richard Ormond et al., *Sargent: Portraits of Artists and Friends*, exh. cat. (London: National Portrait Gallery, 2015), 81–82.

19 Letter, Sargent to Ben del Castillo, Capri, August 10, 1878, quoted in Charteris 1927, 47.

20 "Two New York Exhibitions," *Atlantic Monthly* 43 (June 1879): 781. Quoted in Marc Simpson et al. *Uncanny Spectacle: The Public Career of the Young John Singer Sargent*, exh. cat. (Williamstown, Mass.: Sterling and Francine Clark Art Institute, 1997), 90.

21 Sargent painted three versions of *Dans les oliviers, à Capri*. The first, known as *A Capriote* (1878; Museum of Fine Arts, Boston), was exhibited in New York in 1879 at the second exhibition of the Society of American Artists. It has not been possible to determine which of the other two versions (both in private collections) was shown in the Paris Salon. See Richard Ormond and Elaine Kilmurray, *John Singer Sargent: Complete Paintings*. Vol. 4: *Figures and Landscapes, 1874–1882* (New Haven: Yale University Press, 2006), 158–63.

22 The museum's *Libros de copistas* of 1879 reveals that in October and November Sargent registered to copy nine paintings by the master. See Ormond and Kilmurray 2006, 204–15.

23 For an extensive discussion of the critical reception of *El Jaleo*, see Ormond and Kilmurray 2006, 273.

24 For Sargent's exhibition history up to 1885, see Williamstown 1997. For a detailed exhibition history, see Herdrich and Weinberg 2000.

25 Henry James, "John S. Sargent," *Harper's New Monthly Magazine* 75 (October 1887): 686.

26 Ibid.

27 "The Salon. From an Englishman's Point of View," *Art Journal* (London) 44 (July 1882): 218. Quoted in Williamstown 1997, 136.

28 Vernon Lee letter, June 25, 1818 in Irene Cooper Willis and Gordon Norton Ray, eds. *Vernon Lee's Letters* (London: Privately printed, 1937), 65.

29 Quoted in Charteris 1927, 61.

30 "Mr Sargent a fait un chef d'œuvre du portrait"; Sargent and Gautreau to Allouard-Jouan, summer 1883, John Singer Sargent Archive, Museum of Fine Arts, Boston.

31 "Ma fille est perdue—tout Paris se moque d'elle. Mon genre sera forcé de se battre. Elle mourira de chagrin. etc."; quoted in Charteris 1927, 61–62.

32 Sargent's friend Louis de Fourcaud (1851–1914) was an art critic, art historian, poet, musician and musicologist, and an influential figure in Parisian cultural life.

33 Sargent to Edward Robinson, January 8, 1916, Archives of The Metropolitan Museum of Art.

34 Vernon Lee to her mother, July 16, 1885. Quoted in Williamstown 1997, 121.

35 Quoted in Richard Ormond and Elaine Kilmurray. *John Singer Sargent: Complete Paintings*. Vol. 5: *Figures and Landscapes, 1883–1899* (New Haven: Yale University Press, 2009), 68.

36 Sargent to Emily Sargent, quoted in Charteris 1927, 76–77.

37 Undated letter from Sargent to Robert Louis Stevenson, Stevenson Papers, Beinecke Rare Book and Manuscript Library, Yale University, New Haven, 5427, quoted in London/New York 2015, 99.

38 The title comes from the song "The Wreath" by Joseph Mazzinghi (1765–1844), which was popular in the 1880s. The refrain asks, "Have you seen my Flora pass this way?" to which the answer is "Carnation, Lily, Lily, Rose."

39 Harry Quilter, "Art. The Royal Academy. [First Notice]," *The Spectator* 60 (April 30, 1887): 591.

40 November 1885, Stevenson Papers, Beinecke Rare Book and Manuscript Library, Yale University, quoted in Richard Ormond and Elaine Kilmurray. *John Singer Sargent: Complete Paintings*. Vol. 1: *The Early Portraits* (New Haven: Yale University Press, 1998), 168.

41 Quoted in London/New York 2015, 108.

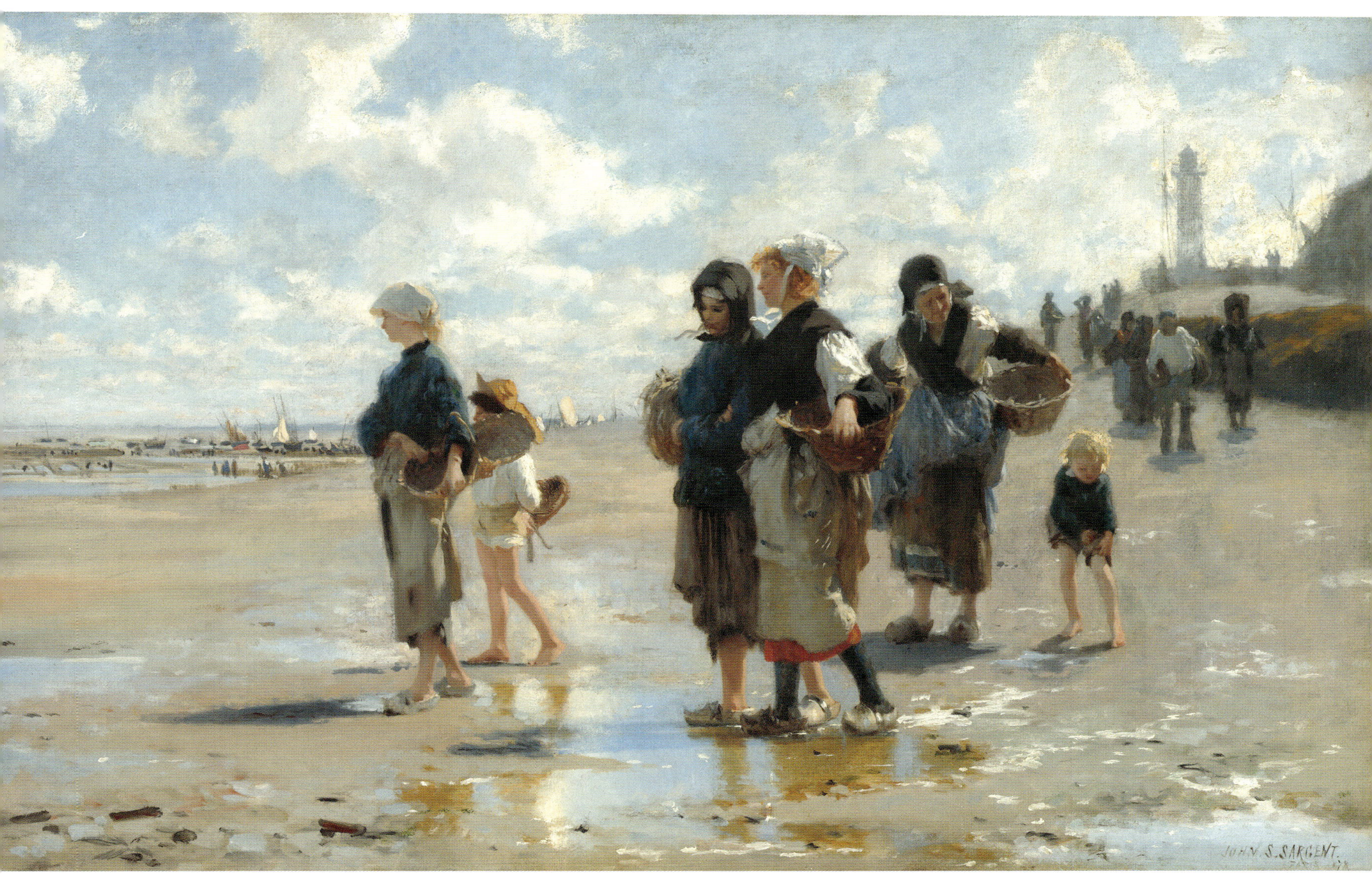

4

En route pour la pêche
(*Setting Out to Fish*)

1878
Oil on canvas, 31 × 48⅜ in. (78.7 × 122.9 cm)
Signed: "JOHN S. SARGENT. / PARIS 1878"
Washington, D.C., National Gallery of Art,
Corcoran Collection [2014.79.32]

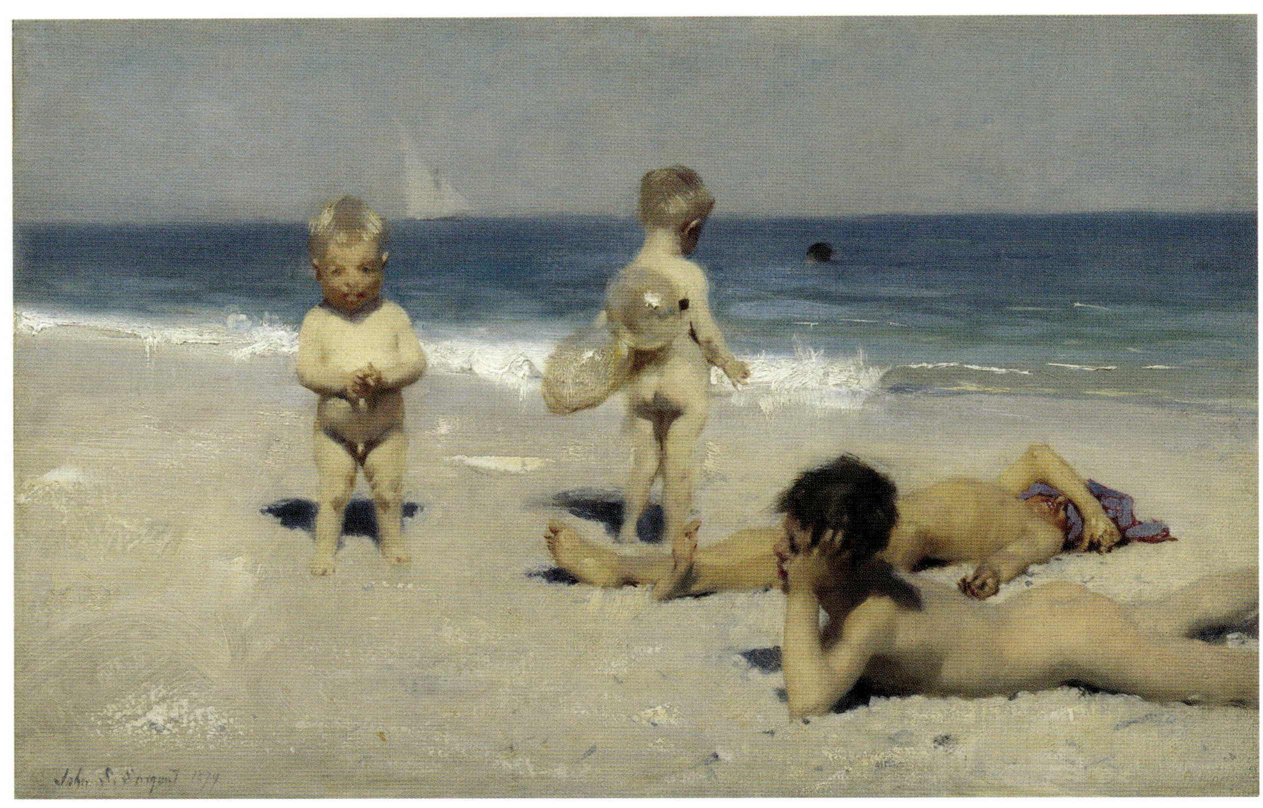

5

Neapolitan Children Bathing

1879
Oil on canvas, 10 9/16 × 16 3/16 in.
(26.8 × 41.1 cm)
Signed: "John S. Sargent 1879"
Williamstown, Massachusetts,
The Clark Art Institute, Acquired
by Sterling and Francine Clark,
1923 [1955.852]

6

A Capriote

1878
Oil on canvas, 30 1/4 × 24 7/8 in.
(76.8 × 63.2 cm)
Signed: "John S. Sargent /
Capri. 1878"
Boston, Museum of Fine Arts,
Bequest of Helen Swift
Neilson [46.10]

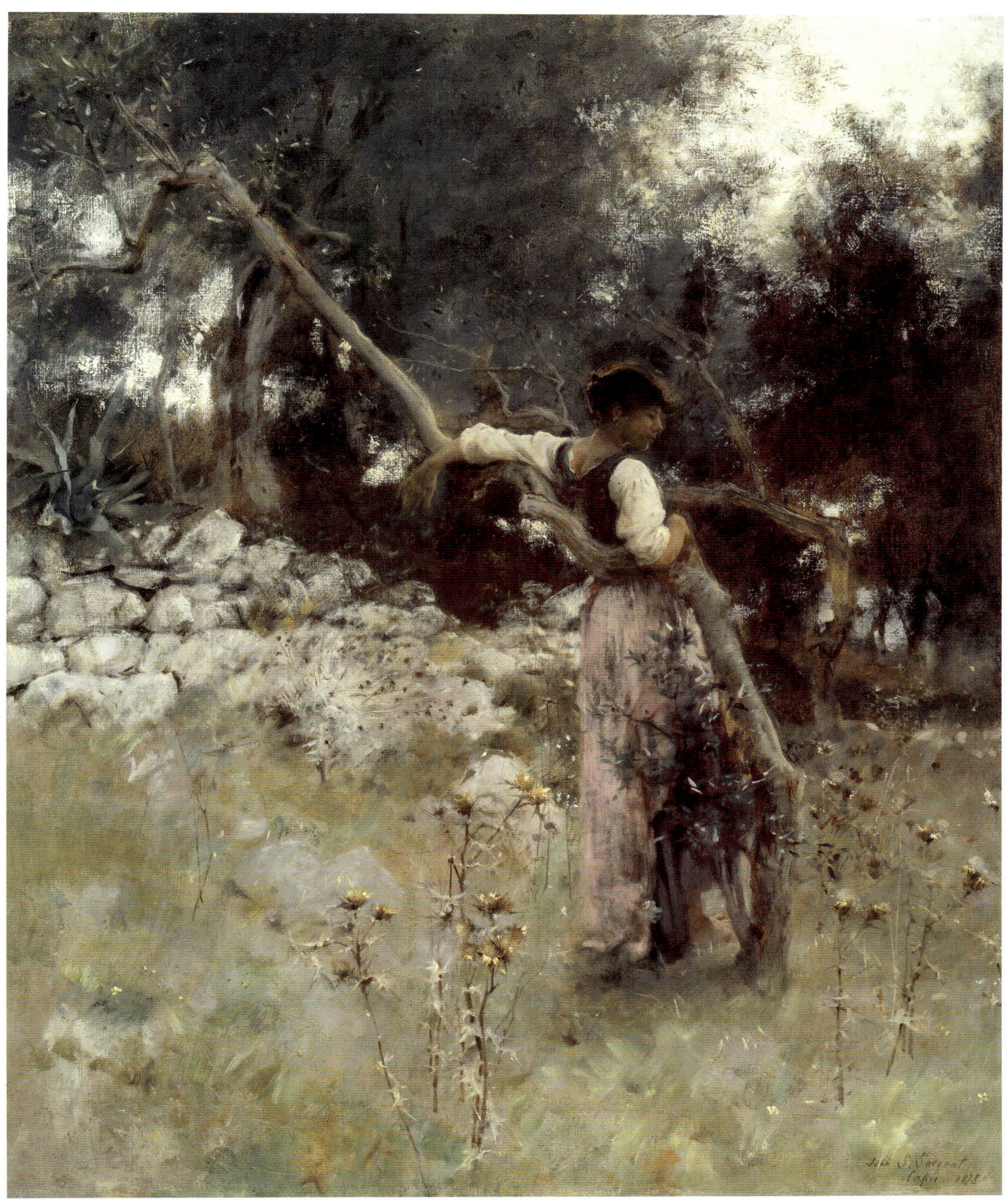

7

Carolus-Duran

1879

Oil on canvas, 46 × 37 13⁄16 in. (116.8 × 96 cm)
Inscription: "à mon cher maître M. Carolus Duran, son élève affectioné / John S. Sargent 1879"
Williamstown, Massachusetts, The Clark Art Institute, Acquired by Sterling and Francine Clark, 1919 [1955.14]

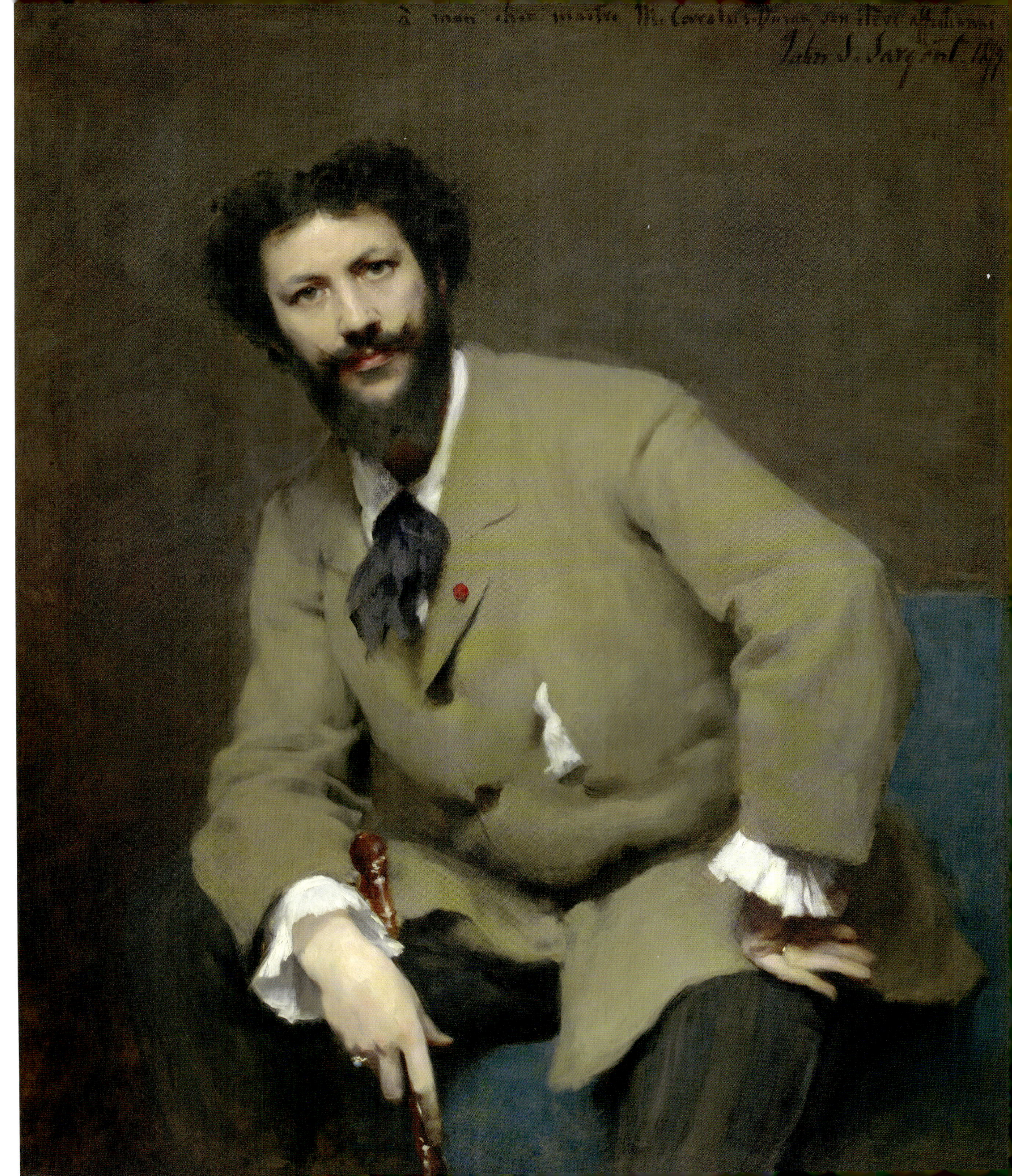
à mon cher maître M. Carolus-Duran son élève affectionné
John S. Sargent 1879

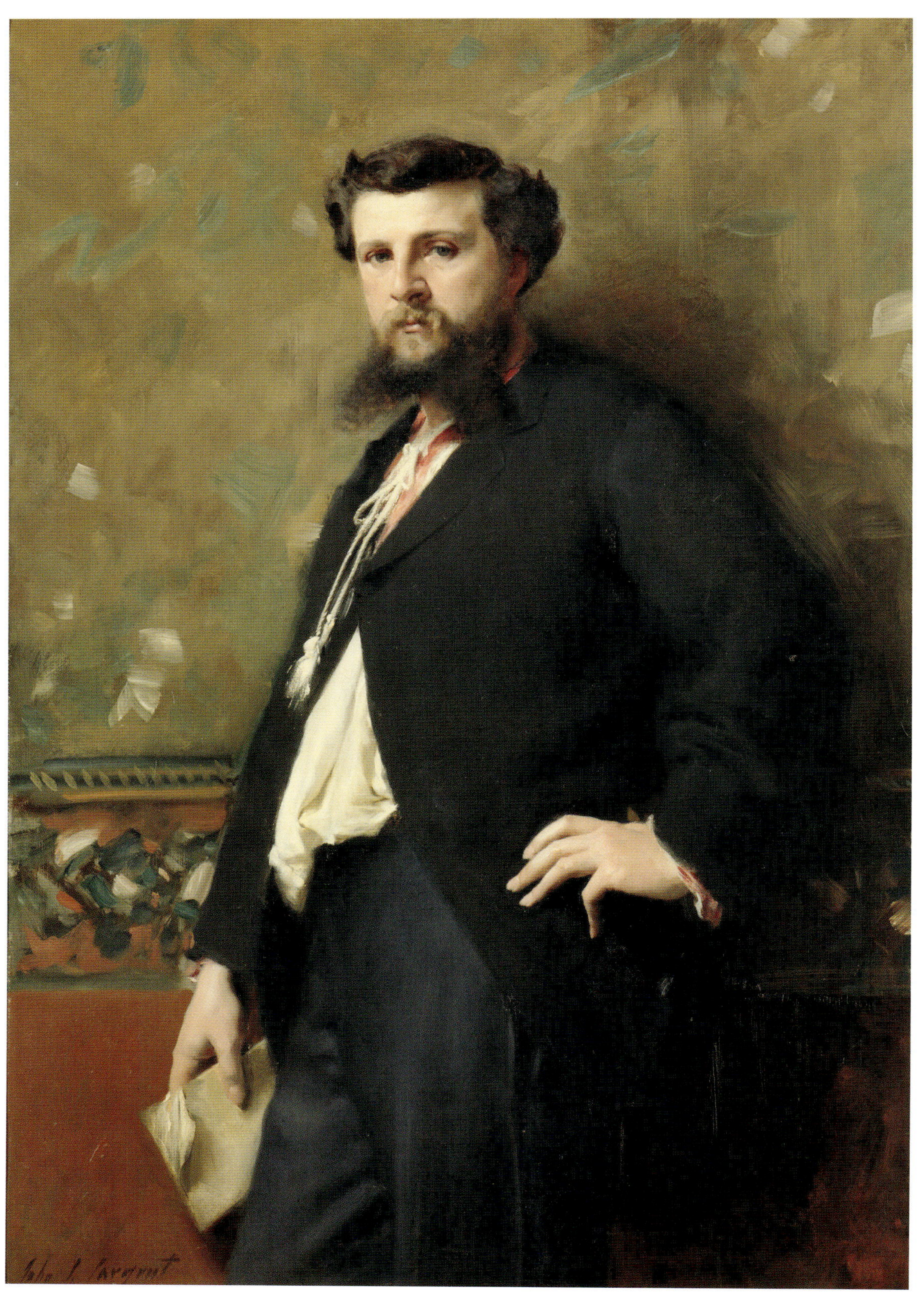

8

Édouard Pailleron

1879
Oil on canvas, 54½ × 37¹³⁄₁₆ in.
(138.5 × 96 cm)
Signed: "John S. Sargent"
Paris, Musée d'Orsay
[DO 1986 17, MV 5623]

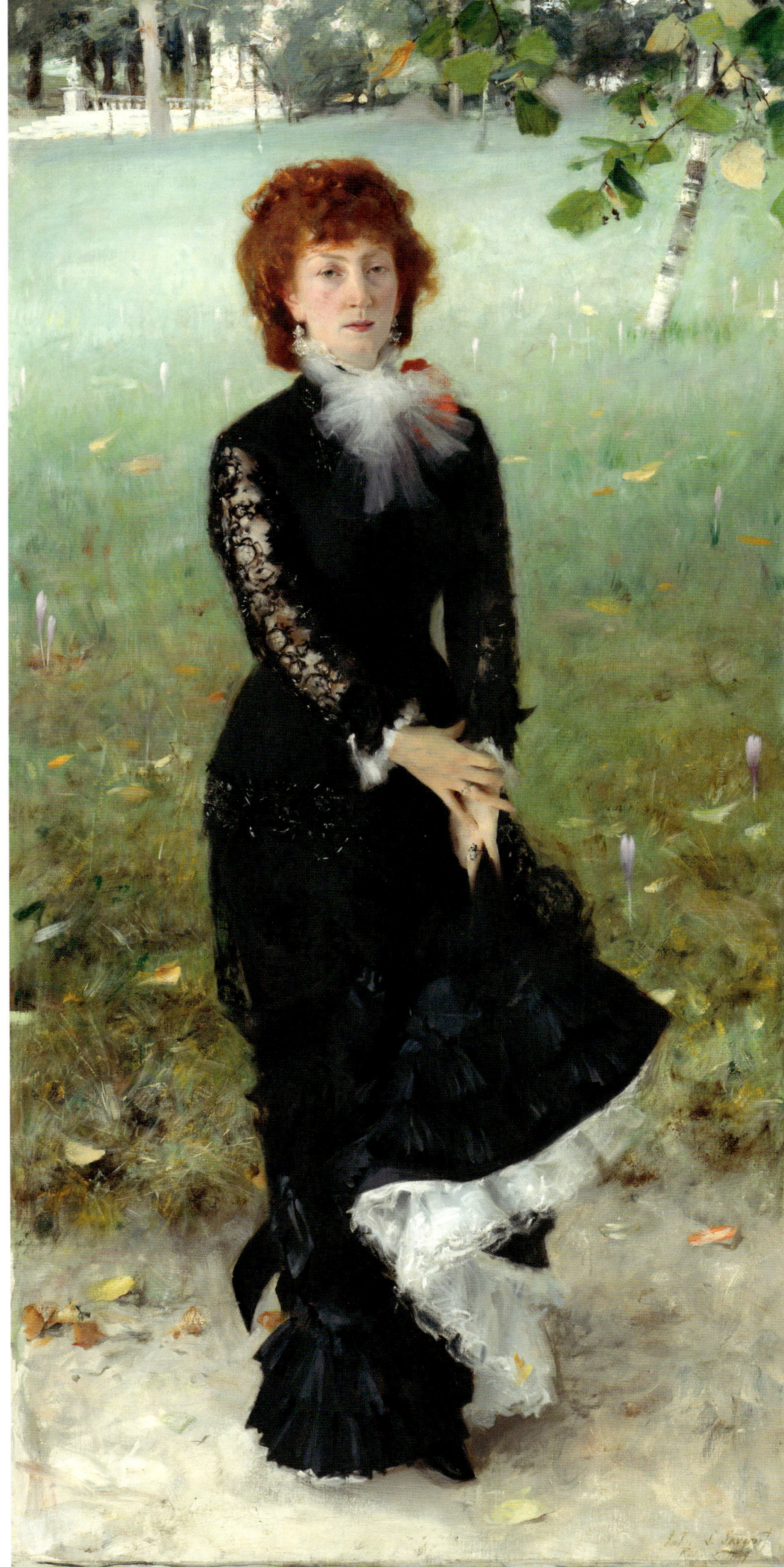

9

Marie Buloz Pailleron (Madame Édouard Pailleron)

1879
Oil on canvas, 83⅛ × 41⅛ in.
(211.2 × 104.4 cm)
Signed: "John S. Sargent / Ronjoux 1879"
Washington, D.C., National Gallery of Art, Corcoran Collection [2014.79.53]

10

Portraits de M.E.P. . . . et de Mlle L.P. (*Portraits of Édouard and Marie-Louise Pailleron*)

1881
Oil on canvas, 60 × 69 in. (152.4 × 175.3 cm)
Signed: "John S. Sargent"
Des Moines, Des Moines Art Center Permanent Collections; Purchased with funds from the Edith M. Usry Bequest, in memory of her parents Mr. and Mrs. George Franklin Usry, the Dr. and Mrs. Peder T. Madsen Fund, and the Anna K. Meredith Endowment Fund [1976.61]

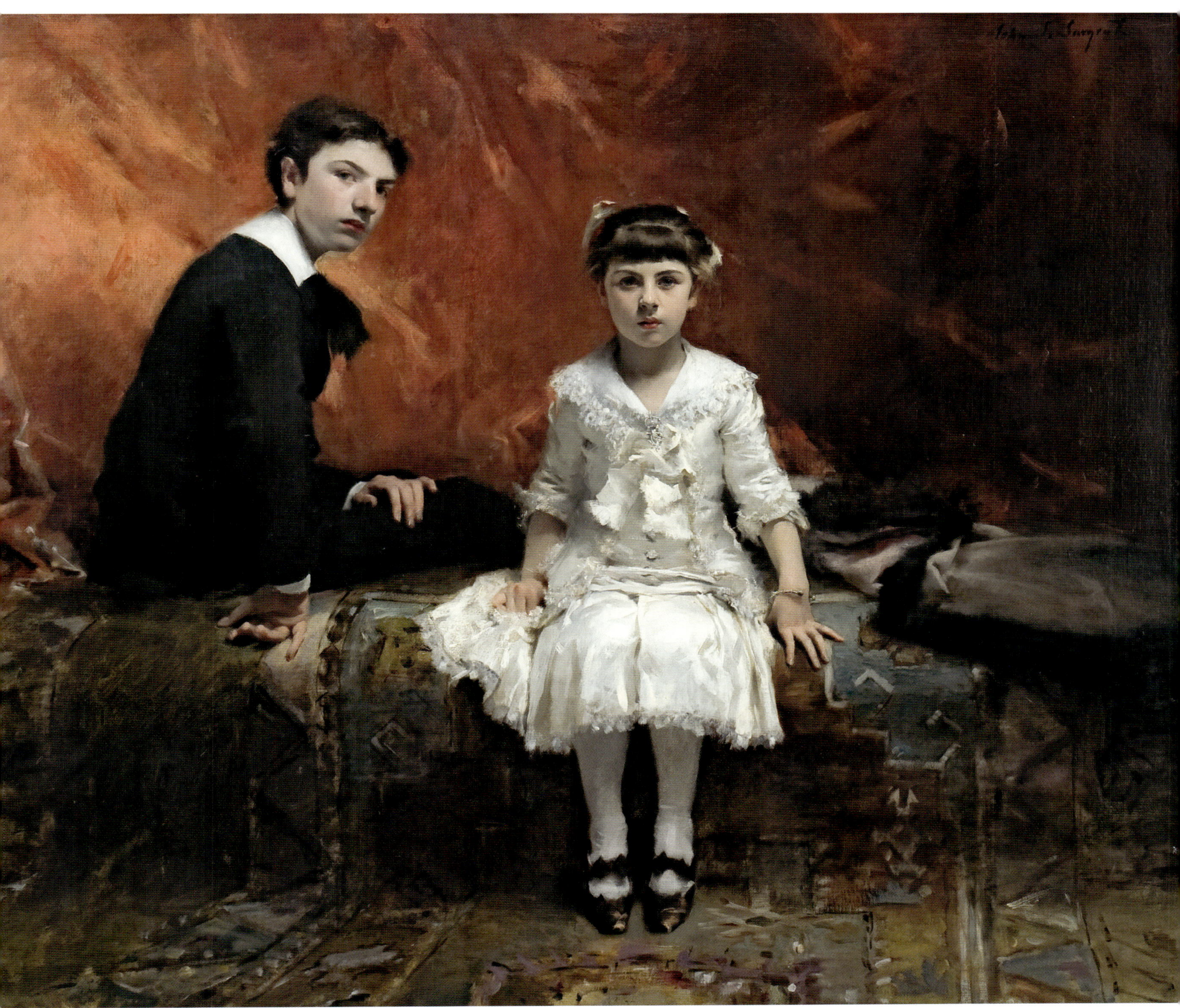

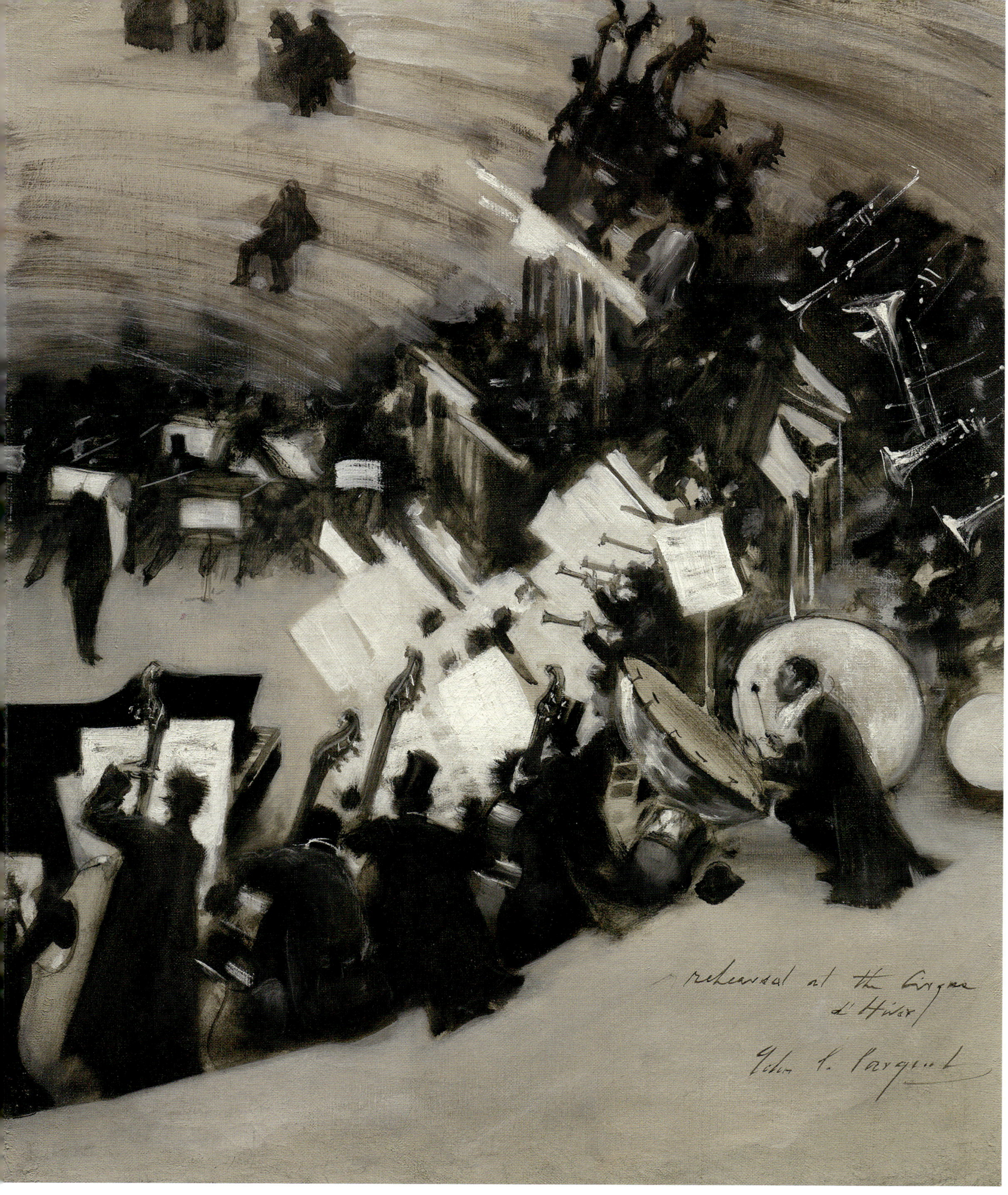
rehearsal at the Cirque d'Hiver
John S. Sargent

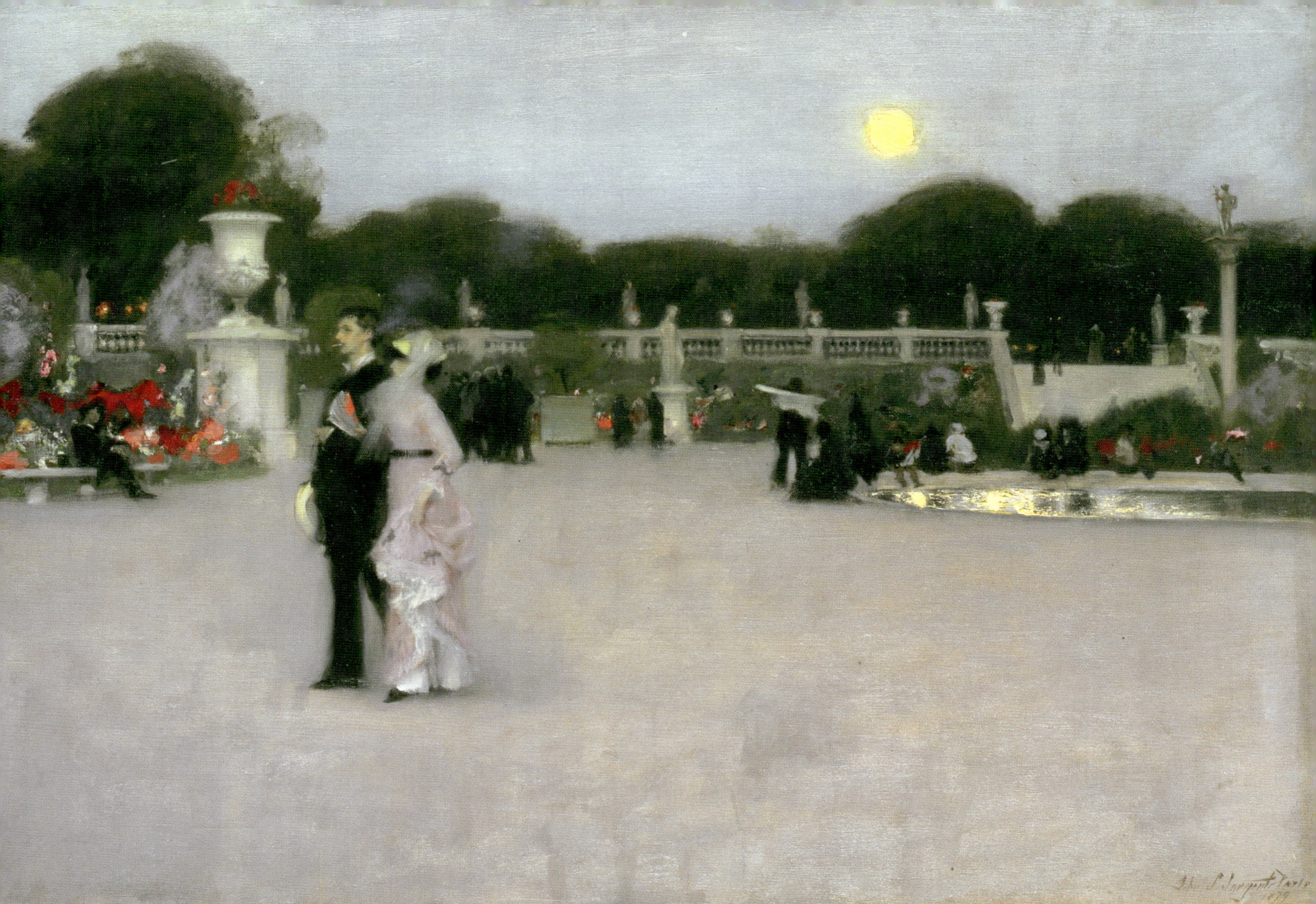

11

Rehearsal of the Pasdeloup Orchestra at the Cirque d'Hiver

ca. 1879
Oil on canvas, 22 ½ × 18 ⅛ in. (57.1 × 46 cm)
Inscription: "rehearsal at the Cirque / d'Hiver / John S. Sargent"
Boston, Museum of Fine Arts, The Hayden Collection—Charles Henry Hayden Fund [22.598]

12

In the Luxembourg Gardens

1879
Oil on canvas, 25 ⅞ × 36 ⅜ in. (65.7 × 92.4 cm)
Signed: "John S. Sargent Paris / 1879"
Philadelphia, Pennsylvania, Philadelphia Museum of Art, John G. Johnson Collection, 1917 [Cat. 1080]

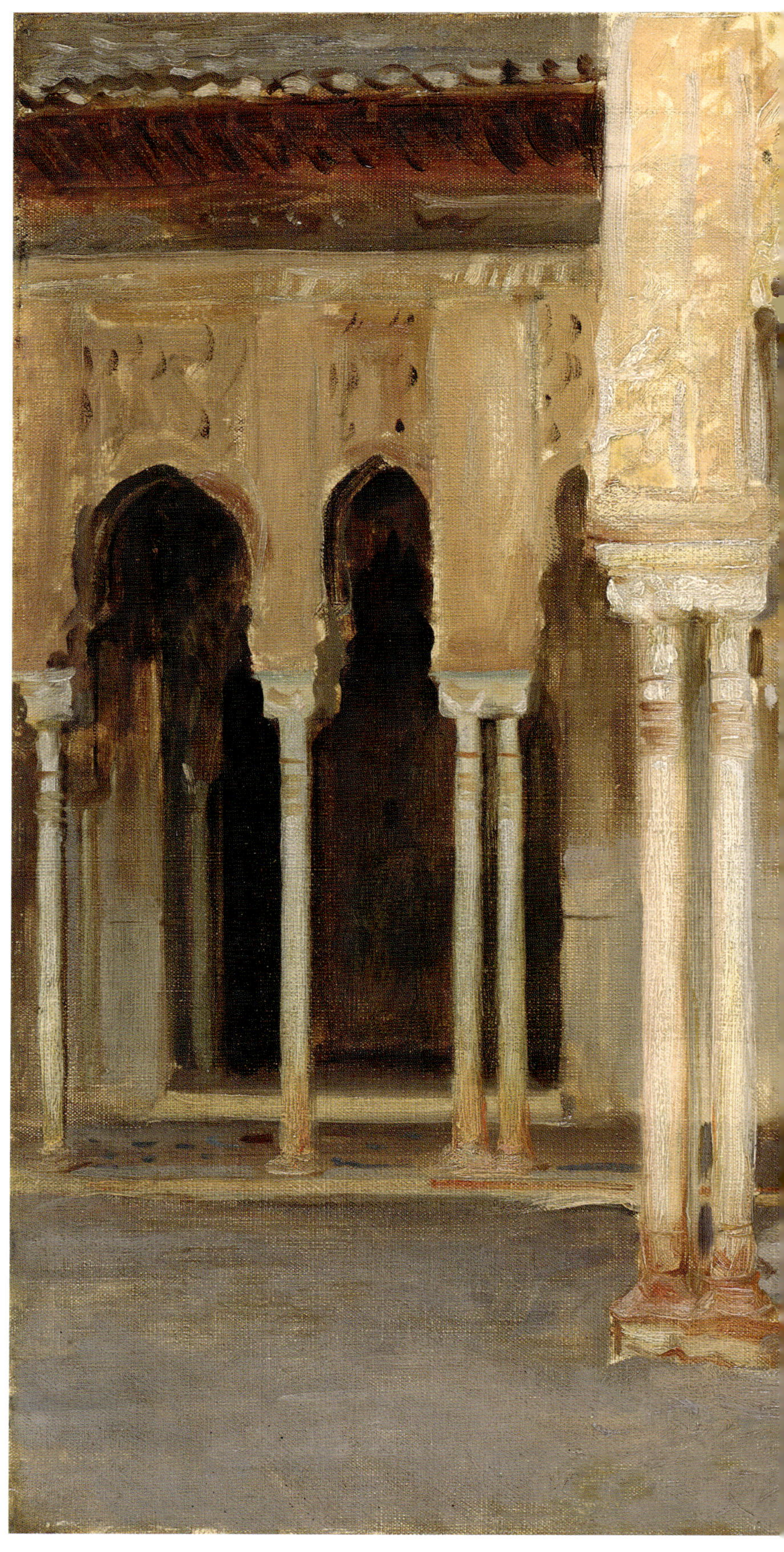

13

Alhambra, Patio de los Leones

1879
Oil on canvas, 18¾ × 31½ in.
(47.7 x 77.5 cm)
Private collection

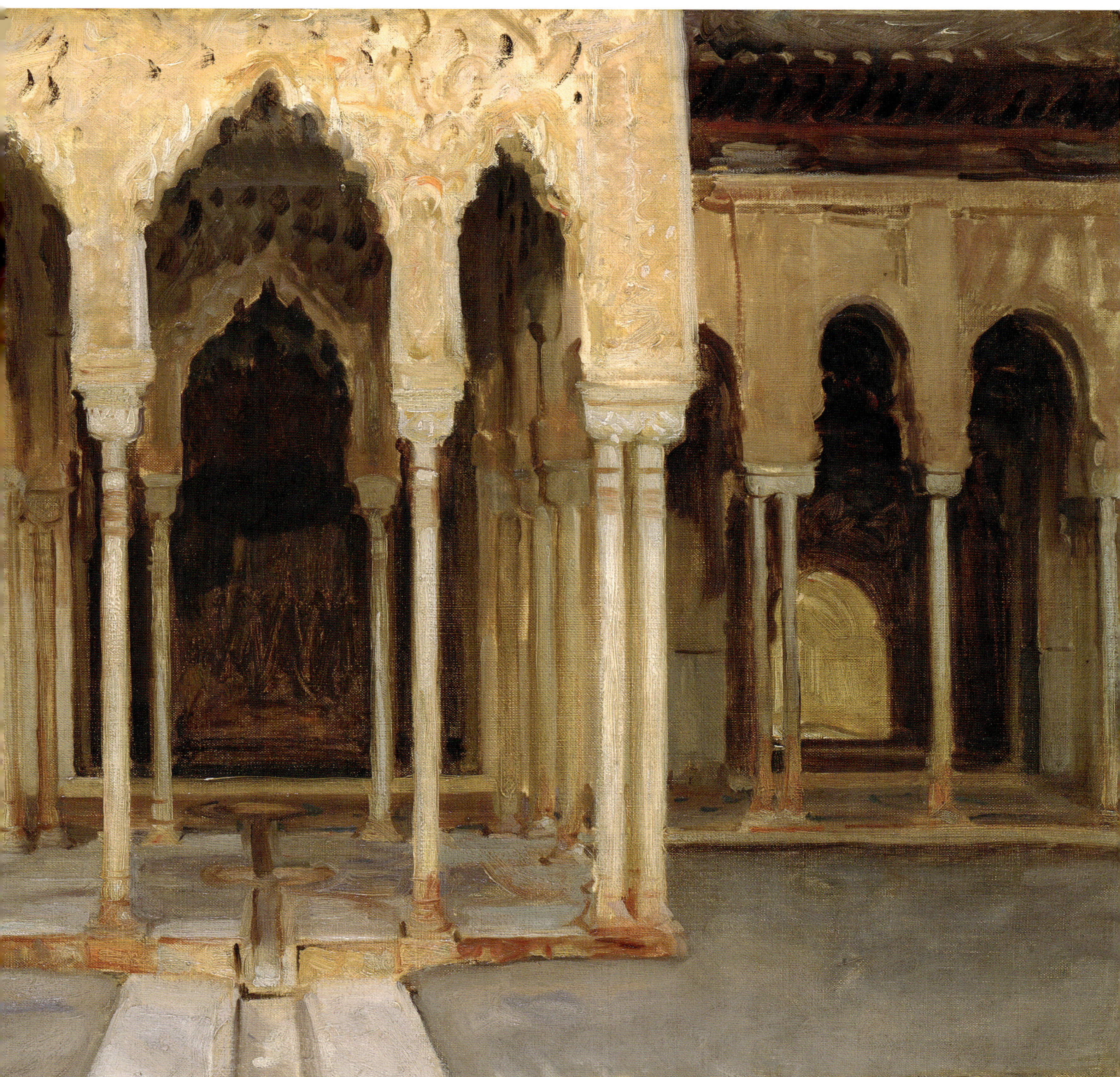

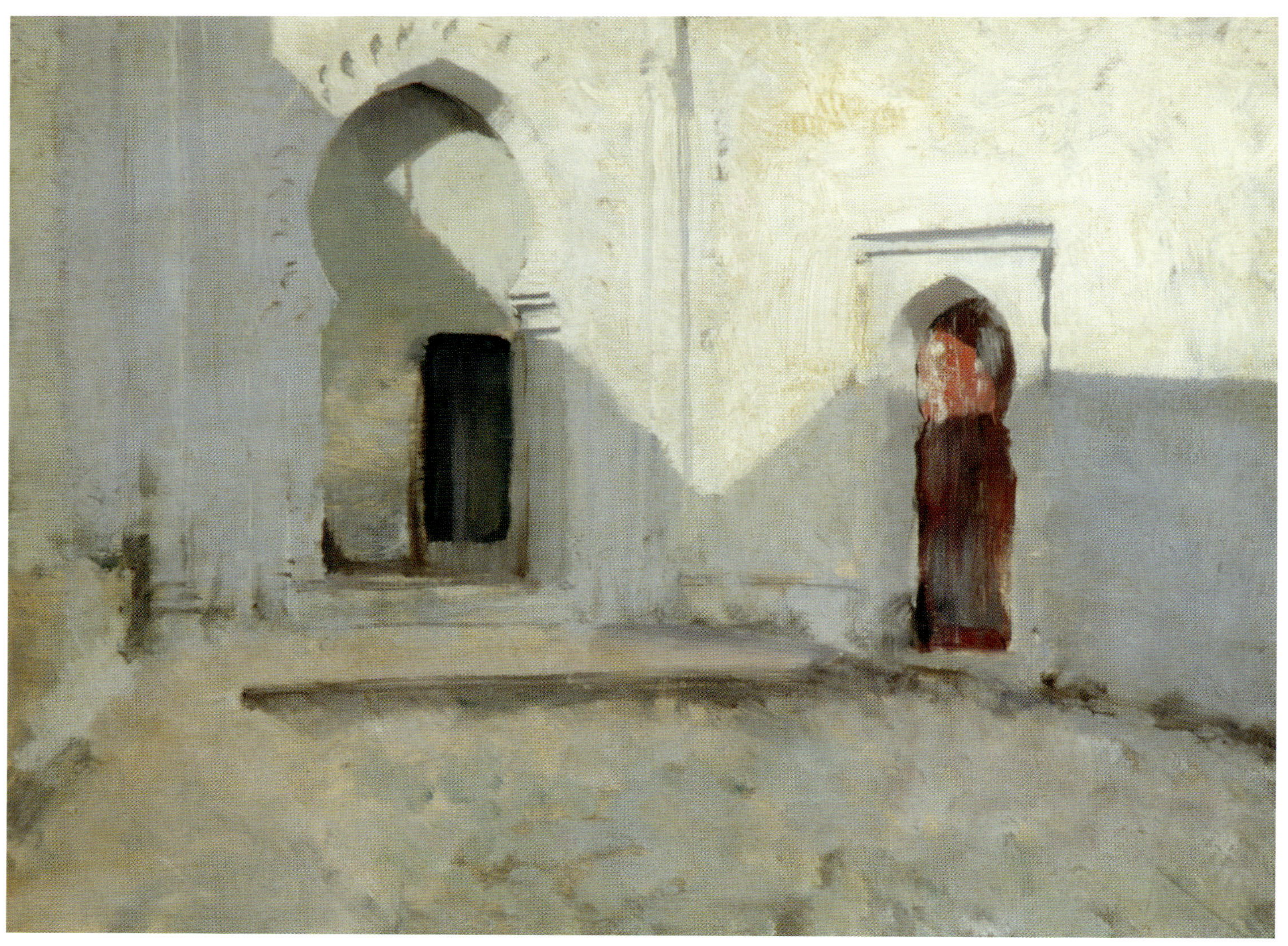

14

Courtyard, Tetuan, Morocco

1880
Oil on wood, 10¼ × 13¾ in. (26 × 34.9 cm)
Inscription: "by J.S. Sargent" (on the back)
New York, The Metropolitan Museum of Art, Gift of Mrs. Francis Ormond, 1950 [50.130.6]

15

Fumée d'Ambre Gris
(*Smoke of Ambergris*)

1880
Oil on canvas, 54¾ × 35 11/16 in. (139.1 × 90.6 cm)
Signed: "John S. Sargent Tanger [*sic*]"
Williamstown, Massachusetts, The Clark Art Institute, Acquired by Sterling Clark, 1914 [1955.15]

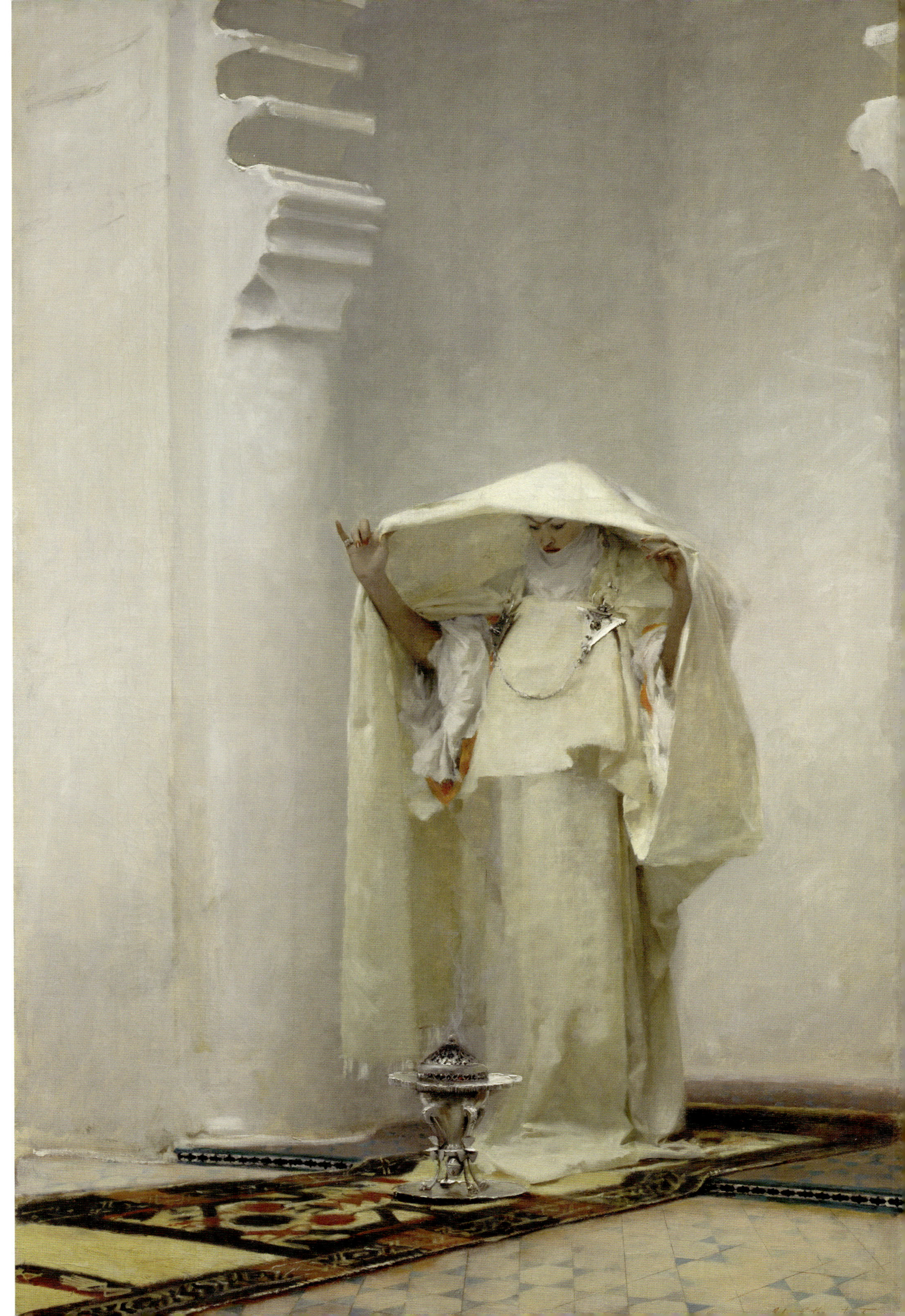

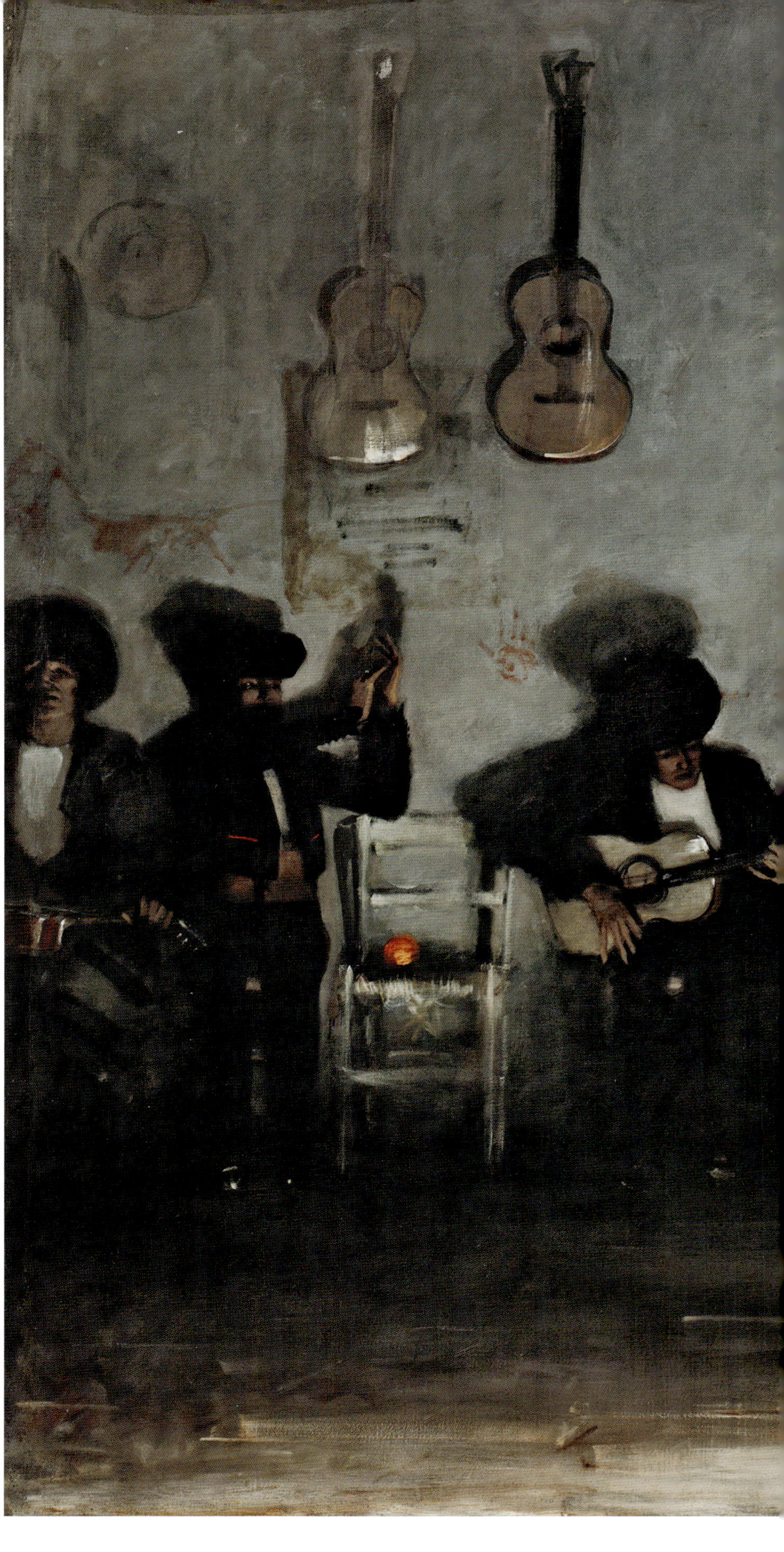

16

El Jaleo

1880–82
Oil on canvas, 91 5/16 × 137 in.
(232 × 348 cm)
Signed: "John S. Sargent 1882"
Boston, Isabella Stewart Gardner Museum [P7s1]

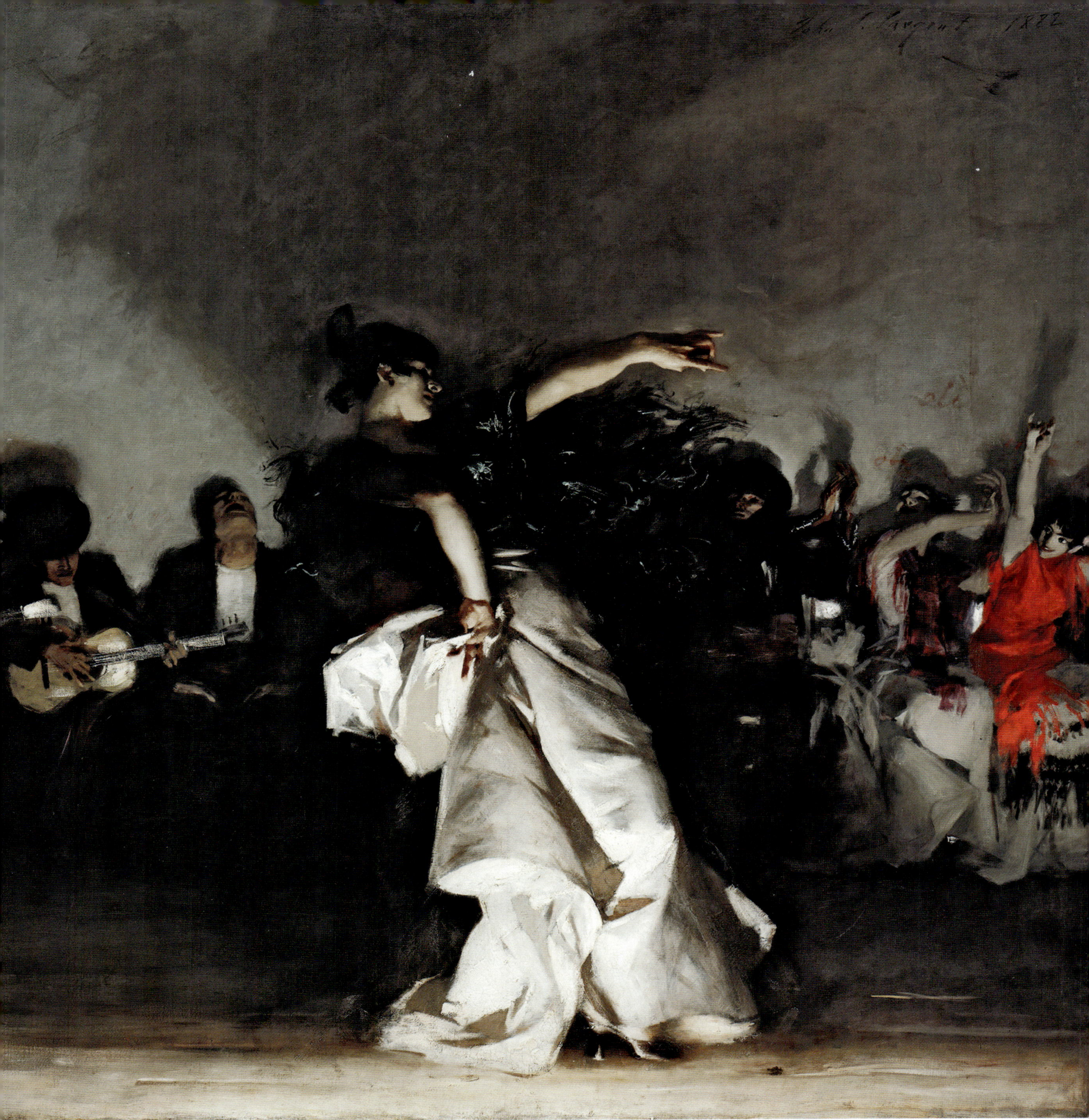

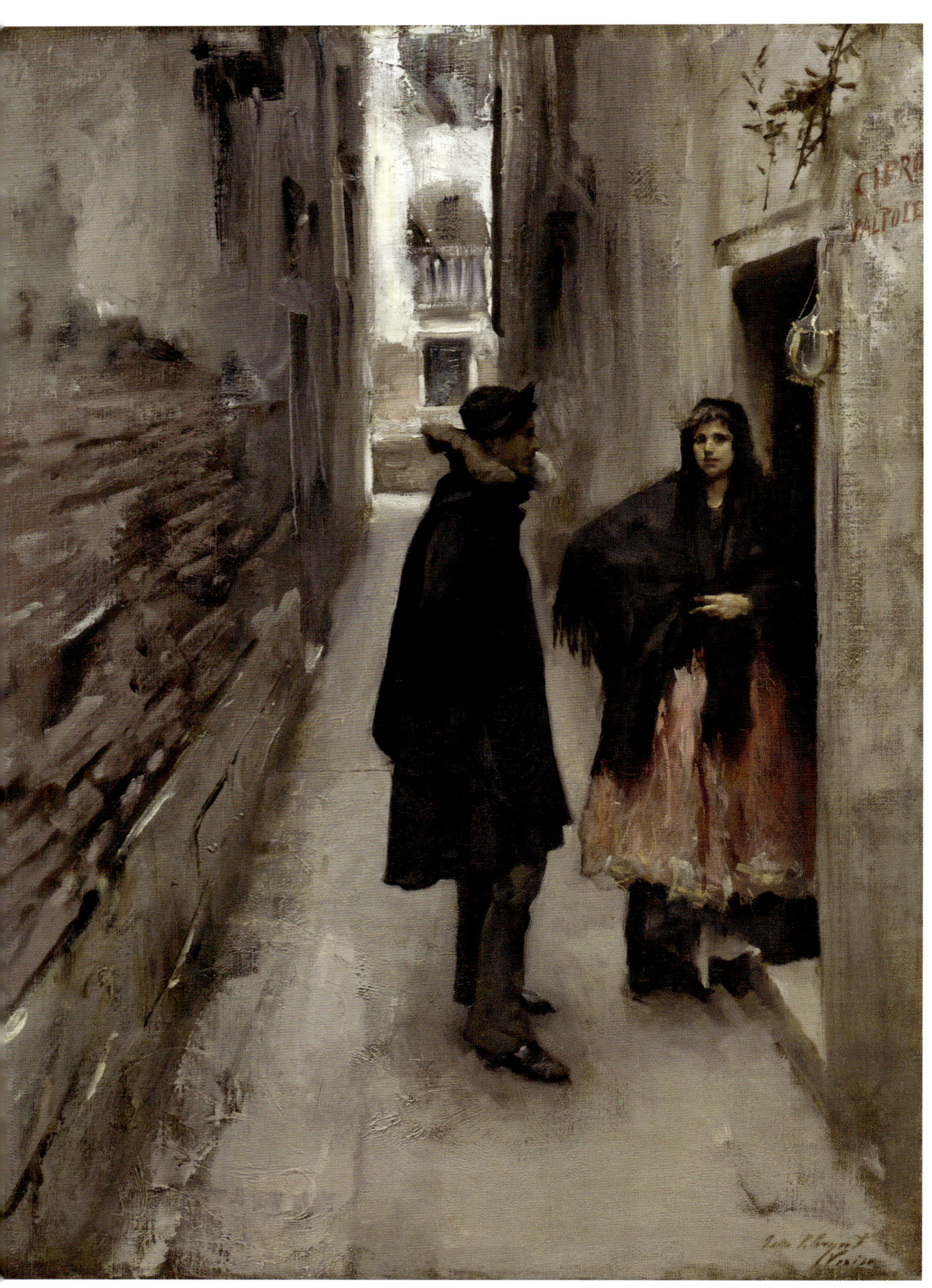

17

Street in Venice

ca. 1880–82
Oil on canvas, 29 9/16 × 20 5/8 in.
(75.1 × 52.4 cm)
Signed: "John S. Sargent / Venise"
Williamstown, Massachusetts,
The Clark Art Institute,
Acquired by Sterling and
Francine Clark, 1926 [1955.575]

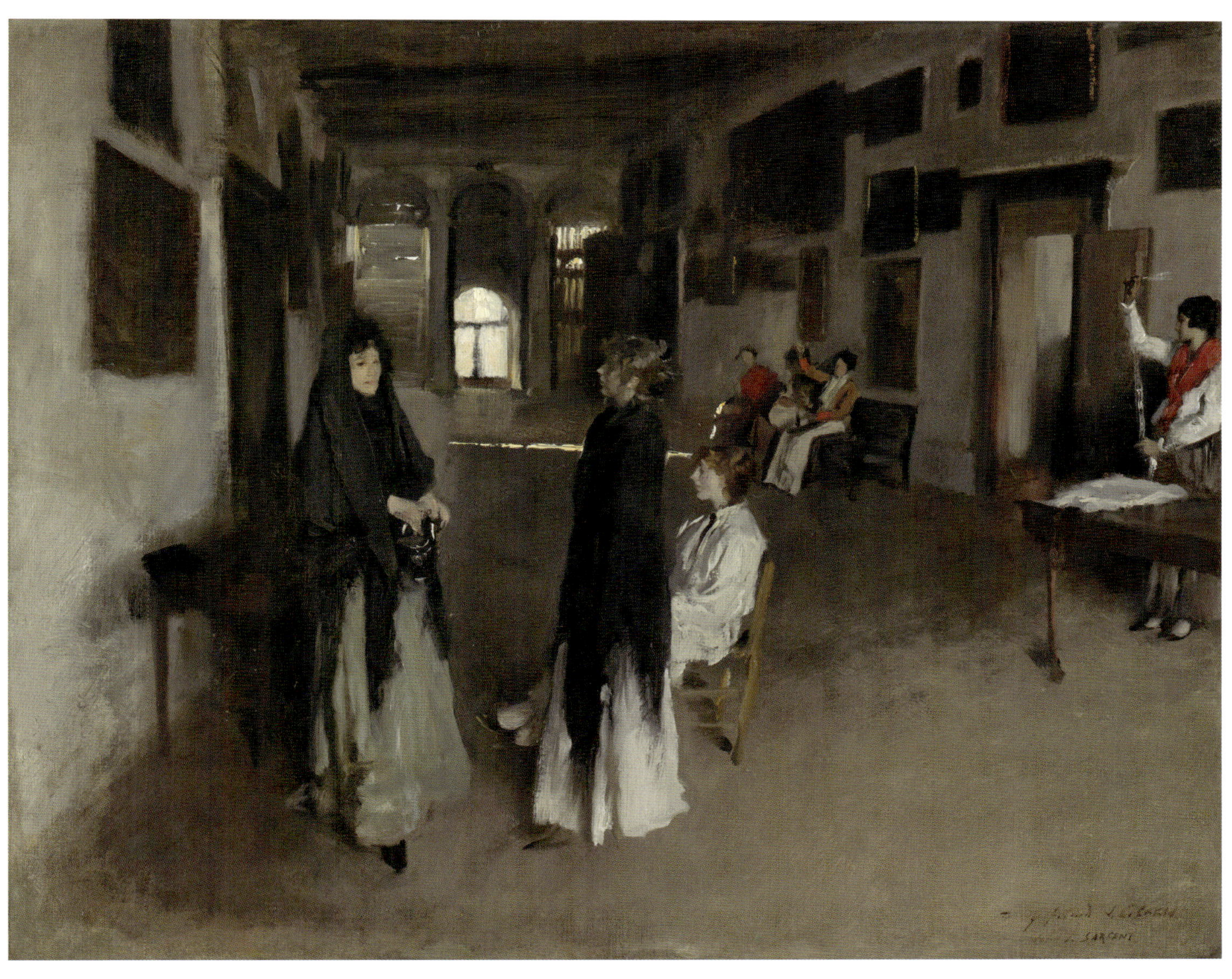

18

A Venetian Interior

ca. 1880–82
Oil on canvas, 19 1/16 × 23 15/16 in. (48.4 × 60.8 cm)
Inscription: "To my friend J. C. Cazin / John S. Sargent"
Williamstown, Massachusetts, The Clark Art Institute, Acquired by Sterling Clark, 1913 [1955.580]

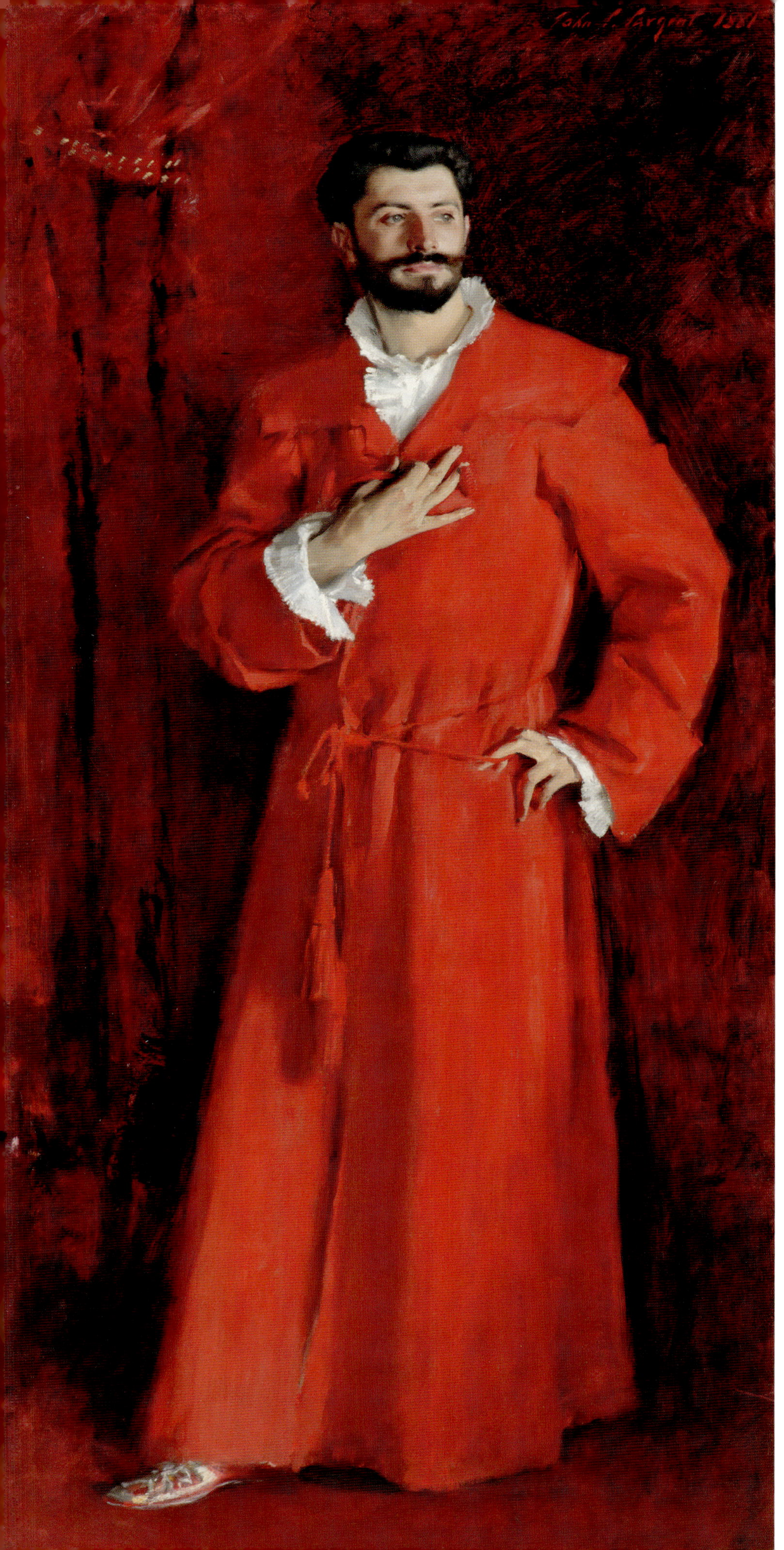

19

Dr. Pozzi or
Dr. Pozzi at Home

1881
Oil on canvas, $79\frac{3}{8} \times 40\frac{1}{4}$ in.
(201.6 × 102.2 cm)
Signed: "John S. Sargent 1881"
Los Angeles, Hammer Museum, The Armand Hammer Collection,
Gift of the Armand Hammer Foundation

20

Lady with the Rose
(*Charlotte Louise Burckhardt*)

1882
Oil on canvas, 84 × 44¾ in.
(213.4 × 113.7 cm)
Inscription: "To my friend Mrs.
Burckhardt / John S. Sargent 1882"
New York, The Metropolitan
Museum of Art, Bequest of Valerie
B. Hadden, 1932 [32.154]

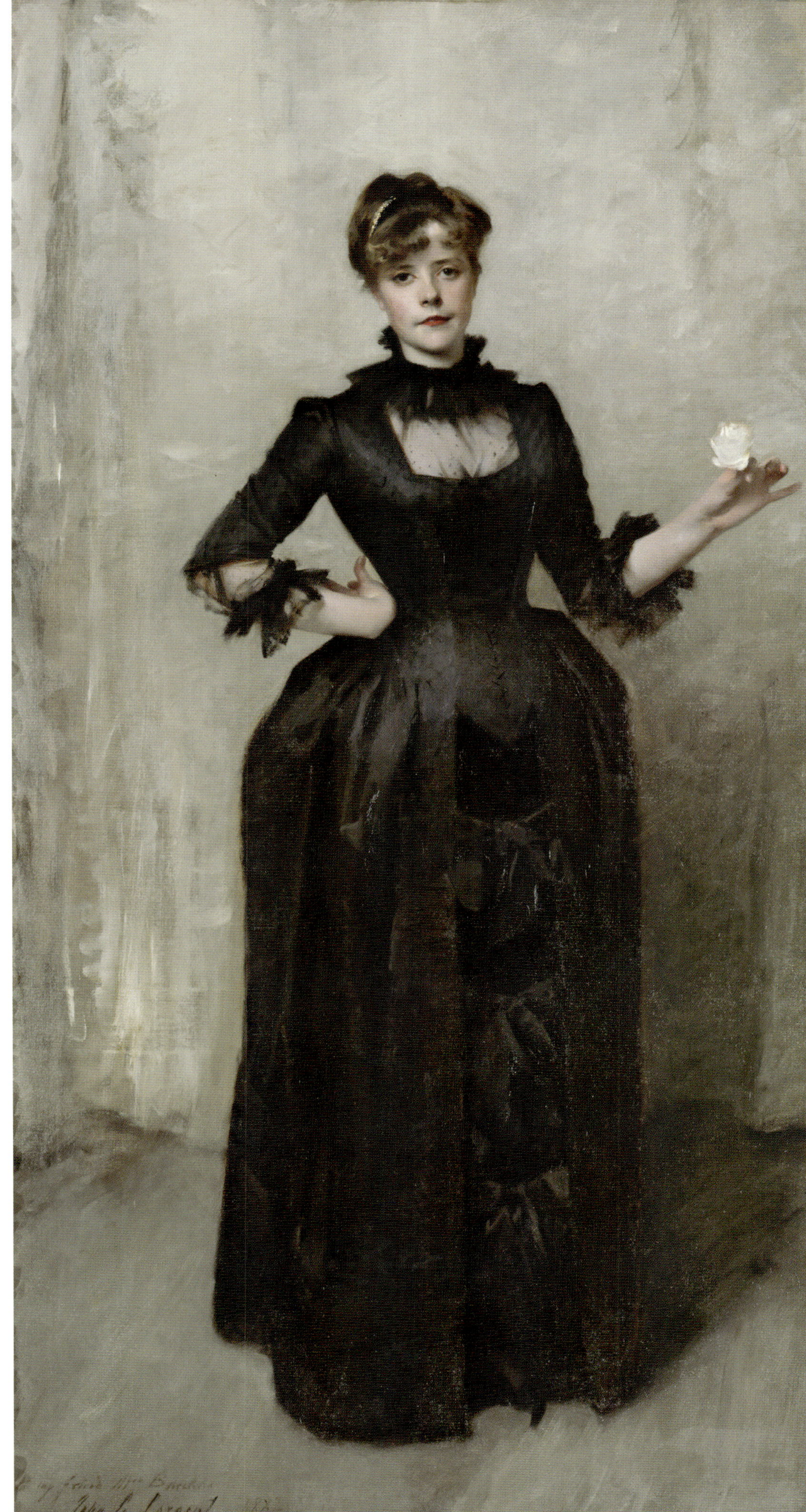

21

The Daughters of Edward Darley Boit

1882
Oil on canvas, 87 3/8 × 87 5/8 in. (221.9 × 222.6 cm)
Signed: "John S. Sargent 1882"
Boston, Museum of Fine Arts, Gift of Mary Louisa Boit, Julia Overing Boit, Jane Hubbard Boit, and Florence D. Boit in memory of their father, Edward Darley Boit [19.124]

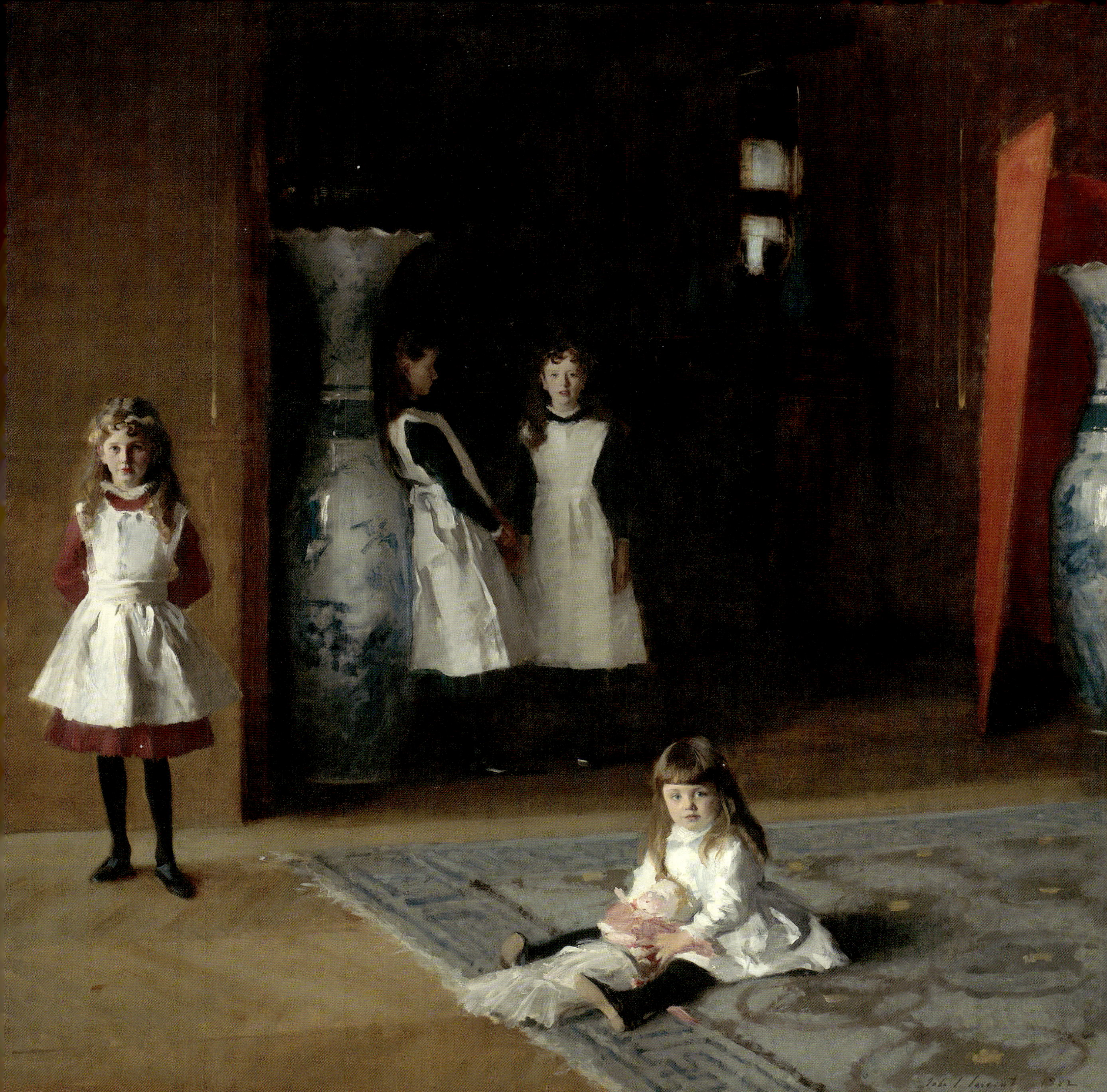

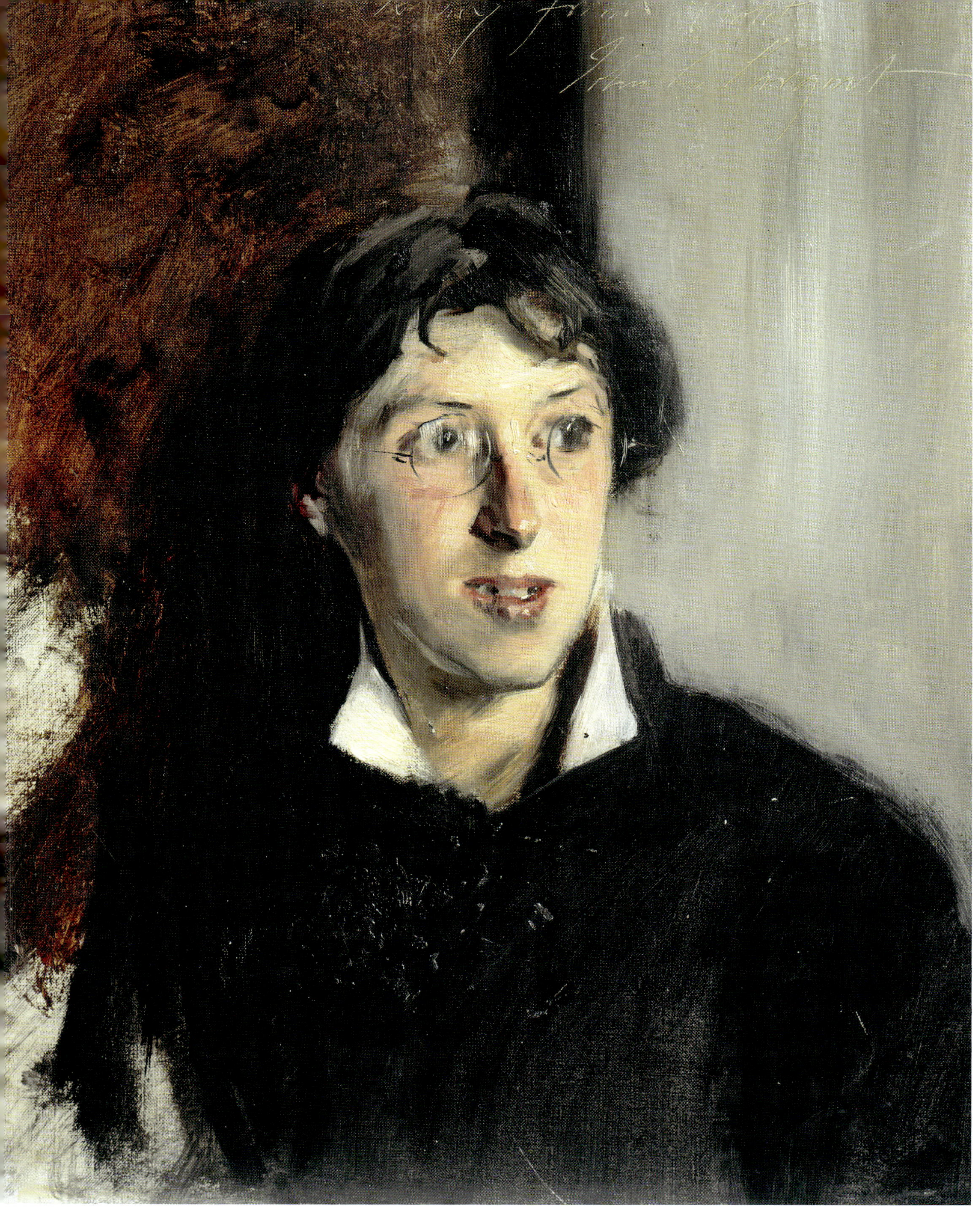

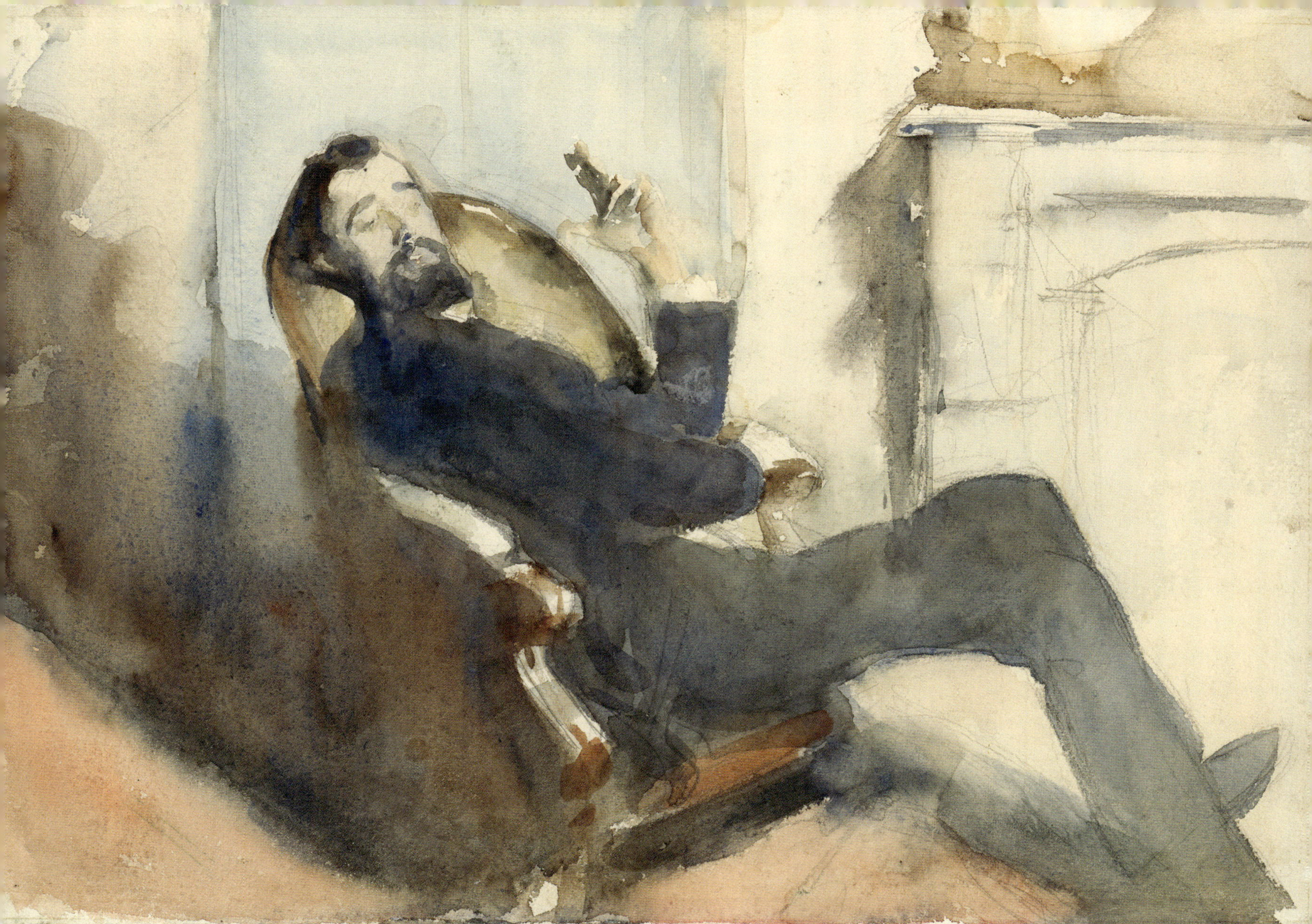

22

Vernon Lee

1881
Oil on canvas, 21⅛ × 17 in. (53.7 × 43.2 cm)
Inscription: "To my friend Violet / John S. Sargent"
London, Tate, Bequeathed by Miss Vernon Lee through Miss Cooper Willis 1935 [N04787]

23

Portrait of Paul-César Helleu

1880s
Watercolor on paper, 9¼ × 14⅜ in. (23.5 × 37.3 cm)
New York, The Morgan Library & Museum, Gift of Rose Pitman Hughes and J. Lawrence Hughes in memory of Junius and Louise Morgan [2005.5]

24

Violet Sargent (*The Breakfast Table*)

ca. 1883
Oil on canvas, 21¼ × 17 11/16 in. (54 × 45 cm)
Inscription: "à mon cher ami Besnard / John S. Sargent"
Cambridge, Massachusetts, Harvard Art Museums/ Fogg Museum, Bequest of Grenville L. Winthrop [1943.150]

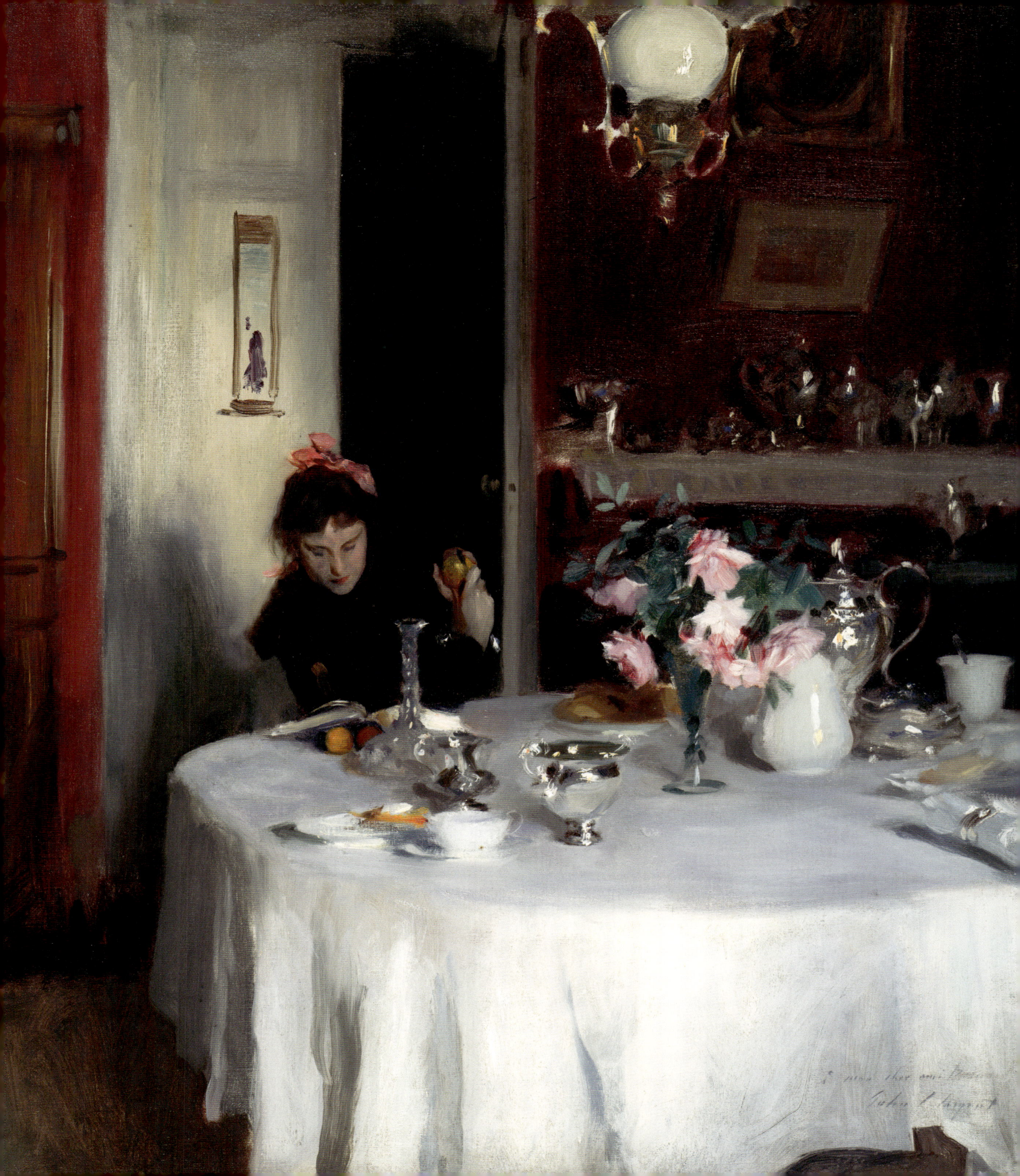

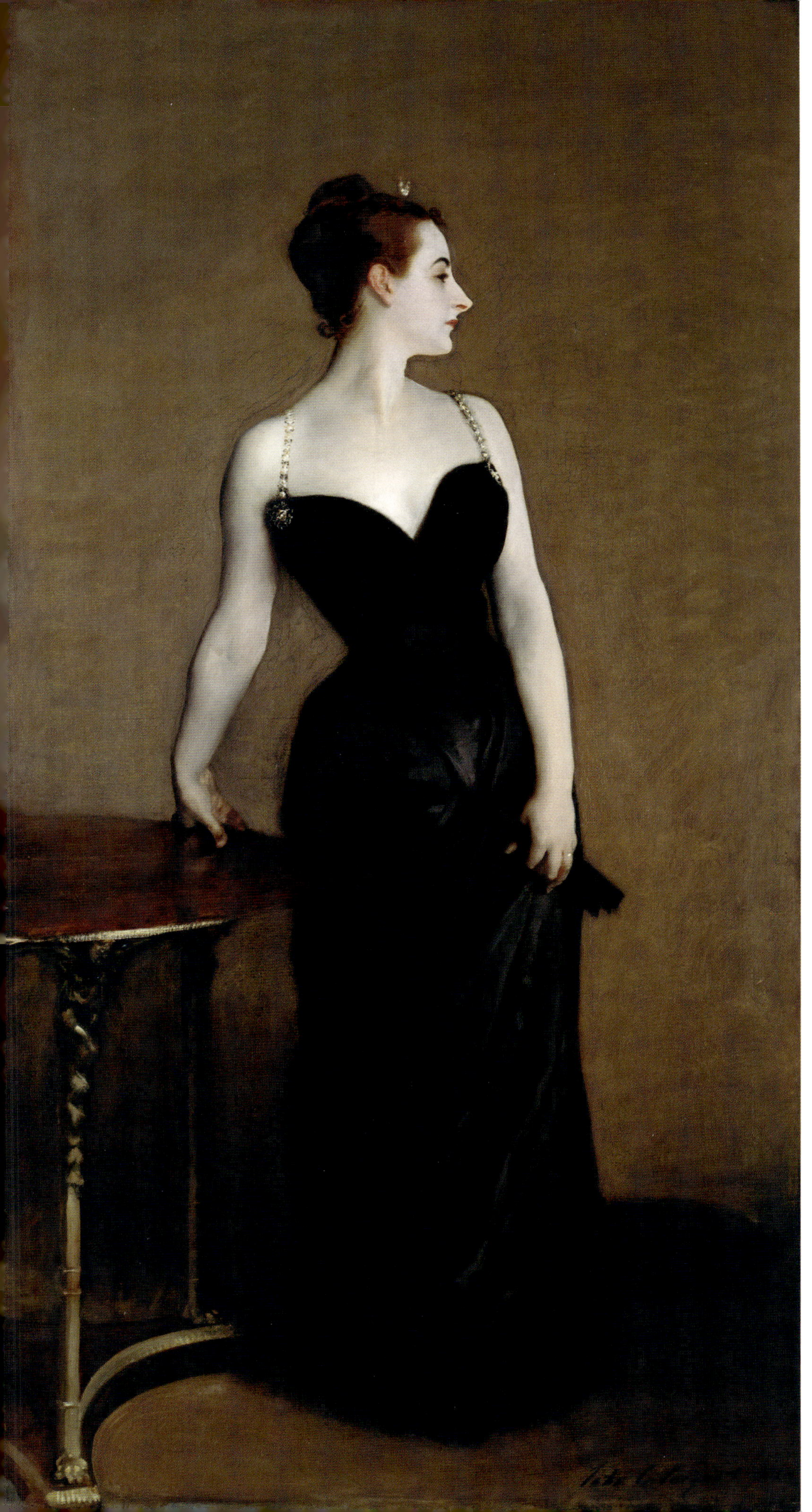

25

Madame X
(*Madame Pierre Gautreau*)

1883–84
Oil on canvas, 82 ⅛ × 43 ¼ in.
(208.6 × 109.9 cm)
Signed: "John S. Sargent 1884"
New York, The Metropolitan Museum of Art, Arthur Hoppock Hearn Fund, 1916 [16.53]

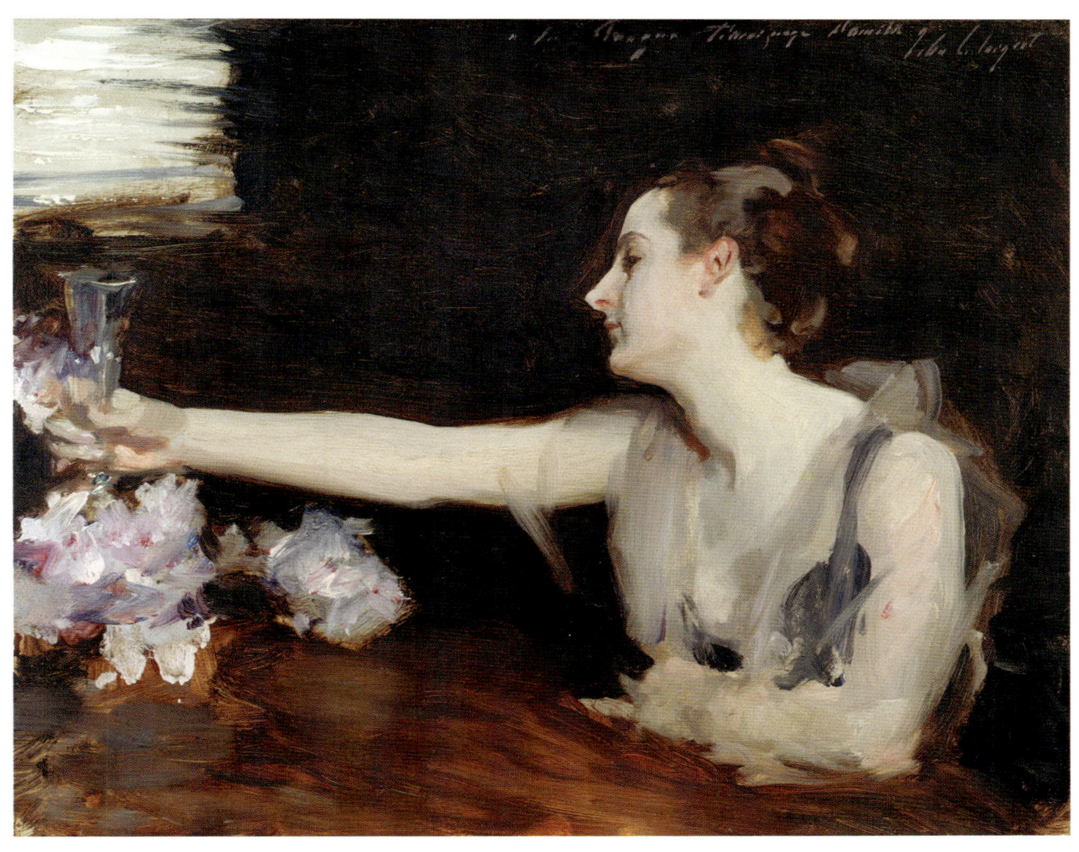

26

Madame Gautreau Drinking a Toast

ca. 1883
Oil on panel, 12 ⅝ × 16 ⅛ in. (32 × 41 cm)
Inscription: "à Me Avegno témoignage d'amitié / John S. Sargent"
Boston, Isabella Stewart Gardner Museum [P3w41]

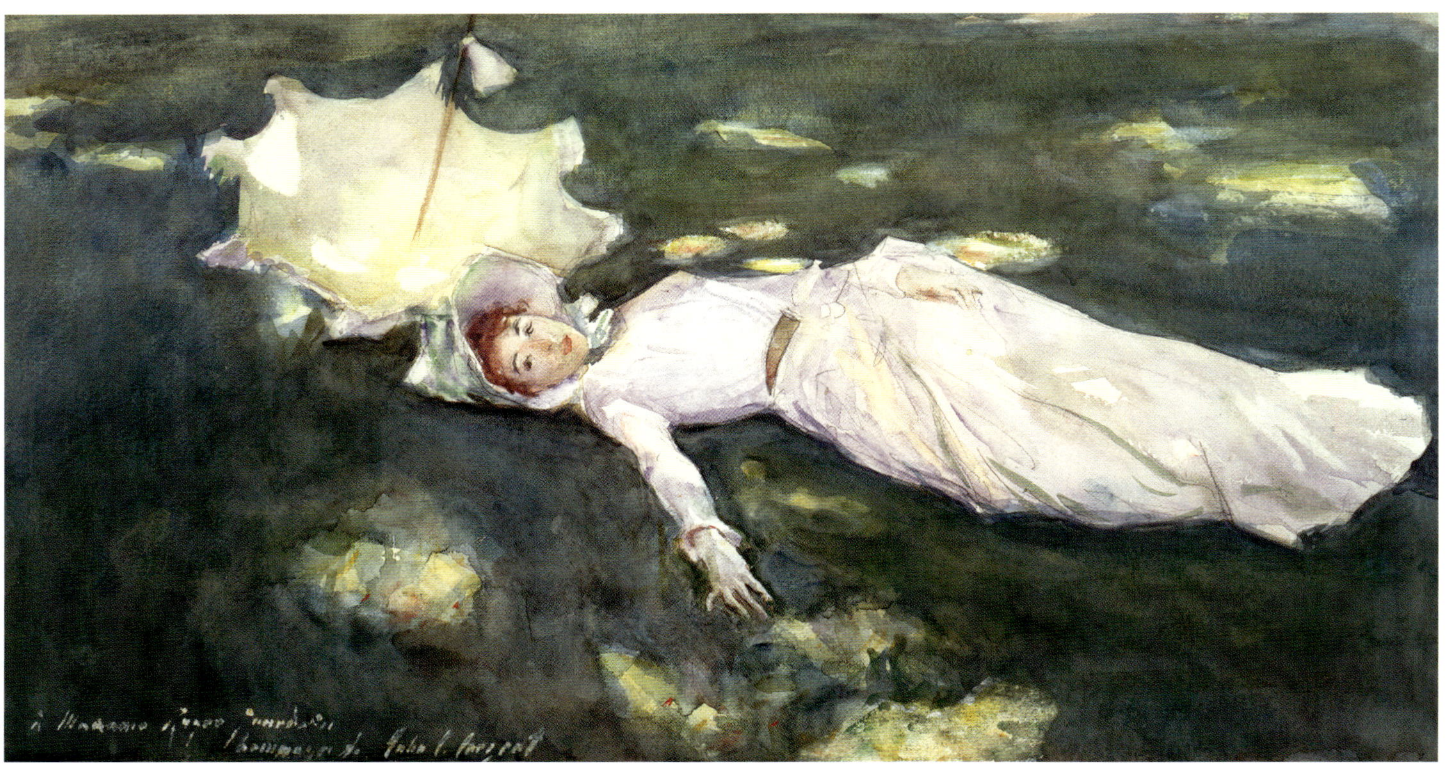

27

Madame Roger-Jourdain

ca. 1883–85
Watercolor on paper, 12 × 22 in.
(30.5 × 55.8 cm)
Private collection

28

Claude Monet Painting by the Edge of a Wood

1885
Oil on canvas, 21¼ × 25½ in. (54 × 64.8 cm)
London, Tate, Presented by Miss Emily Sargent and Mrs. Ormond through the National Art Collections Fund 1925 [N04103]

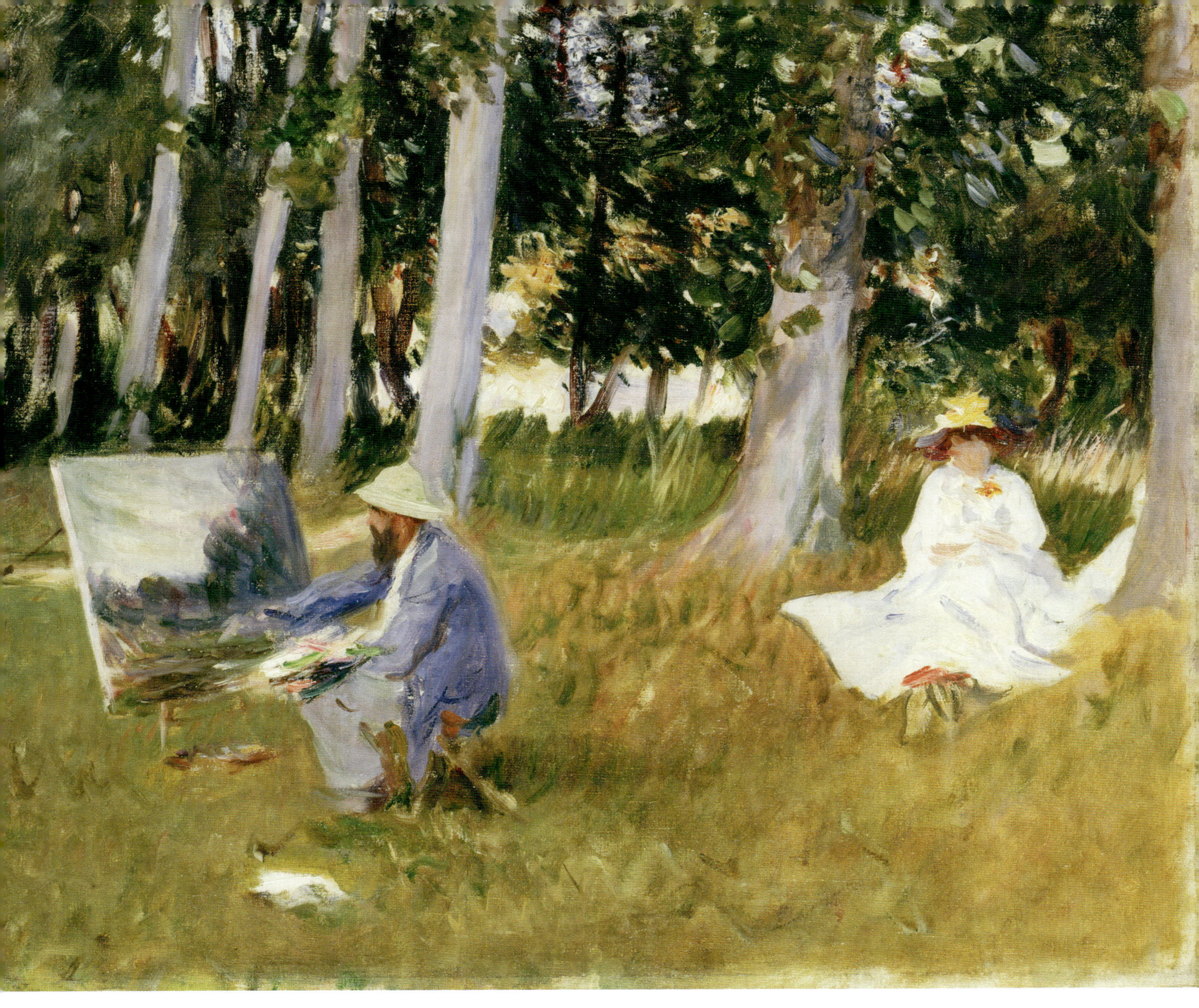

29

Carnation, Lily, Lily, Rose

1885–86
Oil on canvas, 68½ × 60½ in.
(174 × 153.7 cm)
Signed: "John S. Sargent"
London, Tate, Presented
by the Trustees of the Chantrey
Bequest 1887 [N01615]

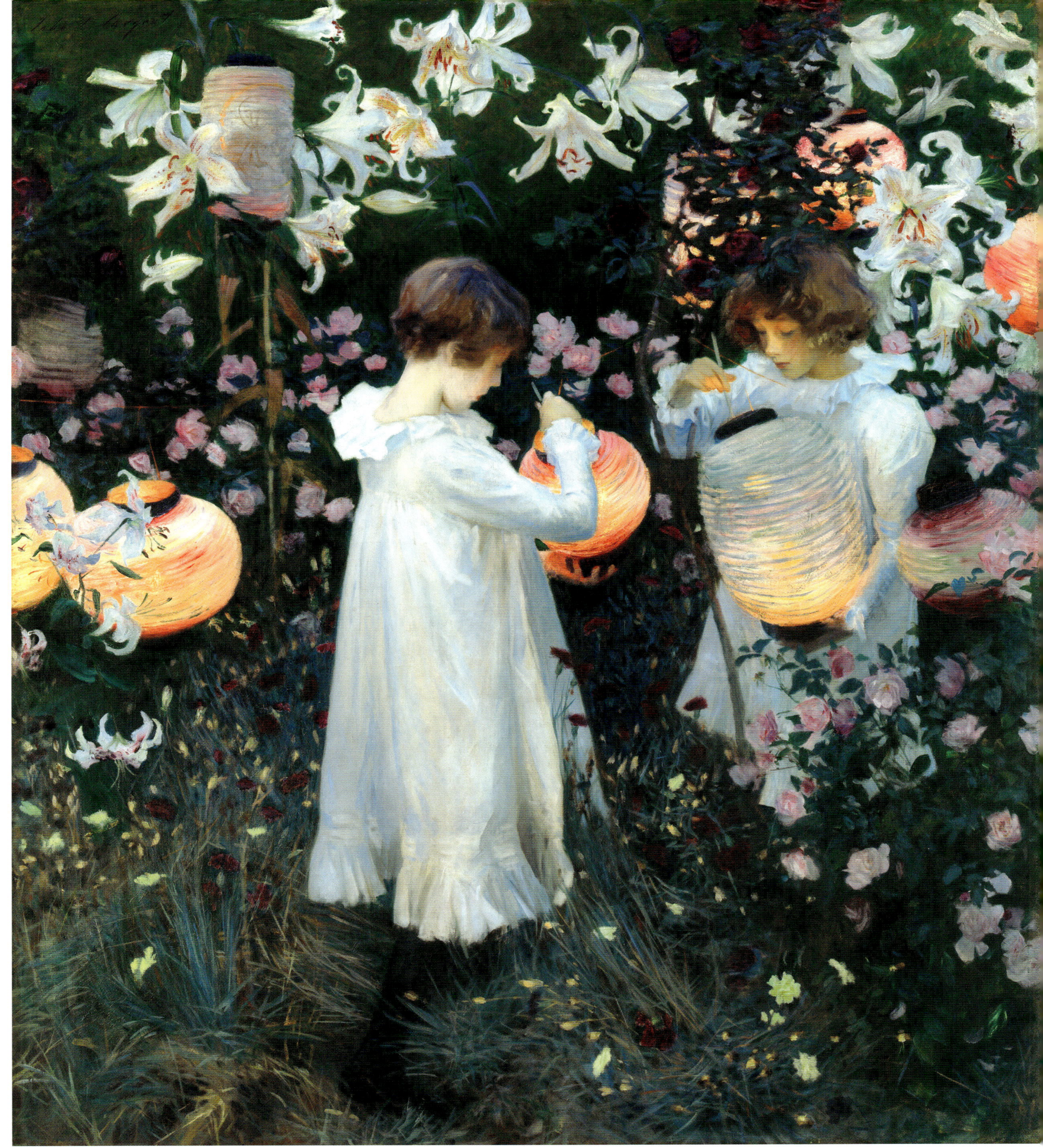

30

Two Women Asleep under the Willows

ca. 1887
Oil on canvas, 22 × 27 in.
(56 × 68.6 cm)
Signed: "John S. Sargent"
Lisbon, Calouste Gulbenkian
Museum [73]

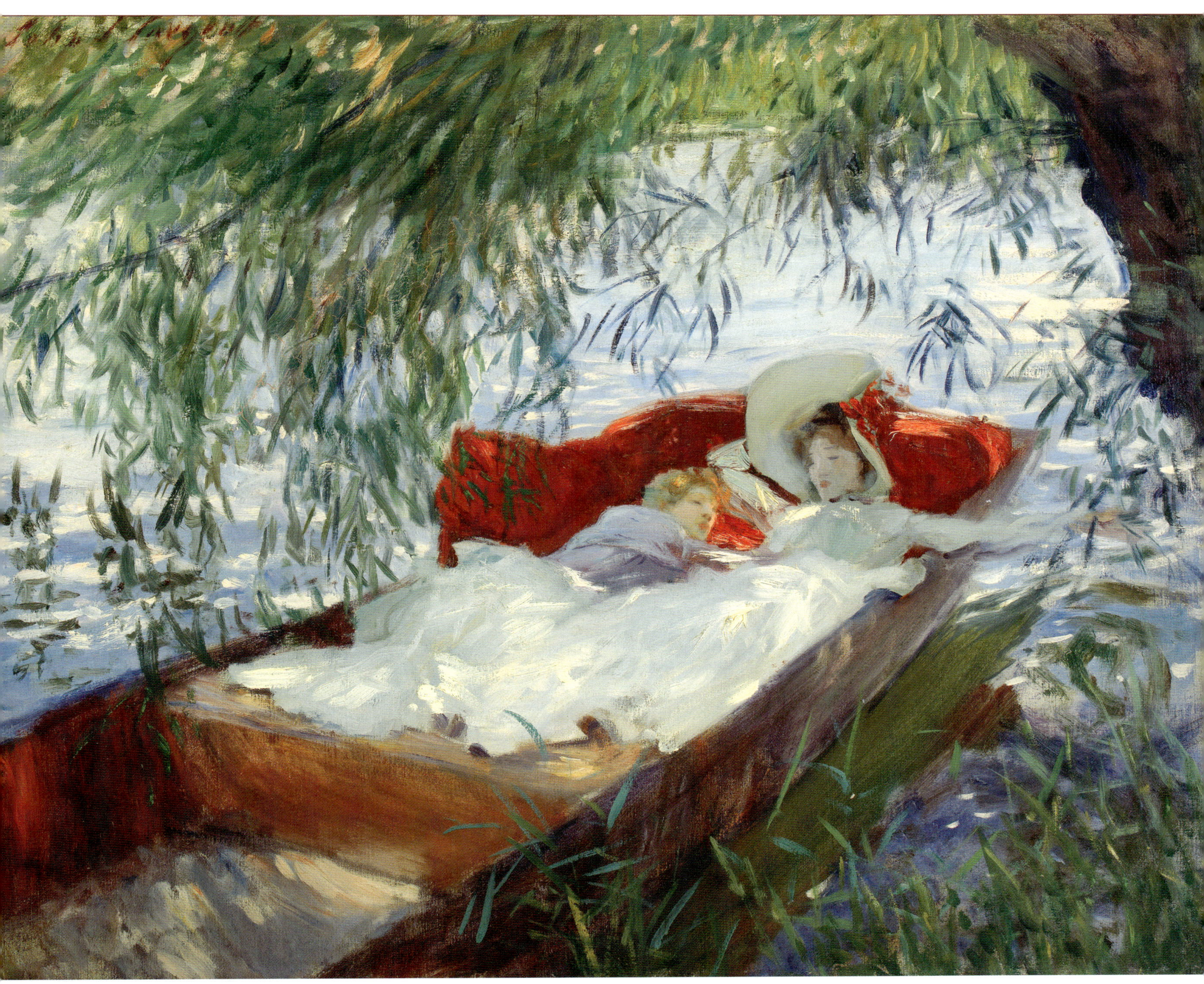

31

Fête Familiale (*The Birthday Party*)

ca. 1885
Oil on canvas, 24 × 29 in. (60.96 × 73.66 cm)
Minneapolis, Minnesota, Minneapolis Institute of Art, The Ethel Morrison Van Derlip Fund and the John R. Van Derlip Fund [62.84]

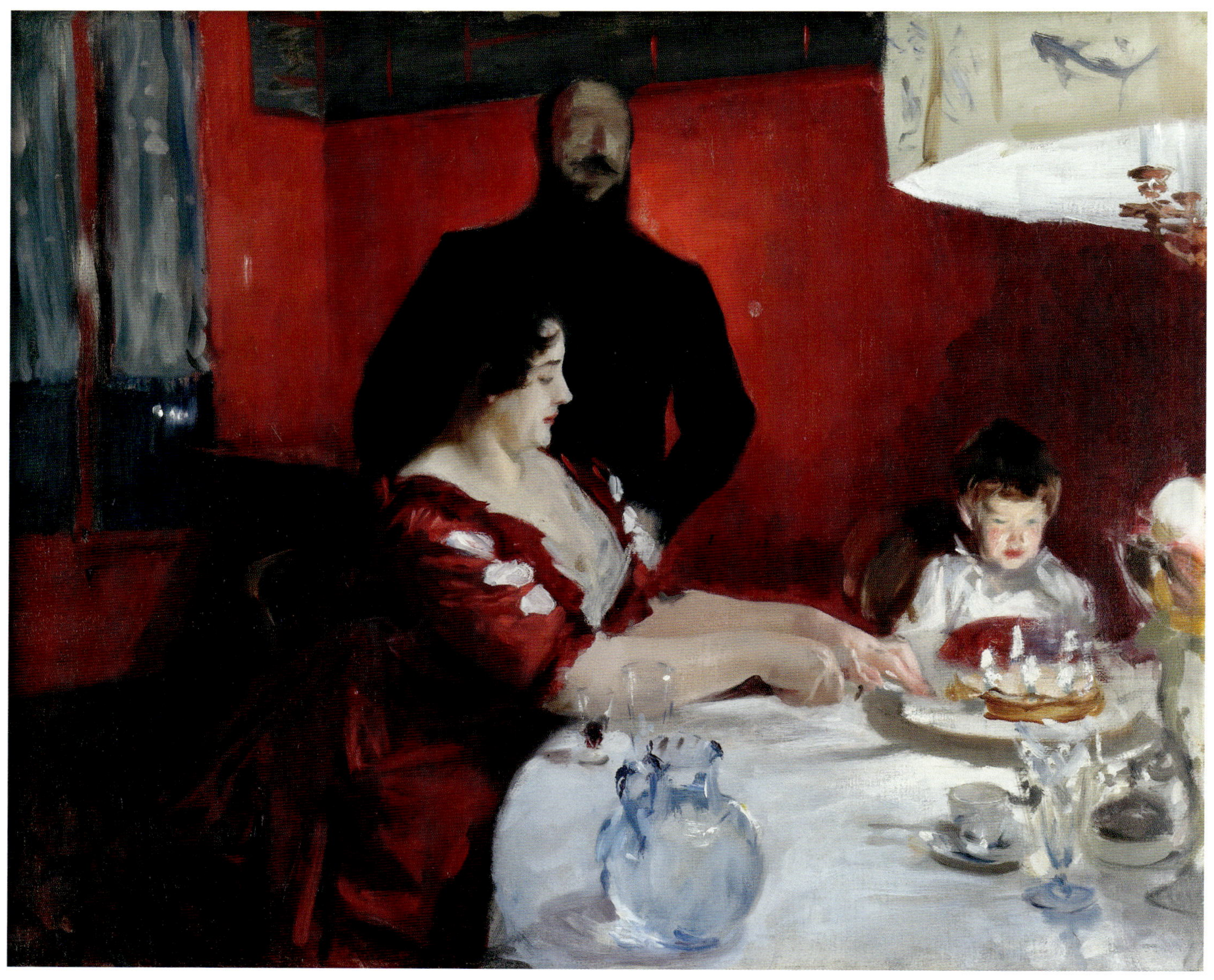

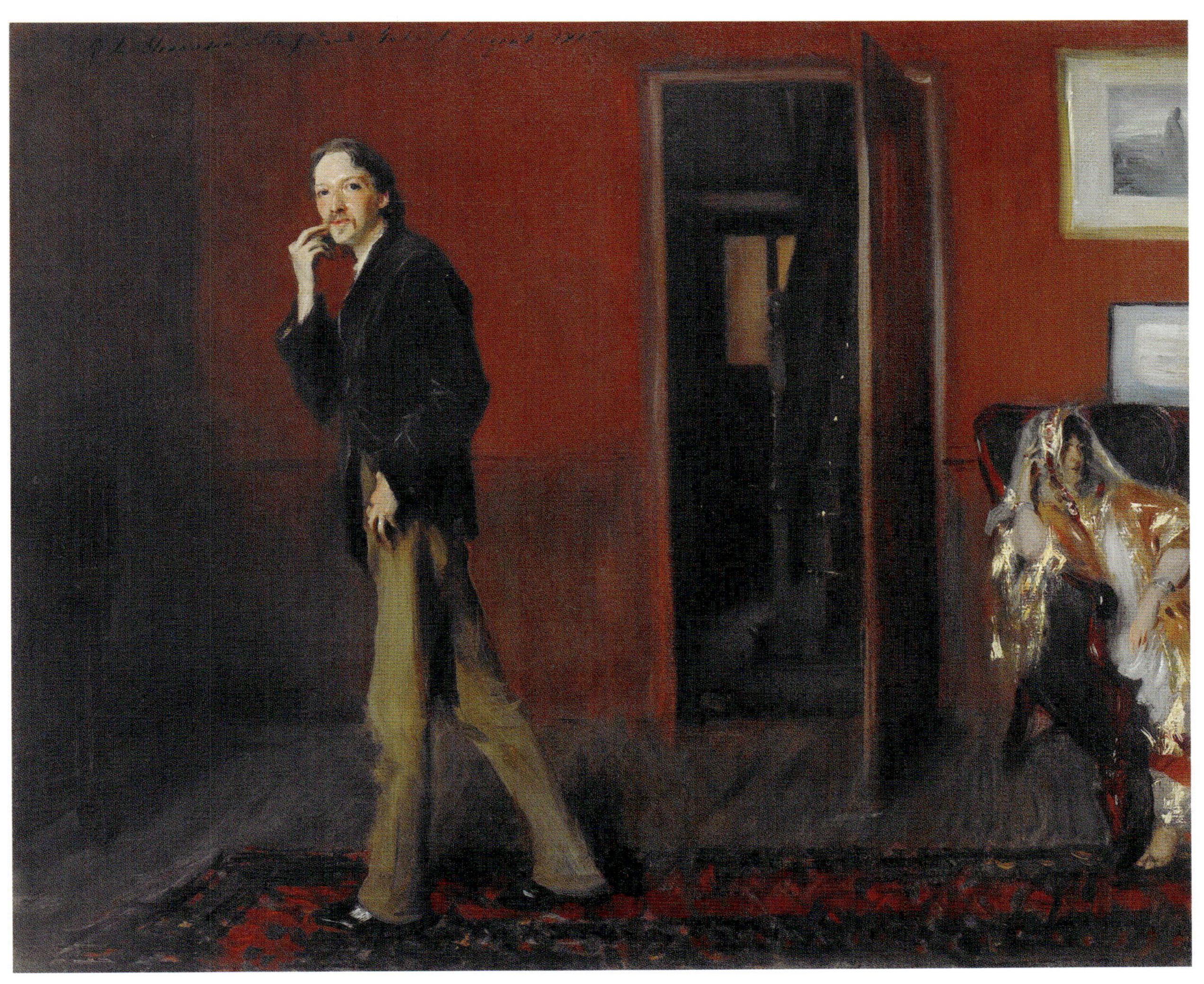

32

Robert Louis Stevenson and His Wife

1885
Oil on canvas, 20¼ × 24¼ in. (51.4 × 61.6 cm)
Inscription: "To R.L. Stevenson, his friend
John S. Sargent 1885"
Bentonville, Arkansas, Crystal Bridges Museum
of American Art [2005.3]

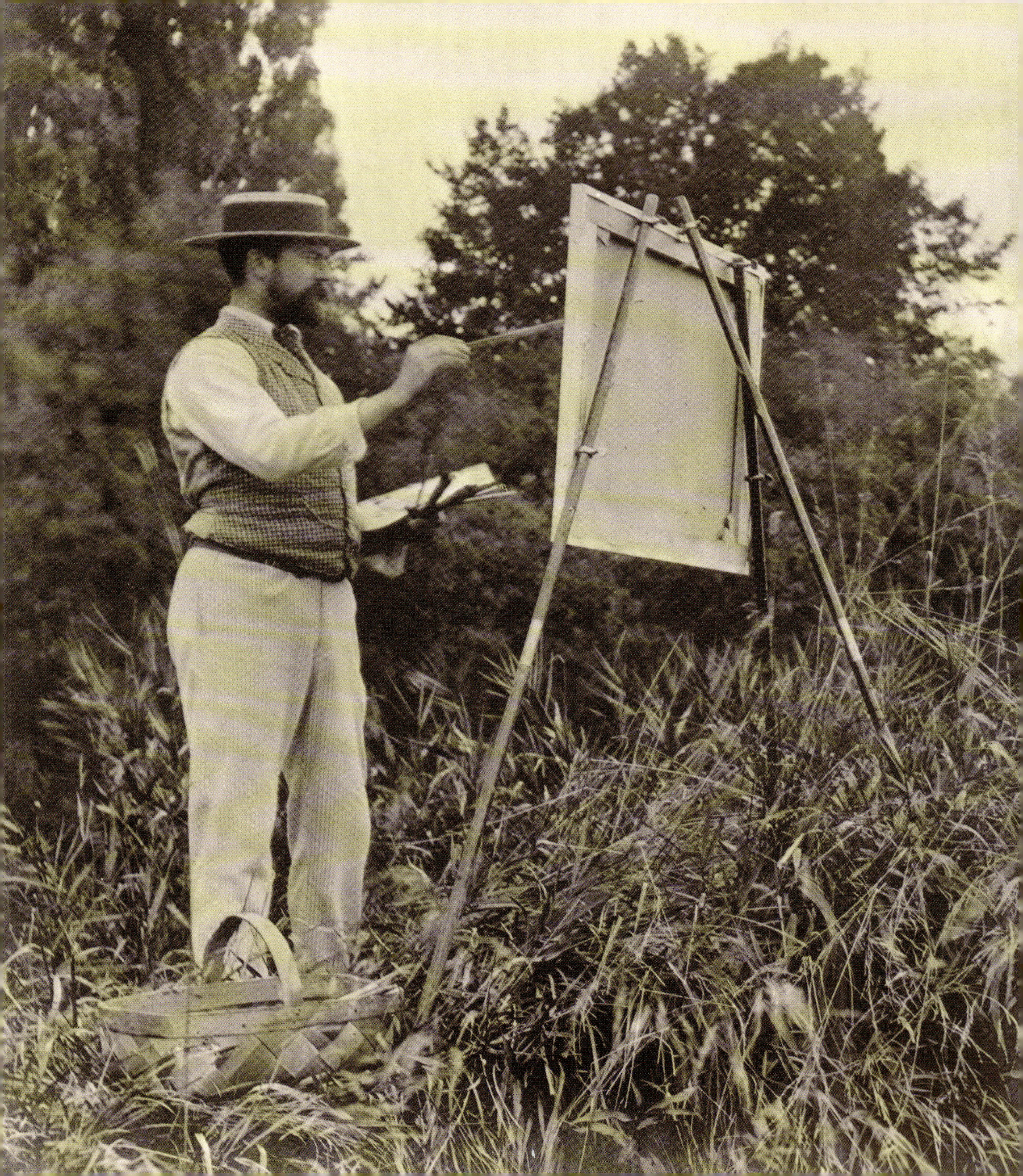

Sargent at Fladbury, Worcestershire, 1889. Museum of Fine Arts, Boston. The John Singer Sargent Archive–Gift of Richard and Leonée Ormond

Professional Success

Sargent in the United States and England 1887–1925

After settling in London in the mid-1880s, Sargent's portrait career languished after the unconventional representation of Virginie Gautreau caused skepticism among potential clients. Though British patrons were reluctant to pose for Sargent, Americans were eager to embrace his cosmopolitan talents. A portrait commission to paint the wife of wealthy financier Henry Marquand in Newport, Rhode Island, came at a fortuitous moment, and in 1887, Sargent crossed the Atlantic in search of additional prospects. Despite his American heritage, he had been to the United States only once, in 1876, when he was a twenty-year-old art student. When he returned in September 1887, he was a rising portraitist with an international upbringing and French artistic training who had already forged connections with prominent American patrons in Europe.

In advance of his first professional visit to the States, Henry James heralded Sargent's talent in a lengthy article in *Harper's New Monthly Magazine*. James used his influence to introduce and endorse his friend to American audiences. He offered an admiring examination of Sargent's career, famously declaring that his works presented "the slightly uncanny spectacle of a talent which on the very threshold of its career has nothing more to learn." James laid claim to Sargent on behalf of the nation while celebrating his European background:

> Is Mr. Sargent in very fact an American painter? The proper answer to such a question is doubtless that we shall be well advised to claim him, and the reason of this is simply that we have an excellent opportunity. . . . He has even on the face of it this great symptom of an American origin, that in the line of his art he might easily be mistaken for a Frenchman. It sounds like a paradox, but it is a very simple truth, that

when to-day we look for "American art" we find it mainly in Paris. When we find it out of Paris, we at least find a great deal of Paris in it.[1]

At a time when the taste for French art dominated American sensibilities, patrons in Boston and New York were primed to embrace the stylish young painter with an American heritage and French artistic training. James dismissed the scandal of *Madame X* and attempted to quash potential patrons' fears by celebrating Sargent as a painter of women who handles "delicate feminine elements . . . with a special feeling for them, and they borrow something of nobleness from his brush."[2] American patrons responded—Sargent painted more than twenty portraits during his nine-month American sojourn in 1887–88. The visit culminated with his first solo exhibition, at Boston's St. Botolph Club, which included many recently completed portraits of the city's most prominent families.[3]

One of the most remarkable—and controversial—portraits was that of Isabella Stewart Gardner [fig. 33], a formidable collector of Old Master works and doyenne of Boston cultural life. Sargent had met Gardner in Paris in 1886, when James brought her to his studio to see the portrait of Gautreau. Gardner—known for her discerning eye; her bold, flamboyant personality; and unconventional behavior—was captivated by the picture. She was eager to sit for Sargent and conspired with the artist to create an exceptional painting, one that she hoped would create a stir in conservative Boston.

Her portrait is a descendent of, and a response to, the portrait of Gautreau, adapted for a discriminating and cultured patron. Sargent forgoes traditionally flattering portrait conventions to create a progressive image that evoked "a Byzantine Madonna with a halo," in the words of Renaissance scholar and advisor Bernard Berenson.[4] Gardner is shown in a simple but austere black dress with a deep plunging neckline. For the background, Sargent selected a swatch of Venetian Renaissance brocade from Gardner's collection that he enlarged and strategically placed. The ornamental pattern radiates from behind her head, its circular nimbus echoed in the curve of Gardner's arms and the swag of lavish strands of pearls draped at her waist and neck. The portrait succeeded in capturing the attention of the critics when it was exhibited at the St. Botolph Club. One critic, known as "Greta," was mystified by the sitter's "aureole" and enigmatic smile, which she claimed as the "prime tour de force of the whole exhibition."[5] In an oft-repeated anecdote, however, Gardner's husband was said to have been less than pleased, allegedly remarking of the painting, "It looks like hell but it looks just like you."[6]

When Sargent returned to England after his successful American trip, he had few portrait commissions to fill his time. As usual, he sought respite from city life in the countryside, often with family members, dear friends, and his community whom he used as models in a series of plein air portraits in which he continued his experiments with Impressionist techniques.

Sargent's portrait of his sister Violet, *A Morning Walk* [fig. 34], painted at Calcot, was inspired by Monet's paintings of his stepdaughter Suzanne Hoschedé [*Essai de figure en plein-air: Femme à l'ombrelle tournée vers la gauche* (1886, Musée d'Orsay) and *Essai de figure en plein-air: Femme à l'ombrelle tournée vers la droite* (1886, Musée d'Orsay, Paris)], which Sargent likely saw during a visit to Claude Monet (1840–1926) at Giverny in 1887. Sargent used an elevated vantage point to set the figure off against the vivid blue water along the vibrant grassy banks. He conveys the optical experience of brilliant and dappled light on her dress in diverse pale tones. Despite the influence of his French friend, Sargent situates the painting in a British context with his title that invokes Thomas Gainsborough's iconic *The Morning Walk* (1758, National Gallery, London).

Sargent's portrait of his dear friend, the French painter Paul-César Helleu (1859–1927) and his young wife, Alice, was painted at Fladbury Rectory in Worcestershire during summer 1889 [fig. 35]. Sargent captures Helleu's intense concentration as he applies his brush to his canvas with a deliberate gesture, recording the creation of his art as if it were a performance. Sargent constructed the composition to focus attention on the easel and Helleu's mark making. The diagonal of the red canoe recedes into the picture at a dramatic angle and compresses the composition. The dynamic brushwork, characterized by long spiky strokes, mimics the effect of reeds and grass, and forms a swirl of motion around the figures. The title, *An Out-of-Doors Study*, highlights the self-reflective nature of the subject—as Helleu paints an out-of-doors study, so, too does Sargent. Nearby, Helleu's wife appears disinterested as she gazes away from the action.

Sargent was continuously attracted to bold personalities and sought them out as subjects for portraits. On December 27, 1888, he attended the opening night of a new production of *Macbeth* at London's Lyceum Theater featuring the great Shakespearean actor Ellen Terry in the role of Lady Macbeth. He was transfixed by her performance, her fiery wig, and her fantastical costume, which had been designed by Alice Comyns Carr, a close friend of his. Sargent exclaimed his admiration for the pictorial possibilities of her costume and her "magenta hair."[7] He was determined to paint her [fig. 36] in the spectacular gown and cloak fabricated from green silk with blue tinsel and adorned with thousands of iridescent beetle wings to look like a serpent. He suggested the shimmering beetle wings with impressionistic dabs of pigment. Sargent depicted Terry placing a crown on her head after the murder of Duncan, the king; an incident that is not included in Shakespeare's text, nor was it a part of her performance. Sargent contrived this dramatic action as a characterization of the role and of Terry's performance. Her intense and powerful gaze enhances this climactic moment.

Sargent returned to the United States in December 1889 for his second professional visit. During his eleven-month stay, he painted another forty portraits, twenty-five of which were commissions.[8] In New York, he saw the Spanish dancer known as La Carmencita perform. After an acclaimed turn in Paris at the 1889 Exposition Universelle, she had traveled to New York and was dancing regularly at a music hall on Twenty-Third Street, where she was rapidly becoming a celebrity.[9] Sargent, who had a lifelong interest in Spanish music and dance, was mesmerized by her and called her a "bewildering superb creature."[10] He invited her to perform for his friends, including Isabella Stewart Gardner, during a party at the studio of the American painter William Merritt Chase (1849–1916). Sargent persuaded her to pose for him [fig. 37], allegedly supplied the bright yellow dress, and made numerous studies of her performing, though for the massive final composition, he presented her standing still, hands on hips, confronting her audience directly. Sargent accentuated her cosmetics, rendering her face pale and masklike and elongated her appearance, making her physique seem more slender and elegant than she appears in contemporary photographs. She is a fierce and indomitable presence. Some viewers indicted the portrait—finding it shocking that Sargent would portray a "common" music hall performer on a grand scale usually reserved for more distinguished personages.

The renowned American sculptor Augustus Saint-Gaudens (1848–1907), who was Sargent's friend since their student days in Paris in the 1870s, had attended La Carmencita's performance. There, he met Sargent's youngest sister, Violet, and determined to make a bas-relief portrait of her playing the guitar, a version of which he presented to Sargent. In return, Sargent painted Saint-Gaudens's ten-year-old son in a tender, candid portrait [fig. 38]. Sargent originally intended to depict just the young boy, but when Homer Saint-Gaudens grew bored during sittings his mother stepped in to entertain him by reading a book and was promptly incorporated into the portrait—almost as a sketched afterthought. The boy confronts the viewer with an informal pose and an earnest expression.

It was thanks, in part, to Augustus Saint-Gaudens that Sargent secured a prestigious mural commission to decorate the Special Collections Hall of Boston's new Public Library on Copley Square, then under construction (1887–94). Saint-Gaudens introduced Sargent to Stanford White (1853–1906) and Charles Follen McKim (1847–1909) of the legendary architectural firm, McKim, Mead & White, who designed the library. Modeled after an Italian Renaissance palazzo, the library was conceived in the spirit of the American Renaissance, a self-conscious moment following the United States Centennial during which artists and architects looked to the great civilizations of the past in order to create a distinctive American art.

In keeping with the Renaissance and the Beaux-Arts traditions, the designers sought to incorporate painting and sculpture into the complete architectural ensemble. In addition to the prominent architects, the creative team included preeminent European-trained artists—sculptor Saint-Gaudens and painters Edwin Austin Abbey (1852–1911), Pierre Puvis de Chavannes (1824–1898), and Sargent. Although Sargent had limited experience as a muralist, he must have seemed an ideal candidate for the project because of his academic training at the École des Beaux-Arts and his extensive knowledge of art history.

In accepting the prestigious commission, Sargent was considering his art historical legacy and announcing his ambitions. A carefully designed program for the murals would allow him to demonstrate his scholarly sophistication. Near the end of his life, Sargent expressed his pleasure in the sustained effort and challenge of painting murals while articulating the deeply personal nature of these projects in an interview with the artist Gutzon Borglum (1867–1941) in 1923. Sargent explained: "What a fine thing it is to have some big work on hand which calls for continued labor and all one's ability! . . . It is an artist's work.

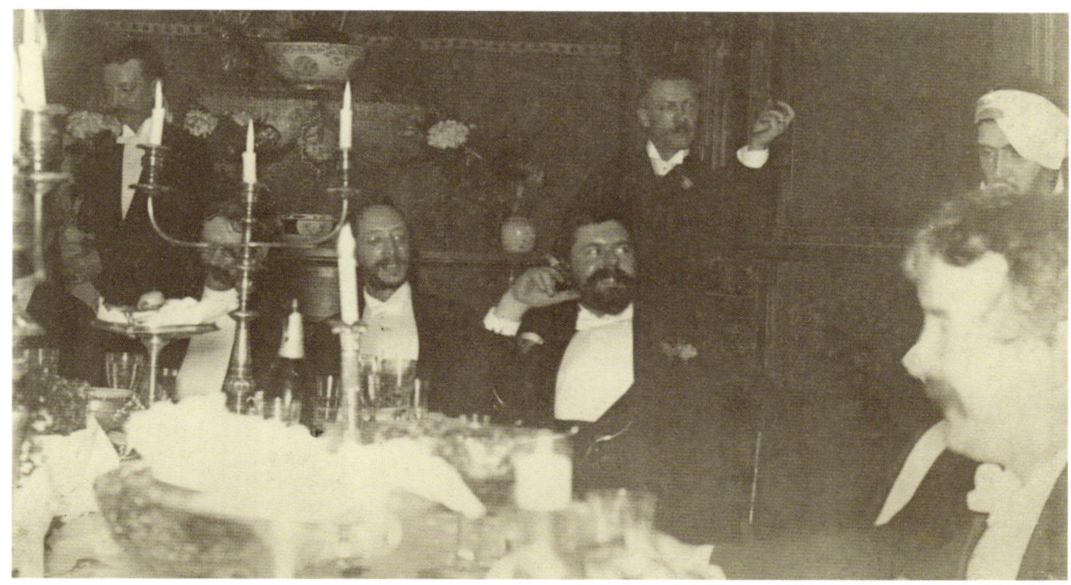

Sargent at an artists' party in New York, ca. 1890. Smithsonian Institution, Archives of American Art, Washington, D. C., Otto Bacher papers, 1873–1938

You can study on and on, and crowd your life into it."[11] The library murals would occupy Sargent for nearly thirty years, from 1890 when he first accepted the commission until 1919 when the final panels were installed.[12]

For the Boston Public Library, Sargent developed an erudite narrative of the history of Western religion. His scheme traces the development of religion from materialist superstition to modern spirituality, highlighting episodes from the Old and New Testaments. Almost immediately after signing the mural contract, Sargent set forth on a research trip to Egypt, Greece, and Turkey. This trip validated and inspired his choice of a religious subject as he explained to Isabella Stewart Gardner, "The consequence of going up the Nile is, as might have been foreseen, that I must do an Old Testament thing for the Boston Library . . . & I saw things in Egypt that I hope will come in play."[13] Candid studies such as *Egyptians Raising Water from the Nile* [fig. 39] and *Interior of Saint Sophia, Constantinople* [fig. 40], which were made during this trip, reflect Sargent's appreciation of life and custom in the biblical lands as well as his consideration of the atmosphere and decor of public spaces.

Sargent completed and installed the first section of the murals in 1895, including *Frieze of the Prophets* [fig. 41]. Moses is seen at center, having received the tablets from God at Sinai, in the frieze to his left and right, is the sequence of prophets who helped disseminate God's law. Sargent explained that the frieze "symbolized the foundation of the religion of Israel upon the structure of the Law."[14] He derived their dress from studies made on his trip. Sargent varies the naturalistic representation and array of expressive poses across the frieze, which was widely reproduced and distributed, helping to secure his reputation.

From the earliest reviews of the first installation, critics associated Sargent's murals in scale and scope with Michelangelo's frescoes for the Sistine Chapel. When critic Frederick W. Coburn called the library murals "an American Sistine Chapel enshrined within a palace of democratic learning," it was an acknowledgment of the mural's position in American art. Coburn admired Sargent's "intensive historical scholarship" and his "power of assimilating ancient styles . . . into vivid, vital and very modern art."[15]

An academically trained artist, Sargent conceived the library murals as grand-scale history painting. He understood that the central narrative element of history painting—which occupied the pinnacle of the academic hierarchy—was the human figure, and he adopted a calculated technical approach to the study of its expressive possibilities for his compositions. For the library and two subsequent mural projects in Boston, Sargent used preparatory drawings to study his models from multiple angles and in seemingly endless variations on poses.[16] Many studies, such as the vivid *Reclining Male Nude* [fig. 45], relate to the murals only tangentially, as renderings of the human figure in dynamic poses. These studies reveal Sargent's delight in depicting the human body and his facility in rendering it with a vigorous, confident technique. Sargent's bold application of charcoal combines expressive lines and broad dark passages, which communicate a sensual immediacy.

Sargent sketched most of his nudes with charcoal, though occasionally he would translate a pose or composition into watercolor. The seductive *Man with Red Drapery* [fig. 46] appears related to Sargent's mural process but transcends it as an immediate, sensuous appreciation of the male figure. Here, apart from his attention to the dramatically foreshortened pose and cropping of the figure, Sargent seems to delight in the fluidity of watercolor. Sargent's model is swathed in red drapery; the luscious rendering of the fabric provides a striking and dramatic note in its variety of tone and opacity against the muted tans and beiges of the model's flesh. Sargent embraced the expressive potential of the human figure in these works. The bold sensuality of such images—and others pertaining to the murals—has provoked curiosity about Sargent's sexuality. Although there is no direct evidence of Sargent's ever having had a relationship with a man or a woman, such drawings seem to represent his attraction to men. Since Sargent was intensely private, any assumptions remain speculative.[17] These evocative figure studies inspired some of the later panels for the library, particularly dramatic scenes such as *Hell* [fig. 42], installed in 1916. Sargent's vision of the inferno included a giant demon devouring writhing, tortured souls against a ornamental gold patterned background.

Before completing the Boston Public Library Murals, in 1916, Sargent began discussions with the Museum of Fine Arts, Boston, to create decorative panels for their entrance rotunda. At Sargent's suggestion, the commission expanded to include the renovation of the dome with eight paintings and twelve bas-relief sculptures with subjects related to the arts and the classical tradition. Above the entrance, Sargent created an allegorical rendering of personifications in *Architecture, Painting, and Sculpture Protected by Athena from the Ravages of Time* [fig. 43] signifying the museum's role as the guardian of culture. When the

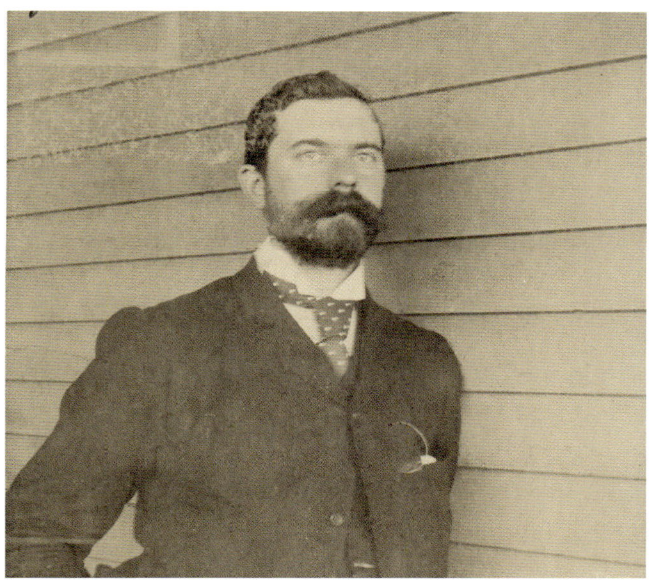

Sargent, 1890. Museum of Fine Arts, Boston. The John Singer Sargent Archive–Gift of Richard and Leonée Ormond

decorations were unveiled in 1921, Sargent immediately accepted a further commission to decorate the ceiling over the staircase; and ambitiously expanded the scope of the project to twelve more paintings of various size and six additional bas-reliefs, again focusing on the classical tradition and incorporating episodes from mythology [fig. 44].

According to architect Thomas Fox (1864–1946), who assisted Sargent on the project, a young African American bellhop whom Sargent met at a hotel in Boston, Thomas E. McKeller, "served as the model for practically all the male figures, and indeed for some of the others [the female figures]" in the murals.[18] Sargent's oil painting of McKeller [fig. 47] doesn't relate directly to any of the mural compositions, though it is painted over a study for the outstretched wings of a bird (probably a study for *Prometheus*, one of the panels for the rotunda). In painting out the underlying sketch, Sargent created a striking silhouette for the figure who appears bathed in glowing light. With his upturned head and averted gaze, he is strong and vulnerable. The portrait is powerful and direct, his frontal pose and spread legs creates a highly sensual image.

Meanwhile, as Sargent planned and executed his murals throughout the last decade of the century, he was becoming the most sought-after portraitist of his era on both sides of the Atlantic. After struggling to win over patrons in England, in the year 1893 he scored a striking success during London's spring exhibition season when he sent *Lady Agnew of Lochnaw* (1892) [fig. 48] to the venerable Royal Academy and *Mrs. Hugh Hammersley* (1892) [fig. 49] to the New Gallery for English Art, a newer institution known to foster modern tendencies in British painting. (Sargent also sent his portrait of *Mrs. George Lewis* [1892, private collection] to the New Gallery, but she was overshadowed by the others.)

Sargent created an astute juxtaposition with the portraits of Agnew and Hammersley. Agnew, the Scottish wife of a baronet, is a study of elegant refinement. In her white dress with its lavender sash, she appears alert but relaxed and at ease, seated in a tastefully appointed interior with its decorative floral upholstered chair and pale blue silk hangings with Japanese motifs. Hammersley, the fashionable society hostess and wife of a London banker, seems to vibrate with energy. Her aniline velvet dress in an assertive fuchsia shade is the main note of color against a pale eighteenth-century-style interior. Sargent has tilted the picture plane to compress the composition, and in contrast to the relaxed of Agnew, Hammersley appears ready to spring into action. Poised on the edge of the settee, Sargent creates a sense of rotation from the swirl of her skirt, the twist of her torso at the waist, and the effect of her left arm, which dissolves into a faint flurry of brushstrokes to suggest her energy and motion. Sargent captured Hammersley's vivacious personality in her energetic pose and her brilliantly colored gown.

Sargent sent the sedate and stable portrait of Agnew to the more traditional venue, the Royal Academy, and the more daring portrait of Hammersley to the more progressive venue, the New Gallery. Sargent's friend Clementina "Kit" Anstruther-Thomson reported on London's response to the portraits in a letter to Vernon Lee, declaring, "As to Mr Sargent London is at his feet. Mrs Hammersley & Mrs Lewis are at the New Gallery, Lady Agnew at the Academy. There are no two opinions this year. He has had a cracking success."[19]

The portrait of Lady Agnew was reassuring, the critic for the *Times* observed, "While Mr. Sargent has abandoned none of his subtlety, he abandoned his mannerisms, and has been content to make a beautiful picture of a charming subject, under conditions of repose."[20] While the portrait of Hammersley signified new directions in Sargent's portraiture, her animated energy (informed by his figural studies for the murals) revealed a new expressiveness in his portraiture. Critics focused on the vivacity of her pose and praised the portrait for its "astonishing vitality"[21] and the "spontaneity of the attitude."[22]

The vibrancy of *Mrs. Hugh Hammersley* in contrast to the relative tranquility of *Lady Agnew* represented options for potential patrons. At least one critic saw the portraits as expressing aspects of Sargent's personality:

> [Sargent's] craftsmanship, his finesse of sight, his captivating *brio*, lead one again and again before his canvases. The personality of his style interests one so powerfully. . . . Yet there are many admirable works in the gallery of a quieter sort, and Mr. Sargent's two portraits [*Mrs. Hugh Hammersley* and *Mrs George Lewis*] themselves cannot match the impeccable *chef d'oeuvre* that he has in the Academy [Agnew]. It is almost with a sense of debauch that one returns to riot in the grand bravura of "Mrs. Hugh Hammersley." One is whirled away by the breadth of mind which covers a whole view in one majestic sweep and recreated the vision through the vivacious play of a touch as rapid as lightning.[23]

The portrait of *Lady Agnew* ensured Sargent's election as an associate to the venerable Royal Academy in 1894. This formal approbation signaled Sargent's acceptance by the British art world and seemingly sealed his fate as the "Van Dyke de l'époque," as Auguste Rodin (1840–1917) would anoint him in 1902.[24] Commissions followed from across the spectrum of British and American society from the upwardly mobile bourgeoisie to established aristocrats. His carefully cultivated, elegant, bravura painting style satisfied his patrons' aspirations and ambitions.

The animated portrait of Mrs. Hammersley is an important precursor to *Mrs. Carl Meyer and Her Children* [fig. 50]. Adèle Meyer was the wife of a prominent international Jewish banker, a vivacious society hostess, and dedicated philanthropist committed to progressive women's issues. Sargent admired the stylish, self-assured young matriarch and portrayed her with her children Elsie and Frank, with a confident poise.[25] Every detail of the sumptuous domestic interior conveys the family's wealth and position and their aesthetic sensibilities. Her gown, a confection of pink-peach *changeant* silk accented with black velvet bows recalls those worn in earlier portraits by French painters François Boucher (1703–1770) or Jean-Honoré Fragonard (1732–1806), albeit with a modern twist.

Sargent referenced the past as he imparts a dynamic immediacy through his lively brushwork and the dramatically tilted composition. Some contemporary viewers found this inventive composition destabilizing: Adèle has just set aside her book and appears ready to emerge from the canvas, a stylish force in a rapidly changing British society—when land ownership was no longer the sole measure of one's wealth and status.

When the painting was exhibited at the Royal Academy in 1897, Henry James celebrated Sargent's bold confidence and the portrait's powerful impact. "Mr. Sargent has made a picture of knock-down insolence of talent and truth of characterization," he wrote, "a wonderful rendering of life, of manners, of aspects, of types, of textures, of everything."[26]

Like *Mrs. Carl Meyer and Her Children*, *The Wyndham Sisters: Lady Elcho, Mrs. Adeane, and Mrs. Tennant* [fig. 51], painted in 1899, is a dazzling display of fin-de-siècle opulence and bravura painting. Amid the extravagance, Sargent's powerful technical virtuosity materializes—his signature brio; his remarkable economy of stroke; his ability to describe detail with the slightest, well-placed daub or swipe of pigment seems effortless. Perhaps the brilliance of Sargent's grand manner painting exists, in part, in the tension between opulence and economy.

In *The Wyndham Sisters*, a monumental depiction of the three elegant daughters of Percy Wyndham, a politician and wealthy Londoner and his wife, the glamorous sisters are shown in the drawing room of their London home at Belgrave Square. Wearing white dresses and poised on an upholstered sofa, they are set against a darkened interior. Sargent creates an unconventional composition in which, at first glance, the upper half of the massive canvas seems empty. Flashes of light illuminate the gilt edges of the frame surrounding a portrait of their mother by the British painter George Frederic Watts (1817–1904). Sargent established the genealogy of the sisters as well as his own artistic heritage, situating himself as a descendent of the tradition of British portraiture.

The sisters—from left to right, Madeline, Pamela, and Mary Constance—appear impossibly graceful. Sargent conveys a mannered elegance in his depiction of their attenuated figures, long necks, and slender arms. The painting is a tour de force of Sargent's mastery of white pigment. In his rendering of their gowns and the upholstery of the sofa, Sargent merges calligraphic strokes and daubs of pigment to represent the shimmering fabrics. Sargent sent *The Wyndham Sisters* and *An Interior in Venice* [fig. 67] to the annual exhibition of the Royal Academy in 1900 where the critic Roger Fry noted that Sargent had been able "to seize the exact cachet of fashionable life."[27]

Sargent's portrait *The Ladies Alexandra, Mary and Theo Acheson* [fig. 52], daughters of the fourth Earl of Gosford and Lady Louisa Montagu, seems to have been commissioned by the young women's grandmother Louisa Cavendish, Duchess of Devonshire, for the magnificent family estate Chatsworth House in the English countryside in Derbyshire. The three unmarried sisters are presented in elegant satin day dresses beneath a large potted orange tree, appropriately symbolizing their purity and chastity. Sargent painted the portrait in his London studio but the setting, with its broadly painted cloudy sky, evokes the pastoral, in keeping with its intended destination at Chatsworth with its historic, grand gardens and notable orangery.

One of Sargent's most devoted patrons was the art dealer Asher Wertheimer, who first commissioned Sargent to paint a pair of likenesses of himself and his wife to celebrate their twenty-fifth wedding anniversary. The portrait of Wertheimer [fig. 53] is a sensitive rendering of a confident man. Posed against a lacquer screen in Sargent's studio, there is a subtlety to Sargent's rendering of his subject's somber suit within the darkened interior. His gestures are understated but expressive. As he tucks his right thumb into his vest, his jacket parts to reveal the glint of his watch chain. In his left hand, he casually gesticulates while holding a cigar, giving the portrait a touch of informality. Sargent included Wertheimer's black poodle, Noble, in the lower left corner, his long bright pink tongue, the sparkle of his eye, and his shiny fur emerge from within the dark background interior. Most critics admired the portrait; one declared, "Happy is the man whose portrait has been painted thus."[28]

Sargent formed a lasting friendship with the family, regularly visiting them at their country estate, Temple. Over the next ten years, Wertheimer would enlist Sargent to paint a sequence of eleven additional portraits of family members, which he later bequeathed to the British nation. The striking double portrait of Wertheimer's eldest daughters, Ena and Betty [fig. 54], is set in the drawing room of the family's London home. The young women are surrounded by symbols of affluence—the trappings of their father's success. Gilded picture frames glimmer in the background, and Ena's hand rests atop a large ceramic urn. Their proximity and casual pose—Ena's arm is wrapped around Betty's waist—highlight their bond. Sargent contrasts the velvety texture of Betty's red dress with the opulent sheen of Ena's white dress. They are alert and energized as they gaze confidently at the viewer.

Sargent's portrait of the aging landscape architect Frederick Law Olmsted (1822–1903) [fig. 55] is humble and unpretentious. In 1895, Sargent traveled to Asheville, North Carolina, at the request of George Vanderbilt, whose massive European-style château, Biltmore, was then nearing completion. He commissioned Sargent for portraits of Richard Morris Hunt (1827–1895), the architect, and Olmsted. The celebrated designer of New York City's Central Park, Olmsted had created Biltmore's impressive Italian-style formal gardens, arboretum, and farm on the 125,000-acre property in rural North Carolina. Olmsted, who

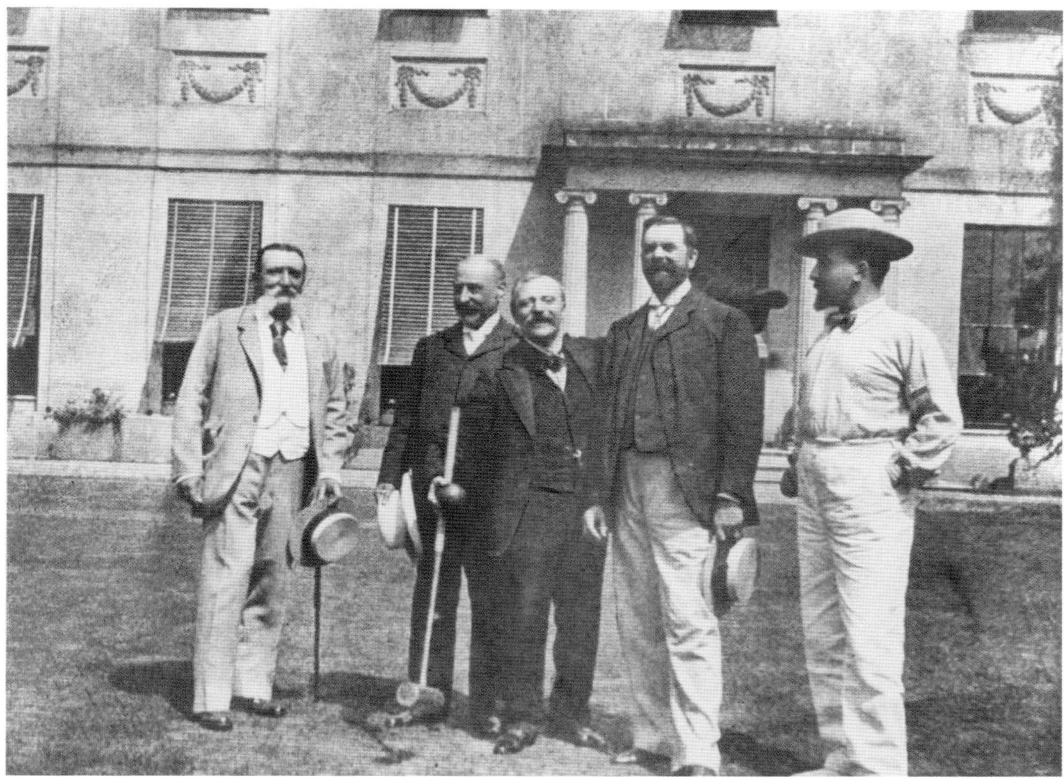

Sargent and friends at Temple, Asher Wertheimer's country house, ca. 1895.
(From left to right: Baron Louis von Solberstein, Asher Wertheimer, Antonio Mancini, Sargent, Edward Wertheimer.) Museum of Fine Arts, Boston. The John Singer Sargent Archive–Gift of Richard and Leonée Ormond

was seventy-three at the time and in failing health, posed for Sargent in a makeshift studio but in the final portrait, he is shown amid the dense native flora of the region: rhododendron, mountain laurel, and dogwood. On occasion, Olmsted's son filled in for his father during the long sittings. He later described Sargent's distinctive painting process:

> He would stand off, some twenty feet or so from his subject and the canvas, very deliberately but very alertly looking back and forth from one to the other and mixing a brush full of paint on his palette, then at last give a little lift of his shoulders and with a very springy motion for so heavy a man walk forward swiftly to the canvas and make a brush-stroke like an arrow going to the bullseye.[29]

Sargent painted the stylish American newlyweds, Mr. and Mrs. Isaac Newton Phelps Stokes [fig. 56], while the couple was in London on their honeymoon. The portrait was a wedding present from a friend. The commission was originally for a portrait only of Edith, a philanthropist who supported progressive causes such as free kindergarten and a sewing school for immigrant women. Sargent first began to paint her in a traditional blue satin evening gown, but after several sittings he decided to portray her instead in the starched white skirt and black

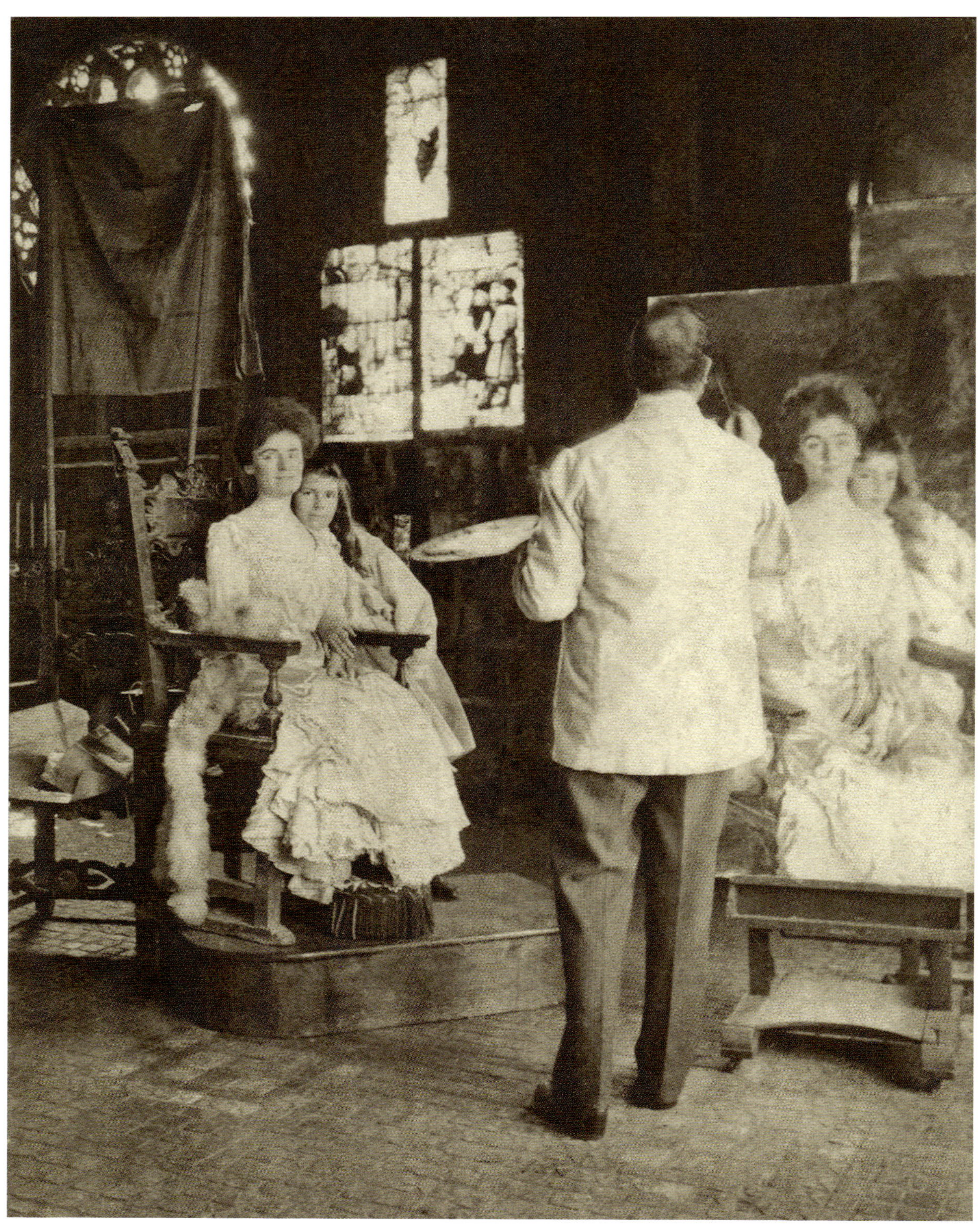

Sargent painting the portrait of Mrs. Fiske Warren and her daughter in the Gothic Room in Fenway Court, 1903. Photograph by John Templeman Coolidge. Isabella Stewart Gardner Museum, Boston.

jacket she had worn to the studio. Sargent intended to include a Great Dane dog in the portrait. But, as Mr. Phelps Stokes would later write in his memoirs, when the dog was unavailable he "had a sudden inspiration, and offered to assume the role of the Great Dane in the picture."[30] Her contemporary "sportswear" and confident poise identify as the quintessential modern American woman; her accomplished husband appears as a cursory afterthought.

For his double portrait of *Mrs. Fiske Warren (Gretchen Osgood) and Her Daughter Rachel* [fig. 57], Sargent contrived an entwined seated pose to depict the relationship between the two generations. Painted in the Gothic Room of Fenway Court, Isabella Stewart Gardner's Italianate Renaissance palazzo in Boston, they are surrounded by precious objects from Gardner's distinguished collection—including a Renaissance chair, a fifteenth-century polychrome sculpture of the Madonna and Child, and gilt candelabra. While the fancy fabrics and opulent details of the setting are painted with a remarkable, urgent fluidity, the composition has a timeless quality that evokes Old Master images of the Madonna and Child.

Sargent's portrait of the 9th Duke of Marlborough (Charles Richard John Spencer-Churchill) and his family [fig. 58] was commissioned as a pendant to an esteemed family heirloom—the great portrait of the 4th Duke of Marlborough and his family (1778) by Sir Joshua Reynolds (1723–1792). Sargent's respect for this tradition and his extensive knowledge of art history, as well as his status in the art world, made him the ideal artist to create a composition suitable for the majestic setting in the Red Drawing Room at Blenheim Palace, where the portrait by Reynolds still resides.

At the height of his success, Sargent grew weary of painting portraits. Beginning about 1900, he raised his fees and began refusing commissions. In 1907, Sargent made an official declaration that he would no longer paint portraits on commission. "No more paughtraits," he wrote to his longtime friend Ralph Curtis (1854–1922), using his personal and satiric spelling of the genre that had made him famous, "I abhor and abjure them and hope never to do another especially of the Upper Classes."[31] His disenchantment with creating commissioned portraits was due, in part, to the difficulty of satisfying his discriminating patrons. Referring to the litany of complaints from his sitters, Sargent once defined a portrait as "a picture in which there is just a tiny little something not quite right about the mouth." The need to engage his sitter's attention while he painted their likeness further challenged the reticent Sargent. He explained to his friend the painter Jacques-Émile Blanche (1861–1942), "Painting a portrait would be quite amusing if one were not forced to talk while working."[32]

As an alternative, he offered clients fluid charcoal portraits drawn on paper, which could be executed in a single sitting that lasted a few short hours. Sargent's fluid technique in charcoal mimics that of his paintings. His portrait sketch of the great Irish poet William Butler Yeats [fig. 59], commissioned as the frontispiece for his volume of *Collected Poems* (1908), amplifies his angular good looks and youthfulness. (Yeats cultivated his image as a poet and an aesthete with flamboyant clothing like the velvet jacket and floppy bow tie seen in Sargent's portrait.) The dashing poet, who appears somewhat younger than his forty-three years, found the portrait "charming" and "very flattering."[33] Sargent's likeness of Lady Elsie Meyer [fig. 60], daughter of Mrs. Carl Meyer, whom Sargent had painted in 1896, conveys the mannered elegance of the artist's late portraits with a simple, yet bold graphic immediacy.

Sargent would occasionally be lured out of "retirement" to paint portraits for cherished friends for special occasions. Sargent painted the lyrical portrait of the Countess of Rocksavage (Sybil Sassoon) [fig. 61] in honor of her marriage: a gift from the artist to his dear friend. The timeless image of his longtime friend Henry James [fig. 62] was commissioned by a group of admirers in honor of the writer's seventieth birthday in 1913. It's a masterly—and sympathetic—study of an older man. The author's intense, penetrating gaze conveys the connection between the dear friends. James admired the portrait, but was mocking in his praise:

> Sargent at his very best and poor old H[enry] J[ames] not at his worst, in short, a living, breathing likeness and a masterpiece of painting. I don't alas exhibit a point in it, but I am all large and luscious rotundity by which you may see how true a thing it is.

In June 1918, Sargent traveled to France as an official war artist for Britain. Commissioned to paint a propagandistic picture commemorating the joint efforts of American and British troops, he spent four months along the western front, sketching and painting in watercolor as he searched for a subject. He ultimately abandoned his assigned topic to depict the horrific effects of modern chemical warfare. *Gassed* [fig. 63]—a monumental friezelike composition of soldiers, blinded by mustard gas, being led to treatment—was based on a scene that Sargent witnessed. The roadside is littered with hundreds of impacted soldiers who convey the senselessness and scale of the Great War. In the distant background, life continues as soldiers are seen relieving tension in a game of soccer.

Sargent's public response to the war incorporated personal associations of loss. Sargent was deeply moved by the death of his beloved twenty-four-year-old niece (and favorite model), Rose-Marie Ormond, who was killed in the bombing of the church of Saint-Gervais in Paris on Good Friday in 1918. Her husband, a soldier, had died in fighting in 1914. Before her death, Rose-Marie had worked as a nurse treating blinded soldiers, and the subject depicted in *Gassed* must have reminded Sargent of her.

Sargent also painted a series of more intimate watercolors, which document the ruin and chaos of war and vignettes of the daily lives of soldiers. On occasion, Sargent found a discreet beauty in the devastation of war. *A Wrecked Sugar Refinery* [fig. 64] conveys the scale of destruction in the mass of tangled and rusted machinery. *The Interior of a Hospital Tent* [fig. 65] has a quiet tranquility as rays of light stream into the tent where soldiers recuperate from their injuries. *Tommies Bathing* [fig. 66] depicts a peaceful, off-duty moment for a group of British soldiers, known as "Tommies," who lounge in the long grass or bathe nearby.[34]

1 Henry James, "John S. Sargent," *Harper's New Monthly Magazine* 75 (October 1887): 683.
2 Ibid., 691.
3 There was no catalogue for this exhibition. For a complete listing of works, see Stephanie L. Herdrich and H. Barbara Weinberg, *American Drawings and Watercolors in The Metropolitan Museum of Art: John Singer Sargent* (New York: The Metropolitan Museum of Art; and New Haven: Yale University Press), V, 2000, 378.
4 Henry James to Miss Reubell, February 22, 1888, Houghton Library, Harvard University; quoted in Richard Ormond et al., *Sargent: Portraits of Artists and Friends*, exh. cat. (London: National Portrait Gallery, 2015), 180.
5 Greta, "Art in Boston," *Art Amateur* 18 (April 1888), 5.
6 Quoted in Richard Ormond and Elaine Kilmurray, *John Singer Sargent: Complete Paintings*. Vol. 1: *The Early Portraits* (New Haven: Yale University Press, 1998), 210.
7 Quoted in Ormond and Kilmurray 1998, 188.
8 According to Richard Ormond and Elaine Kilmurray, *John Singer Sargent: Complete Paintings*. Vol. 2: *Portraits of the 1890s* (New Haven: Yale University Press, 2002), 11, Sargent painted forty portraits in total during the 1889–90 trip to the United States.
9 La Carmencita was so renowned, she became the first woman to be recorded on film in the studio of Thomas Edison in 1894. See their website: https://www.loc.gov/item/00694116/.
10 Undated letter, Archives of the Isabella Stewart Gardner Museum, Boston; quoted in London/New York 2015, 183.
11 Gutzon Borglum, "John Singer Sargent—Artist. The Greatest of American Portrait-Painters." *Delineator* [no volume] (February 1923): 15.
12 The paintings, which were executed almost entirely in England, were installed in four phases: 1895, 1903, 1916, and 1919. Sargent shared a studio with Edwin Austin Abbey, who had also accepted a mural commission for the library, Fairford, Gloucestershire, about forty miles south of Broadway, where Abbey, Francis David Millet (1846–1912), Sargent, and others lived and worked during the 1880s. Sargent later established his own mural studio on Fulham Road, London, in 1895.
13 Sargent to Isabella Stewart Gardner [August] 1891, Bursa, Turkey, Isabella Stewart Gardner Papers, Archives of American Art; quoted in Herdrich and Weinberg 2000, 369.
14 Boston Public Library, *Handbook of the Boston Public Library* (Boston: Association Publications, 1916), 48.
15 Frederick W. Coburn, "The Sargent Decorations in the Boston Public Library," *American Magazine of Art* 8 (February 1917): 129–30.
16 Sargent painted a mural program with mythological subjects for the Museum of Fine Arts, Boston (1916–25), and two mural panels commemorating students who died during World War I for the Widener Memorial Library at Harvard University (1922).
17 Homosexual behavior was illegal in England until 1967. For the typical response to this issue, Elaine Kilmurray and Richard Ormond, *John Singer Sargent*, exh. cat. (London: Tate Gallery, 1998), 14. Compare Trevor J. Fairbrother, *John Singer Sargent* (New York: Harry N. Abrams, 1994), 8, 83. Although the identity of the model is unknown, he resembles Nicola d'Inverno, whom Sargent hired as a model in the early 1890s. Nicola became a trusted companion, assuming greater responsibilities around the studio, before becoming Sargent's valet, a position he held until about 1918, when he was dismissed after a fight in a bar. Fairbrother has speculated that d'Inverno and Sargent were lovers. *Man with Red Drapery* came to The Metropolitan Museum of Art from Sargent's estate. When his sisters made their initial dispersal of the contents of his studio, many experimental and personal works were retained by the family. The bold sensuality of these watercolors may have prompted his sisters to initially keep them private to protect Sargent's reputation.
18 Fox, "As Sargent goes to rest." Quoted in Trevor J. Fairbrother, *John Singer Sargent: The Sensualist*, exh. cat. (Seattle: Seattle Art Museum and New Haven: Yale University Press, 2000), 176.
19 Letter from Kit Anstruther-Thomson to Vernon Lee, spring 1893, quoted in Kilmurray and Ormond 1998, 34.
20 *Times* [London] (April 29, 1893), 13, quoted in Ormond and Kilmurray 1998, 66.
21 The critic for the *New Standard* declared that "it is a record of astonishing vitality and unsurpassed aplomb." "The New Gallery," *New Standard* (May 1, 1893): 6. Clipping from a scrapbook of reviews compiled by Mrs. Hammersley in the collection of the American Wing at The Metropolitan Museum of Art.
22 Another reviewer noted that "what chiefly distinguishes the picture is its intense vitality, the lifelike expression of the face, and the spontaneity of the attitude." "The New Gallery" (May 6, 1893), no page. Clipping from a scrapbook of reviews compiled by Mrs. Hammersley in the collection of the American Wing at The Metropolitan Museum of Art.
23 "The New Gallery," *Pall Mall Gazette* (May 1, 1893), no page; clipping from a scrapbook of reviews compiled by Mrs. Hammersley in the collection of the American Wing at The Metropolitan Museum of Art.
24 "M. Rodin in London," *New York Times* (May 18, 1902), 4.
25 This discussion of *Mrs. Carl Meyer and Her Children* first appeared as Stephanie L. Herdrich, "Meet the Meyers at the Jewish Museum," *Magazine Antiques* CLXXXIII, no. 5 (September/October 2016): 32–33.
26 Henry James, *The Painter's Eye: Notes and Essays on the Pictorial Arts* (London: R. Hart Davis, 1956), 257.
27 Roger Fry, "Royal Academy," *Pilot* 1 (May 12, 1900): 321.
28 *Athenaeum* (June 1898), 762. Quoted in Ormond and Kilmurray 2002, 133.
29 Letter from Olmsted Jr. to Thomas A. Fox, September 13, 1933, quoted in Ormond and Kilmurray 2002, 104.
30 Quoted in Doreen Bolger Burke, *American Paintings in the Metropolitan Museum of Art. Vol. 3: A Catalogue of Works by Artists Born between 1846 and 1864* (New York: The Metropolitan Museum of Art, 1980), 248.
31 Sargent to Ralph Curtis, ca. 1907; quoted in Evan Charteris, *John Sargent* (New York: Charles Scribner's Sons, 1927), 155.
32 Excerpts from letters are quoted in Stanley Olson, *John Singer Sargent: His Portrait* (New York: St. Martin's Press, 1986), 237. This passage was originally published as Stephanie L. Herdrich, "'No More Paughtraits': Final Thoughts on Sargent: Portraits of Artists and Friends," Sargent Exhibition Blog (October 6, 2015), http://www.metmuseum.org/exhibitions/listings/2015/sargent-portraits-of-artists-and-friends/blog/posts/no-more-paughtraits.
33 Allan Wade (ed.), *The Letters of W. B. Yeats* (London: Rupert Hart Davis, 1954), 509.
34 The nickname "Tommies," for British soldiers came from the name "Thomas Atkins," which was the generic name used on government documents (similar to the American "John Doe").

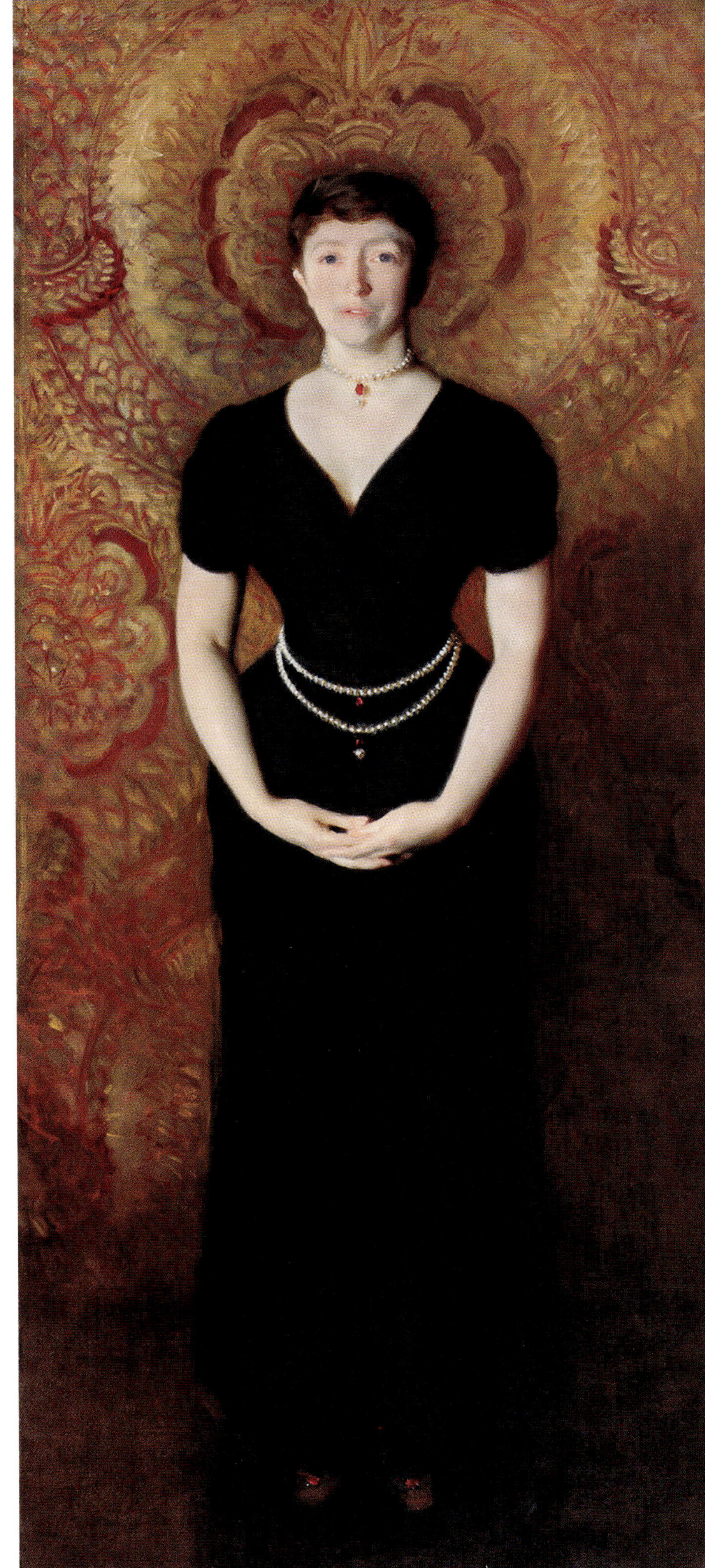

33

Isabella Stewart Gardner

1888
Oil on canvas, 74 13/16 × 31 ½ in.
(190 × 80 cm)
Signed: "John S. Sargent"
Dated: "1888"
Boston, Isabella Stewart Gardner
Museum [P30w1]

34

A Morning Walk

1888

Oil on canvas, 26½ × 19¾ in.
(67.3 × 50.2 cm)
Signed: "John S. Sargent"
Private collection

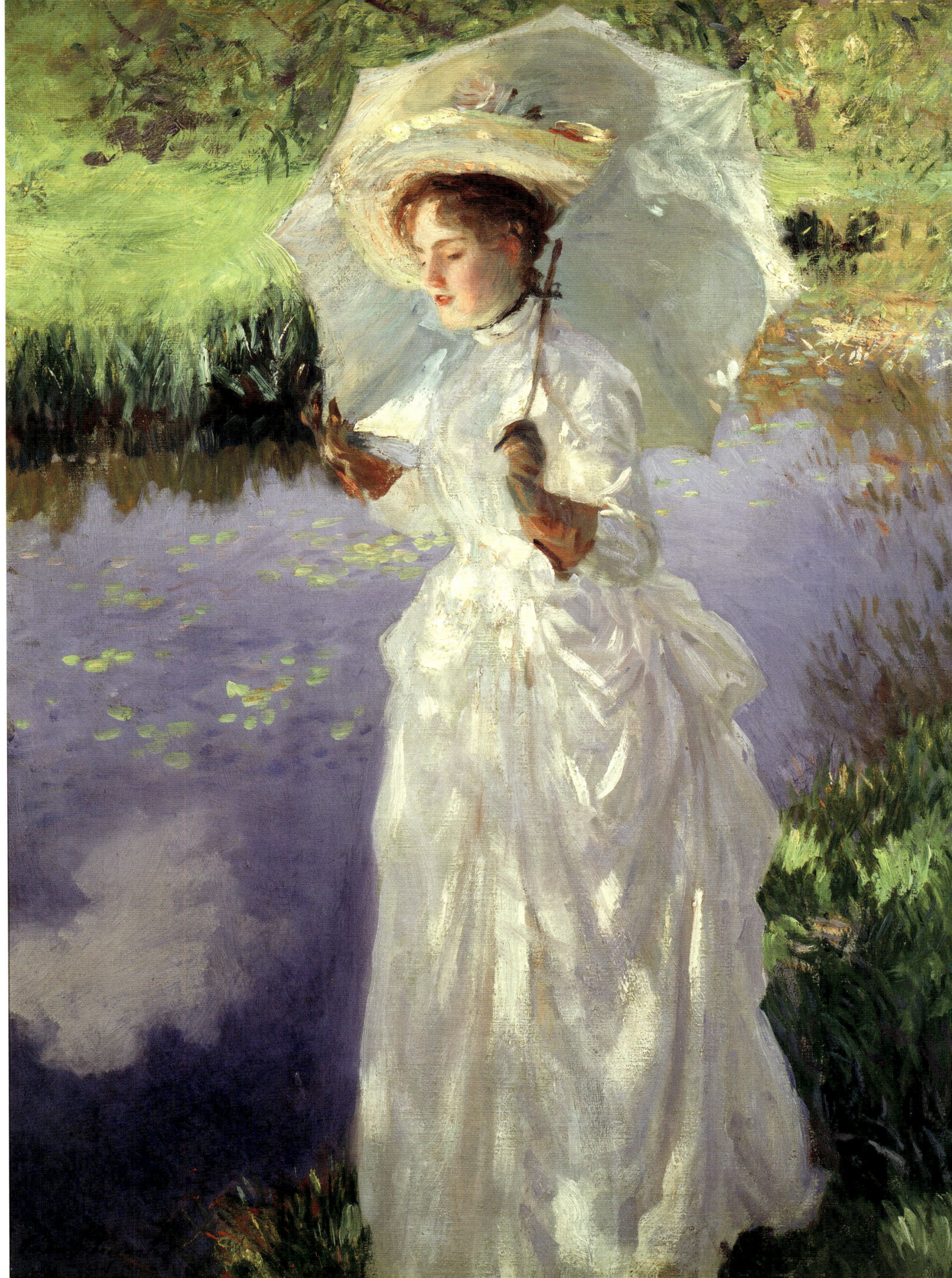

35

An Out-of-Doors Study

1889
Oil on canvas, 25 15/16 × 31 3/4 in.
(65.9 × 80.7 cm)
Signed: "John S. Sargent"
New York, Brooklyn Museum,
Museum Collection Fund [20.640]

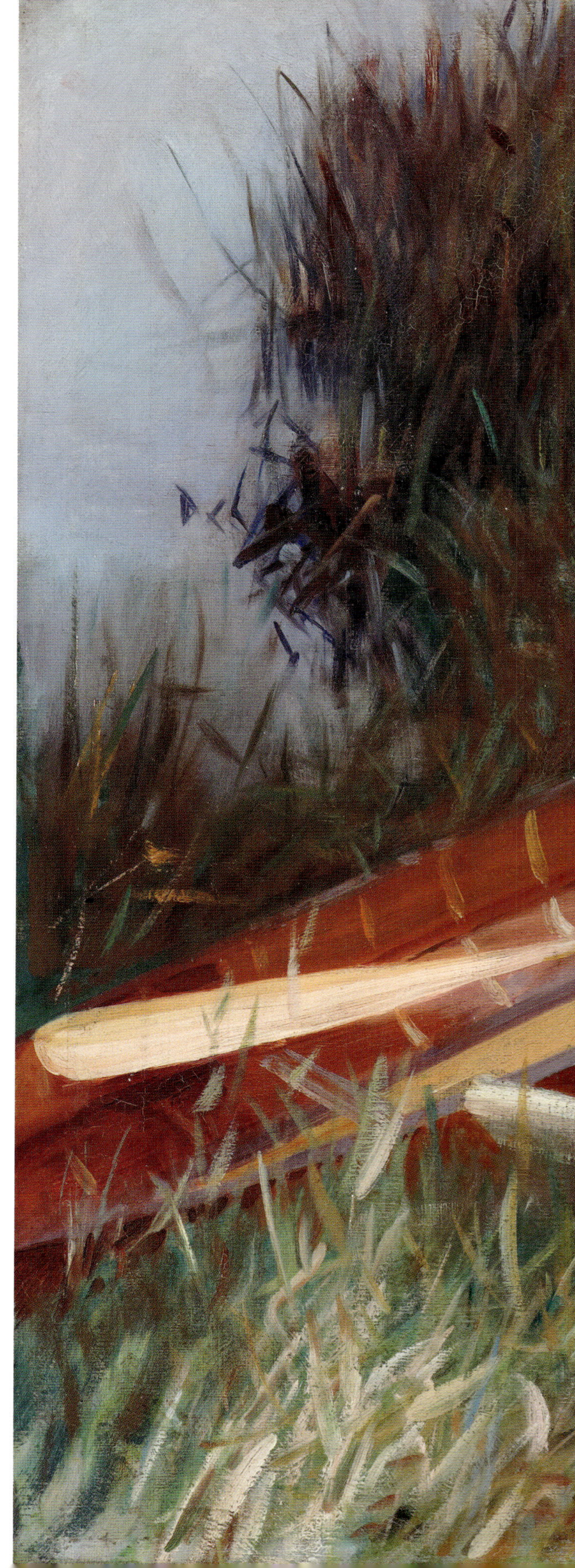

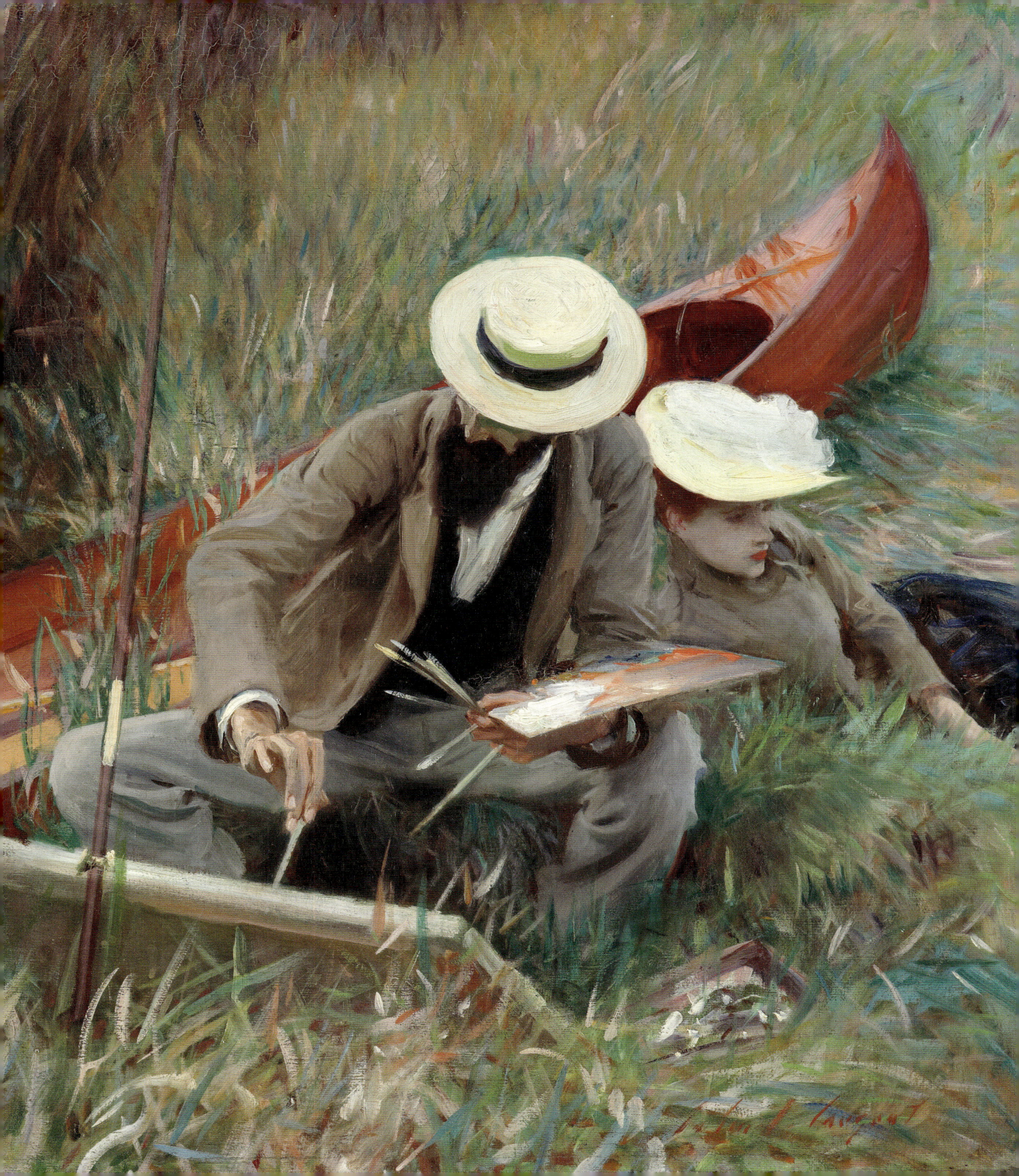

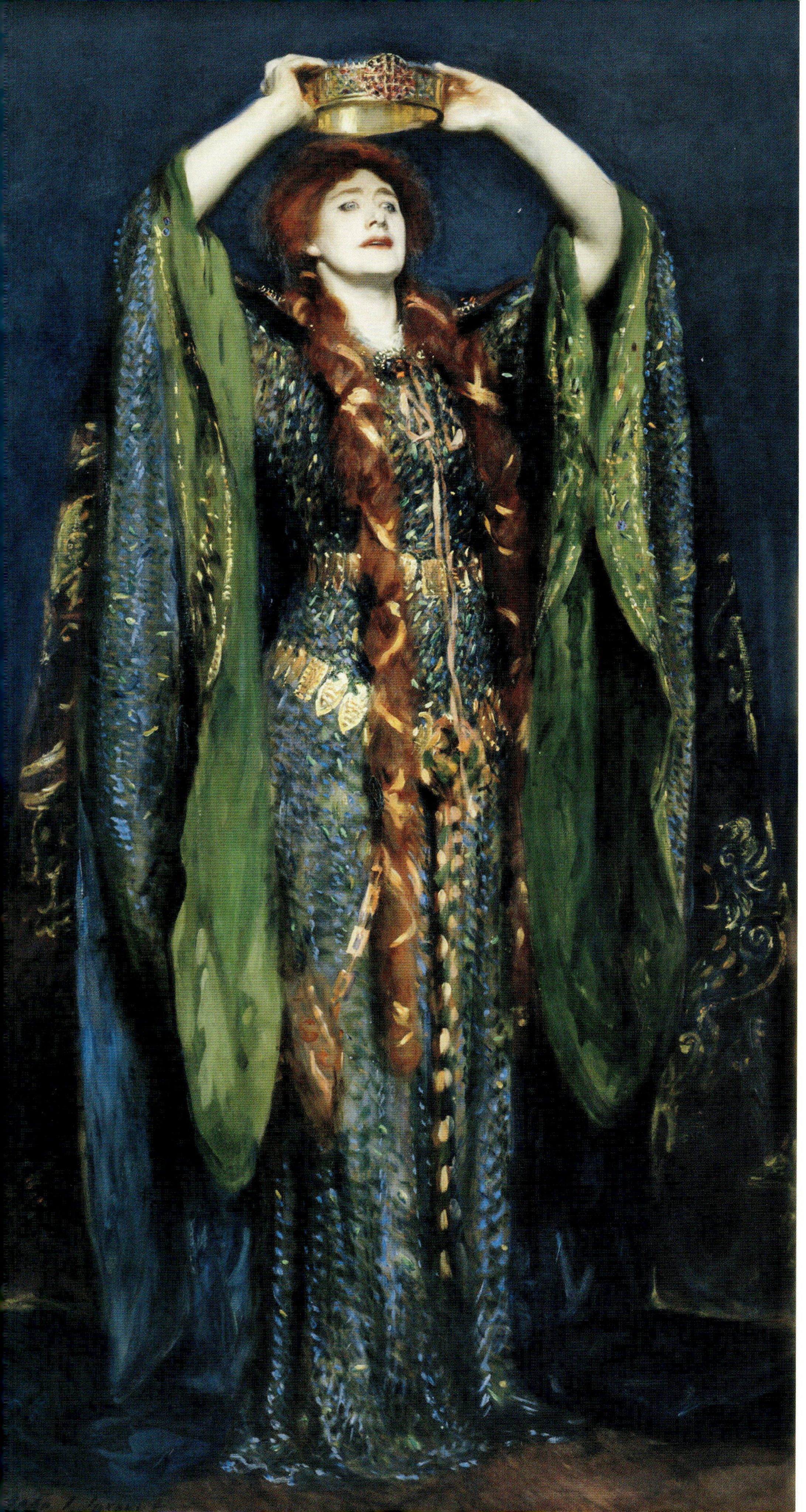

36

Ellen Terry as Lady Macbeth

1889
Oil on canvas, 87 × 45 in.
(221 × 114.3 cm)
Signed: "John S. Sargent"
London, Tate, Presented by Sir
Joseph Duveen 1906 [N02053]

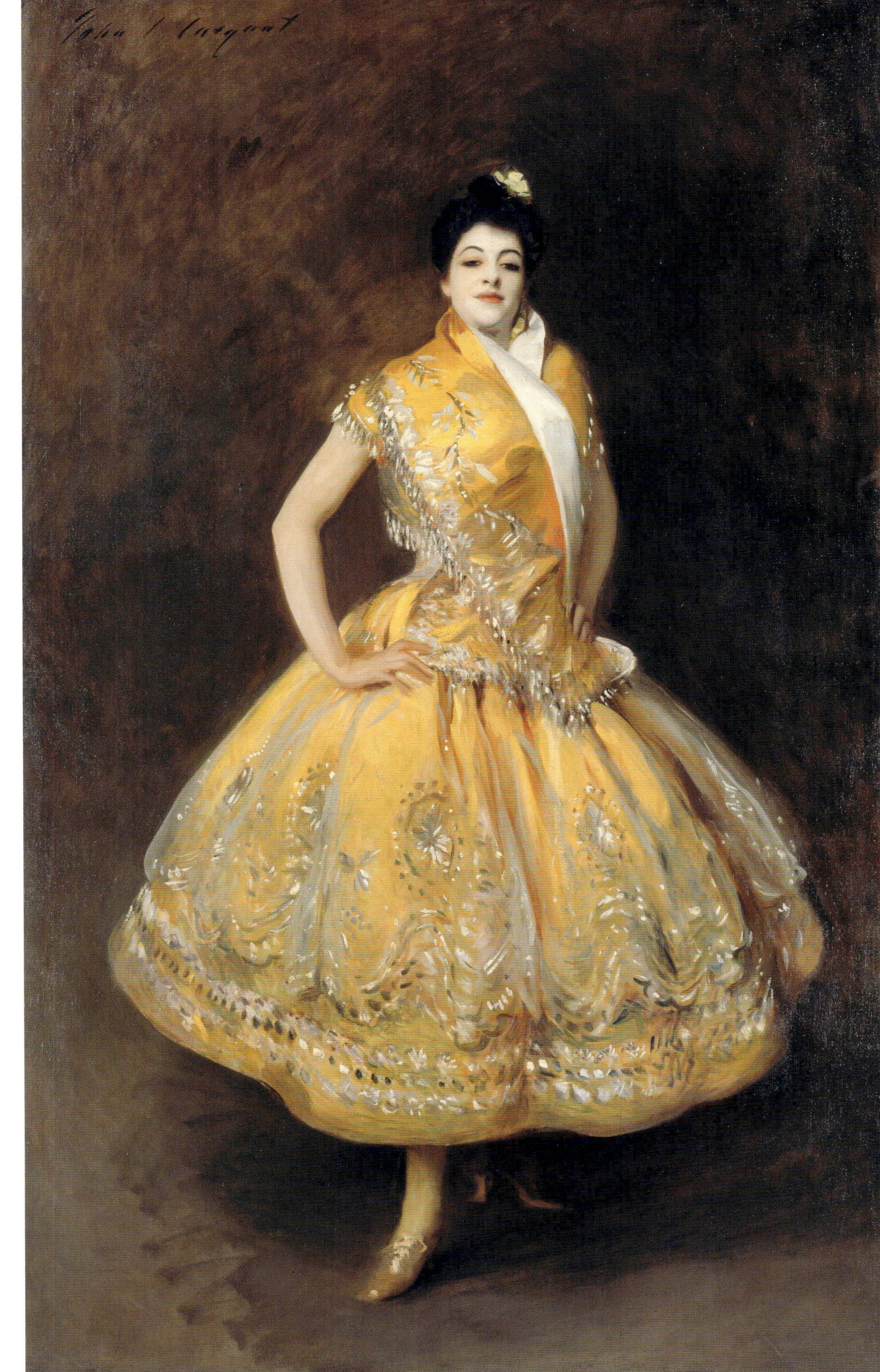

37

La Carmencita

1890
Oil on canvas, 90⅛ × 55 in.
(229 × 140 cm)
Signed: "John S. Sargent"
Paris, Musée d'Orsay
[RF 746]

38

Portrait of a Boy
(*Homer Saint-Gaudens and His Mother*)

1890
Oil on canvas, 69¼ × 52¼ in. (175.9 × 132.7 cm)
Pittsburgh, Carnegie Museum of Art [32.1]

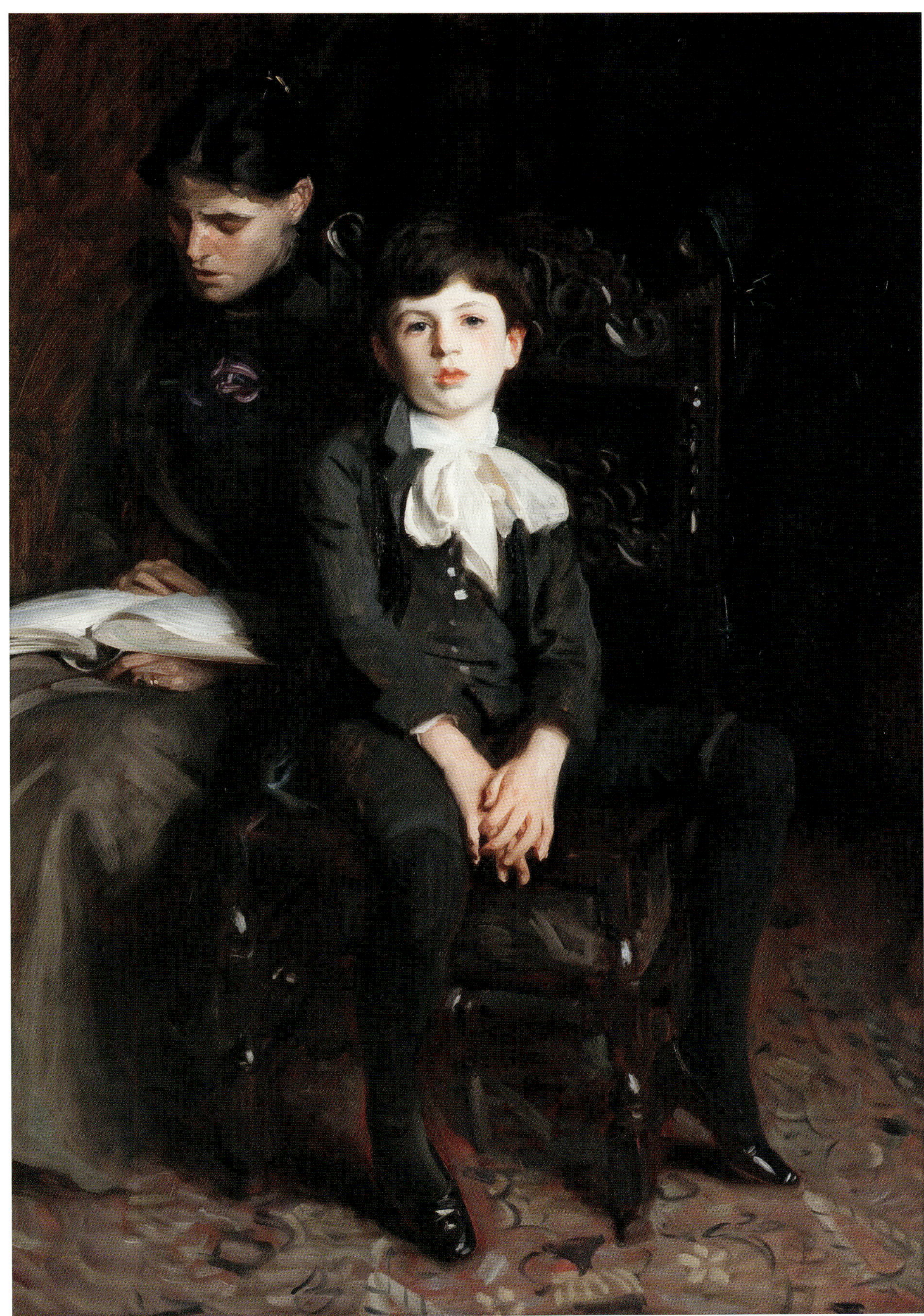

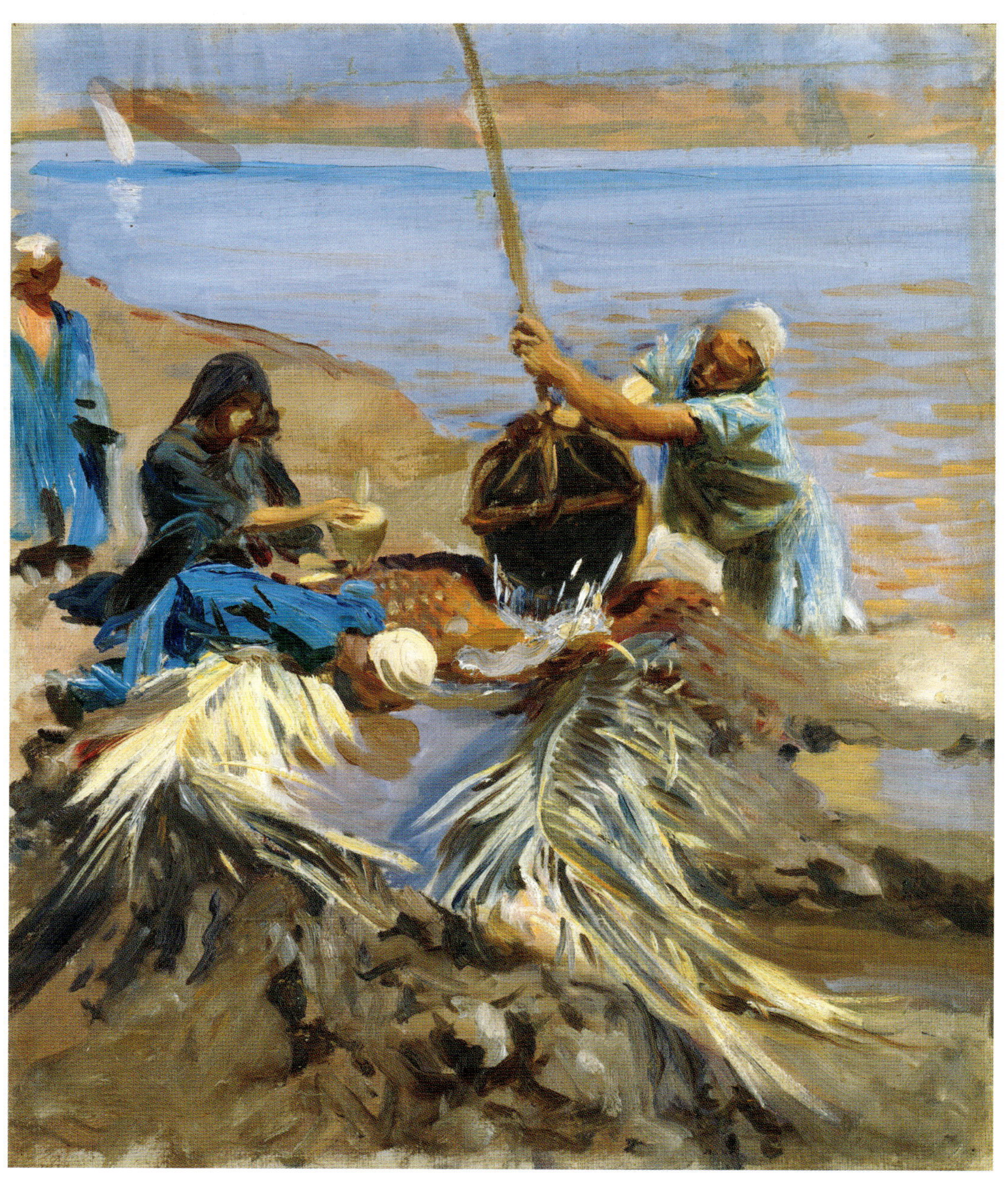

39

Egyptians Raising Water from the Nile

1891
Oil on canvas, 25 × 21 in. (63.5 × 53.3 cm)
New York, The Metropolitan Museum of Art,
Gift of Mrs. Francis Ormond, 1950 [50.130.16]

40

Interior of Saint Sophia, Constantinople

1891
Oil on canvas, 32 × 24 5/8 in.
(81.3 × 62.6 cm)
Louisville, Kentucky,
Speed Art Museum, Purchase,
Museum Art Fund [1960.5]

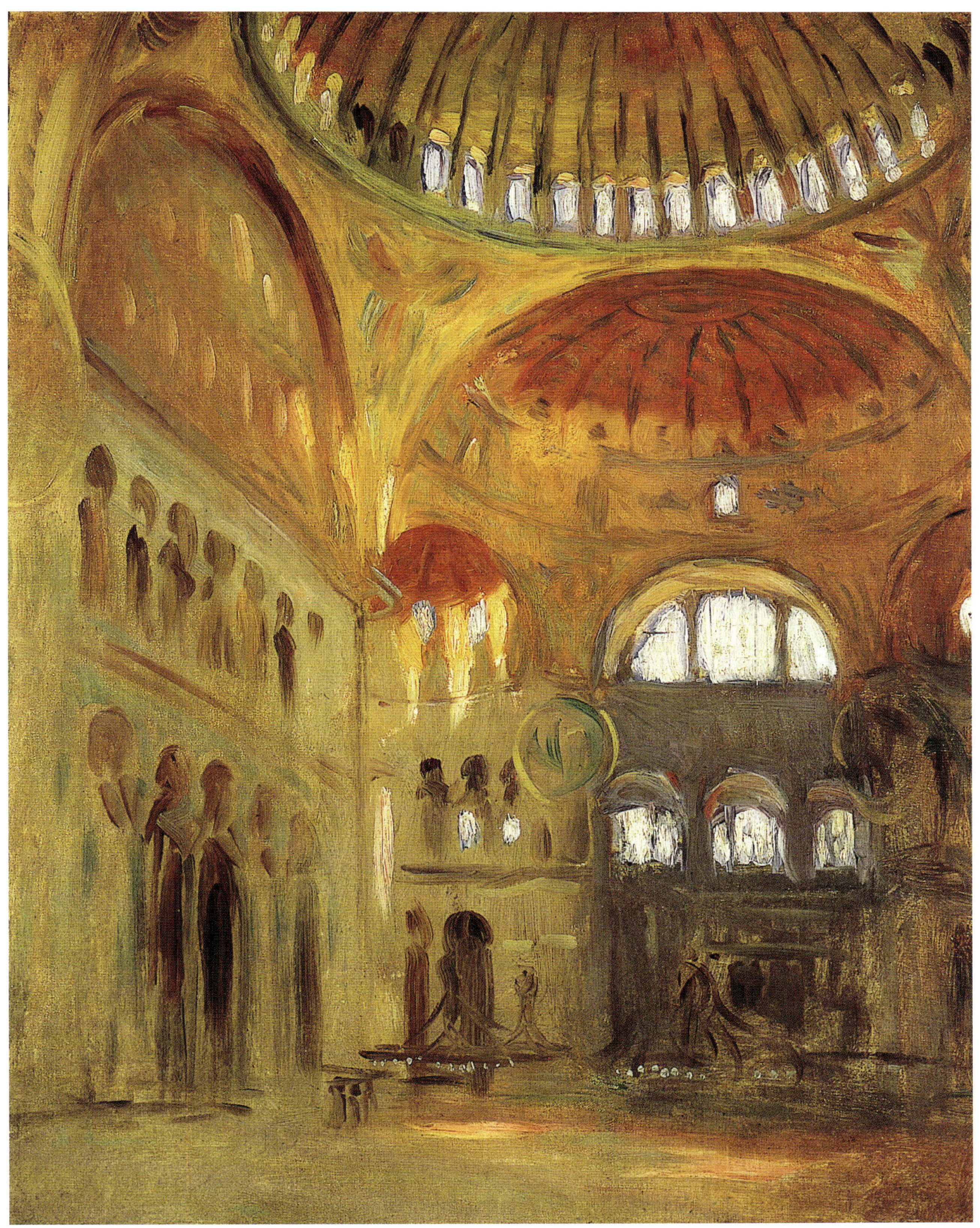

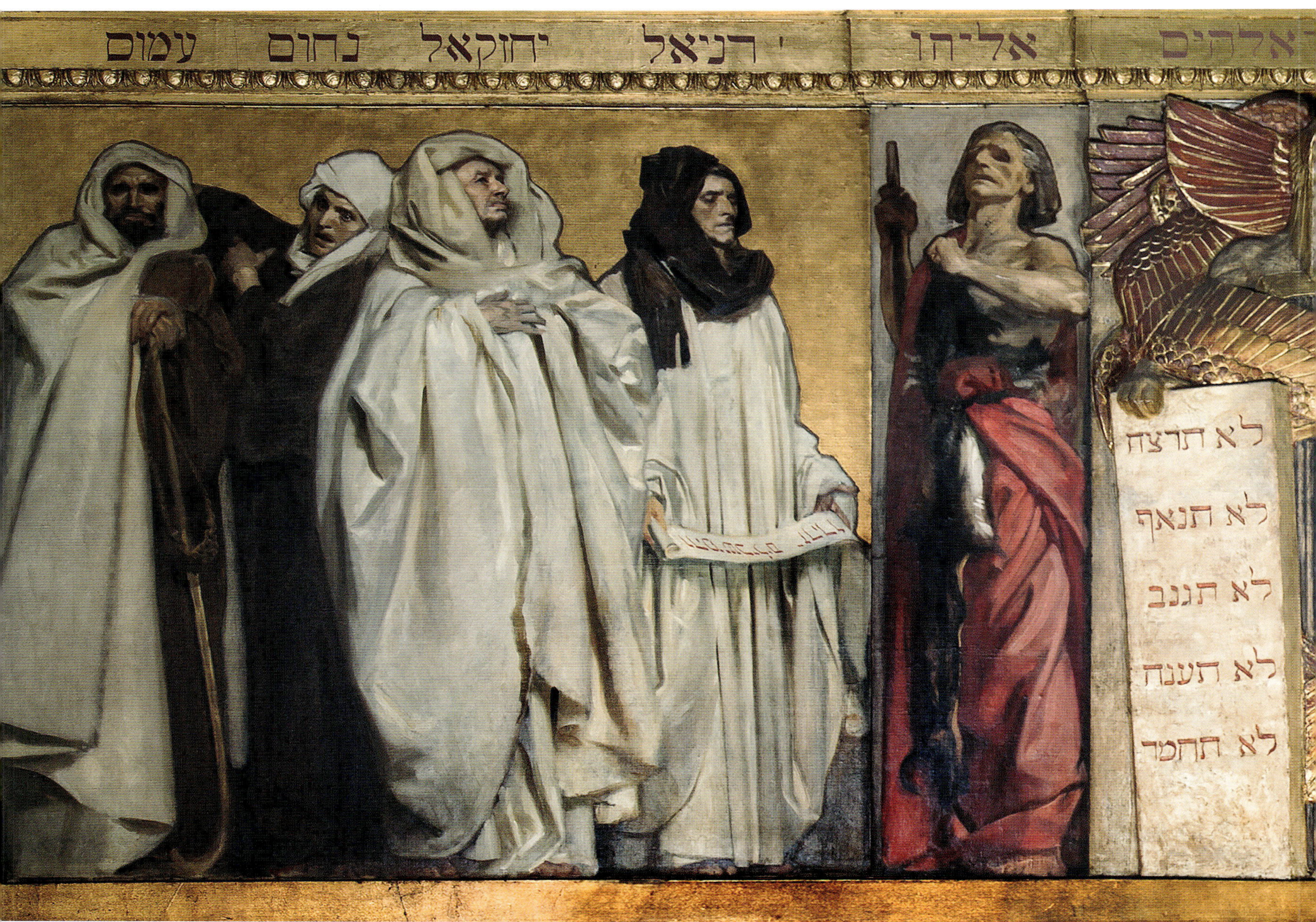

41

Frieze of the Prophets
Installed 1895
Oil on canvas (with relief elements),
approx. 84 × 253 in. (213 × 673 cm)
Boston, Boston Public Library

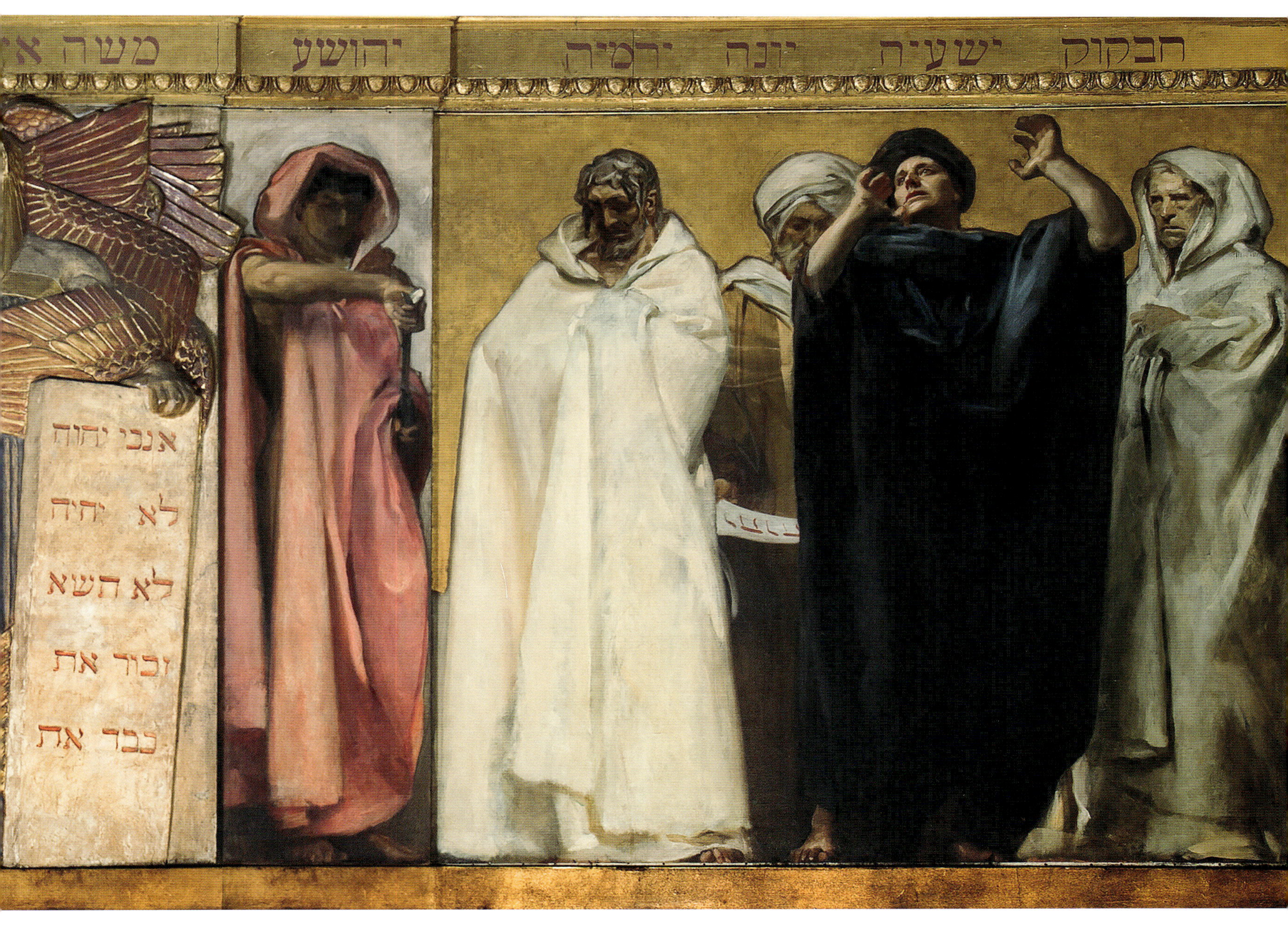
משה
יהושע
ירמיה
יונה
ישעיה
חבקוק
אנכי יהוה
לא יהיה
לא תשא
זכור את
כבד את

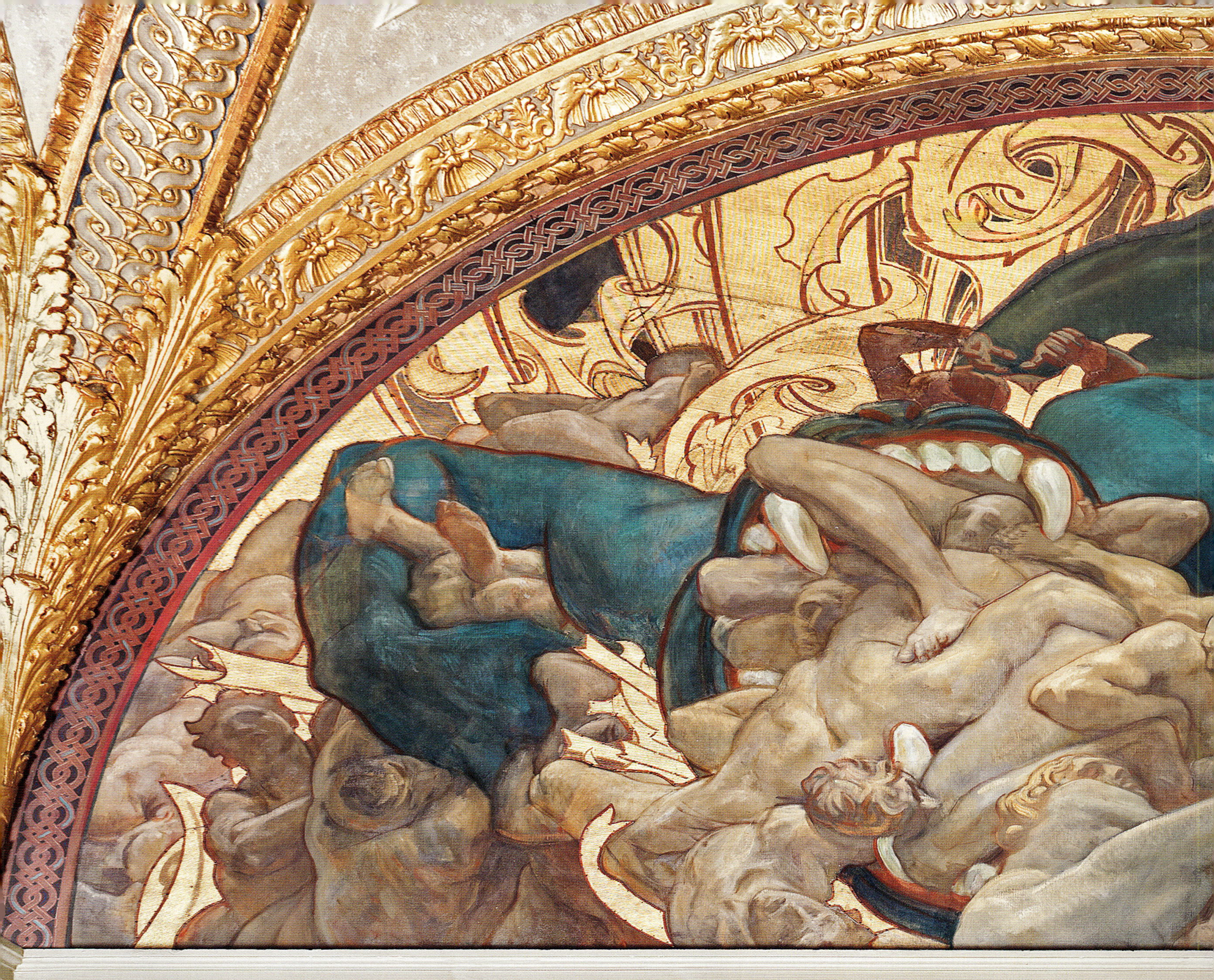

42

Hell

Installed 1916

Oil on canvas, approx. 100 × 200 in.

(254 × 508 cm)

Boston Public Library

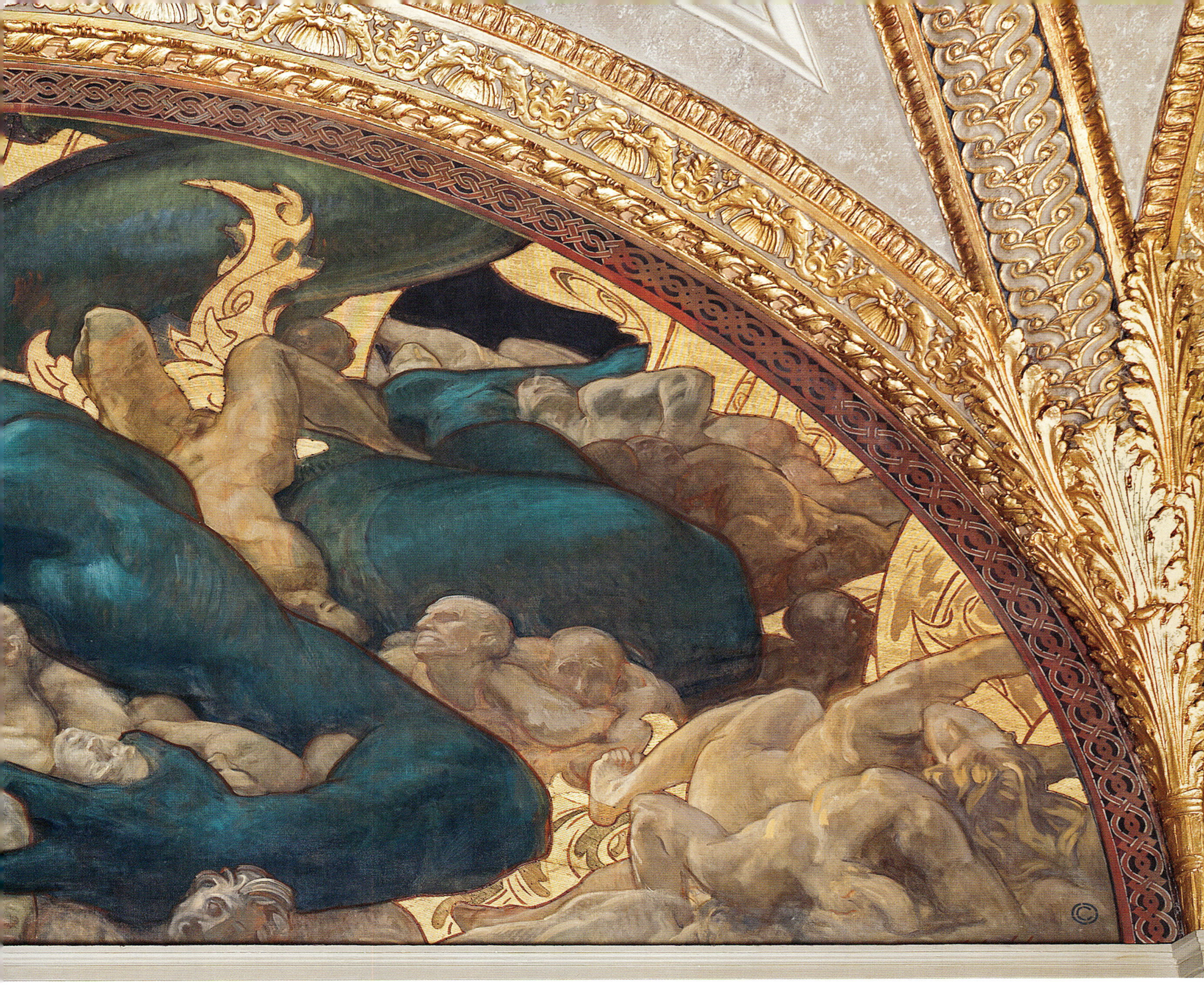

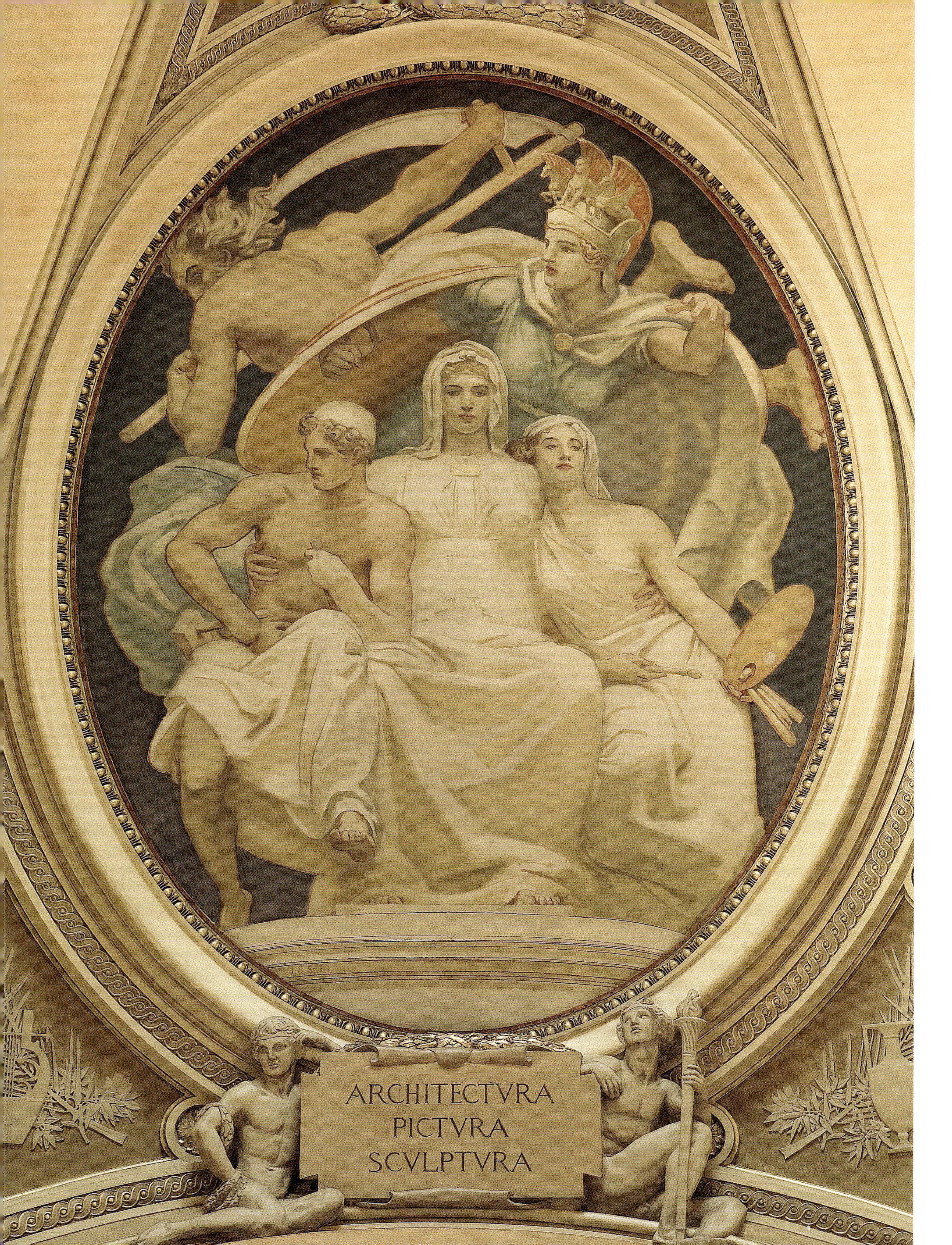
ARCHITECTVRA
PICTVRA
SCVLPTVRA

43

Architecture, Painting, and Sculpture Protected by Athena from the Ravages of Time

1921
Oil on canvas, $126\frac{1}{8} \times 102\frac{7}{8}$ in.
(320.4 × 261.3 cm)
Signed: "J S S"
Boston, Museum of Fine Arts,
Francis Bartlett Donation of 1912
and Picture Fund [21.10513]

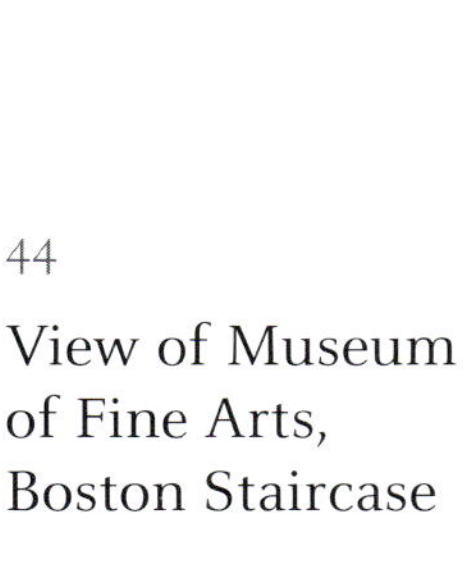

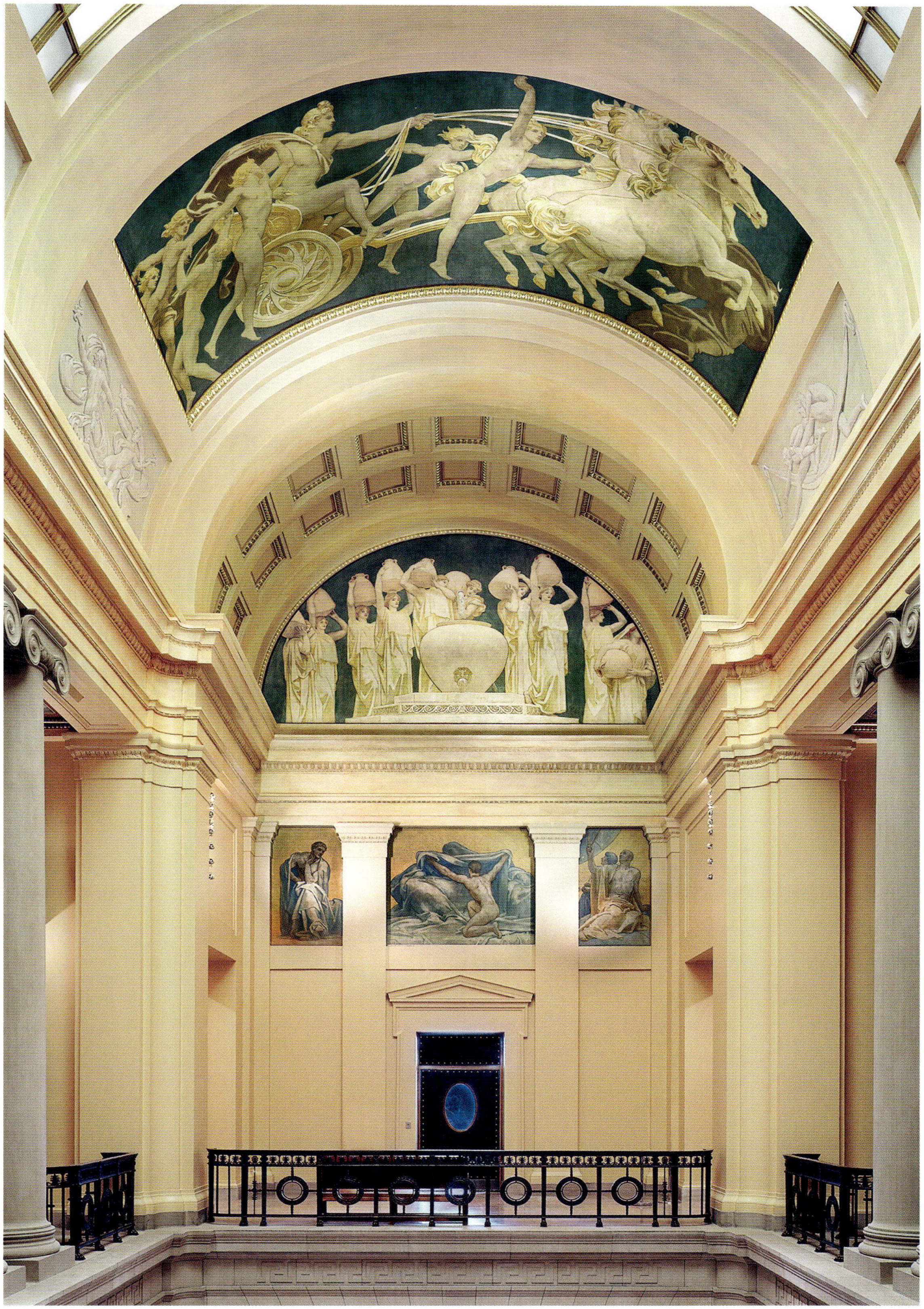

44

View of Museum of Fine Arts, Boston Staircase

1921
Boston, Museum of Fine Arts
Francis Bartlett Donation of 1912
and Picture Fund

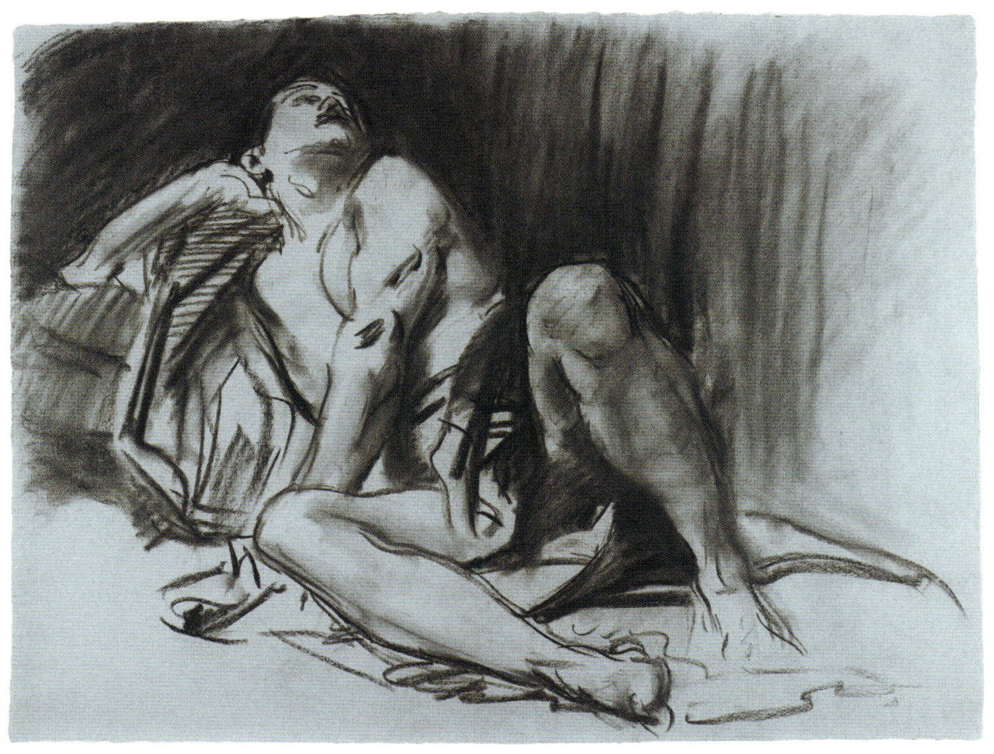

45

Reclining Male Nude

ca. 1890–1915
Charcoal on paper, 18 ½ × 24 7⁄16 in.
(47 × 62 cm)
Cambridge, Massachusetts,
Harvard Art Museums/
Fogg Museum, Gift of
Mrs. Francis Ormond
[1937.9.18]

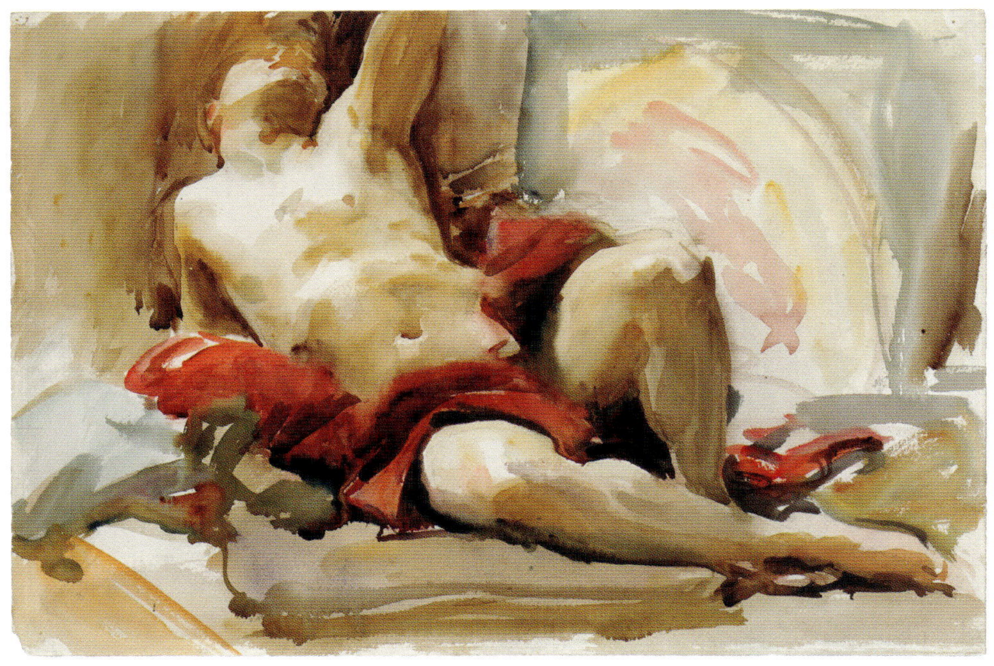

46

Man with Red Drapery

ca. 1904
Watercolor and graphite on paper,
14 ⅜ × 21 ⅛ in. (36.5 × 53.7 cm)
New York, The Metropolitan
Museum of Art, Gift of
Mrs. Francis Ormond, 1950
[50.130.73]

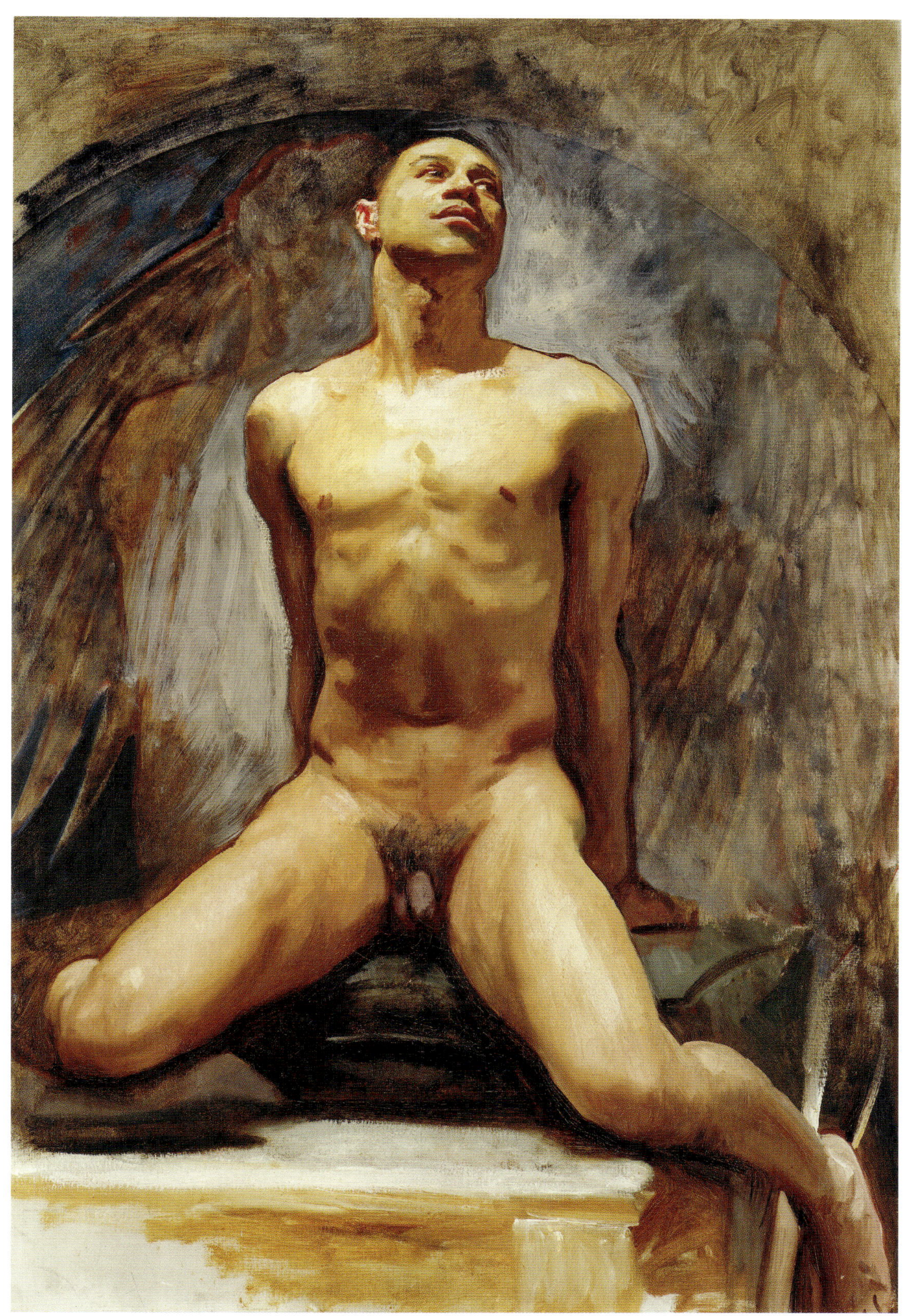

47

Nude Study of Thomas E. McKeller

1917–20
Oil on canvas, 49½ × 33¼ in.
(125.7 × 84.4 cm)
Boston, Museum of Fine Arts,
Henry H. and Zoe Oliver
Sherman Fund [1986.60]

48

Lady Agnew of Lochnaw

1892
Oil on canvas, 50 × 39¾ in.
(127 × 101 cm)
Signed: "John S. Sargent"
Edinburgh, National Galleries of Scotland, Purchased with the aid of the Cowan Smith Bequest Fund 1925 [NG 1656]

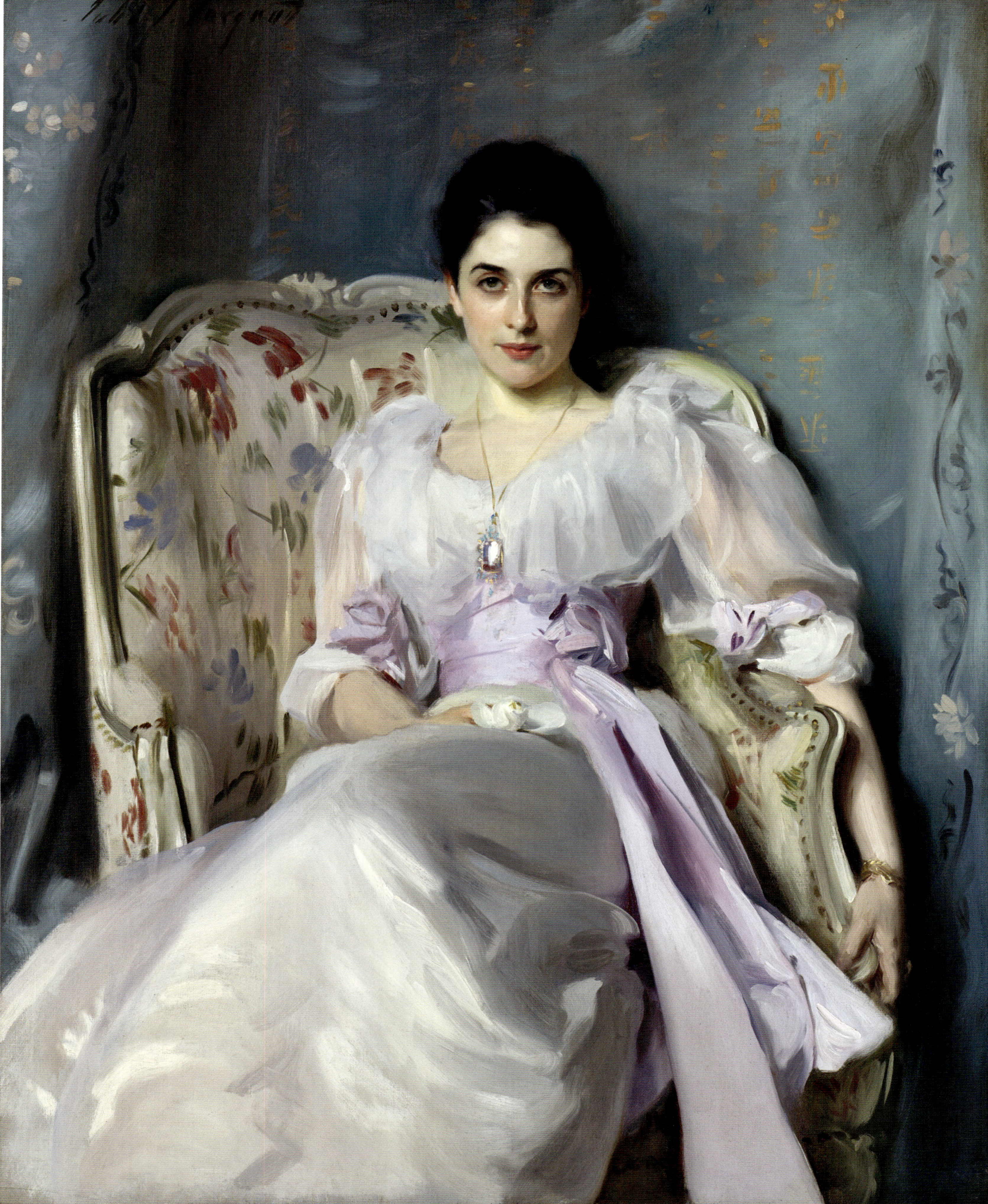

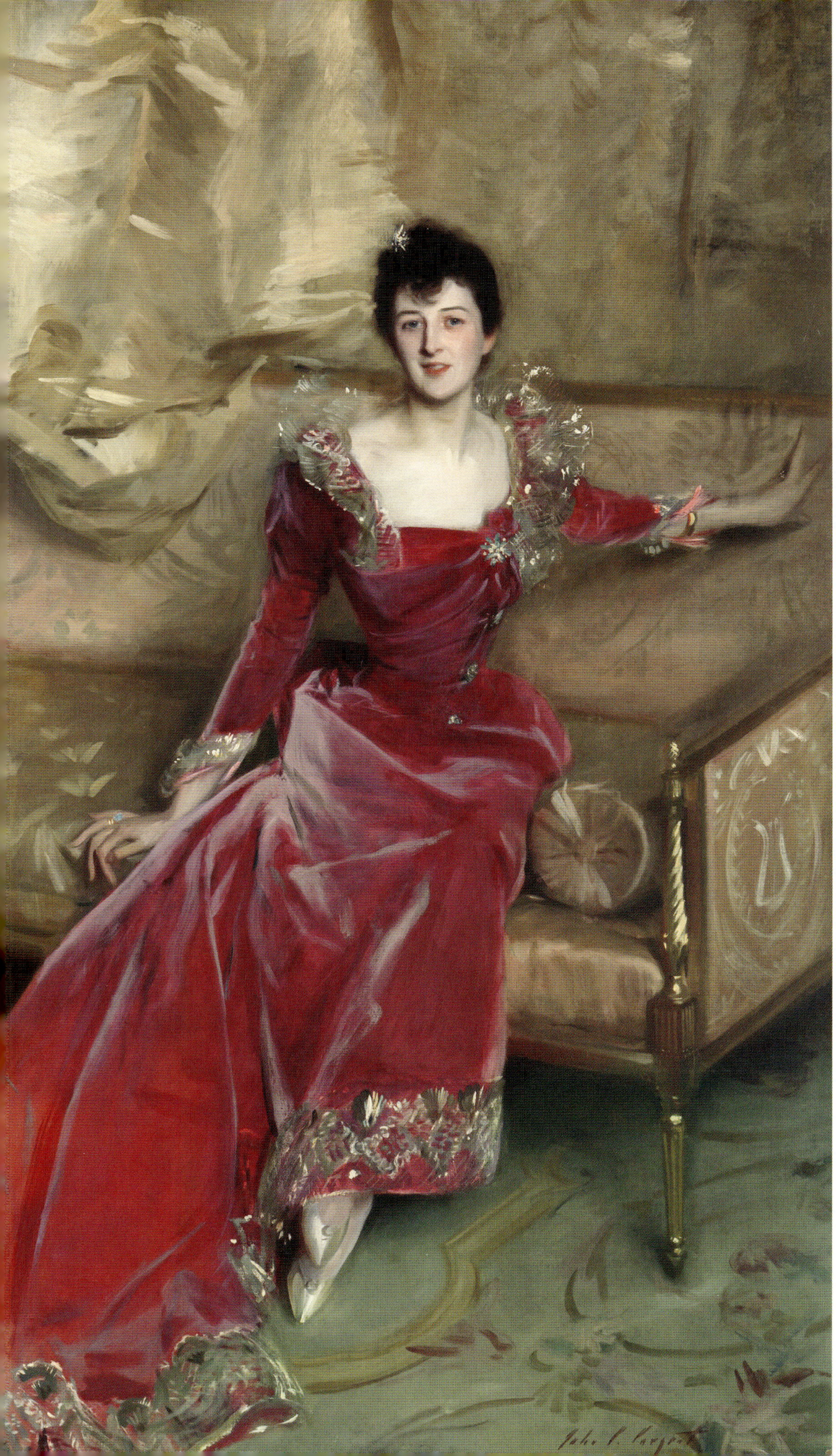

49

Mrs. Hugh Hammersley

1892
Oil on canvas, 81 × 45½ in.
(205.7 × 115.6 cm)
Signed: "John S. Sargent"
New York, The Metropolitan Museum of Art, Gift of Mr. and Mrs. Douglass Campbell, in memory of Mrs. Richard E. Danielson, 1998 [1998.365]

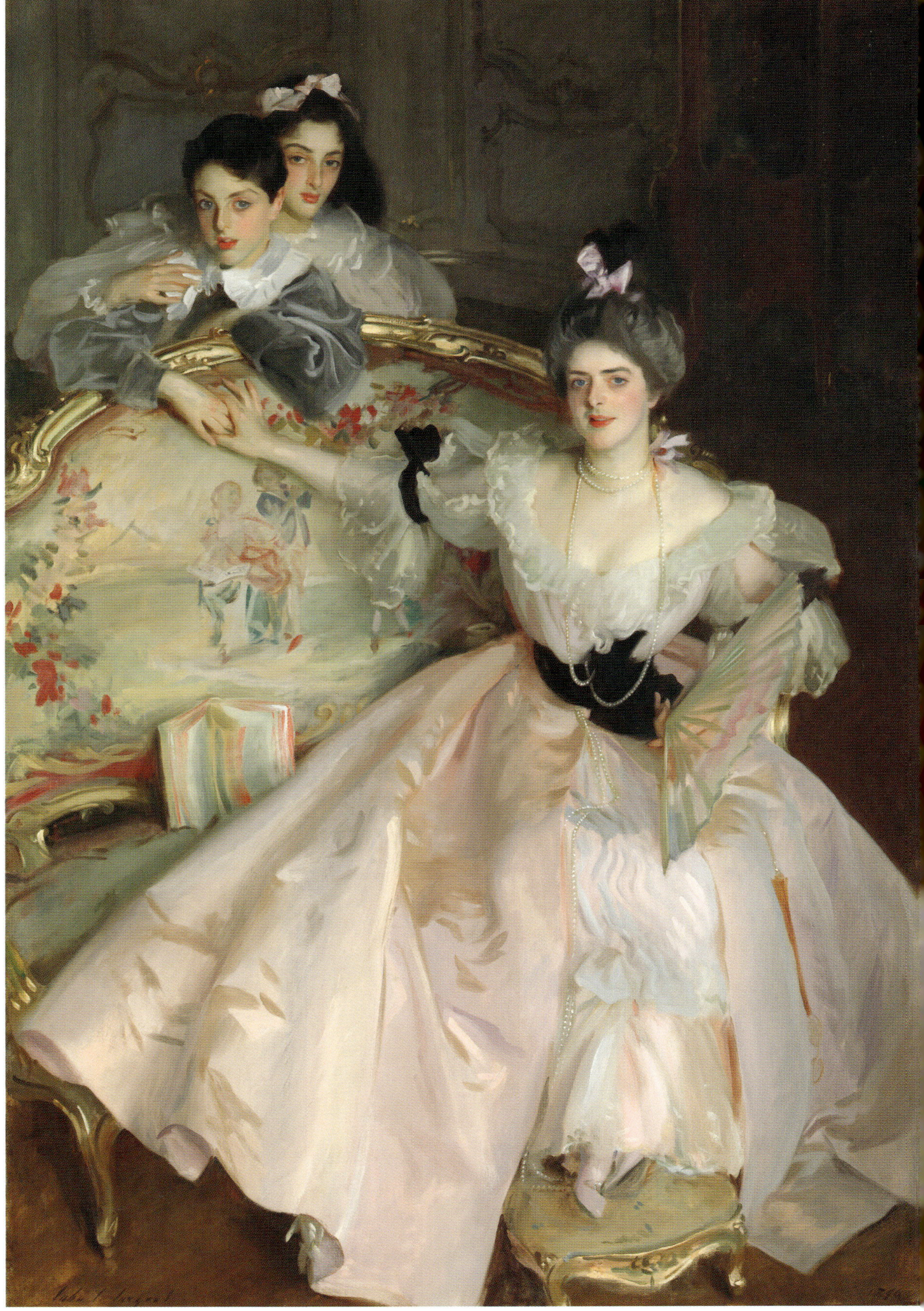

50

Mrs. Carl Meyer and Her Children

1896
Oil on canvas, 79¼ × 52¾ in.
(201.4 × 134 cm)
Signed: "John S. Sargent"
London, Tate, Bequeathed by Adèle, Lady Meyer 1930, with a life interest for her son and grandson and presented in 2005 in celebration of the lives of Sir Anthony and Lady Barbadee Meyer, accessioned 2009
[T12988]

51

The Wyndham Sisters: Lady Elcho, Mrs. Adeane, and Mrs. Tennant

1899
Oil on canvas, 115 × 84 1/8 in.
(292.1 × 213.7 cm)
Signed: "John S. Sargent"
New York, The Metropolitan Museum of Art, Catharine Lorillard Wolfe Collection, Wolfe Fund, 1927 [27.67]

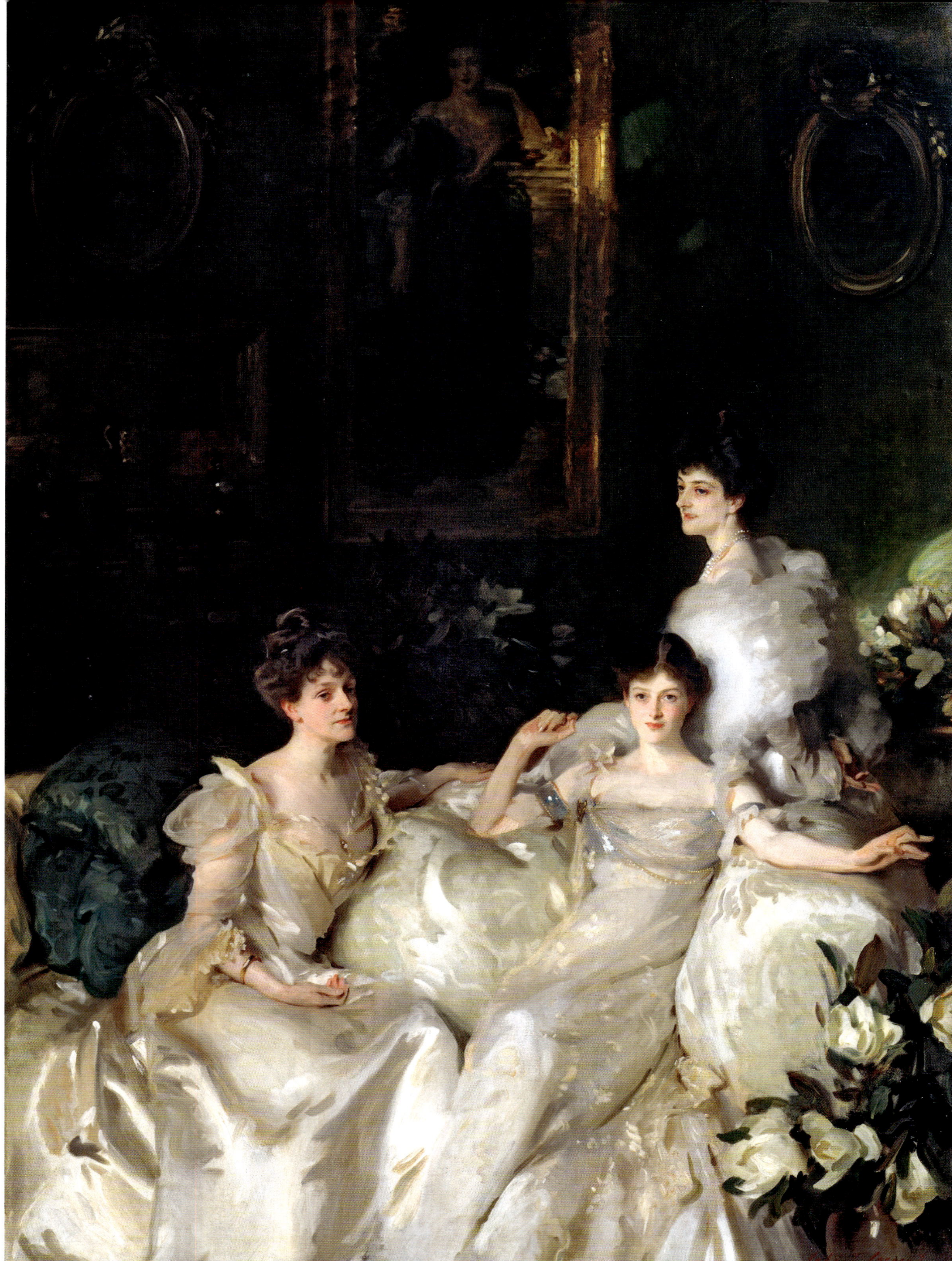

52

The Ladies Alexandra, Mary and Theo Acheson

1902

Oil on canvas, 106 × 78 in. (269.2 x 198 cm)

Signed: "John S. Sargent 1902"

Chatsworth, Devonshire Collection,
The Duke of Devonshire and the Chatsworth Settlement Trustees

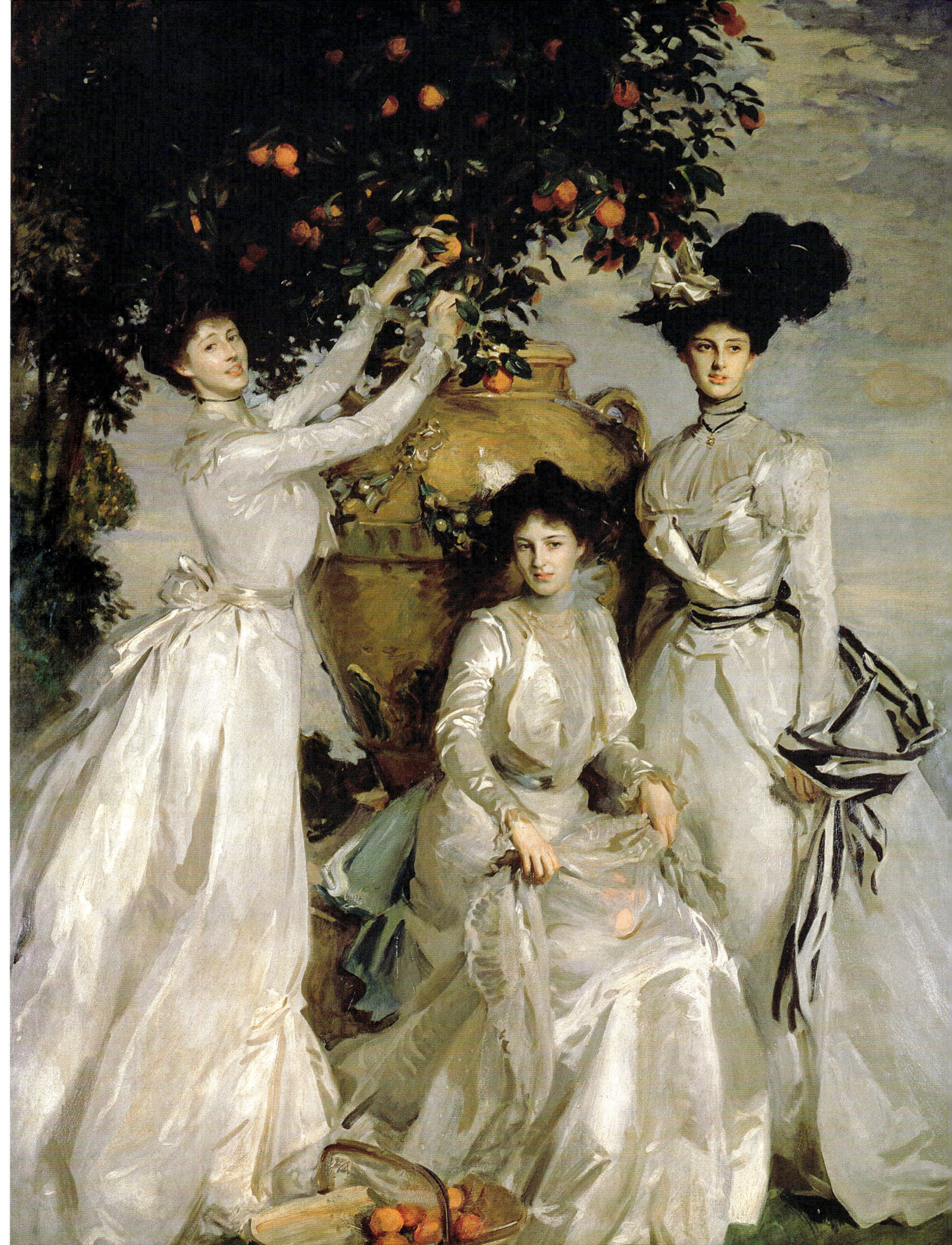

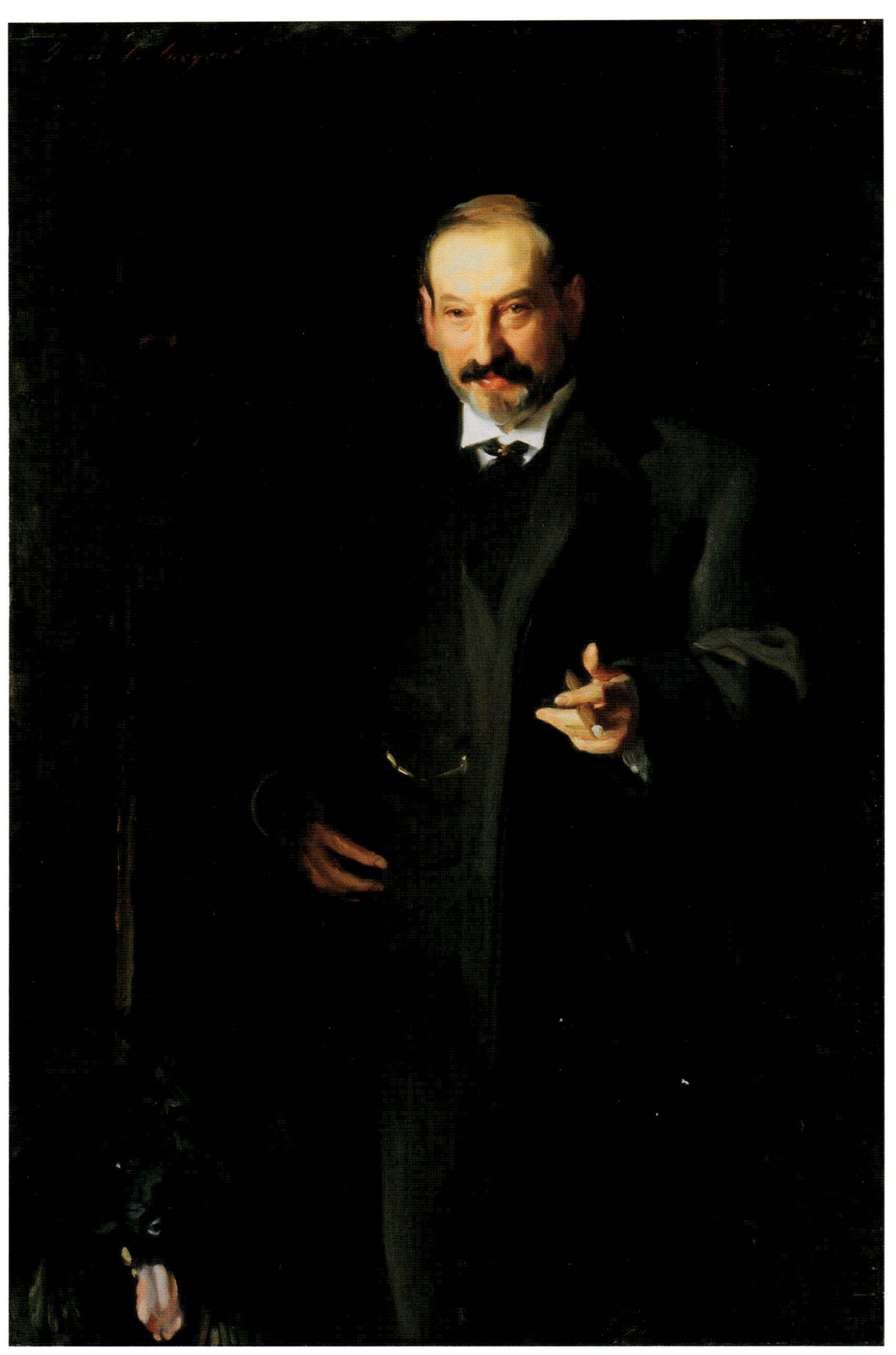

53

Asher Wertheimer

1898
Oil on canvas, 58 × 38½ in.
(147.3 × 97.8 cm)
Signed: "John S. Sargent"
Dated: "1898"
London, Tate, Presented by the widow and family of Asher Wertheimer in accordance with his wishes 1922 [N03705]

54

Ena and Betty, Daughters of Asher and Mrs. Wertheimer

1901
Oil on canvas, 73 × 51½ in.
(185.4 × 130.8 cm)
Signed: "John S. Sargent 1901"
London, Tate, Presented by the widow and family of Asher Wertheimer in accordance with his wishes 1922 [N03708]

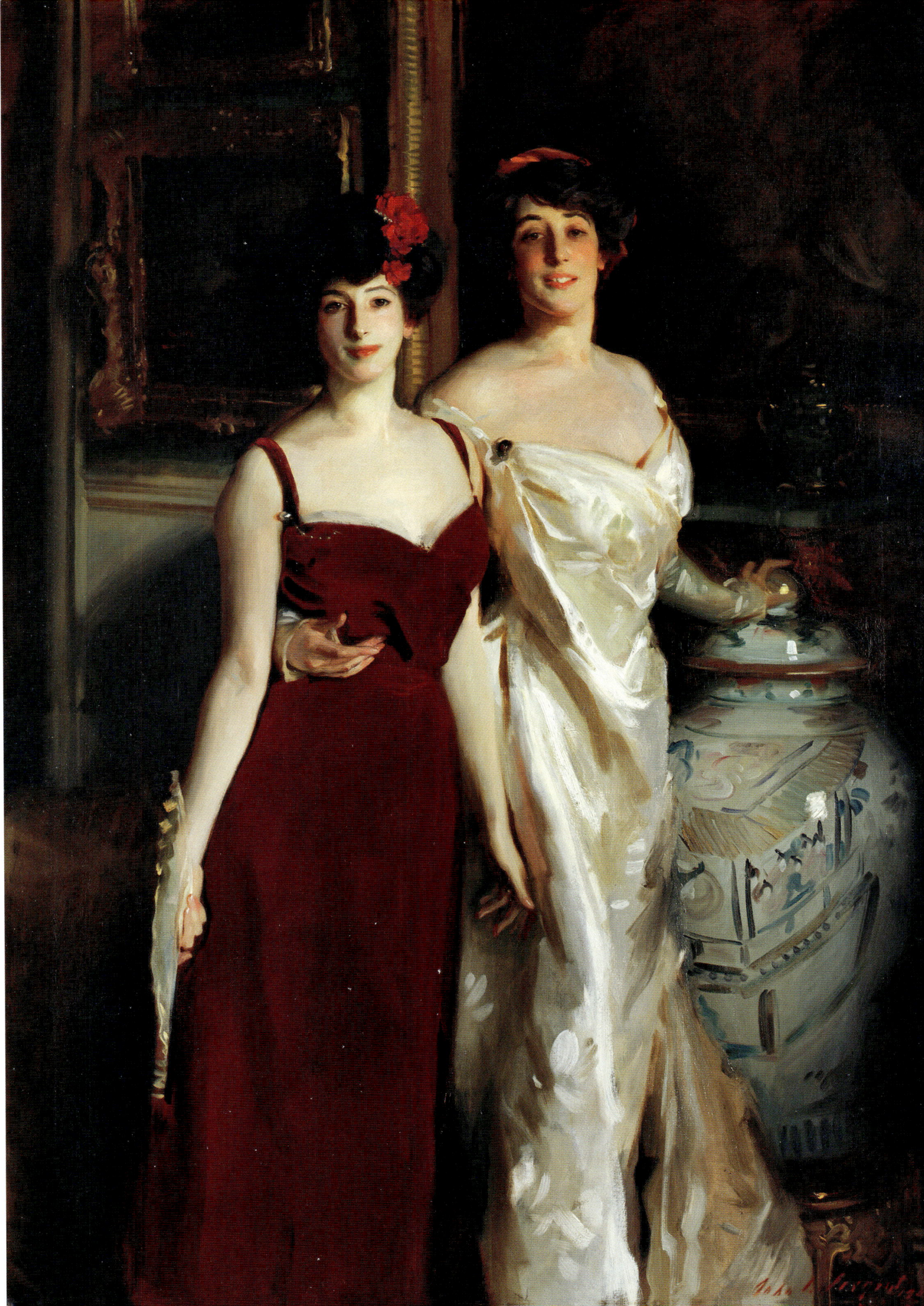

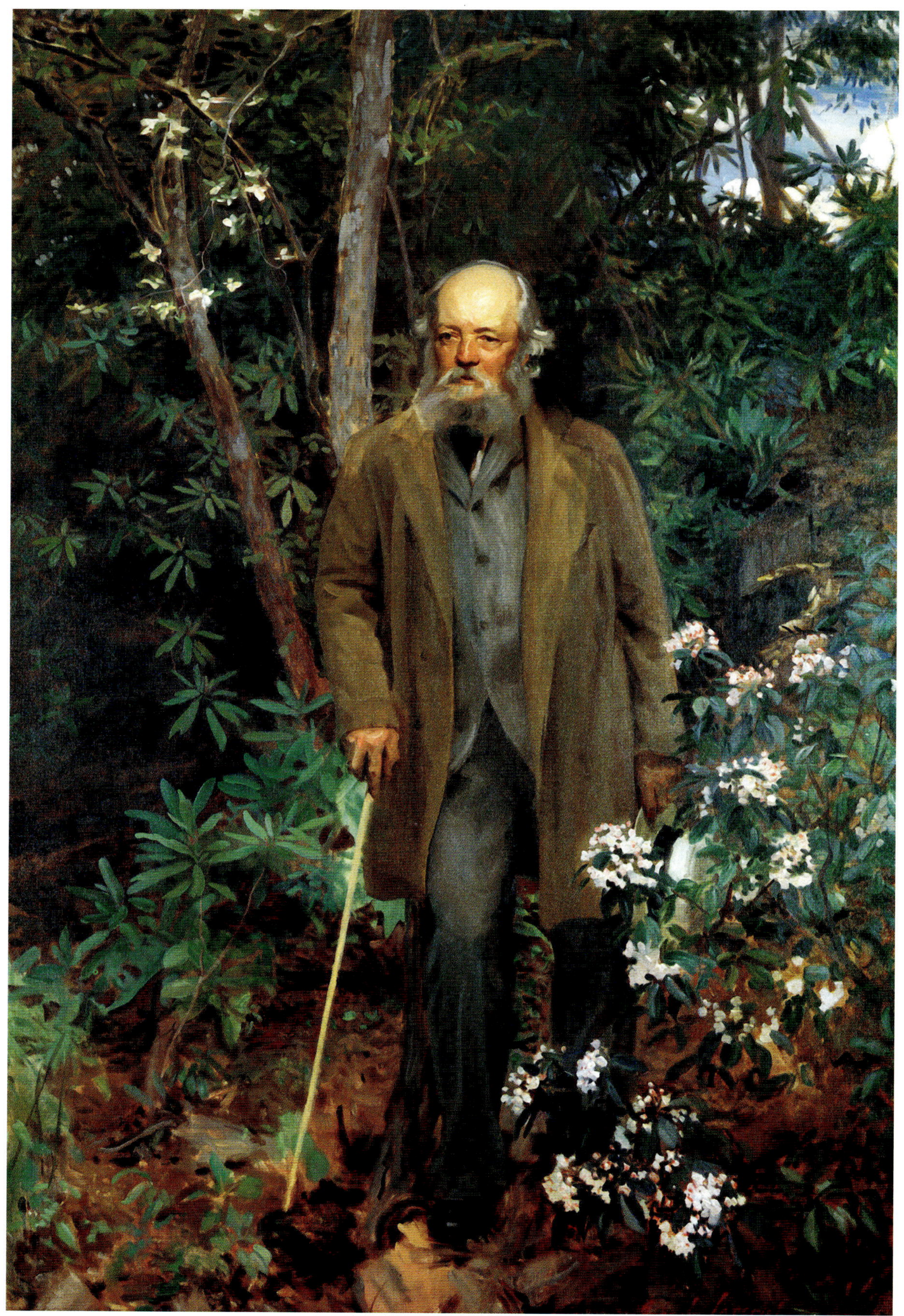

55

Frederick Olmsted

1895
Oil on canvas, 100 × 55 in.
(254 × 139.7 cm)
Signed: "John S. Sargent"
Asheville, North Carolina,
Biltmore House,
The Biltmore Company

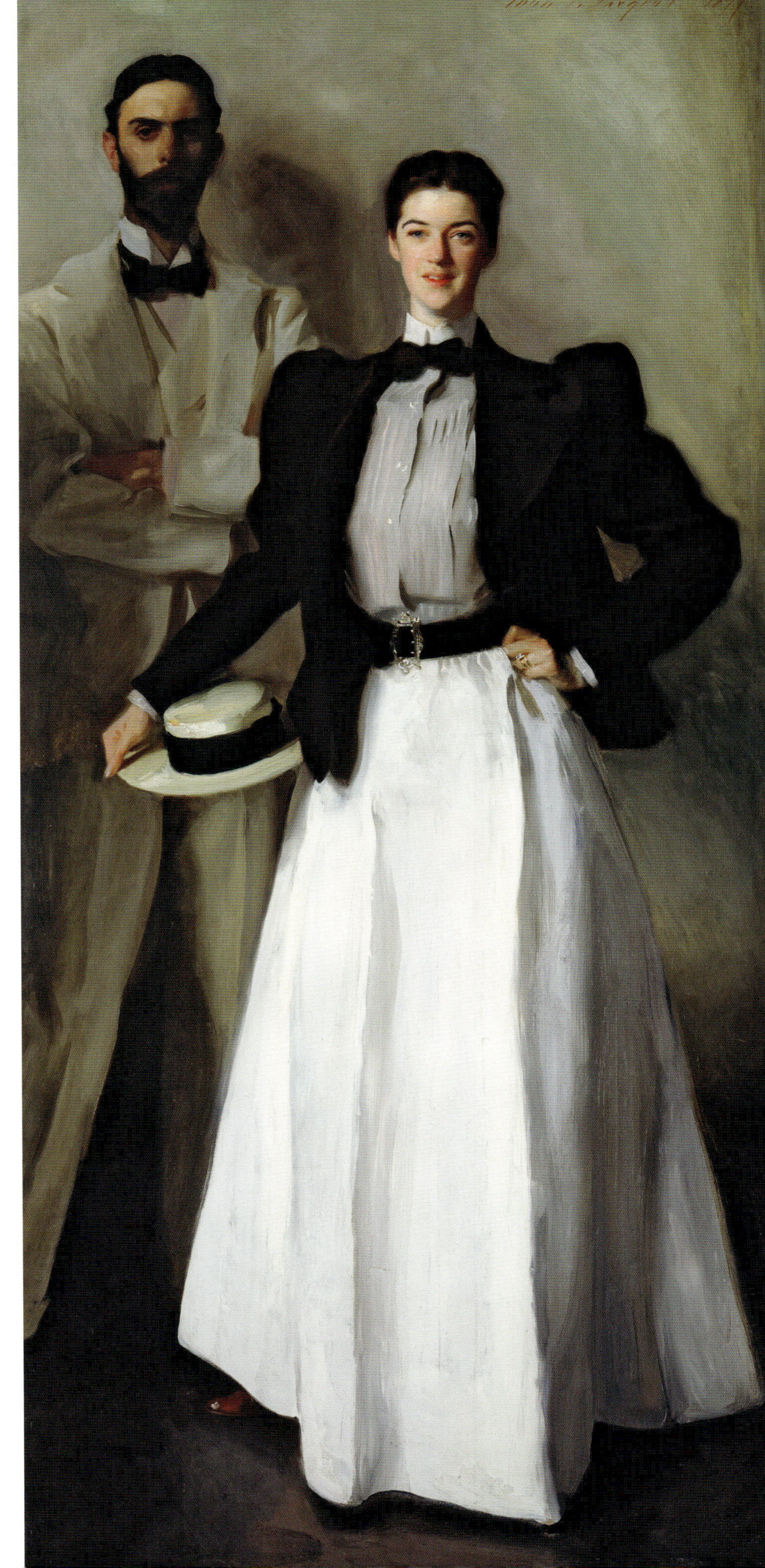

56

Mr. and Mrs. I. N. Phelps Stokes

1897
Oil on canvas, 84¼ × 39¾ in. (214 × 101 cm)
Signed: "John S. Sargent 1897"
New York, The Metropolitan Museum of Art,
Bequest of Edith Minturn Phelps Stokes
(Mrs. I. N.), 1938 [38.104]

57

Mrs. Fiske Warren (Gretchen Osgood) and Her Daughter Rachel

1903
Oil on canvas, 60 × 40⅜ in.
(152.4 × 102.6 cm)
Signed: "John S. Sargent 1903"
Boston, Museum of Fine Arts,
Gift of Mrs. Rachel Warren Barton
and Emily L. Ainsley Fund [64.693]

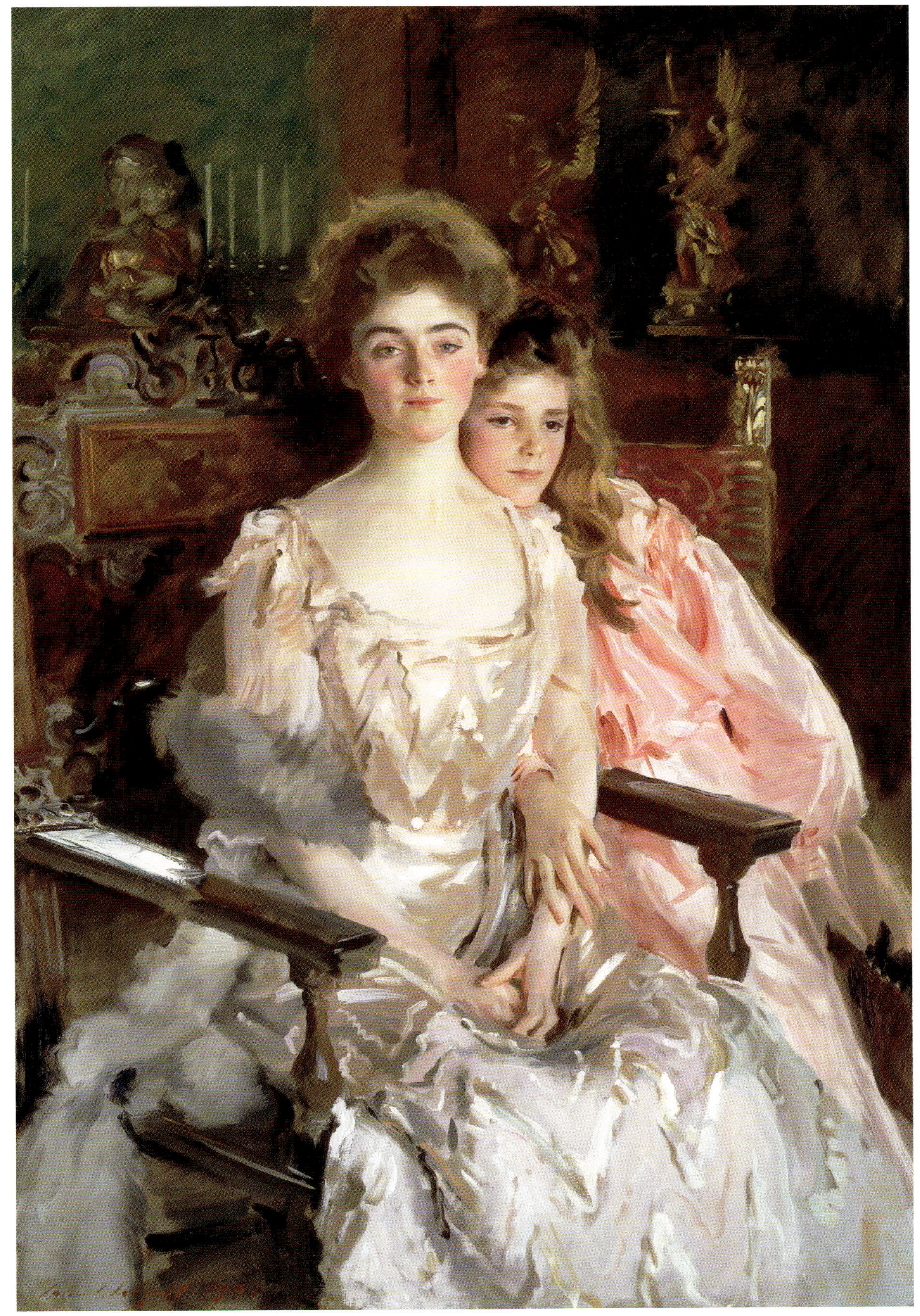

58

The Marlborough Family

1904–5
Oil on canvas, 113 × 94 in.
(287 × 238.7 cm)
Signed: "John S. Sargent 1905"
Inscription: "Charles Spencer Churchill, Duke of Marlborough. Consuelo, Duchess of Marlborough. John, Marquess of Blandford. Lord Ivor Spencer-Churchill"
Woodstock, Oxfordshire, Blenheim Palace

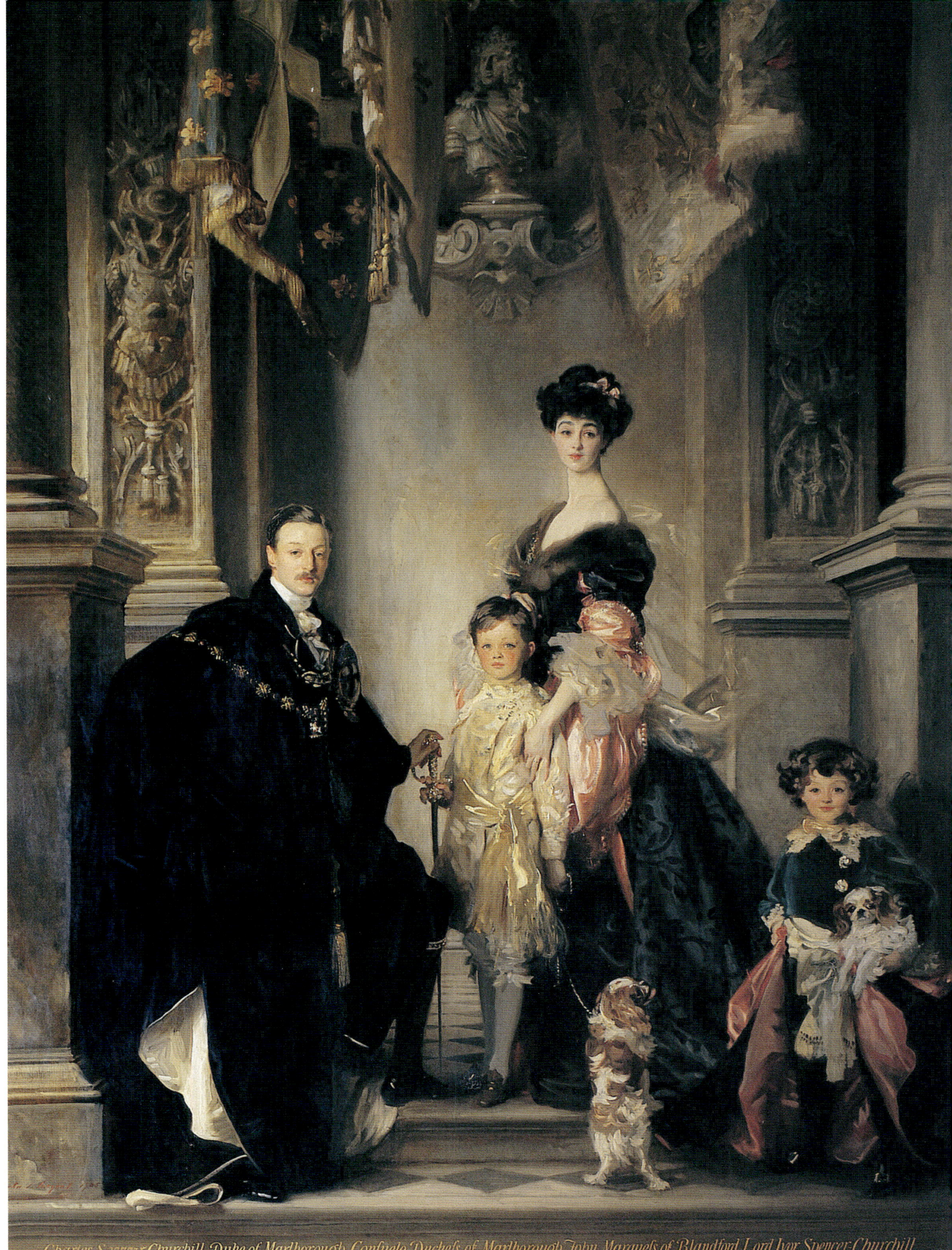
Charles Spencer-Churchill. Duke of Marlborough. Consuelo. Duchess of Marlborough. John. Marquess of Blandford. Lord Ivor Spencer-Churchill.

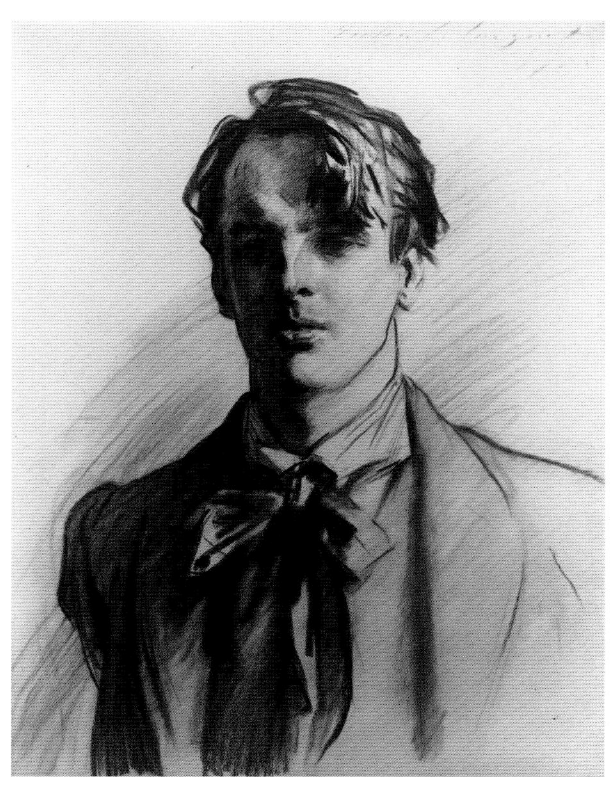

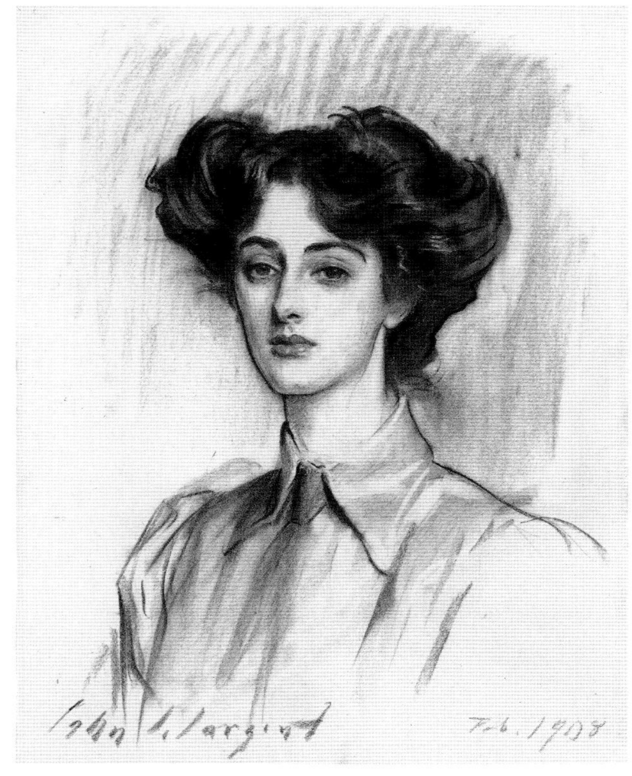

59

William Butler Yeats

1908
Charcoal on paper, 24½ × 18½ in.
(62.2 × 47 cm)
Signed: "John S. Sargent"
Dated: "1908"
Private collection

60

Portrait of Lady Elsie Meyer

1908
Charcoal on paper, 24¼ × 18¾ in.
(61.6 × 47.6 cm)
Signed: "John S. Sargent"
Dated: "Feb. 1908"
Private collection

61

The Countess of Rocksavage

1913
Oil on canvas, 34 × 26½ in.
(86.4 × 67.3 cm)
Inscription: "to Sybil / from her friend / John S. Sargent"
Dated: "1913"
Private collection (Houghton Hall)

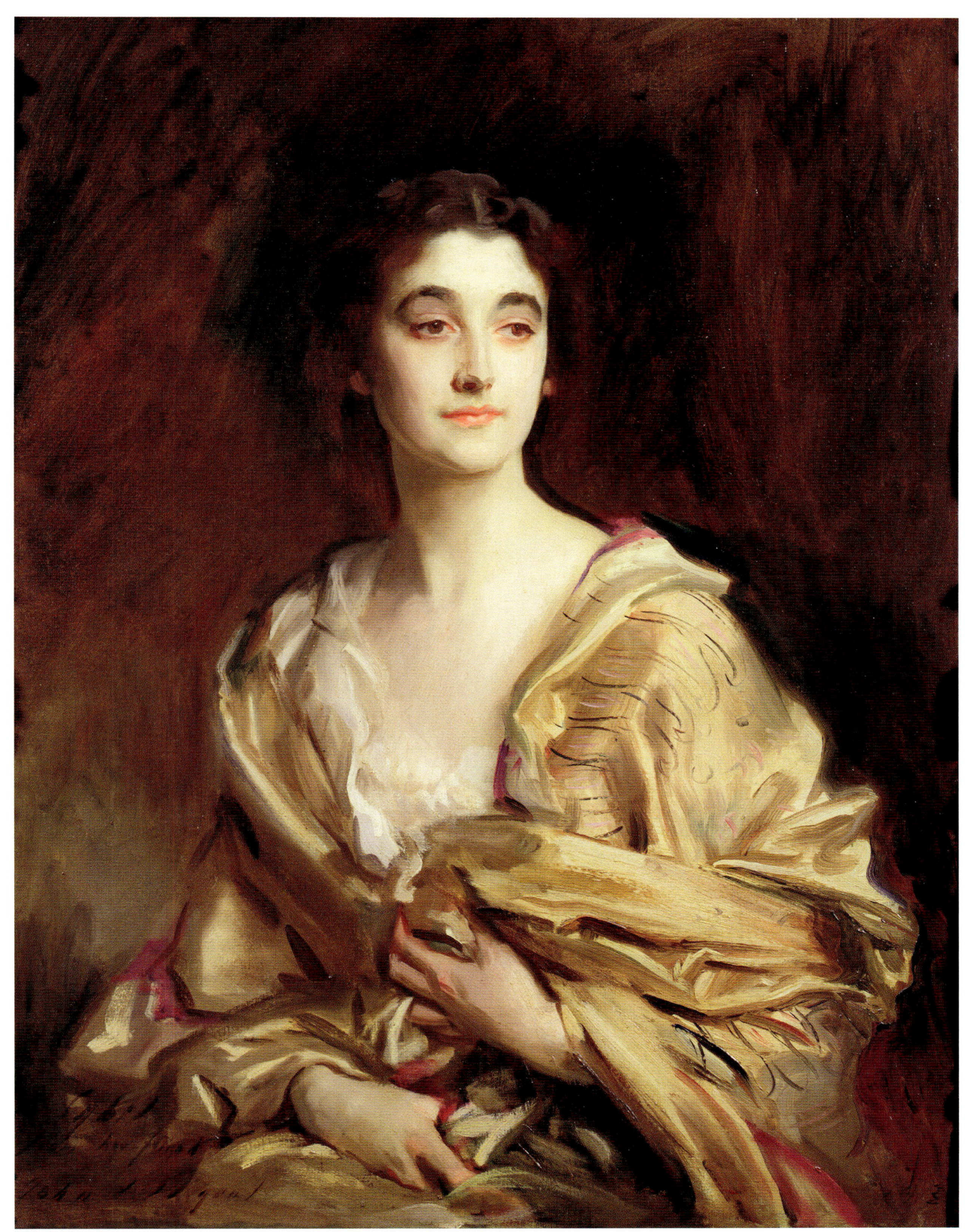

62

Henry James

1913
Oil on canvas, 33½ × 26½ in.
(85.1 × 67.3 cm)
Signed: "John S. Sargent"
Dated: "1913"
London, National Portrait Gallery,
Bequeathed by Henry James, 1916
[NPG 1767]

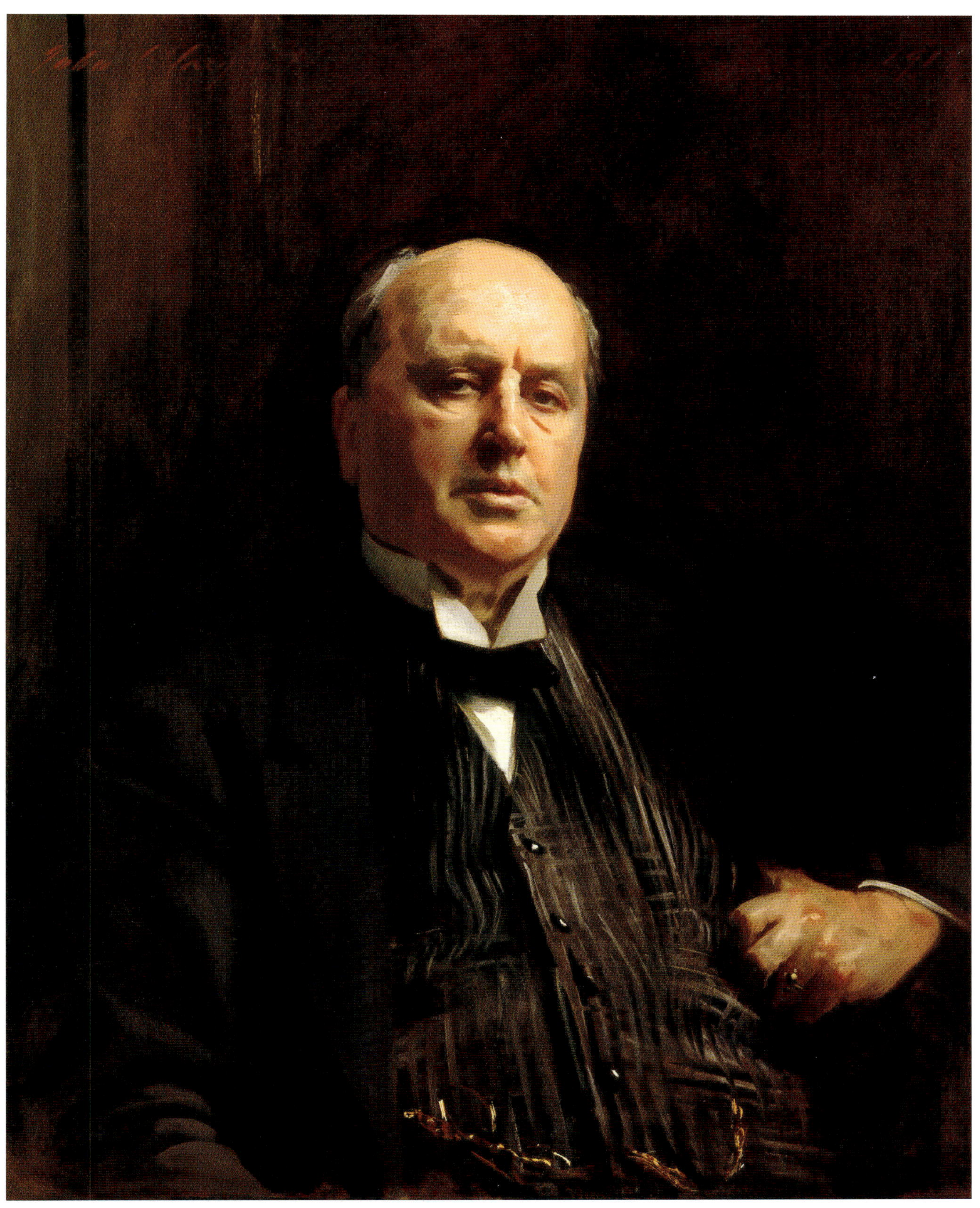

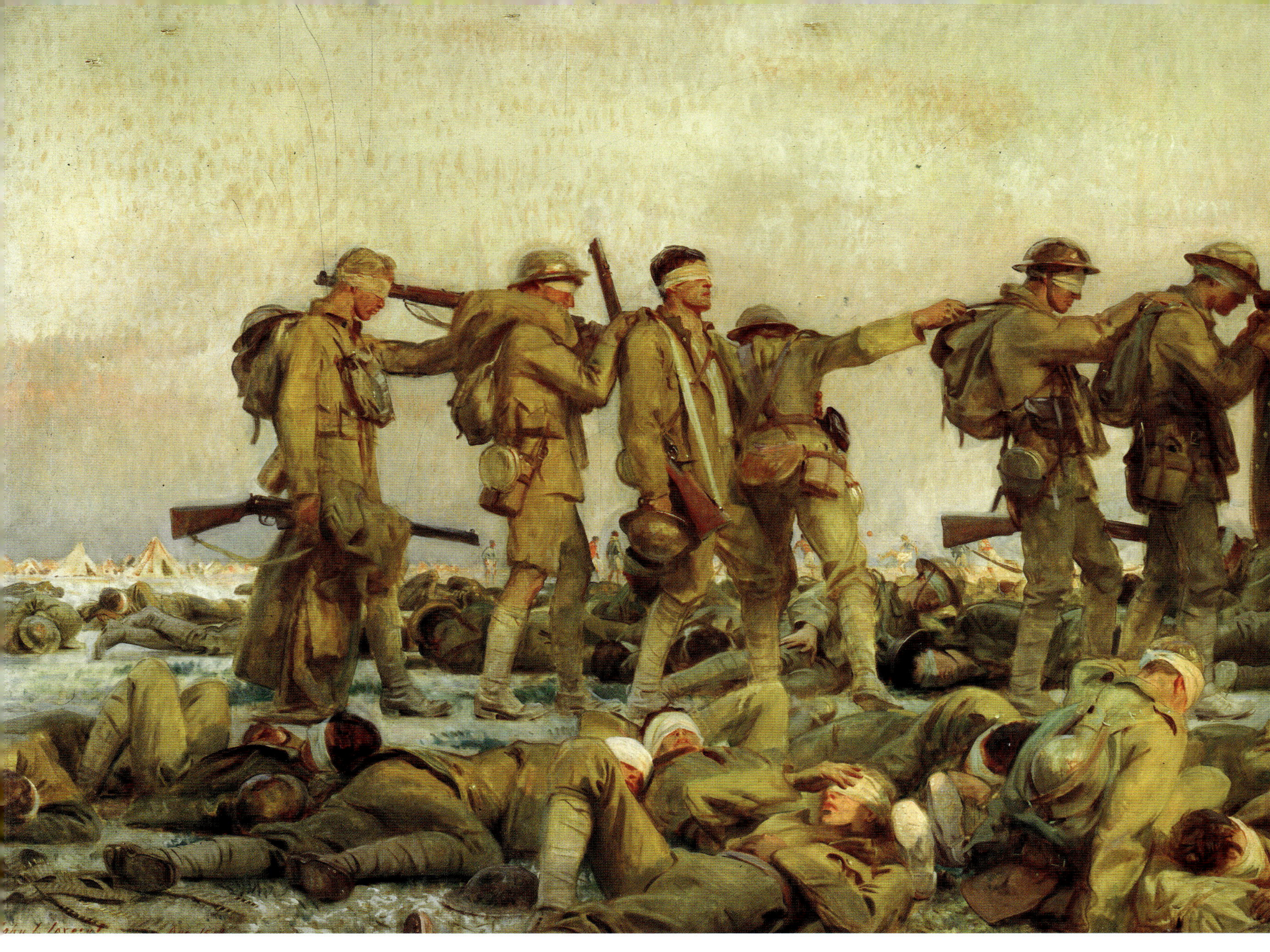

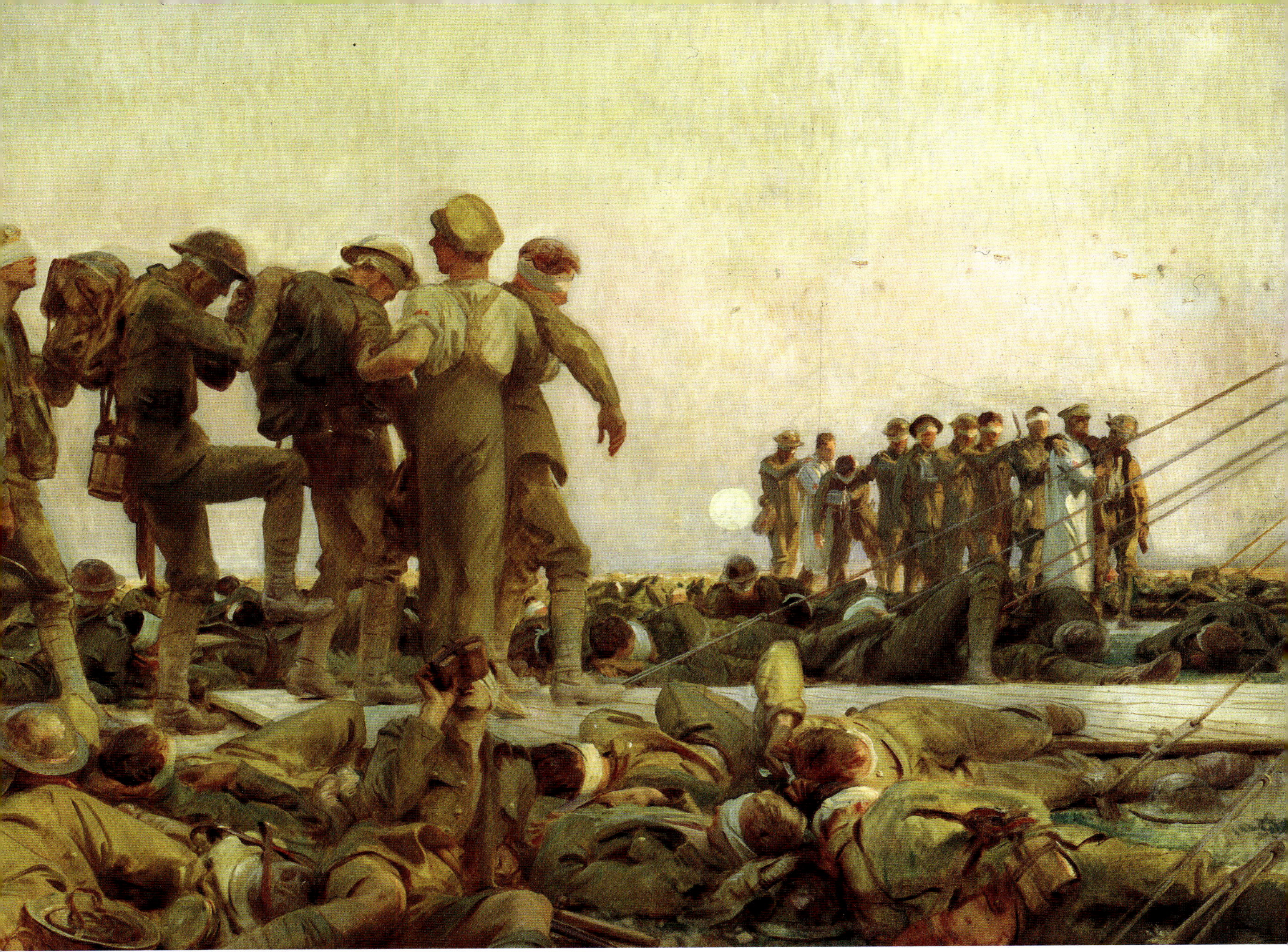

63

Gassed

1919
Oil on canvas, 91 × 240¾ in. (231.1 × 611.1 cm)
Signed: "John S. Sargent Aug 1918"
United Kingdom, Imperial War Museums
[Art. IWM ART 1460]

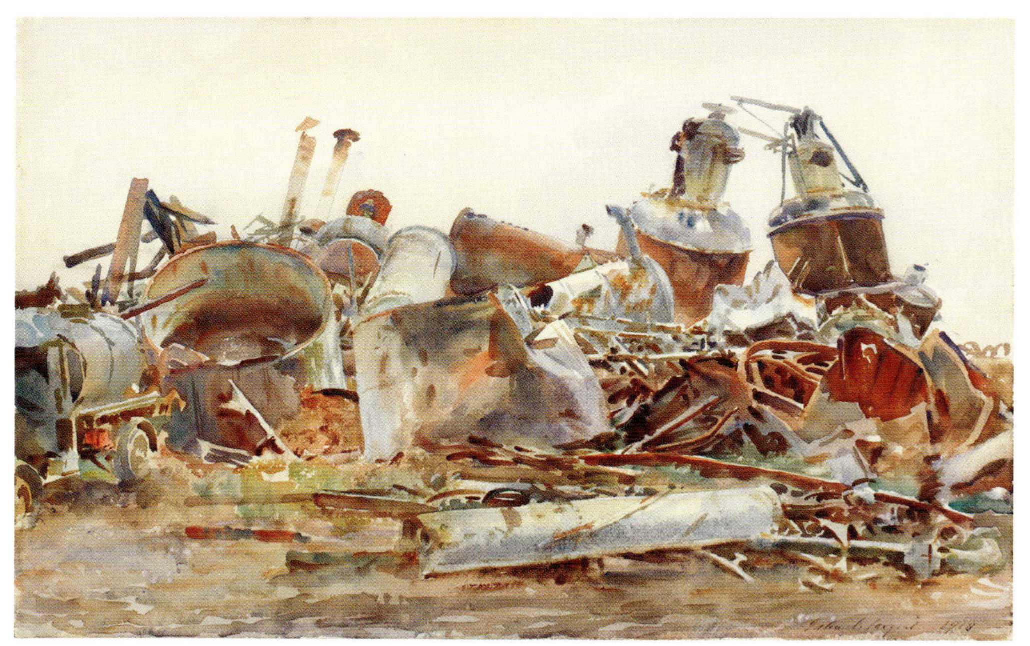

64

A Wrecked Sugar Refinery

1918
Watercolor on paper,
$13\frac{1}{4} \times 20\frac{3}{4}$ in.
(33.6×52.7 cm)
Signed: "John S. Sargent 1918"
United Kingdom,
Imperial War Museums,
Gift of the artist, 1919
[Art.IWM ART 1612]

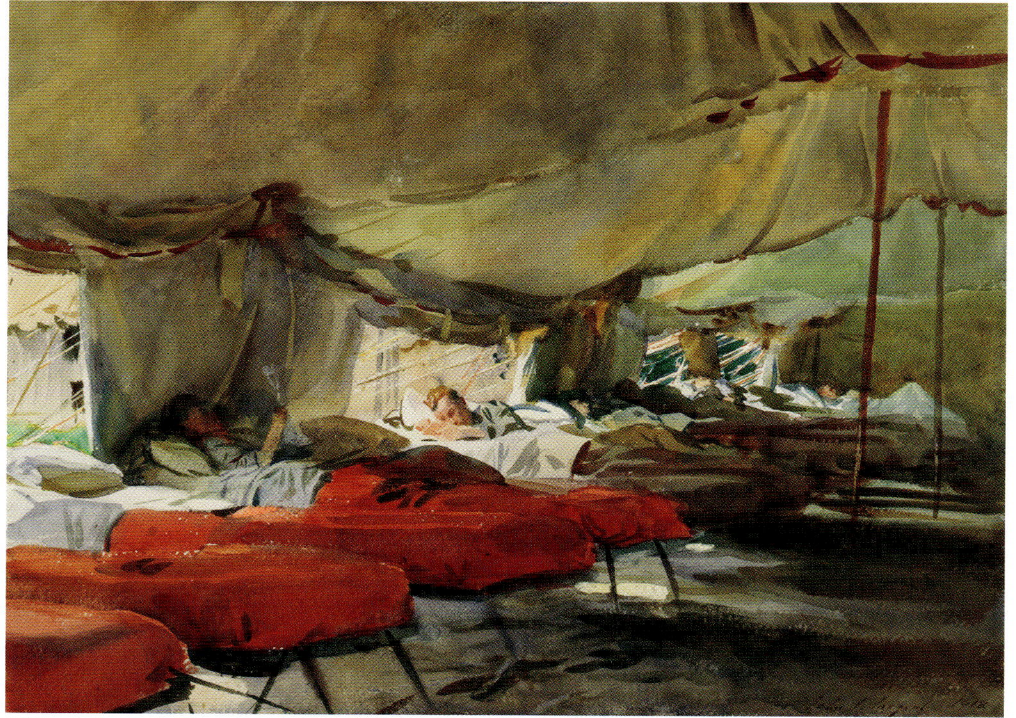

65

The Interior of a Hospital Tent

1918
Watercolor on paper,
$15\frac{1}{2} \times 20\frac{13}{16}$ in.
(39.3×52.8 cm)
Signed: "John S. Sargent 1918"
United Kingdom,
Imperial War Museums,
Gift of the artist, 1919
[Art.IWM ART 1611]

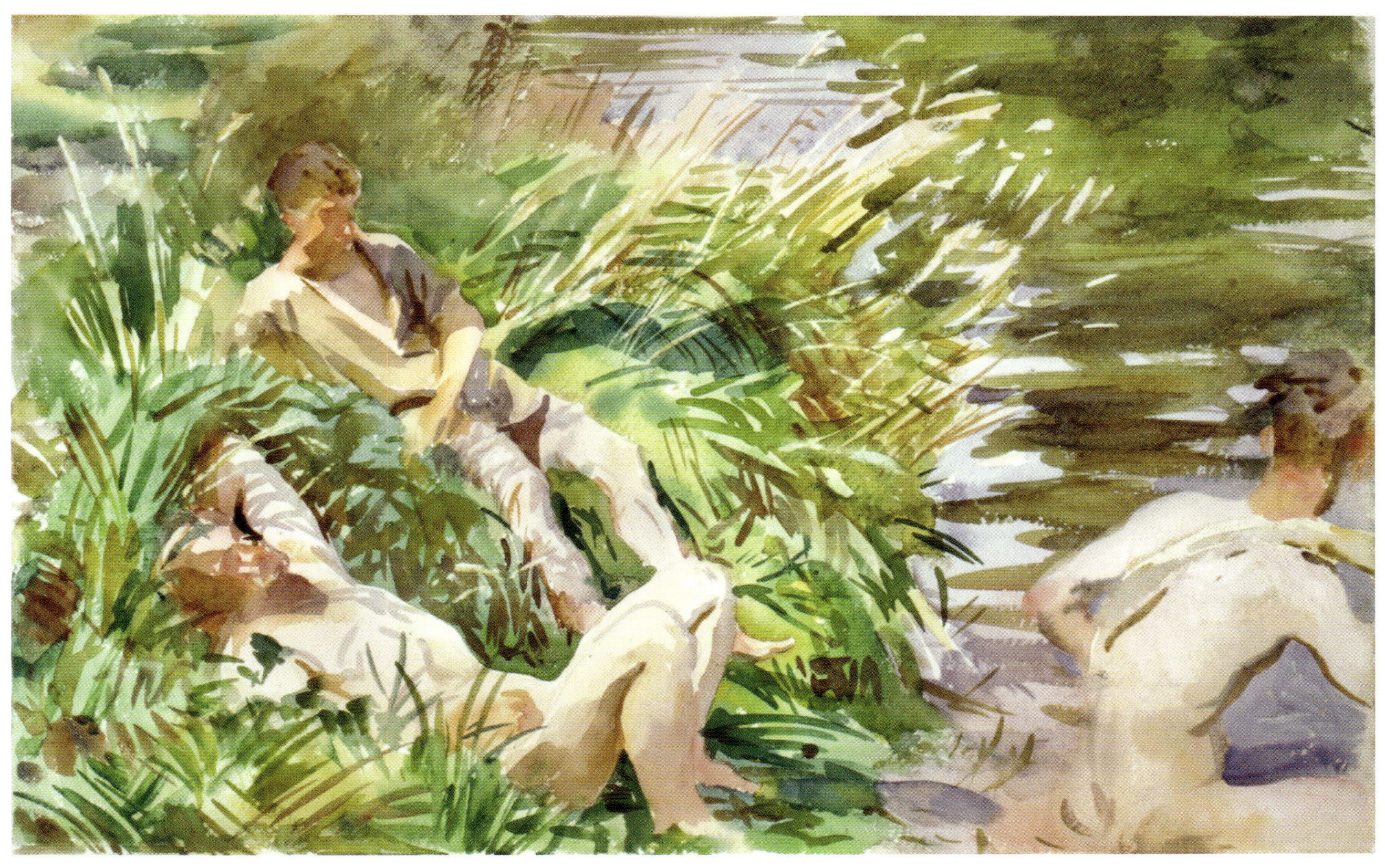

66

Tommies Bathing

1918
Watercolor, gouache, and graphite on paper, 13 5/8 × 20 15/16 in. (34.6 × 53.2 cm)
Inscriptions: "151 / By J.S.Sargent"; "[0?] /3"; "V.O. (Trust) / W W"; "990" (on verso)
New York, The Metropolitan Museum of Art, Gift of Mrs. Francis Ormond, 1950 [50.130.58]

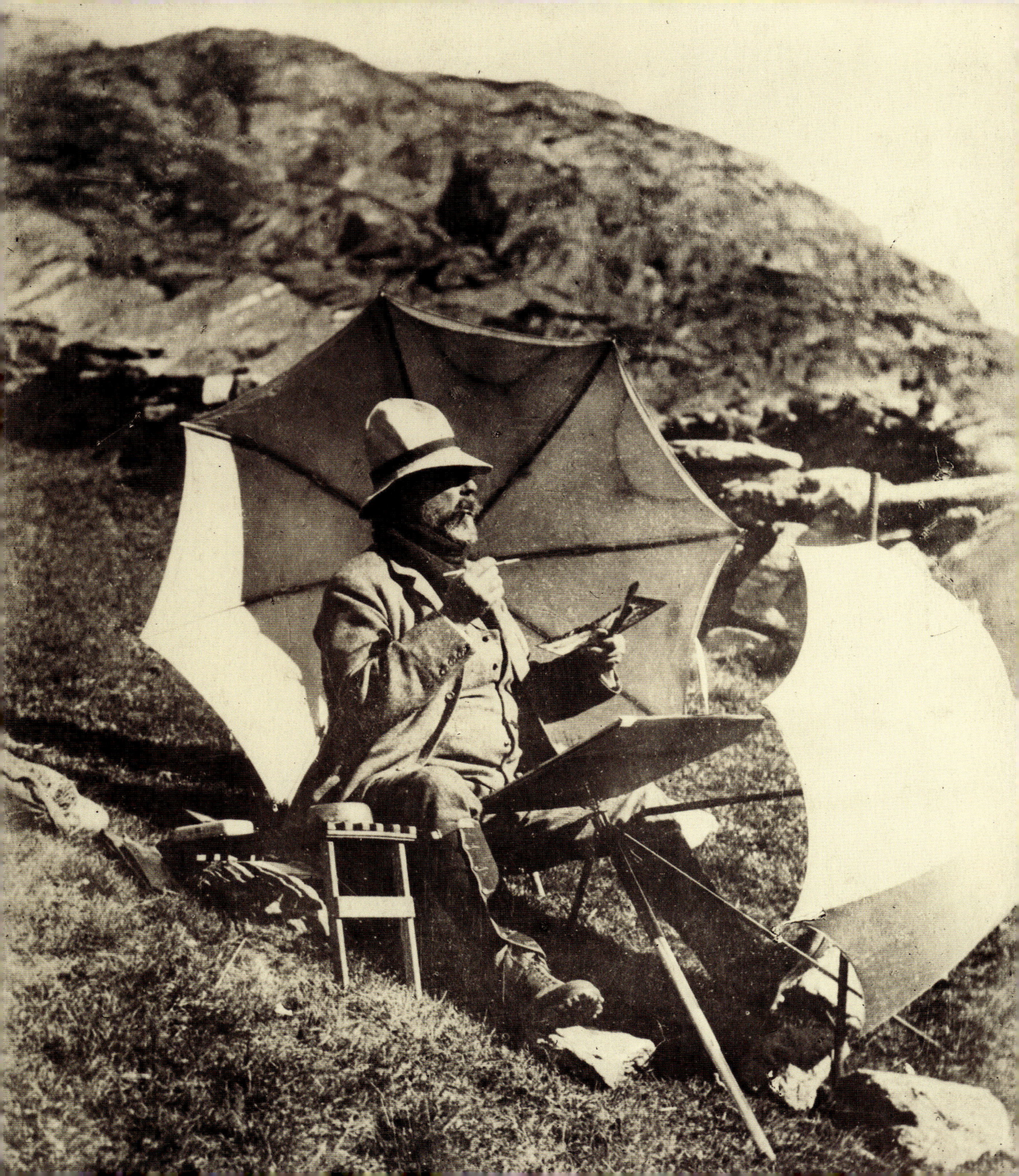

Sargent painting a watercolor in the Simplon Pass, ca. 1910–11. Museum of Fine Arts, Boston. The John Singer Sargent Archive–Gift of Richard and Leonée Ormond.

Beyond the Portrait Studio

1900–1925

During the first decade of the twentieth century, Sargent balanced his professional commitments—portrait and mural work—with a dynamic travel schedule. He traveled in order to fill commissions, conduct research for his murals, and for the pleasure of exploring new places. In some ways, this lifestyle echoed the pattern established during his childhood, of moving with the seasons. Each summer, he retreated from his London studio to picturesque locations in Europe. These "holidays" offered respite from his commissioned portraits, a chance for leisure, and inspiration. As was his habit, he seems to have painted and sketched constantly.

When Sargent was elected a full member of Britain's Royal Academy in 1897, a distinction that secured his position in that country's art establishment, he was obligated to submit a representative work to the collection as his diploma picture. The work he selected, *An Interior in Venice* [fig. 67], blends aspects of portraiture and genre painting and signifies new directions in his art at the cusp of the new century. The composition commemorates his first visit to Venice since 1882 by depicting his hosts—his father's cousin Daniel Sargent Curtis and his wife, Ariana, their son Ralph, and daughter-in-law, Lisa—in the grand ballroom of their residence at the Palazzo Barbaro, a famed fifteenth-century palace on the Grand Canal.

The older generation, at lower right, anchors the composition. As Ariana gazes directly at the viewer, her husband leafs through a book of prints. To the left, Ralph is casually perched upon an ornate gilt table; his long legs extend into the room, while his wife, Lisa, reaches for the silver tea service. As Ariana appears to pose for Sargent, the others enact the daily rituals of their privileged fin-de-siècle life in the ornate ballroom, a masterpiece of seventeenth-century architectural decor known for its gilded stucco relief and paintings by Giovanni

Battista Piazzetta (1682–1754) and Sebastiano Ricci (1659–1734). Insomuch as Sargent is at ease in this setting, he is also a dispassionate observer, slightly removed by virtue of his elevated vantage point. Light emanates from the Grand Canal through unseen windows at right, illuminating details of the furnishings and energizing the setting. Sargent's friend, the painter Jacques-Émile Blanche (1861–1942) remarked of the picture, "Out of this rootless, idle group, Sargent has fashioned a painting of great poignancy. They reveal to him his natural environment."[1] The composition creates a tension between the two generations, which is reinforced by their formal and informal attitudes. Painted at the precipice of the new century, the elder Curtises, especially Ariana with her matronly dress and cap, seem tied to the historical past of the opulent room while the younger generation affects a casual nonchalance.

In the early years of the twentieth century, Sargent would become a frequent guest at the Palazzo Barbaro. Ralph Curtis (1854–1922) was Sargent's friend since his student days in the atelier of Carolus-Duran (1837–1917), and the expatriated Bostonians welcomed Sargent readily into their congenial social circle. The palazzo was a renowned gathering spot for the Anglo-American community in Venice, including Robert Browning and Henry James, who wrote *The Aspern Papers* (1888) in the palazzo's library and modeled the setting for *The Wings of the Dove* (1902) after the grand ballroom. Painters Claude Monet (1840–1926) and James McNeill Whistler (1834–1903) also visited and worked at the palazzo. Shortly after his stay in 1898, Sargent expressed his delight and nostalgia in a letter to Mrs. Curtis: "The Barbaro is a sort of *fontaine de jouvence*, for it sends one back twenty years, besides making the present seem remarkably all right."[2]

Sargent planned to present *An Interior in Venice* to the Curtises in appreciation for their hospitality, but the formidable Mrs. Curtis was offended by the painting because it anticipated her "advancing years," and she disapproved of her son's indecorous pose on the table.[3] Their mutual friend Henry James tried to reassure her writing: "The Barbaro saloon thing . . . I absolutely and unreservedly adored. . . . I've seen few things of [Sargent's] that I've ever craved more to possess!"[4] Unable to convince the Curtises to accept his gift, Sargent deposited *An Interior in Venice* at the Royal Academy.

Sargent increasingly incorporated aspects of landscape and genre painting into his portrait work as in *On His Holidays* [fig. 68], painted during a visit to Norway in the summer of 1901. His patron was George McCulloch, a wealthy businessman and noted collector of Victorian painting. The unconventional *On His Holidays*, depicts his son, fourteen-year-old Alexander, casually reclining on the edge of a picturesque Norwegian stream. His fishing hook, net, and recent catch—two salmon, shown in the lower right corner—represent his "holiday" pastime. Sargent seems to delight in rendering the expanse of the flowing water and rocky banks of the river. In this sense, the work's title seems playful—referring to the boy's holiday, but also Sargent's holiday from the confines of the studio.

Sargent's mural project for the Boston Public Library continued to prompt travel. His childhood "education by Baedeker's and Murray" had conditioned him to learn through direct encounter with a variety of actual and artistic sources for inspiration and accuracy.[5] His choice of a historical, religious subject for his Boston murals compelled him to return to ancient lands in 1905–6, when he explored in Syria, Palestine, and Lebanon. (He had visited Egypt, Greece, and Turkey in 1890–1.)

Seeking authenticity in his mural research, Sargent planned an excursion into the desert to visit the nomadic Bedouin people, inspired by the then common belief that, in shunning aspects of modern life, they represented a link to a biblical past. His trip into the desert inspired a great series of independent watercolors.[6] *Bedouins* [fig. 69] combines carefully observed portrait details with Sargent's expressive handling of watercolor. The figures' faces are set off by their vivid blue headscarves, and Sargent captures their piercing gazes. Brilliant highlights suggest bright desert light, as the bottom of the composition dissolves into fluid liquid washes of color. Sargent exploited the coarse texture of the paper to convey the immediacy of the study.

The subject of boats in port interested Sargent throughout his Mediterranean travels; *In a Levantine Port* [fig. 70] could represent any one of a number of ports from Alexandria to Jaffa that he passed through during his visit to the Holy Land. (He would revisit the subject in Venice, Majorca, and the Italian lakes.) Here Sargent cropped out the full height of the tall masts to concentrate on the prows of the boats and the shimmering surface of the water. Warm, saturated light permeates the scene and is reflected throughout the undulating pools of color on the surface of the water and the bright highlights sparkling on the underside of the boats.

Sargent's peripatetic lifestyle is made visible in the evocative oil sketch *An Hotel Room* [fig. 71]. Diffuse light filters through the closed shutters and gauzy curtains, and the entire room is imbued with a soft glow. An open suitcase fills the foreground floor, its contents—difficult to determine—are splayed across the floor. The artist's presence is felt throughout the room—a shirt rests on the windowsill, and a towel hanging from the washbasin at right seems to have been recently used.

Increasingly, Sargent's summer holidays signified a retreat from his portrait work. As Sargent grew weary of the endless demands of portrait sittings and the need to please his patrons, he found respite in returning to favorite locales on the Continent with robust groups of family, friends, and artists. In autumn 1901 he wrote his friend, the sculptor Augustus Saint-Gaudens (1848–1907), that he had come to Italy, where he was born and had spent much of his childhood, "to avoid portraits."[7] Increasingly, he focused his considerable energy on painting landscapes and subject pictures, seeking subjects that interested him—particularly around the themes of light and water. Sargent most often visited Italy, making at least fifteen trips there between 1897 and 1913. He traveled the full length of the country from Sicily and Naples in the south to Venice, Bologna, Milan, and the Alps in the north. He continuously studied Italian art across the eras as inspiration for his murals while producing brilliant independent images of friends and family in the Italian landscape.

One of Sargent's favorite locales was Venice, which he visited at least nine times between 1898 and 1913, painting upward of 140 oils and watercolors of Venetian scenes.[8] Sargent was enchanted by the pictorial possibilities of the city, and his Venetian watercolors are often celebrated as the pinnacle of his accomplishment in the medium. The watery canals suited his fluid technique, and the marble architecture allowed him to indulge his obsession with light on stone. (Sargent expressed his preference for Venice over Rome to his friend Henry Tonks (1862–1937) in terms of the stone: "It is a pity that so many things in Rome are built of that ugly porous travertine—the marble of Venice is much more paintable.")[9] The interplay of water, stone, and sparkling light, which had captivated so many artist-visitors to La Serenissima, became the leitmotif of Sargent's Venetian oeuvre.

Sargent's most characteristic Venetian works are painted from a gondola as he traveled through the city's canals. He avoided the broad views of the city that were characteristic of the great *vedute* painters of the past such as Canaletto (1697–1768), Francesco Guardi (1713–1793), and Joseph Mallord William Turner (1775–1851). (He also tended to eschew Turner's evocative atmospheric effects.) As he sketched from the low vantage point of the canals, he most often selected near and fragmentary views of the city's buildings in which he could focus on the interplay of light, water, and stone. He delighted in rendering the ornate details of the city's Gothic and Renaissance architecture and repeatedly studied certain architectural details. He made a series of images of the emblematic Santa Maria della Salute, the seventeenth-century church built in celebration of the city's recovery from the plague in 1630. He focused on partial views of the building that he could see from the water, such as *Santa Maria della Salute* [fig. 72], in which he cropped out the majesty of the church's recognizable dome to depict the lower register of the building with its grand doors and a crowd of gondoliers in the foreground.

He was as likely to paint less easily identifiable or seemingly inconsequential and oblique views of the city. In *Giudecca* [fig. 73] Sargent avoided easily recognizable monuments to present a picturesque view of this distinctive neighborhood, south of the main city. In *Gondoliers' Siesta* [fig. 74], he used the base of the Palazzo Contarini delle Figure on the Grand Canal as a setting for his depiction of two gondoliers taking a break from their duties. Not surprisingly, Sargent also found beauty in the graceful movements of the gondoliers: *Vue de Venise (sur le canal)* [fig. 75] attempts to characterize their dynamic energy as they guide their vessels through the canal—their extended figures frozen in time.

Sketching on the Giudecca [fig. 76] records his friend the painter Wilfrid de Glehn (1870–1951) at work in his "floating studio" on a canal. Jane (1873–1961), his wife, is shown at center wearing a broad-brimmed white hat, observing her husband paint.[10] The newly married couple was actually on their honeymoon, when Sargent—the unseen presence—observed and captured this scene from the adjacent gondola, the prow of which intrudes into the composition at the lower left. Sargent and the de Glehns were friends and became frequent traveling companions; Jane would become a favorite model and muse in Sargent's later pictures. The sheet has much of the apparent fluid spontaneity of Sargent's watercolors, but it is very carefully composed. His composition accentuates an emotional and physical distance from his subjects. Both sitters turn away from Sargent, and the sense of separation is enhanced by the sweeping diagonal of the mooring line that comes between the two gondolas.

Initially, Sargent's Venetian watercolors were created for his own pleasure. For many years, he refused to sell them (though he occasionally presented them to friends as gifts). He explained to friend William Rathbone: "These sketches keep up my morale & I never sell them. At the Watercolour Society they may be marked sold, but they are really not for sale."[11] Sargent's images of Venice occupied a special place in his oeuvre, representing his personal vision of the city. Sargent finally agreed to sell a group of his watercolors to the Brooklyn Museum in 1909—setting off a frenzy among major museums to acquire his work.[12]

THE ALPS

Between 1904 and 1909, Sargent made annual summer visits to the Italian Alps, where he indulged his interest in depicting figures in the landscape. These summer holidays involved his artist friends and his extended family, including his sister Violet Ormond and her six children. Written accounts, family folklore, and photographs reveal that these vacations were exuberant, happy occasions when Sargent's companions took turns serving as his models.[13] Between 1904 and 1907 the group gathered at the town of Purtud, Italy, a few miles south of Mont Blanc. In 1908 and 1909 they stayed near Breuil, Italy, just south of the Matterhorn. And, in 1910 and 1911, they lodged near the Simplon Pass. Sargent's paintings range from the formal to the informal—fully developed compositions for exhibition and candid informal sketches. They almost always show his delight in rendering details of the landscape—typically not broad alpine vistas but rocks, boulders, forests, and streams. Sargent posed his models outdoors, often lounging, reading, or painting, sometimes in the exotic costumes he had brought from London.

The dazzling *Group with Parasols* (*Siesta*) [fig. 77] depicts four of Sargent's artist-friends dozing in an alpine meadow. At left, two women, Dos Palmer and Lillian Mellor, nap beneath white parasols. To the right Leonard ("Ginx") Harrison rests with his head in Lillian's lap next to his brother Lawrence ("Peter") Harrison. There's a sensuality to their languorous attitudes. Their limbs and bodies intertwine. Their casual poses, particularly the men's splayed legs, seem to flaunt contemporary ideas about propriety and are the opposite of composed formal portraits. They seem utterly oblivious to the artist's alert observation. The high vantage point and close cropping amplify this voyeuristic aspect. Sargent eliminates the horizon and compresses the space creating an intimacy to the scene. Sargent's technical virtuosity is evident in his bold brushstrokes, which delineate forms, light, and color. Passages dissolve into near abstraction, an effect that is intensified by his depiction of the dappled sunlight.

A variation of this composition, in watercolor, is the broadly painted sheet known simply by the descriptive title *Group* or *Siesta in a Swiss Wood* [fig. 78]. In this freely painted and candid study, Sargent again portrays brothers Ginx and Peter Harrison, this time with family friend Polly Barnard. In the rendering of the parasol and Peter Harrison's pale suit, the absence of paint is remarkable—Sargent leaves broad passages of the white sheet unpainted and gently layers pale gray strokes to suggest the folds of his suit. In contrast, Polly's vivid blue skirt, accentuated with brown shadows, anchors the composition and becomes a pillow for Peter's head.

Sargent would continue to paint his friends and companions lounging in alpine meadows at the Simplon Pass on the border of Switzerland and Italy between 1909 and 1911. Watercolors such as *Simplon Pass: The Tease* [fig. 79] replace the languorous sensuality of *Group with Parasols* and *Group* with a decidedly playful and jovial mood. The young woman on the left good-humoredly "teases" the woman on the right with a minute, unseen object (possibly an insect?) as Sargent delights in the rendering of their billowing skirts nestled into the lush growth.

Sargent's portrait of the local "botanizing priest," *Padre Sebastiano* [fig. 80], painted at Purtud, incorporates genre details. The young cleric is shown at his desk, absorbed in his thoughts. His pen is poised above his notebook as he pauses from taking notes about the flowers and plants that are spread across the desk. Within his modest home, he is surrounded by his worldly possessions: behind him, his discarded coat and hat rest on his unmade bed while other clothes and belongings hang on a rope against the wall. Within the cluttered interior, light streams in from the right and highlights the rumpled white sheets.

Sargent painted *The Hermit* (*Il Solitario*) [fig. 81], an image of a lone ascetic man—most likely modeled by the painter Ambrogio Raffele (1845–1928)—and two deer set in the woody foothills of the Alps, at the very moment he announced he would no longer paint portraits on commission. The symbolism is suggested by the painting's title: a hermit represents one who has withdrawn from society or, in Sargent's case, society portraits. Raffele, a painter and frequent traveling companion, is once again a surrogate for Sargent. The painting distinguishes itself from other works of this period through its novel approach and strong intellectual and philosophical underpinnings. The composition exploits the effect of dappled sunlight filtering through the trees, across the rocky ground, the figure, and the animals. Sargent used a limited palette to represent the diffuse light, creating the effect of camouflage. (The figure and the animals seem to emerge from the setting only after a few moments of looking.) The contrast of light and shade is created with a pale, earthy palette and multiple layers of mixed pigment, which emphasize the materiality of the paint.

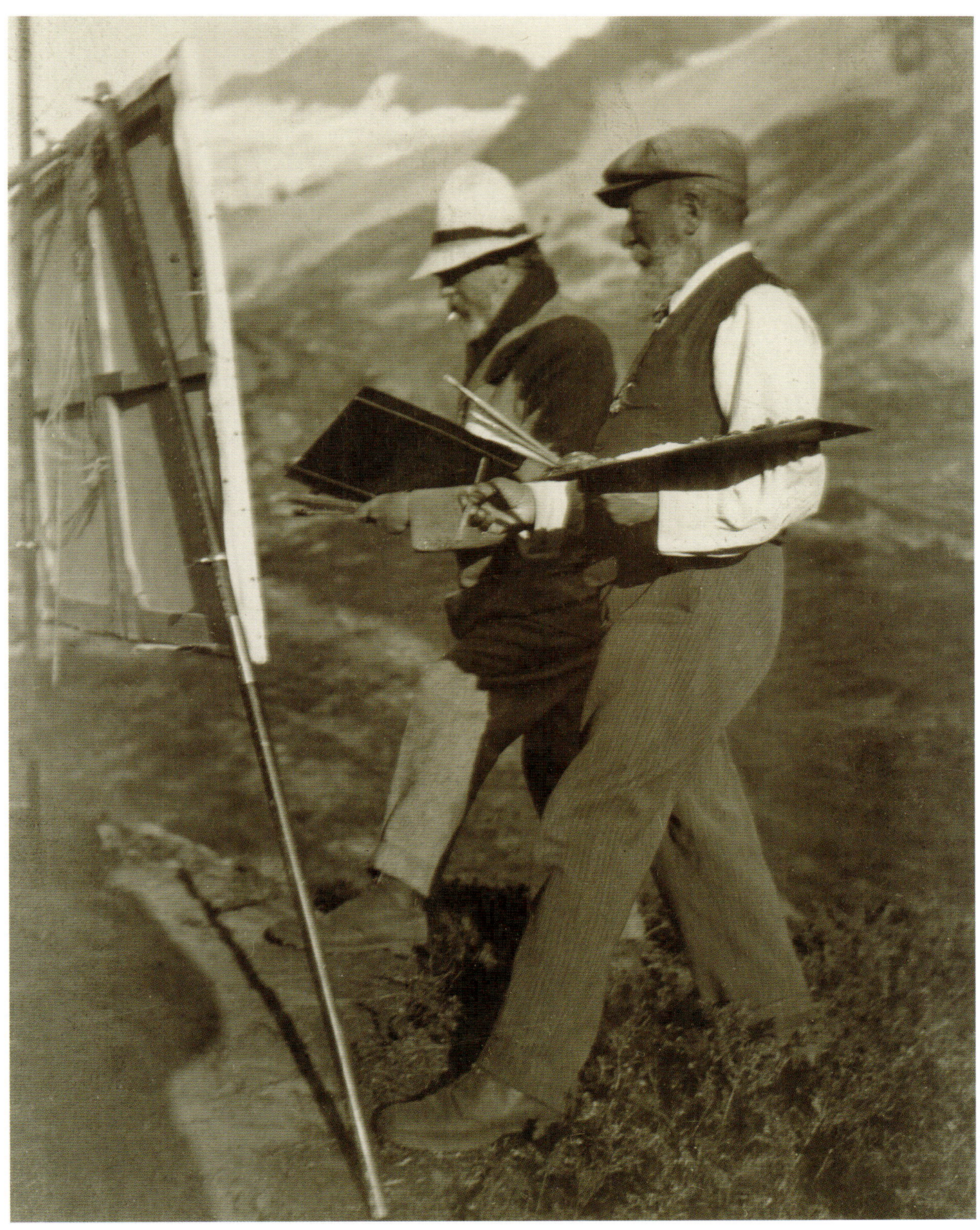

Sargent and Ambrogio Raffele sketching, ca. 1904–7. Museum of Fine Arts, Boston.
The John Singer Sargent Archive–Gift of Richard and Leonée Ormond.

Sargent's biographer Evan Charteris recalled the artifice of the creation of *The Hermit* by revealing that "[o]ne year [Sargent] travelled with a stuffed gazelle . . . which was to figure in some landscape."[14] Critic Kenyon Cox elaborated on Sargent's technique in a lengthy appreciation of the painting, suggesting that in it "one sees the essential John Sargent, working for himself alone without regard to external demands and doing what he really cares most to do."[15] When Sargent sold the painting to The Metropolitan Museum of Art in 1911, he expressed concern about the title. He explained, "'Hermit' is all right. I wish there were another simple word that did not bring with it any Christian association, and that rather suggested quietness or pantheism."[16] For Sargent, *The Hermit* signified an important transitional moment in his career. In his retreat from society, he sought spirituality through nature.

The Brook [fig. 82] indulges Sargent's fascination with exotic and Orientalist imagery in an Aesthetic mode. Sargent posed his nieces, Rose-Marie and Reine, in exotic costumes he had brought with him from London; he depicts them lounging by the side of an alpine stream. He takes pleasure in rendering the folds and patterns of the costumes, particularly Rose-Marie's Turkish-style coat (right), and other decorative aspects. The pose of Rose-Marie's lithe body mimics the curve of the meandering brook. The colors of her dress echo the landscape: the blue of her pants appears in the stream, the golden yellow of her slippers in the warm grassy knoll. Her head sinks and blends into a mossy pillow. At left, Reine's green dress connects her to the verdant landscape behind her. Even though Sargent did exhibit *The Brook* to great acclaim in London, one senses the personal nature of the subject and Sargent's attachment to his nieces—particularly in the tender portrait of Rose-Marie. Sargent presented the painting to his sister Violet, mother of the two models, as a gift. The portrait was a precious family record of these Italian holidays and Sargent's devotion to his nieces.

In *Cashmere* [fig. 83], Sargent seems to have aimed for loftier themes in his mysterious frieze like composition of seven young women parading across a verdant background. Sargent's young niece Reine (then only eleven years old) seems to have been the model for all the figures, variously draped in Sargent's "exotic" cashmere shawl.[17] The setting and costume are evocative and timeless. The composition is at once highly decorative in its rhythmic repetition of the figures yet also appears symbolic. The various poses and attitudes of the young women across the composition suggest the passage of time and the transition from adolescence to womanhood. The painting received high praise when exhibited at the summer exhibition of the Royal Academy in London in 1909:

> What matters their uniformity of type when their faces—seen full or in profile, some shawl-veiled, others free—are so fair, the rhythmic lines of their draped figures, the patterns wrought by them in sequence, sing with a music that hold memories of the immortal Parthenon frieze? This is Sargent unmannered, full of gracious impulse, which is in its kind all but faultless.[18]

The cashmere shawl reappears in the painting *Nonchaloir* (*Repose*) [fig. 84] swaddling Sargent's favorite niece, Rose-Marie Ormond. She lounges in a luxurious setting, surrounded by gilt-trimmed furniture, an upholstered sofa, and a large gilt frame above her head. Sargent seems fascinated by the rendering of the deep folds of her luscious skirt, the patterned textile of the sofa, and the decorative elements of the room—while she appears listless and submissive to his scrutiny.

ITALY AND ITS GARDENS

In autumn 1906 Sargent visited and painted at several villas and their gardens around Rome with his friend and patron Mary Hunter. He expressed his admiration for the sites in a letter to Ralph Curtis:

> In spite of scirocco and lots of rain we have been seeing the villas within miles round thanks to Mrs. Hunter's motor. They are magnificent and I should like to spend a summer at Frascati and paint from morning till night at the Torlonia or the Falconieri, ilexes and cypresses, fountains and statues—ainsi soit il—amen.[19]

He crafted a similar excursion for September–October of 1907, when he toured the villas of Frascati with his sister Emily and friend Eliza Wedgwood, before meeting the de Glehns to paint at the gardens of Tivoli, Villa Falconieri, Villa d'Este, and Villa Torlonia. It is not surprising that the concept of the villa appealed to Sargent. The very idea of the villa, originating in antiquity and enduring in the Renaissance, was that of a retreat from urban life, exactly what Sargent was seeking as he moved away from his career as a portraitist.

Sargent's interest in Italian villas and gardens corresponds with Edith Wharton's work on the subject. Sargent and Wharton moved in similar expatriate circles and had met briefly about 1899. Her book *Italian Villas and Their Gardens* (with illustrations by Maxfield Parrish), published in 1905 (and dedicated to Sargent's friend Vernon Lee), is a thorough accounting of more than eighty villas that combines serious research with an appreciation for "Italian garden-magic."[20]

At the Villa Torlonia in 1907, Sargent conceived a major exhibition picture that blends art and nature in the villa garden setting. Wharton praised the gardens and fountains at Torlonia as "the most beautiful example of fountain-architecture in Frascati."[21] Sargent chose this celebrated setting for *The Fountain, Villa Torlonia, Frascati, Italy* [fig. 85], which shows Jane de Glehn painting while her husband observes. The composition is organized around Sargent's careful study of the ornate balustrade. Poised there, Jane is alert and very much in command of her art. Wilfrid affects a casual pose behind the easel at left. (Sargent inverted the scene in *Sketching on the Giudecca* [fig. 76], which shows Wilfrid painting and

Jane watching.) The asymmetrical composition focuses attention at the moment Jane's brush touches the canvas. Behind them, the forceful spout of the fountain creates a swirl of energy that leads back to Jane's head—the source of her creativity.

Sargent continued to explore the Italian villa garden as a setting for paintings through autumn 1910, when he settled at the fifteenth-century Villa Torre Galli, southwest of Florence, with his sister Emily, the painters Jane and Wilfrid de Glehn, and William Blake Richmond (1842–1921) and his wife, Clara. Sargent depicted the introspective and restorative aspect of villa life in the oil painting *Villa Torre Galli: The Loggia* [fig. 87], an idyllic image of his companions relaxing in the loggia off the cloistered garden behind the villa. Sargent positioned himself at one end of the colonnade, directly opposite a copy of Giambologna's *Bathing Venus* (1573), who seems to preside over the scene. Sargent arranged his friends across the loggia, creating a dynamic triangle that leads the viewer through the composition. Jane de Glehn is seen in the right foreground, cocooned in the exotic cashmere shawl, but cropped at the waist; she holds a book on her lap and faces away from the villa and toward nature and the garden. She invites the viewer into the picture, through the open alleyway down the center of the composition—to her husband, Wilfrid, who is painting at the opposite end of the loggia. He sits beneath the *Venus*, who seems to gaze over his shoulder as he creates his painting. At left, in the middle ground, Richmond is at his easel; his wife stands nearby reading a book. Sargent creates a scene of quiet concentration in which each individual is engaged and absorbed in his or her own activity. The sense of isolation—from each other and the outside world—is palpable. Sargent's painting embodies the concept of villeggiatura, the ideal state of country living. He celebrates the villa as a place of retreat and rejuvenation from city living, but also as the "center of the contemplative life" for a privileged leisure class[22] (a subject he would reiterate in *A Garden at Corfu* in Greece [fig. 86]).

Sargent painted a distinctive series of watercolors in the nearby *giardino della limonaia* at Villa Reale at Marlia in which he translated the decorative elements of the Italian garden—the potted lemon trees, the balustrade and fountain basins, and the statuary—into startling snapshots of light, color, and form. These unpopulated watercolors convey a timelessness and nostalgia for the past combined with a vivid sense of the immediate present in the rendering of light and shadow.

In *Villa di Marlia, Lucca: A Fountain* [fig. 88], Sargent contrasts the acidic yellow greens of the sunlit grass and lemon trees with the cool greens of the darkened background. The garden statuary (at center) is defined by the cool blue and gray shadows. Sargent conveys the shimmer and intensity of light through the building of layers of pigment, exploiting the transparency and opacity of his medium. Broken down, the variations of color and tone seem extreme; but viewed as a complete ensemble, Sargent captured the immediacy of the optical experience of Italian sunlight. As Charteris averred, "[Sargent's] watercolors are fragmentary—pieces of the visible world broken off because they appealed to his eye."[23]

Sargent saw the pictorial possibilities of mundane subjects. *La Biancheria* [fig. 89] transforms laundry hanging on a clothesline into a study of light. Only the title hints that the subject is Italian. *La Biancheria*, literally "the washing" or "the laundry" is derived from the Italian word for white, *bianco*. The simplicity of the subject is enlivened by the zigzag of the clothesline, creating dynamic angles and recessions into space. As contemporary critic Martin Hardie enthused, "[I]t is just some white clothes and sheets hanging on a line by a hedgerow—but a masterpiece."[24]

In the range of Sargent's subjects, one senses that Sargent was constantly painting and didn't hesitate to spontaneously start a composition when something caught his eye. In *Mountain Fire* [fig. 90], a panoramic vista of mountain peaks form the background for an atmospheric study of a dramatic alpine fire. The foreground is a chaos of freely painted gray-blue brushstrokes that suggest smoke and red dabs of fire. Rising smoke billows across the composition at a diagonal from lower right to upper left, and the painting seems to glow with fading daylight and burning embers. Sargent was likely captivated by the atmospheric effect and the transitional time of day. *Mountain Fire* stands out in Sargent's oeuvre as a highly abstracted and unconventional composition.

In 1911, Sargent visited the historic marble quarries of Carrara, Italy. The quarry had been renowned since antiquity for its particularly pure marble, which had been used for the greatest monuments of the ancient world, such as the Pantheon, and Renaissance masterpieces such as Michelangelo's colossal sculpture of David. Throughout his oeuvre, Sargent was attracted to depicting marble and other stone for their ability to reflect and absorb light and color, whether the architecture of buildings of Venice or garden statuary in Italy and Spain. Sargent spent several weeks at Carrara, impressing the local workmen with his dedication and commitment. One witness described how Sargent "slept for weeks in a hut so completely devoid of all ordinary comforts that his companions, far younger men, fled after a few days, unable to stand the Spartan rigors tolerated by their senior with such serene indifference."[25] (Sargent was then fifty-five years old.) Sargent made dozens of sketches, some photographs, and sixteen watercolors of the workmen engaged in various aspects of their perilous labor, which was still conducted using ancient techniques.

Bringing Down the Marble from the Quarries to Carrara [fig. 91] conveys the magnificence of the rugged landscape and the timeless labor of the workmen. Sargent emphasized the massive scale of the quarries by choosing a low vantage point gazing up the steep marble cliffs. Here the strong workmen are at once dwarfed by the epic landscape and seem to be part of it. They are positioned at either end of the long ropes, which were used to lower the enormous blocks. The diagonal lines sweep across the composition emphasizing the grandeur of the landscape. In a series of more intimate watercolor sheets, Sargent focused on depicting the laborers from a near vantage point at work or at rest. In *Carrara: Workmen* [fig. 92], three workers seem to emerge from the stone as they take a break for nourishment.

In 1908, Sargent was lured to the island of Majorca by its reputation; as he wrote to Ariana Curtis before his first visit there in 1908, "If it is as delightful as they say, I daresay Emily and I, and perhaps Miss Wedgwood, may go there in the autumn."[26] The Balearic island lived up to his expectations, and he returned there that fall accompanied by his sister and friend and painted dozens of works, which are particularly vibrant and expressive. He found pleasure in familiar subjects such as *Melon Boats* [fig. 93], an especially vivid harbor scene that is characterized by dense layers of fluid pigment used to suggest the azure water and dynamic flashes of opaque yellow and blue paint, which seem to dart across the composition. The sheet is dominated by the sweep of the massive sail across the upper left of the composition, and the melons of the title are barely suggested in the boat at center. *Gourds* [fig. 94] has a similar dynamic flair in its technical virtuosity, and one senses Sargent's delight in rendering the pattern of color and light across the dense tangle of leaves and vines painted in various effervescent shades of green.

Among the artists whom Sargent befriended in Majorca was a young landscape painter from Argentina, Francisco Bernareggi (1878–1959). According to local reports, Sargent's spontaneous portrait study of the handsome artist [fig. 95] was dashed off in a mere two-and-a-half hours. (Sargent's haste is evident along the bottom edge of the canvas, which appears unfinished.) Bernareggi's olive-skinned good looks were a type that appealed to Sargent—and his enthusiasm seems reflected in his highly charged, sensual technique. The remarkable pale yellow-golden background is painted with energetic squiggles of the brush, which transform Bernareggi's silhouette into a glowing halo.

A trip to Spain in late summer 1912, prompted a celebrated series of watercolors that exploited his favorite themes. Sargent was returning to familiar locations; he had visited Granada and the Alhambra as a child (in 1868) and as a younger man (in 1879 and 1895). Light on stone is the subject of two masterful watercolors *Spanish Fountain* [fig. 97] and *Escutcheon of Charles V of Spain* [fig. 98]. In his depiction of the Renaissance fountain in the courtyard of the hospital of San Juan de Dios in Granada, Sargent took a near, cropped view to focus on the flow of water between the fountain's upper and lower basins. As a stream of water cascades from above, it creates ripples in the pool of water below. Sargent suggests the undulating surface of the water with arcing brushstrokes in blue-violet tones atop the golden reflection. Light flashes across the decorative carved putti who support the upper basin.

In *Escutcheon of Charles V of Spain*, Sargent chose a monochromatic subject—a carved stone relief of the coat of arms of the emperor—and transformed it into a dazzling study of light and shadow. Sargent found the escutcheon above a fountain near the Puerta de la Justicia, an entrance to the Alhambra Palace. He masterfully describes the optical experience of warm Mediterranean light on pale stone. The composition was very carefully drawn and measured; Sargent used a ruler to delineate the horizontal architrave and a compass to inscribe the semicircle of the crest. He eradicated his effort with his application of broad pools of color, delicate washes, broad bravura brushstrokes, and carefully articulated details to create a work that astonishes. As one critic mused,

> Sargent, the pure painter, has seen the sun striking across it, has noted the glitter of light on the projecting bosses, the sharp forms of blue shadows, the warm reflections; and with astonishing rapidity and simplicity of means has so set down these things as to create an absolute illusion. The thing is there before you and you feel sure that by going a little closer you can make out the exact forms that have caused this confusion of light and shade.[27]

At the Alhambra, Sargent also returned to a favorite theme—artists at work—creating a luscious watercolor of his sister Emily, an amateur painter, working at her easel in the gardens of the Palacio del Generalife, the fourteenth-century summer palace of the Moorish sultans [fig. 96]. Her friends Jane de Glehn (muse and frequent model) and Dolores (about whom little is known) observe her efforts. Sargent created careful and precise portrait studies of these companions, in contrast to the blurred face of his sister. Dolores and Emily, in their dark clothing, seem to emerge from the cool verdant foliage of the gardens while Jane is distinguished by her pale garments and fanciful hat. Despite the bold, bright passages in the foliage and the swirling pattern of the decorative pavement, the figures appear firmly anchored despite the tilted perspective. In addition to their dazzling execution, these compositions provide great insight into Sargent's life during these painting holidays.

WORLD WAR I, THE TYROL, AND THE UNITED STATES

World War I would force Sargent to change his habits. He was painting in the Austrian Tyrol, on one of his customary summer excursions, when England and France declared war on Austria on August 4, 1914. Without his passport, Sargent was unable to return to England until late November when he finally obtained the necessary travel documents. Faced with few options, Sargent continued to paint. One of his traveling companions, the painter Adrian Stokes (1854–1935), would later suggest that Sargent was unperturbed by the war as he continued to work, but poignant letters to his dear niece Rose-Marie in Paris reveal otherwise. Sargent expressed his concern for the safety of her young husband who had joined the French army on the western front and offered her words of comfort. When news reached Sargent of the young man's death in battle in October, his consoling letter suggests his sadness and empathy: "I pity you with all my heart—your sorrow must be dreadful—and it will be a long while before you become aware of what those who love you are attempting to say to make your grief less painful."[28]

During this time, not surprisingly, Sargent painted some unusually somber pictures, such as *Graveyard in the Tyrol* [fig. 99], that suggest the solemn mood that infiltrated the holiday. Sargent depicts the ornate grave monuments of the cemetery at Colfuschg, Austria, against a broad panoramic vista of the Sella Mountains. The prominent funerary monuments intimate mortality. Beneath the stunning alpine vista and atmospheric sky, two figures in local garb tend to the grounds of the cemetery with scythes, evoking association with death and the grim reaper.

Sargent would also paint some of his more typical subjects in the Tyrol, such as the vivid watercolor *Mountain Stream* [fig. 100], an elaborate study of rushing water, rocks, and surfaces in an alpine wood. A lone figure, probably modeled by Sargent's trusted companion and manservant, Nicola d'Inverno, lowers himself into the stream at right.

With the start of the Great War and nearing the final phases of his murals for the Boston Public Library, Sargent settled in Boston to focus on the completion of that project. By the summer of 1916, his wanderlust struck. He told his friend Edwin Blashfield (1848–1936), "When the American summer comes I am frightened. I have to get away to the top of a mountain somewhere to breathe."[29] He planned a visit to the Canadian Rockies, certainly thinking that the splendid mountains would be the North American solution to his usual summer holiday. After a long journey across the continent from Boston, Sargent expressed relief upon his arrival, "After the heat of the last days in Boston and of the many days railway journey across the endless plains it is delicious to be here among crags and glaciers and pine woods."[30]

While visiting Florida in 1917, Sargent found a counterpart to his beloved Italian and Spanish villas and gardens. The purpose of his trip was a rare portrait commission for business magnate John D. Rockefeller, but Sargent also visited his old friend Charles Deering, whom he had known since his student days in Paris. Deering had briefly studied painting before joining his family's agricultural machinery business. Sargent was drawn to the nearby elaborate Italianate villa, Vizcaya, then being built for Charles's brother James. Sargent wrote to his cousin, "There is so much to paint . . . at my host's brother's villa. It combines Venice and Frascati and Aranjuez, and all that one is likely never to see again. Hence this linger-longing."[31] For Sargent, Vizcaya conjured memories of his favorite painting sites in Europe, which were then inaccessible because of World War I. *Shady Paths, Vizcaya* [fig. 101] evokes the grandeur of Sargent's European garden watercolors with nostalgia.

Sargent also painted a dazzling series of vivid watercolors in the uncultivated, natural landscape of Florida using the muscular laborers who were then constructing Vizcaya's garden as his models. He combined his sensuous delight in rendering the male nude figure with his favorite themes of sunlight and water. Set among the dense mangrove growth and shallow pools along the coast, the most elaborate composition from the series is *The Bathers* [fig. 102], which likely shows one figure in a variety of poses. The candid and more broadly painted *Man and Pool, Florida* [fig. 103] evokes images of Narcissus, the handsome hunter of Greek mythology who fell in love with his own reflection. Despite Sargent's complaint

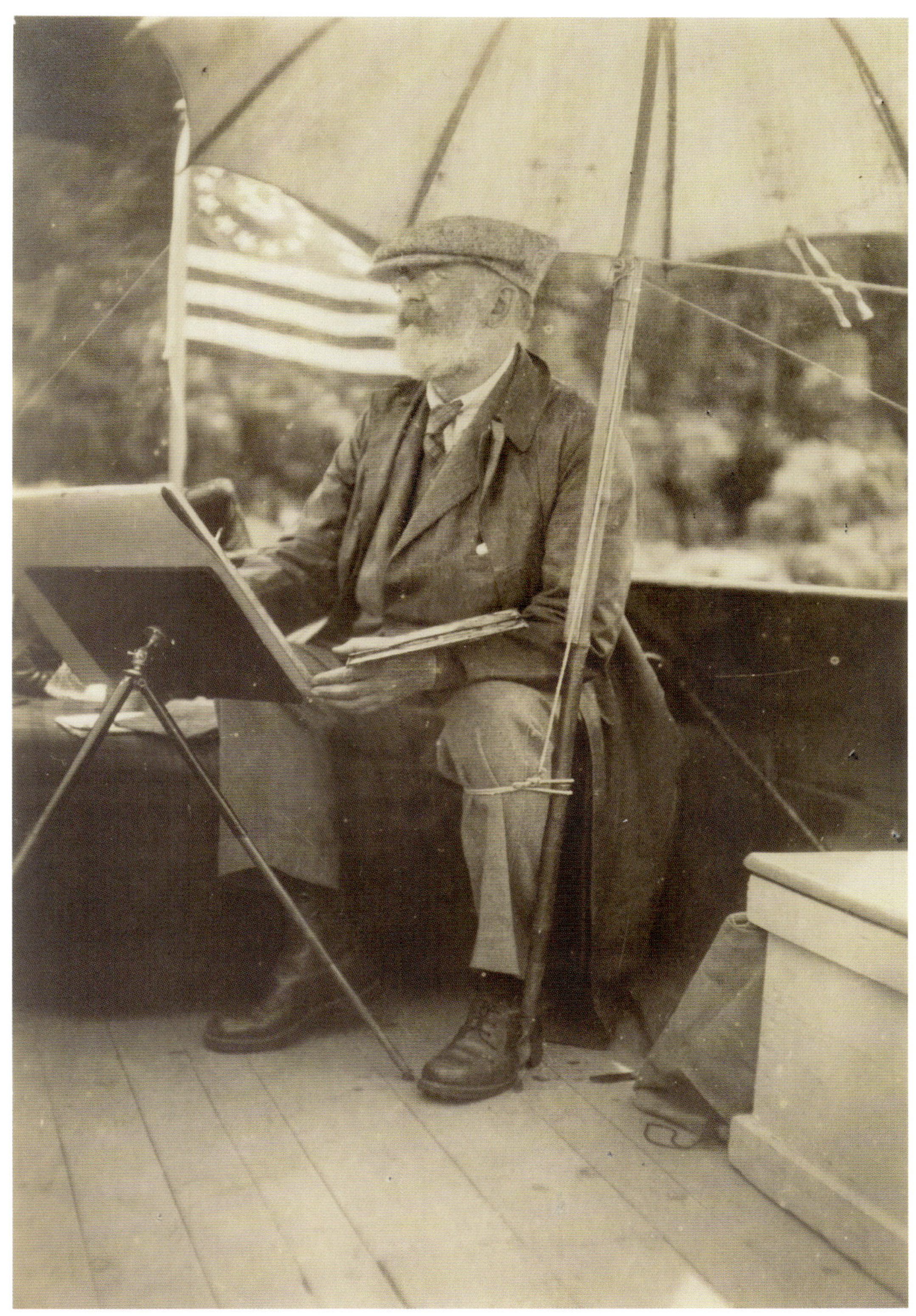

Sargent sketching, Ironbound Island, Maine, 1922. Museum of Fine Arts, Boston. The John Singer Sargent Archive–Gift of Richard and Leonée Ormond

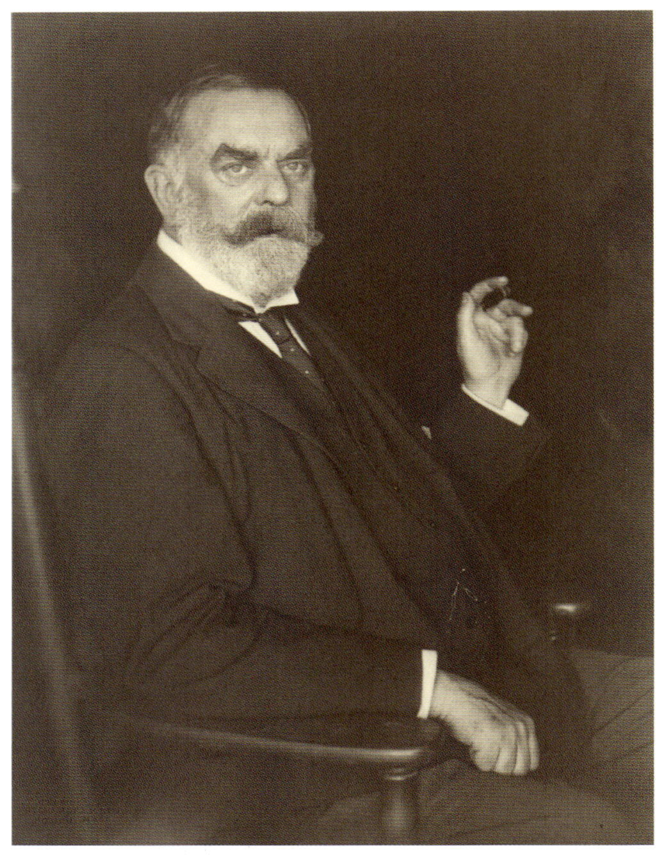

John Singer Sargent, Boston, 1924. Photograph by H. H. Pierce. Museum of Fine Arts, Boston. The John Singer Sargent Archive–Gift of Richard and Leonée Ormond.

that "aligators [*sic*] don't make very interesting pictures," one of his most fascinating Florida watercolors is the unusual *Muddy Alligators* [fig. 104].[32] Sargent exploits the full range of his technique to suggest the rough texture and scales of the prehistoric-looking reptiles in a complex composition.

Sargent may have painted the portrait of his host Charles Deering [fig. 105] as a token of gratitude; it's inscribed "to my friend / Charles Deering." Painted forty-one years after the two men first met, the portrait reflects the comfortable familiarity of old friends. It blends aspects of portraiture and landscape painting to create a unique and candid masterpiece. The tropical setting is described with a bright palette and fluid style that echo Sargent's watercolor technique. His bravura rendering of light and shadow across the sitter's crinkled white suit recalls the fancy gowns of his lavish society patrons. The striking informality of the composition—evident in Deering's unbuttoned collar and casual pose, the disarray of the landscape with its scattered palm fronds and coconuts, and the casual wicker furniture—seems to reject the formal opulence of Sargent's earlier society portraits. This candid, noncommissioned likeness reflects the liberty of Sargent's work late in his life but also his steadfast commitment to remarking on shifting social structures.

Sargent continued to paint and travel until his death in 1925. He challenged himself, accepting his commission as a war artist in 1918 and working tirelessly to complete his murals for the Museum of Fine Arts, Boston. Early in 1925, as he prepared the last panels for shipment to the United States, he told his friend Adrian Stokes, "Now the American things are done, and so, I suppose, I may die when I like."[33] Four days before he was scheduled to sail for Boston, after returning home from a farewell party hosted by his sister Emily, he suffered a heart attack in his sleep and died. He had dozed off while reading Voltaire's *Dictionnaire philosophique*. His untiring devotion to creating art was commemorated on his tombstone, which reads Laborare est Orare ("To Work is to Pray").

1 Quoted in Elizabeth Anne McCauley, Alan Chong, Rosella Mamoli Zorzi, and Richard Lingner, *Gondola Days: Isabella Stewart Gardner and the Palazzo Barbaro Circle*, exh. cat. (Boston: Isabella Stewart Gardner Museum, 2004), xvii.

2 Sargent to Mrs. Curtis, May 27, 1898, John Singer Sargent Collection. Boston Athenaeum, box 1, folder 11; quoted in Richard Ormond and Elaine Kilmurray, *John Singer Sargent: Complete Paintings.* Vol. 2: *Portraits of the 1890s* (New Haven: Yale University Press, 2002), xvi.

3 Evan Charteris, *John Sargent* (New York: Charles Scribner's Sons, 1927), 163.

4 Henry James to Ariana Curtis, March 16, 1899; quoted in Richard Ormond et al., *Sargent: Portraits of Artists and Friends*, exh. cat. (London: National Portrait Gallery, 2015), 210.

5 Stanley Olson, *John Singer Sargent: His Portrait* (New York: St. Martin's Press, 1986), 18.

6 Richard Ormond and Elaine Kilmurray, *John Singer Sargent: Complete Paintings.* Vol. 7: *Figures and Landscapes, 1900–1907* (New Haven: Yale University Press, 2012), 148.

7 Sargent to Saint-Gaudens, November 2, 1901, Saint-Gaudens Papers, Dartmouth College Library; quoted in Richard Ormond and Elaine Kilmurray, *John Singer Sargent: Complete Paintings.* Vol. 3: *The Later Portraits* (New Haven: Yale University Press, 2003), xi.

8 These statistics are based Richard Ormond and Elaine Kilmurray, *John Singer Sargent: Complete Paintings.* Vol. 5: *Figures and Landscapes, 1883–1899* (New Haven: Yale University Press, 2009); Ormond and Kilmurray 2012; and Richard Ormond and Elaine Kilmurray, *John Singer Sargent: Complete Paintings.* Vol. 8: *Figures and Landscapes, 1908–1913* (New Haven: Yale University Press, 2014).

9 Sargent to Henry Tonks, August 20, 1920, private collection; quoted in Ormond and Kilmurray 2009, 31.

10 Wilfrid's birth name was "von Glehn." He changed it to de Glehn during World War I.

11 Sargent to William Gair Rathbone, April 13, 1904, Private collection; quoted in Ormond and Kilmurray 2009, 50.

12 For more about the collection of Sargent's watercolors, see Stephanie L. Herdrich and H. Barbara Weinberg, *American Drawings and Watercolors in The Metropolitan Museum of Art: John Singer Sargent* (New York: The Metropolitan Museum of Art; and New Haven: Yale University Press), V, 2000, 2–5; and Erica E. Hirshler and Teresa A. Carbone, *John Singer Sargent Watercolors*, exh. cat. (New York: Brooklyn Museum and Boston: Museum of Fine Arts Publications, 2013), 27–47.

13 Ormond, one of Violet's grandchildren, has described the jovial camaraderie of these holidays via the recollections of his aunts and uncles. One legendary anecdote recounts that the children would try to avoid making eye contact with Sargent for fear of being enlisted as that day's model (Richard Ormond, oral communication, June 2015).

14 Charteris 1927, 170.

15 Kenyon Cox, "Two Ways of Painting," *Scribner's Magazine* 52 (October 1912): 509.

16 Sargent to Edward Robinson, March 16, 1911, The Metropolitan Museum of Art, archives.

17 Dorothy Barnard likely modeled some of the drapery.

18 *Glasgow Herald* (May 1, 1909), quoted in Ormond and Kilmurray 2014, 123.

19 Sargent to Ralph Curtis, Rome (1907); quoted in Charteris 1927, 171.

20 Wharton wrote, "The traveller returning from Italy, with his eyes and imagination full of the ineffable Italian garden-magic, knows vaguely that the enchantment exists; that he has been under its spell, and that it is more potent, more enduring, more intoxicating to every sense than the most elaborate and glowing effects of modern horticulture; but he may not have found the key to the mystery." Edith Wharton, *Italian Villas and Their Gardens* (New York: Century Co., 1905), 6.

21 Ibid., 156.

22 David R. Coffin, *The Villa in the Life of Renaissance Rome* (Princeton: Princeton University Press, 1988), 11, 15.

23 Charteris 1927, 224.

24 Martin Hardie, *Queen* (May 20, 1911), quoted in Ormond and Kilmurray 2014, 233.

25 "Memories of Sargent," *Living Age* 325 (May 30, 1925): 446.

26 Sargent to Ariana Curtis, May 15, 1908, Curtis Papers, Boston Athenaeum. Quoted in Ormond and Kilmurray 2014, 35.

27 Kenyon Cox, "The Sargent WaterColors," *Bulletin of The Metropolitan Museum of Art* 11, 2 (February 1916): 37.

28 JSS letter to Rose-Marie Ormond, October 20, 1914, private collection, quoted in Richard Ormond and Elaine Kilmurray. *John Singer Sargent: Complete Paintings.* Vol. 9: *Figures and Landscapes, 1914–1925* (New Haven: Yale University Press, 2016), 83.

29 Edwin H. Blashfield, "John Singer Sargent: Recollections," *North American Review* 221 (June–August 1925): 645.

30 Sargent to Evan Charteris, July 25, 1916. Quoted in Charteris, 1927, 207.

31 John Singer Sargent letter to Mary Hale, quoted in Ormond and Kilmurray 2003, 242.

32 Sargent to Thomas Fox, March 5, 1917, Thomas A. Fox-John Singer Sargent papers, Boston Athenaeum.

33 Adrian Stokes, "John Singer Sargent, RA, RWS", *Old Water-Colour Society's Club* 3 (1925–26): 52.

67

An Interior in Venice

1899
Oil on canvas, 26 × 33 in. (66 × 83.5 cm)
Signed: "John S. Sargent Aug 1899"
London, Royal Academy of Arts, Diploma Work given by John Singer Sargent, R.A., accepted 1900 [03/1387]

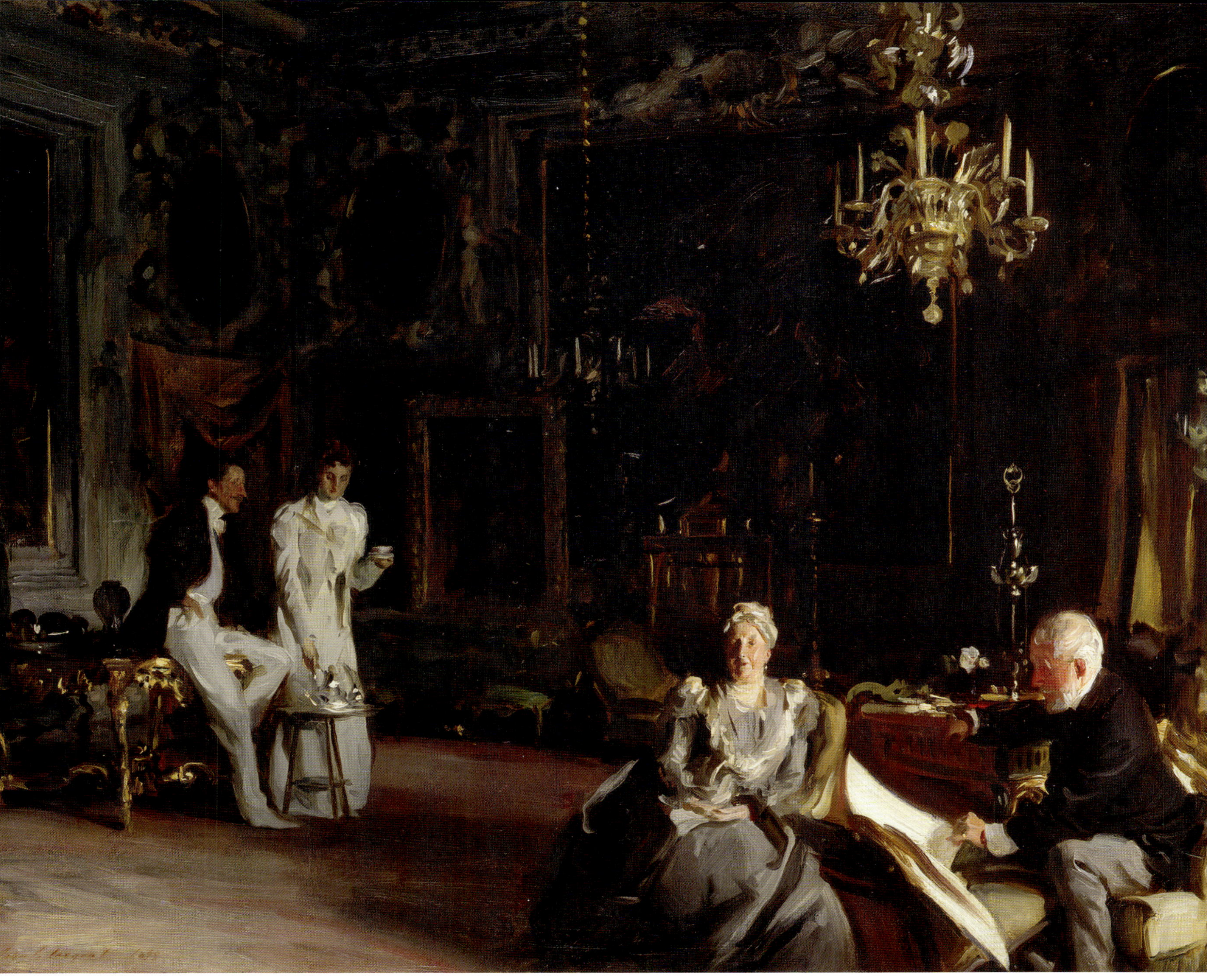

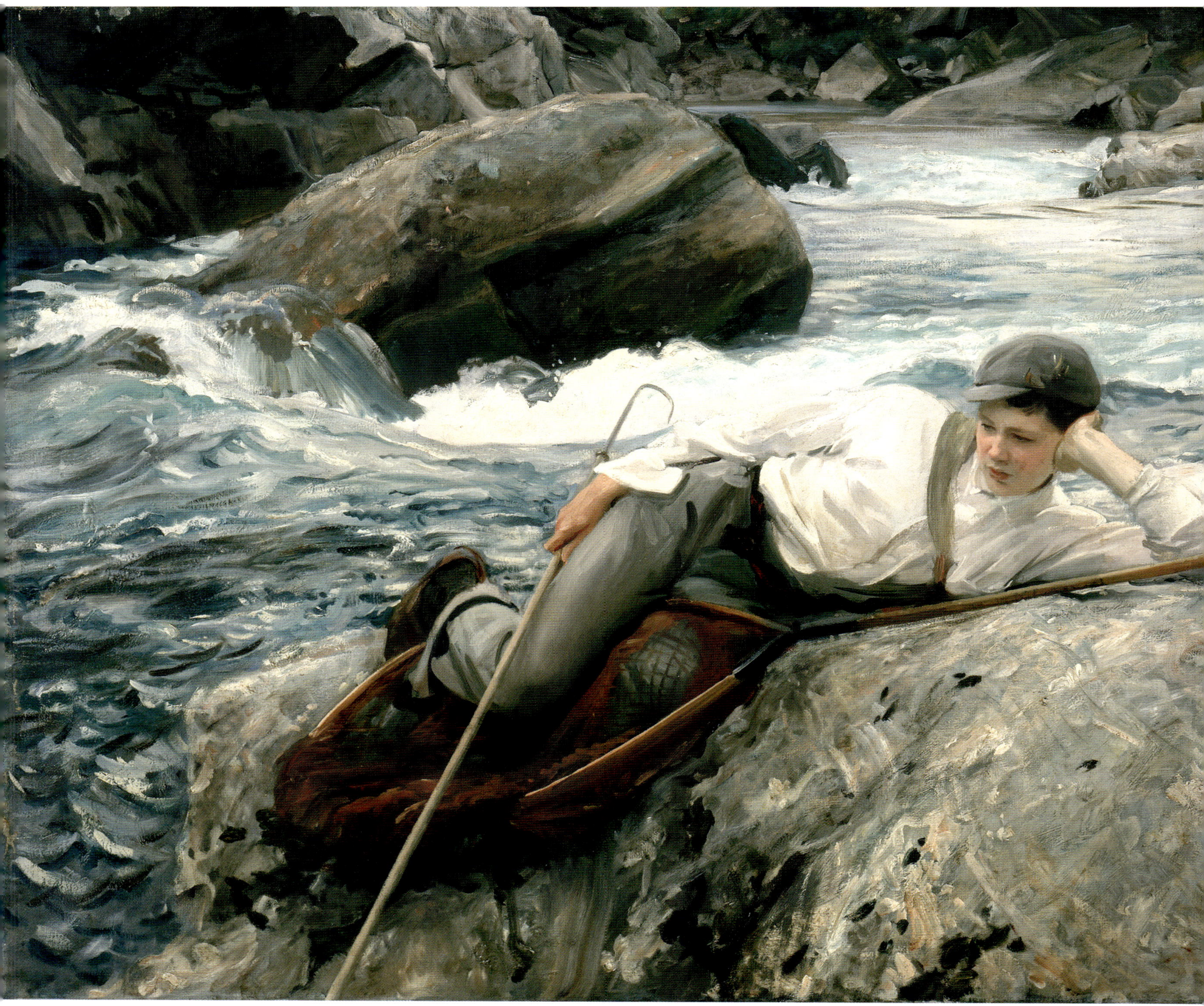

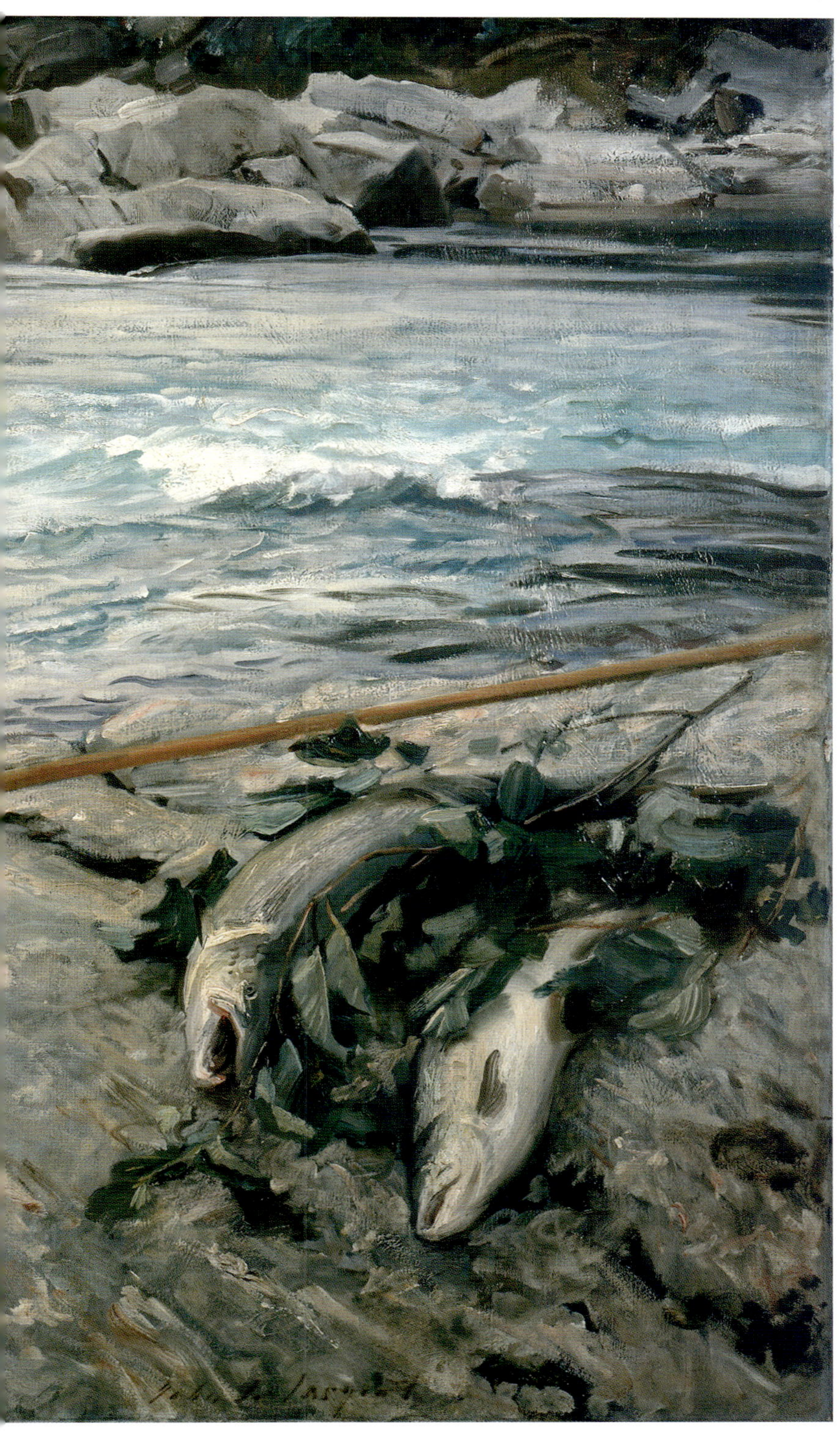

68

On His Holidays

1901
Oil on canvas, 53½ × 95½ in.
(137 × 244 cm)
Signed: "John S. Sargent"
Port Sunlight Village, Wirral,
Lady Lever Art Gallery [LL3136]

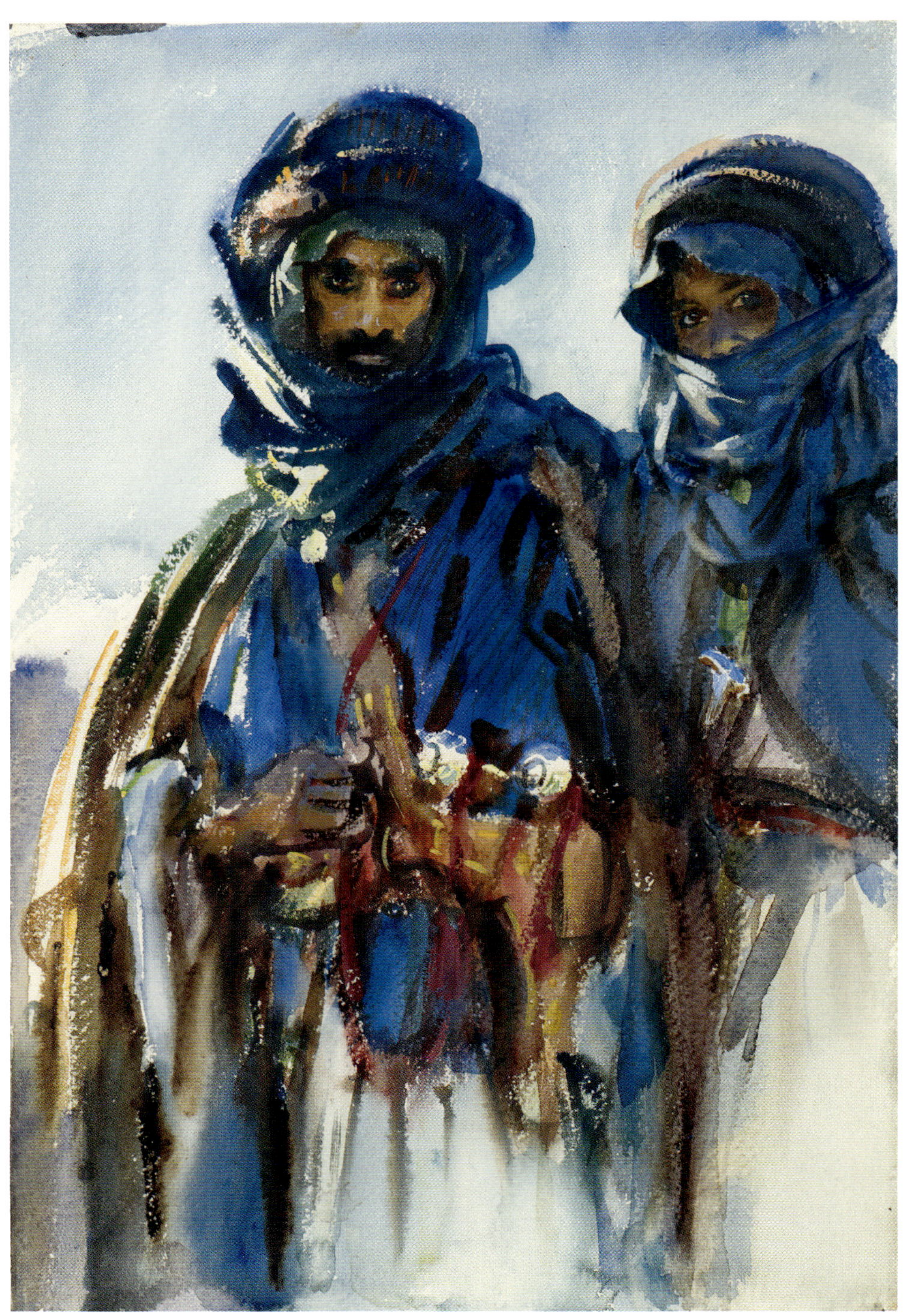

69

Bedouins

1905–6
Watercolor and gouache on paper,
18 × 12 in. (45.7 × 30.5 cm)
New York, Brooklyn Museum,
Purchased by Special Subscription
[09.814]

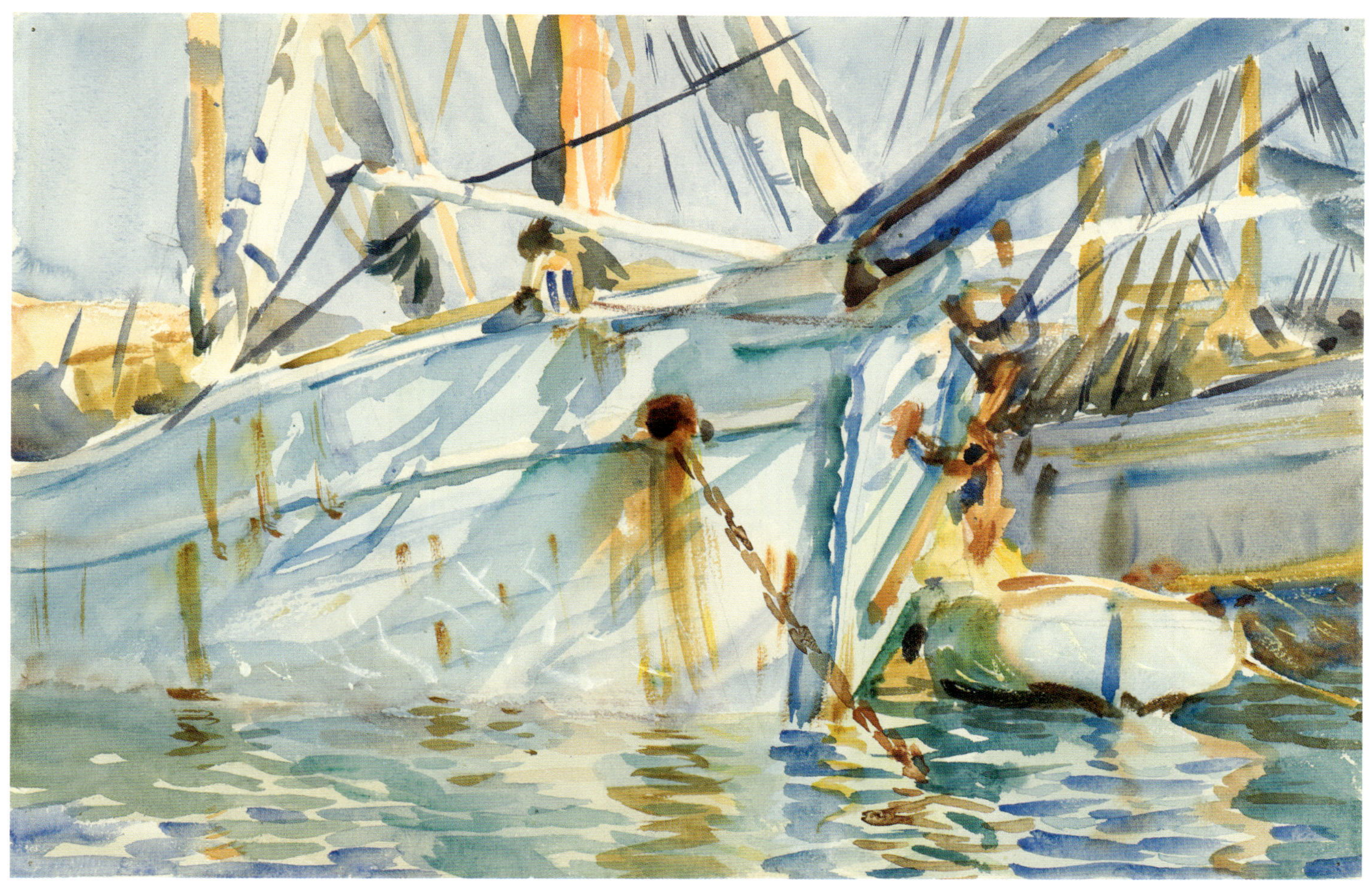

70

In a Levantine Port

1905–6
Watercolor, gouache, and graphite on paper, 12 1/16 × 18 1/8 in. (30.6 × 46 cm)
New York, Brooklyn Museum, Purchased by Special Subscription [09.825]

71

An Hotel Room

ca. 1904–6

Oil on canvas, 24 × 17½ in.

(61 × 44.5 cm)

Private collection

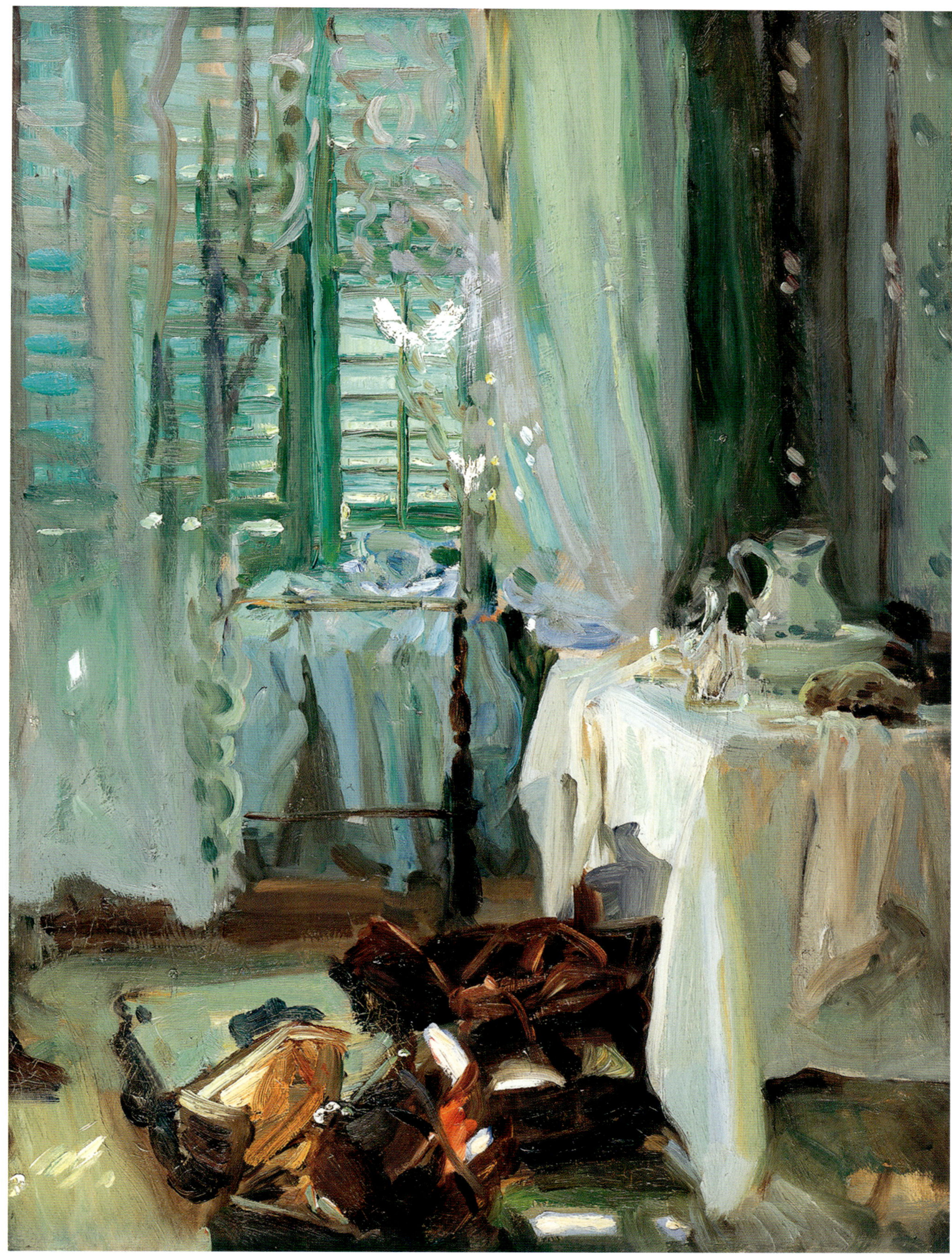

72

Santa Maria della Salute

1904
Watercolor and graphite on paper,
18 3/16 × 22 15/16 in. (46.2 × 58.3 cm)
Signed: "John S. Sargent 1904"
New York, Brooklyn Museum,
Purchased by Special Subscription
[09.838]

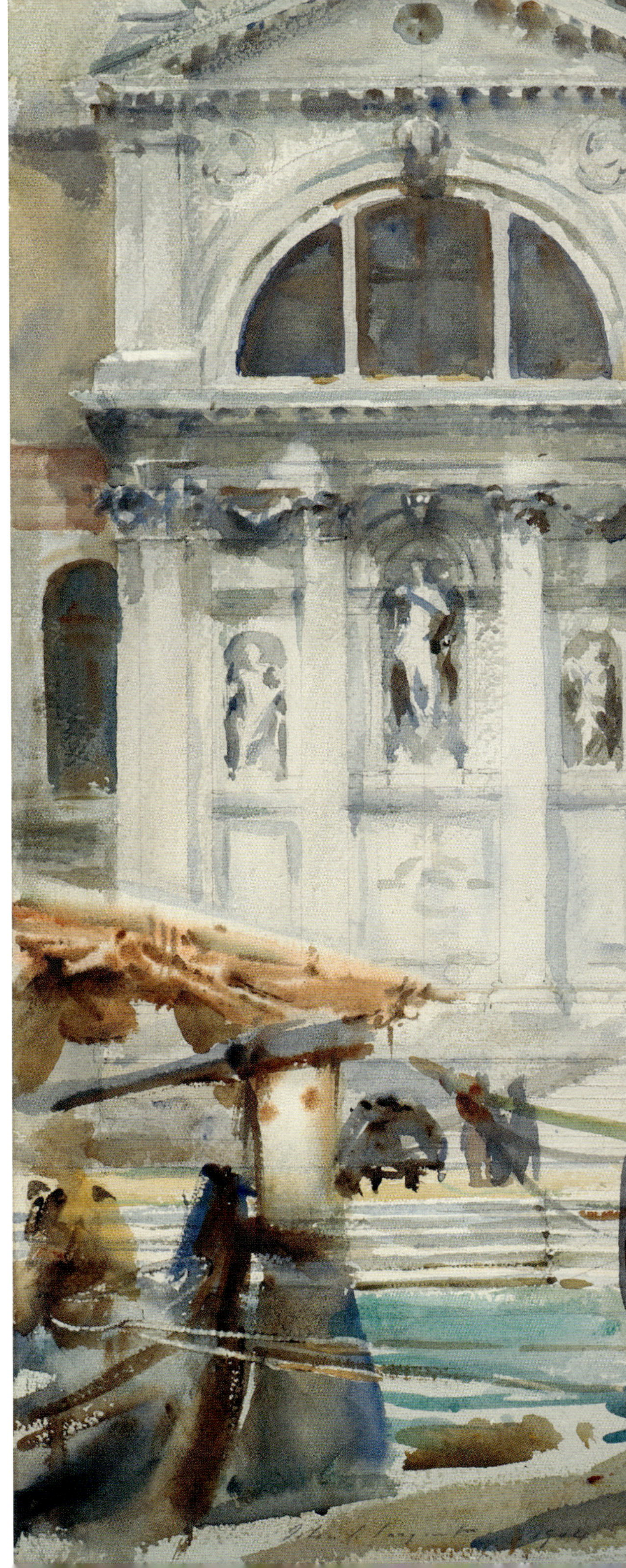

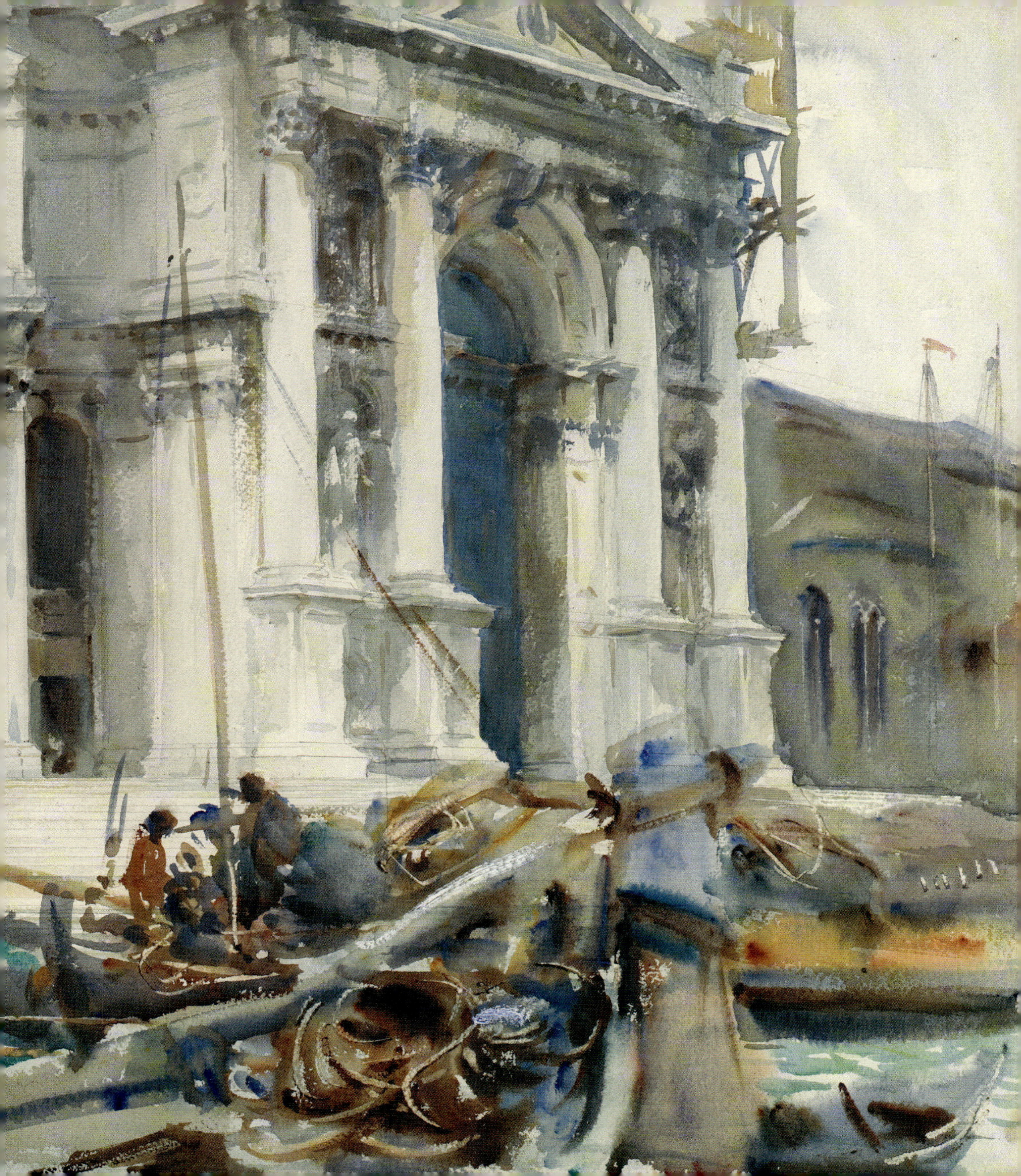

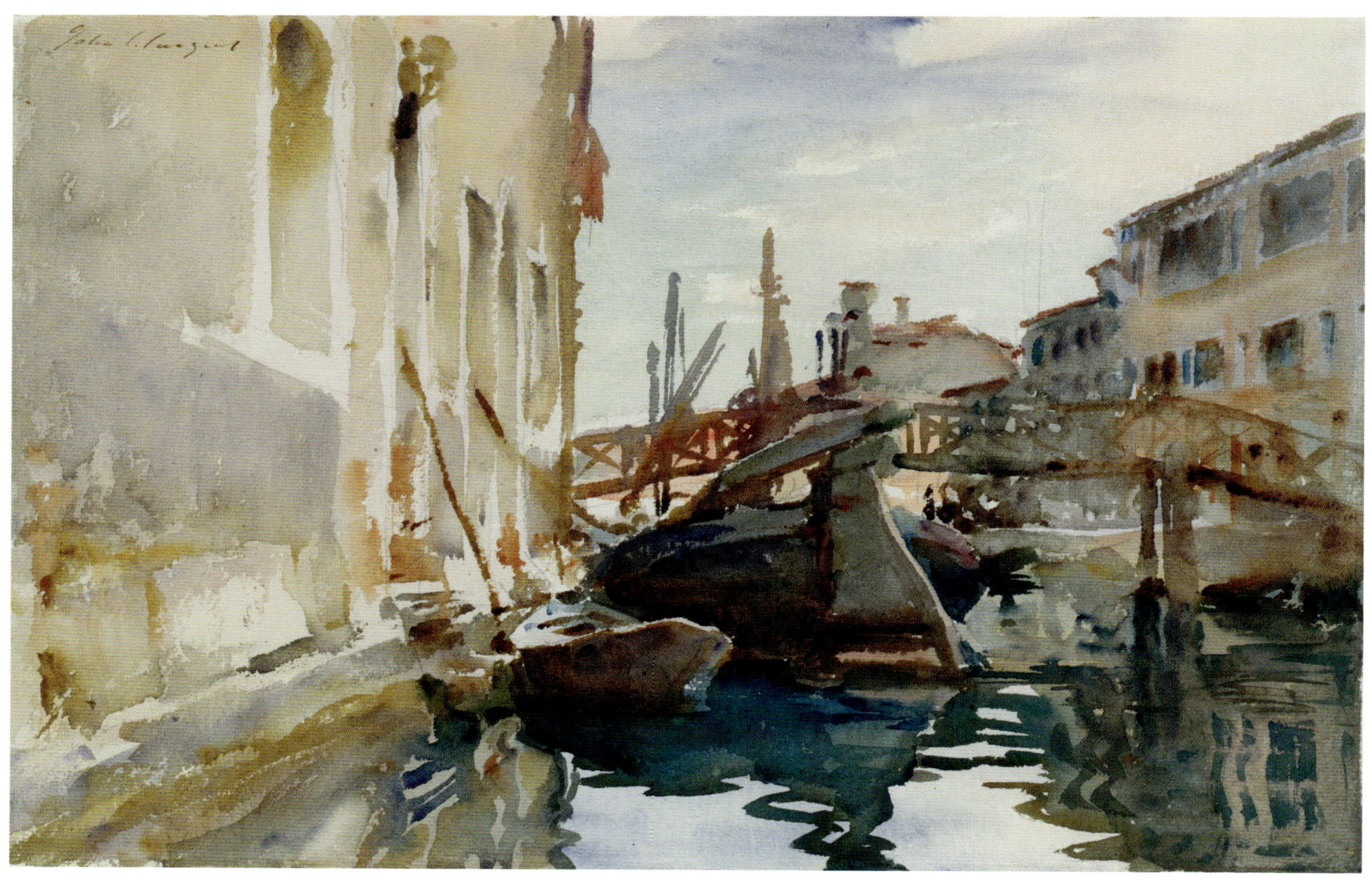

73

Giudecca

1913
Watercolor and graphite on paper,
$13\frac{1}{16} \times 20\frac{15}{16}$ in. (33.2 × 53.2 cm)
Signed: "John S. Sargent"
Inscriptions: "1574"; "(2)" (on verso)
New York, The Metropolitan Museum of Art,
Purchase, Joseph Pulitzer Bequest, 1915
[15.142.4]

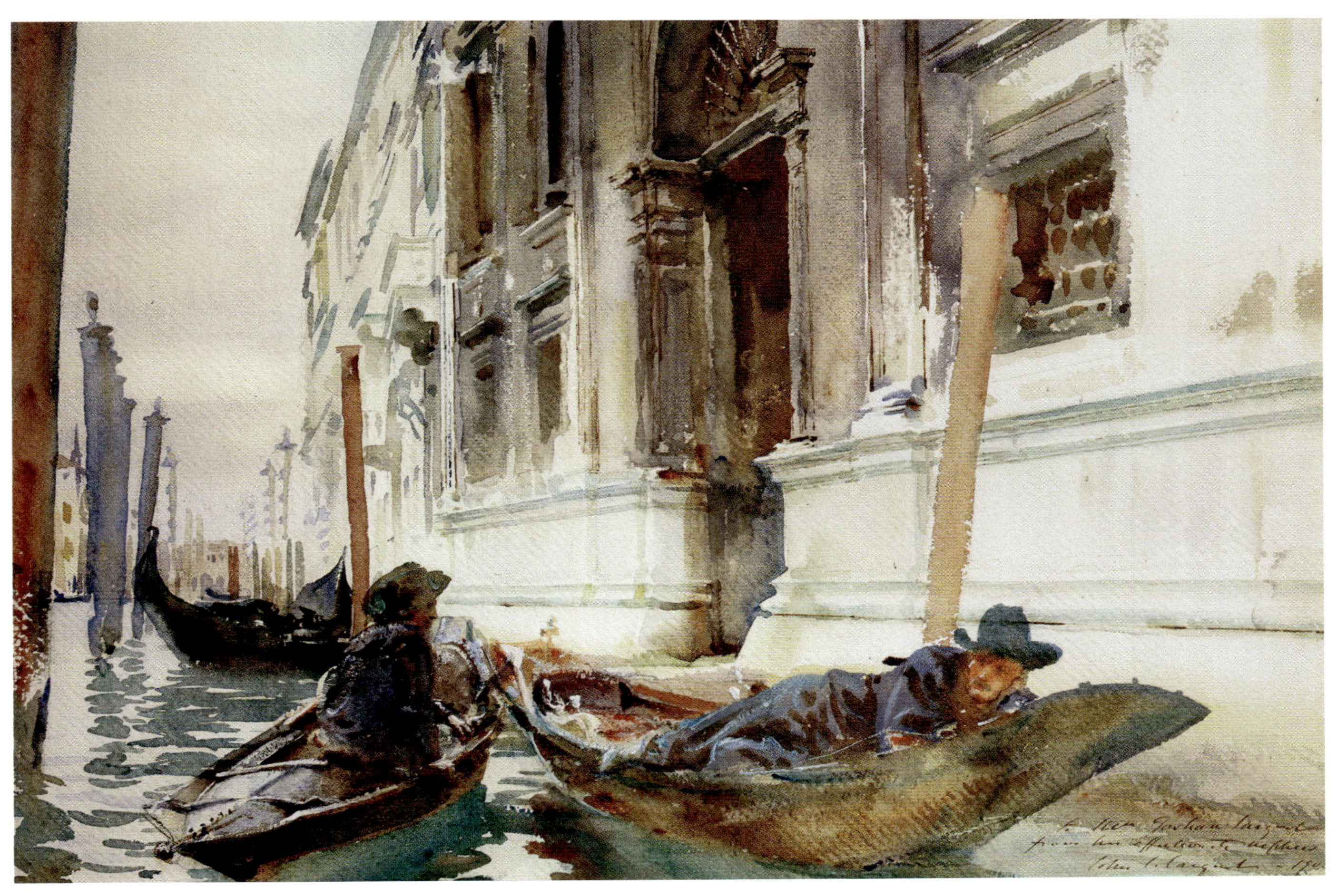

74

Gondoliers' Siesta

ca. 1902–3
Watercolor over pen and ink on paper,
14 × 20 in. (35.6 × 50.8 cm)
Inscription: "to Mrs Gorham Sargent / from her affectionate nephew / John S. Sargent-1905"
Private collection

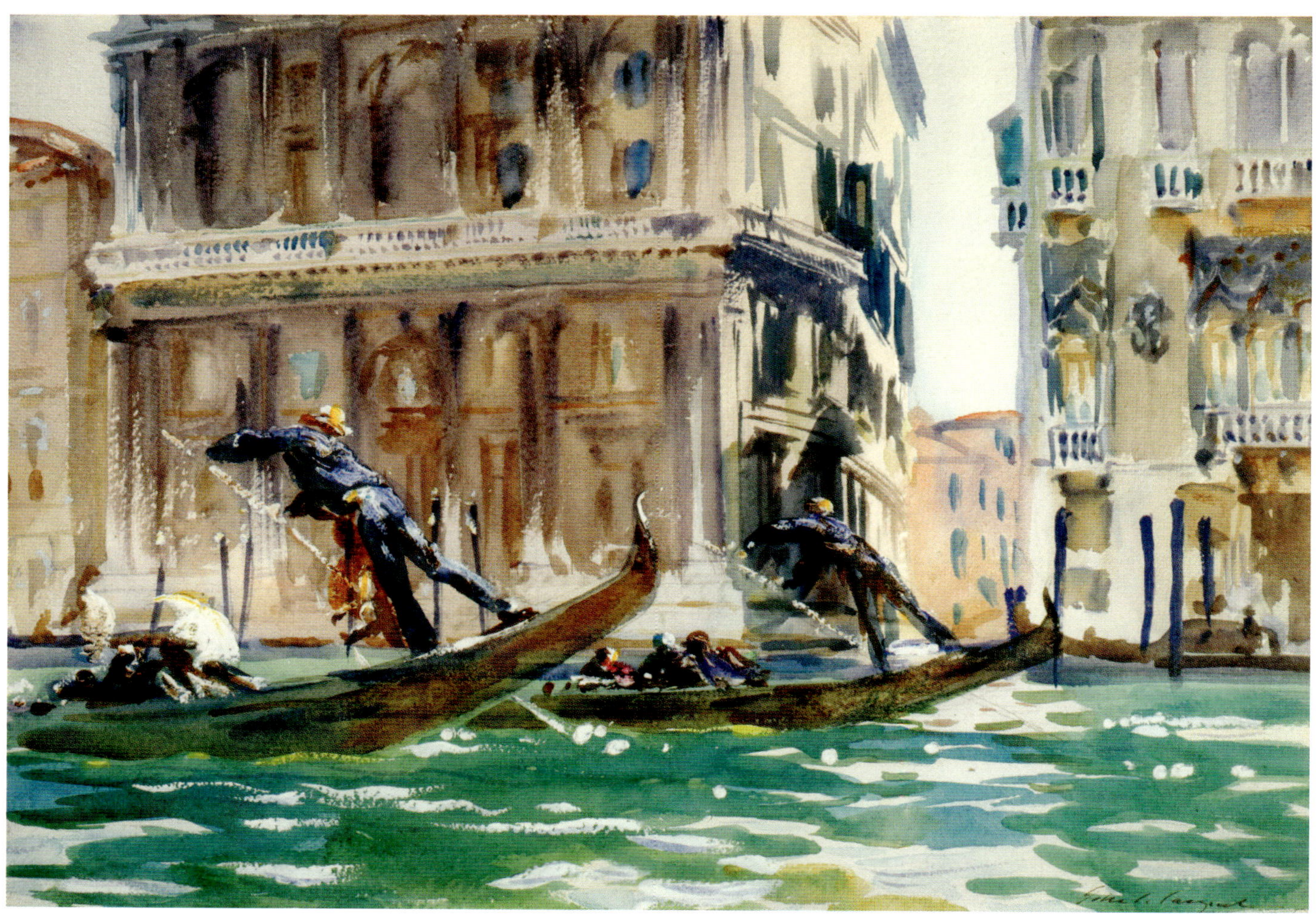

75

Vue de Venise (sur le canal)

ca. 1903
Watercolor and gouache on paper,
13½ × 19½ in. (35.1 × 49 cm)
Signed: "John S. Sargent"
Paris, Petit Palais, Musée des Beaux-Arts
de la Ville de Paris [PPD788]

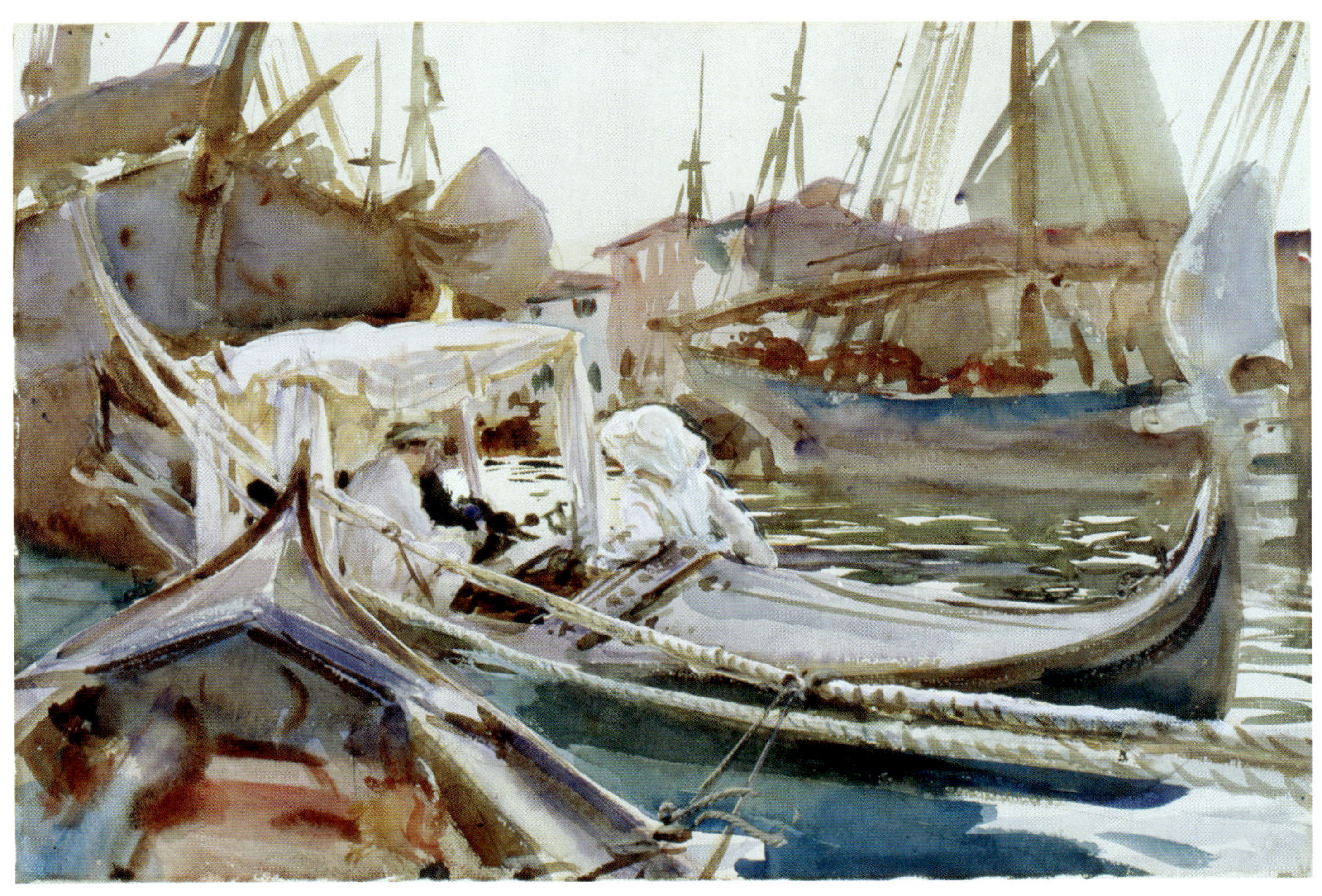

76

Sketching on the Giudecca

ca. 1904
Watercolor and pencil on paper, $14\frac{1}{2} \times 21$ in. (36.8×53.3 cm)
Private collection

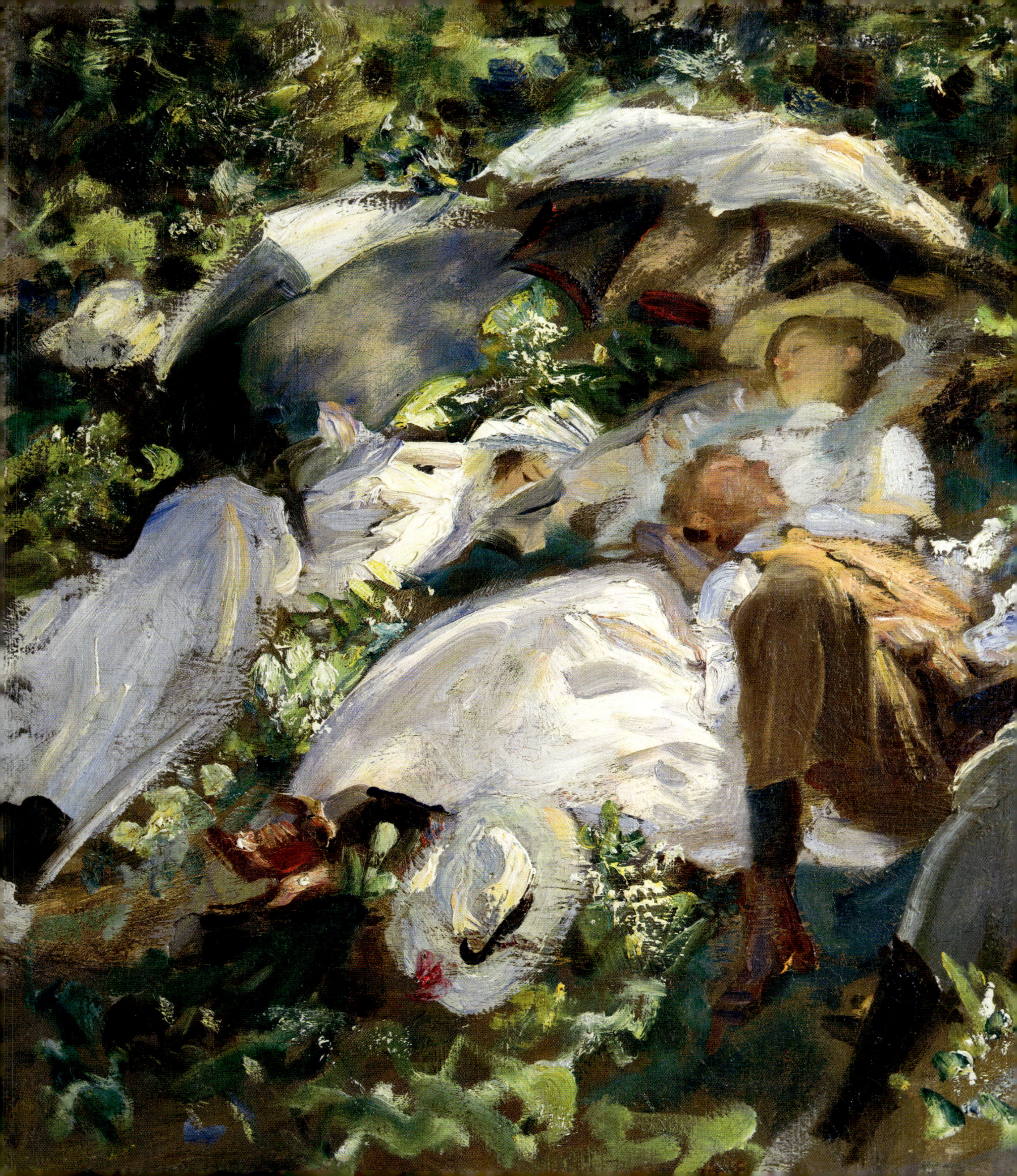

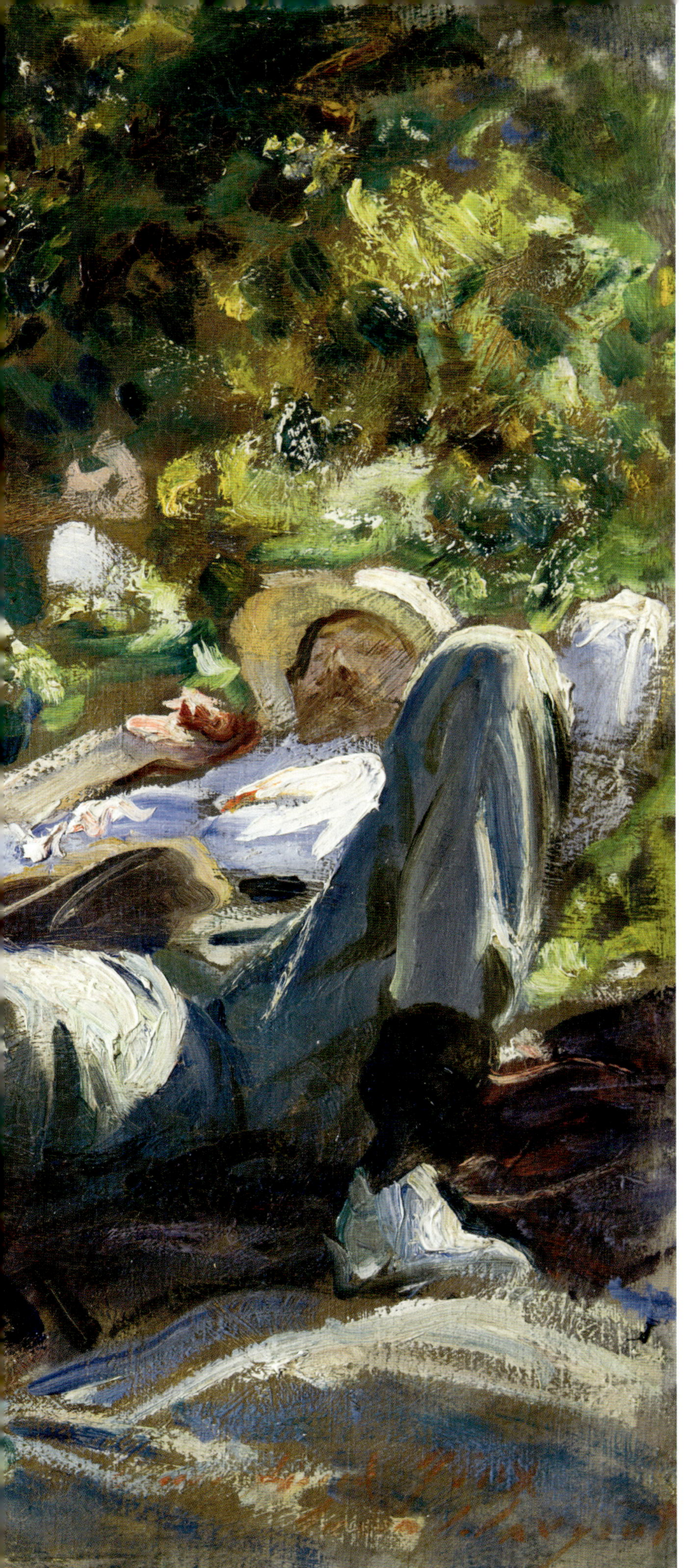

77

Group with Parasols (*Siesta*)

ca. 1904–5
Oil on canvas, 21 ¾ × 27 ⅞ in. (55.3 × 70.8 cm)
Inscription: "to my friend Ginx / John S. Sargent"
Private collection

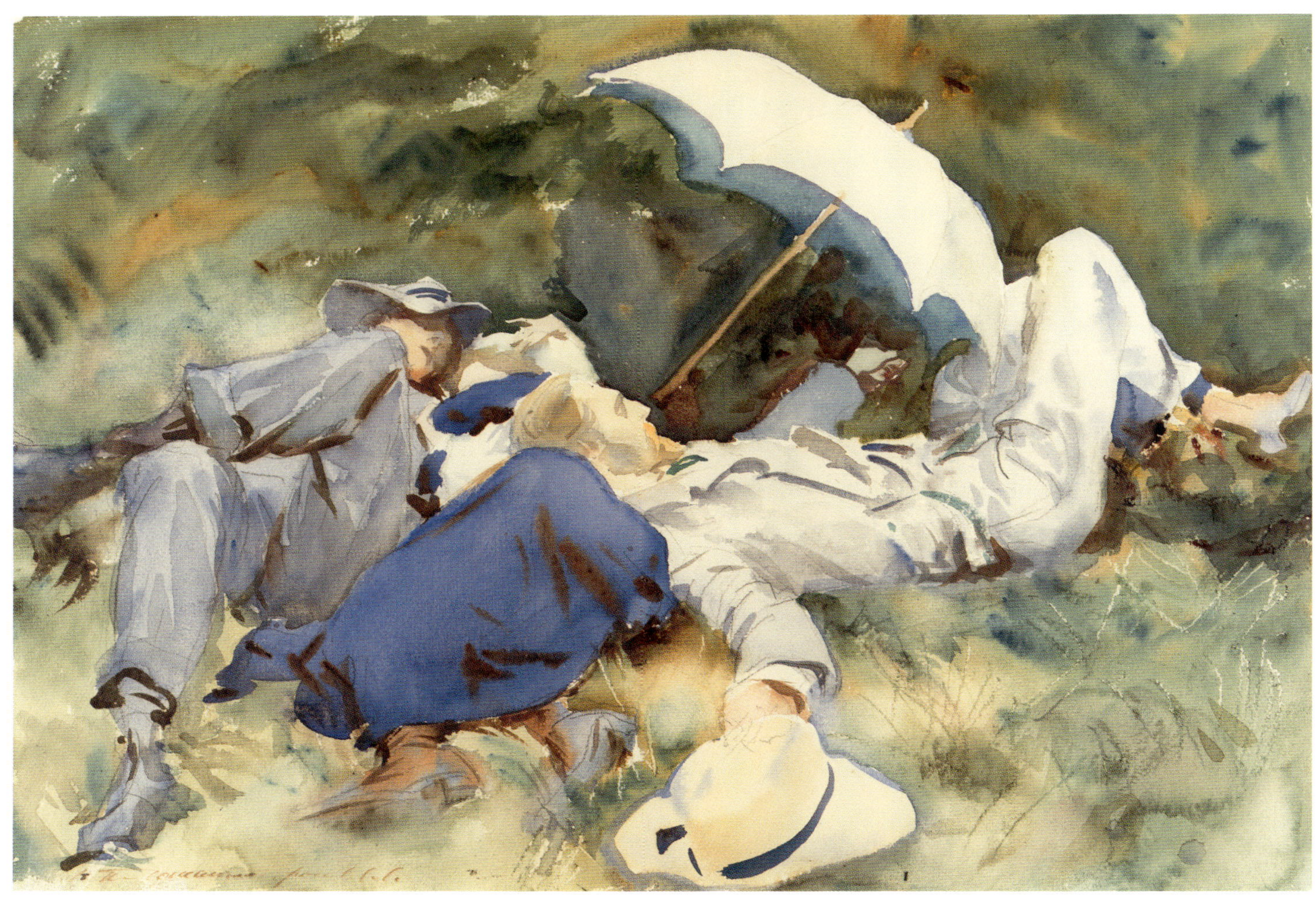

78

Group (*Siesta in a Swiss Wood*)

ca. 1904–5
Watercolor and graphite on paper, 13¾ × 19¾ in.
(34.9 × 50.2 cm)
Inscription: "to the comaniac from J. S. S."
John and Susan Klein

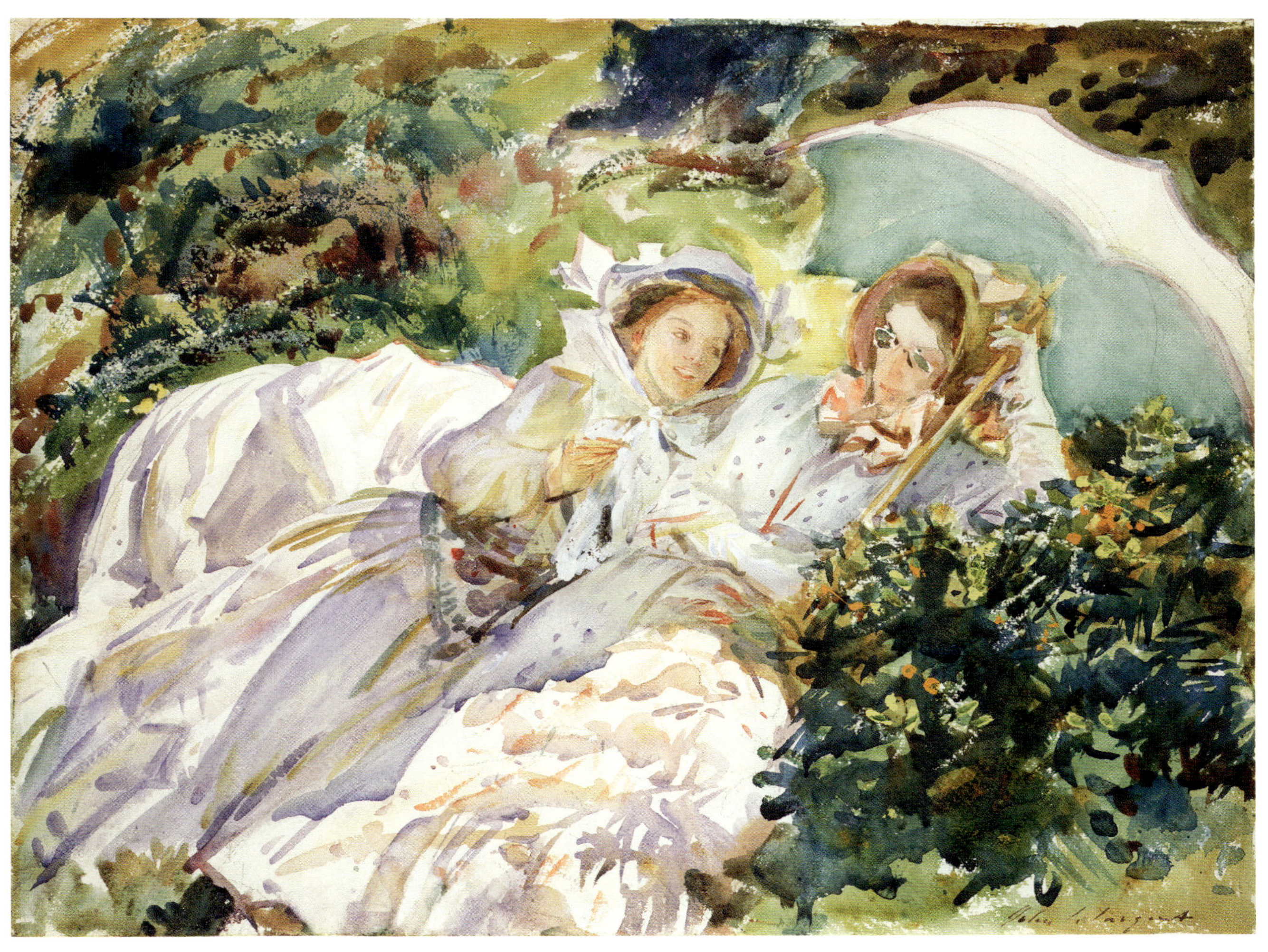

79

Simplon Pass: The Tease

ca. 1911
Watercolor, gouache, graphite, and wax resist on paper, 15 13/16 × 20 13/16 in. (40.2 × 52.9 cm)
Signed: "John S. Sargent"
Boston, Museum of Fine Arts, The Hayden Collection–Charles Henry Hayden Fund [12.216]

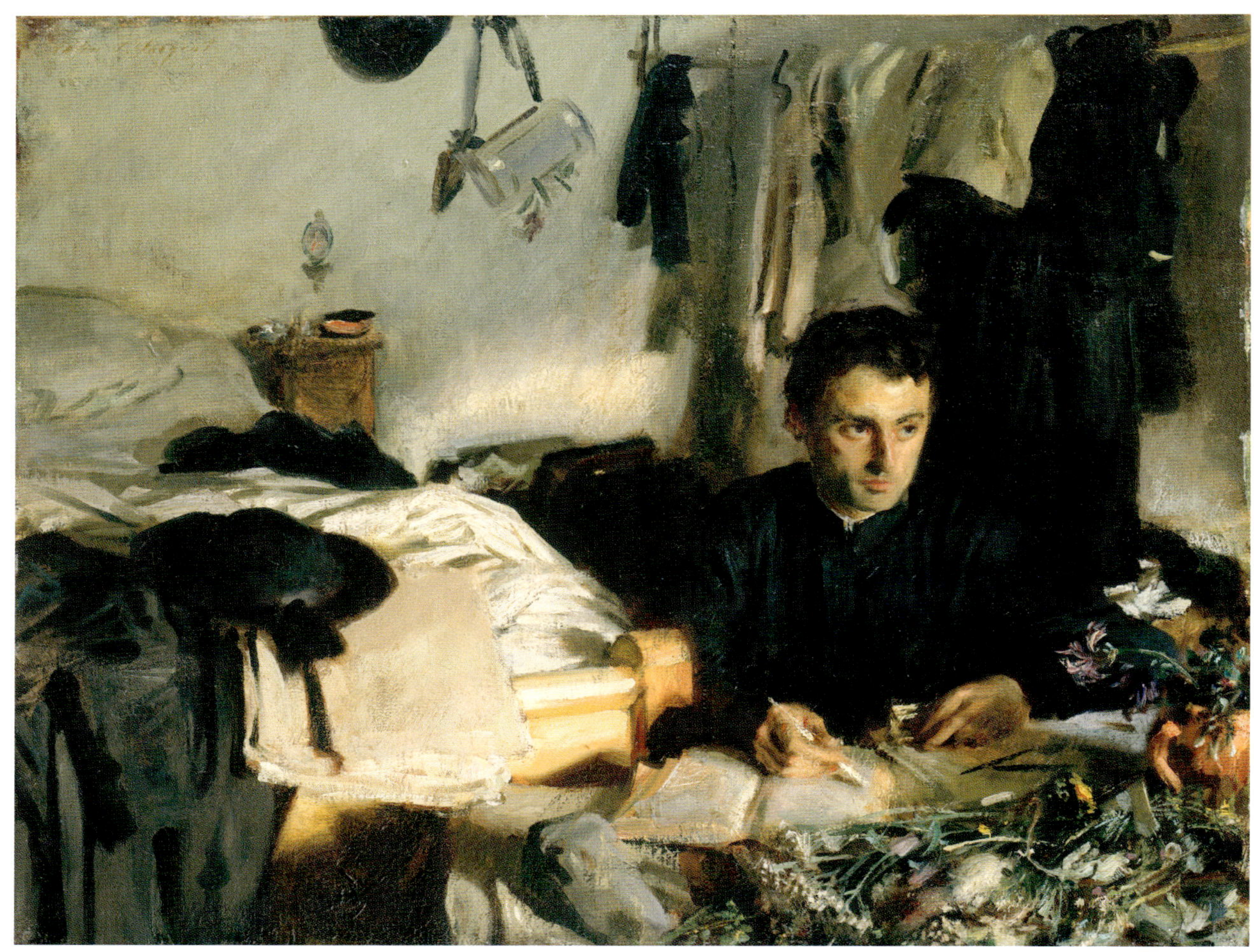

80

Padre Sebastiano

ca. 1905
Oil on canvas, 22¼ × 28 in. (56.5 × 71.1 cm)
Signed: "John S. Sargent"
New York, The Metropolitan Museum of Art,
Rogers Fund, 1910 [11.30]

81

The Hermit (*Il Solitario*)

ca. 1907
Oil on canvas, 37¾ × 38 in. (95.9 × 96.5 cm)
Signed: "John S. Sargent"
New York, The Metropolitan Museum of Art,
Rogers Fund, 1911 [11.31]

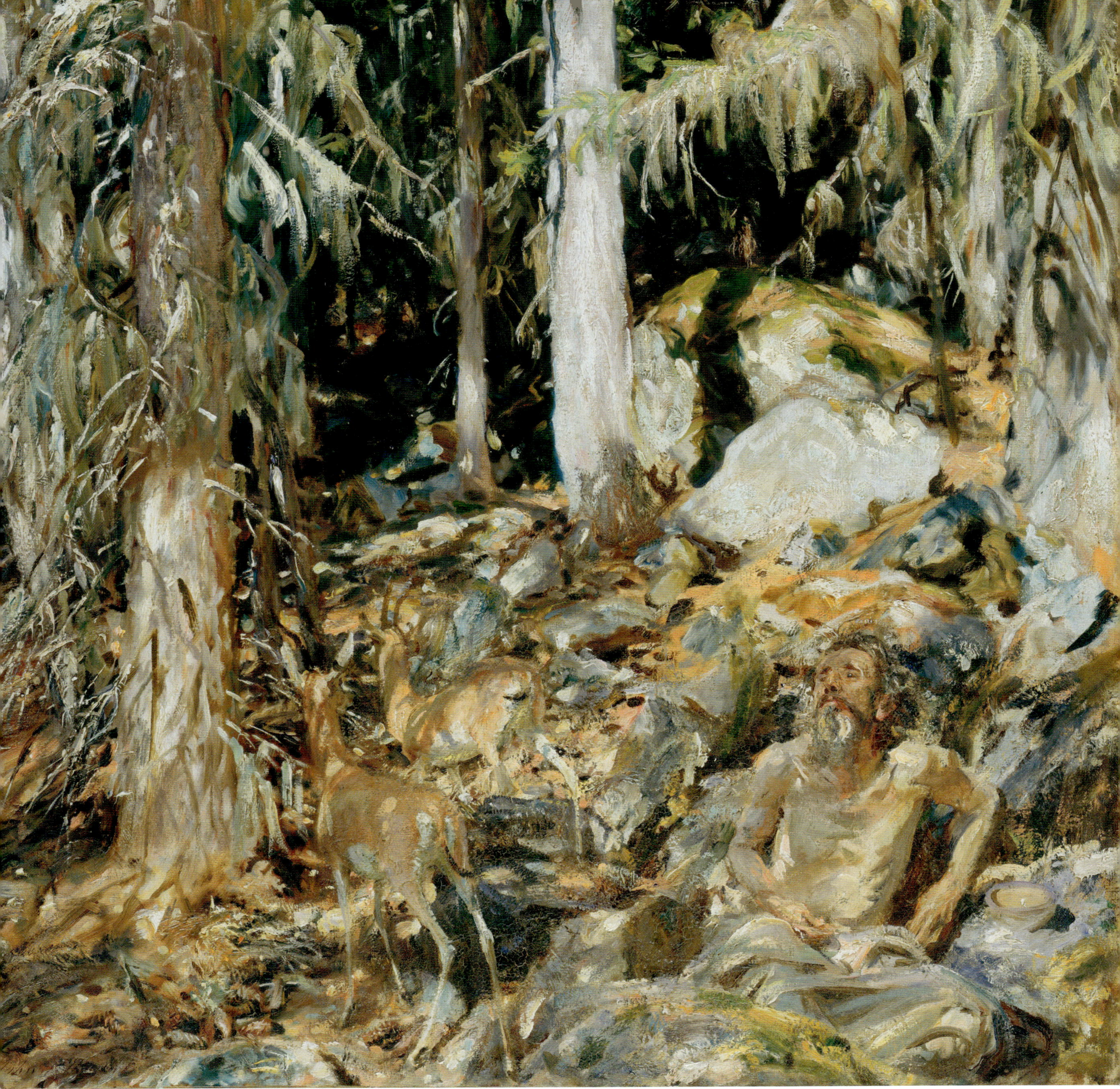

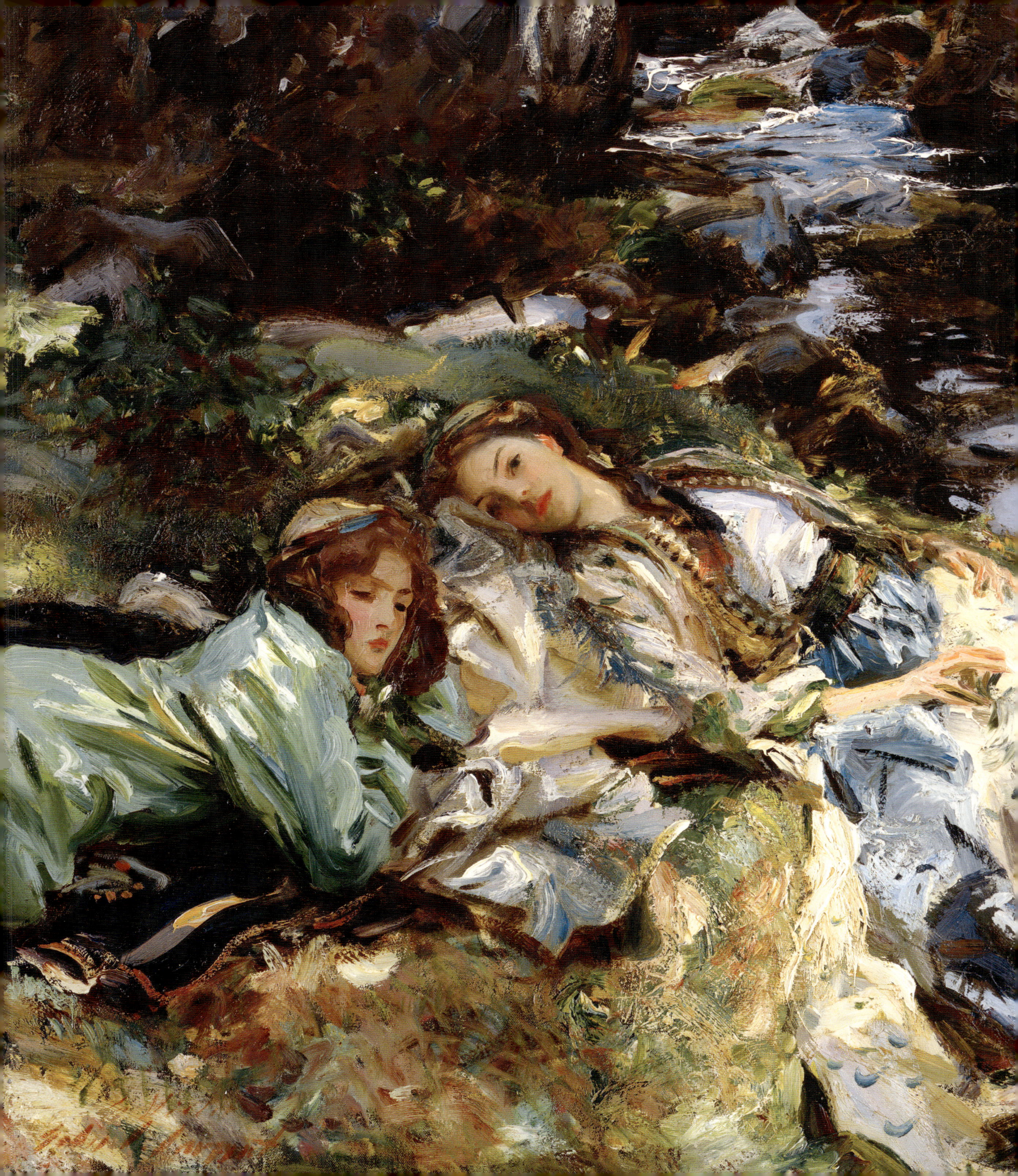

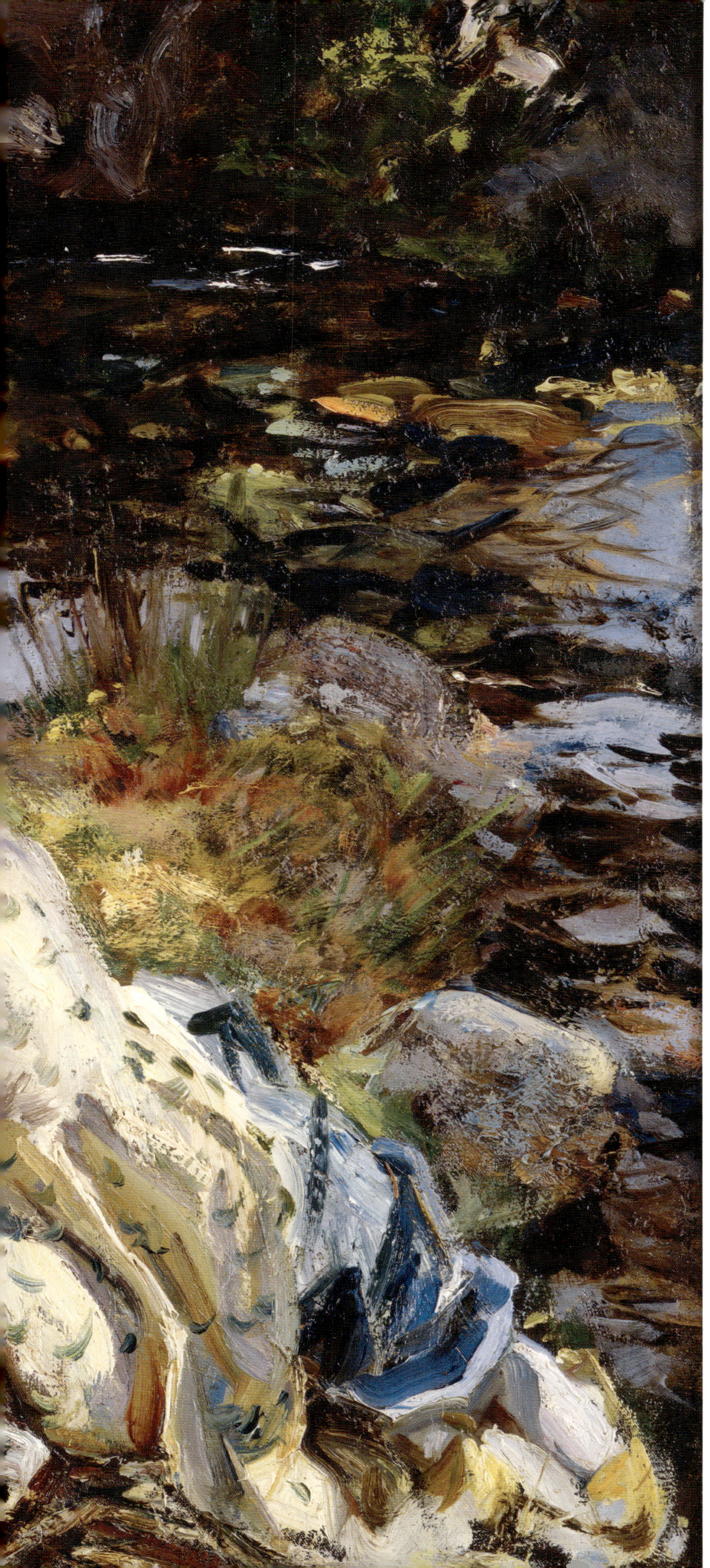

82

The Brook

1907
Oil on canvas, 21 × 27½ in. (53.3 × 69.9 cm)
Inscription: "to Violet / John S. Sargent"
Private collection

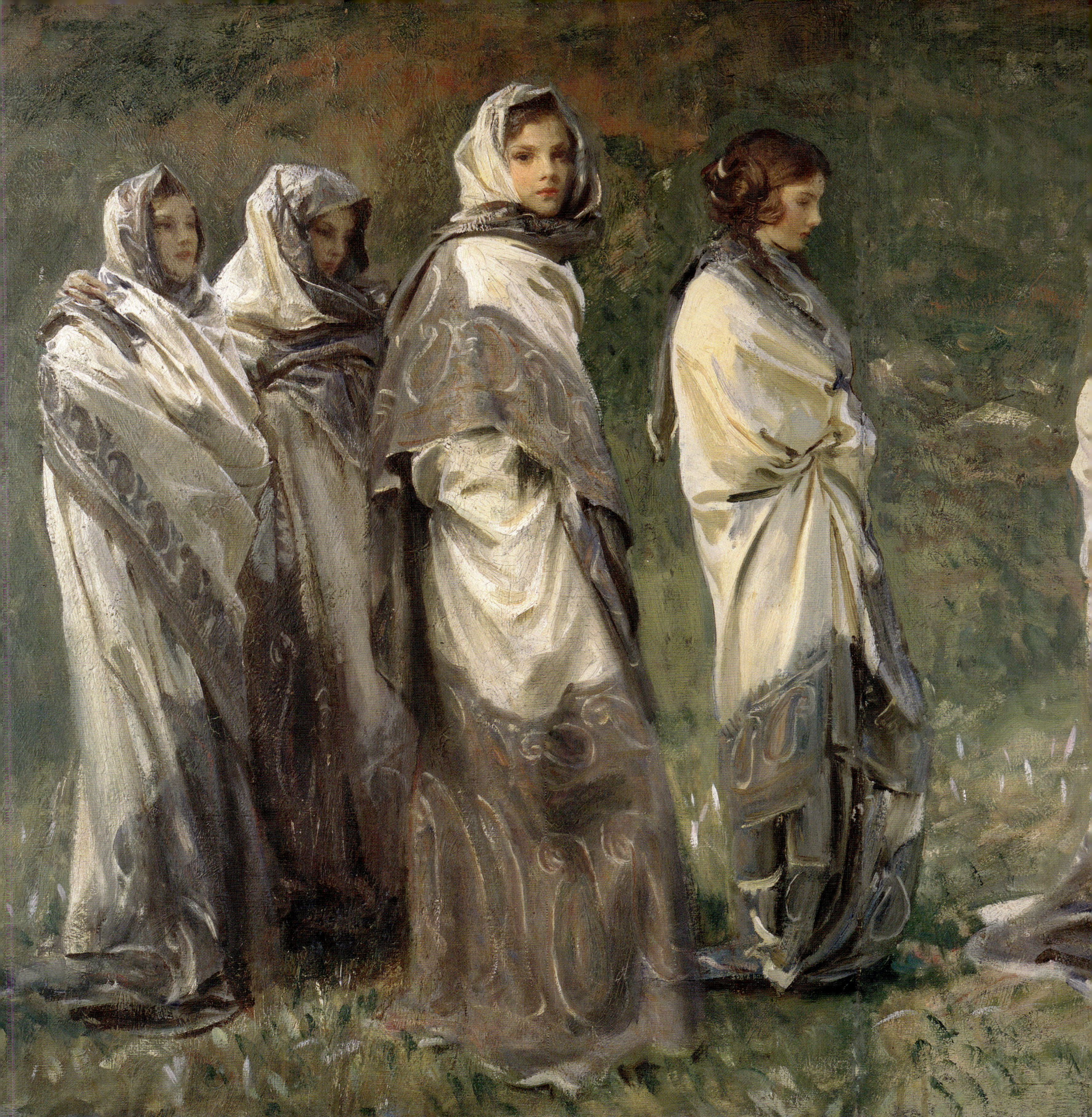

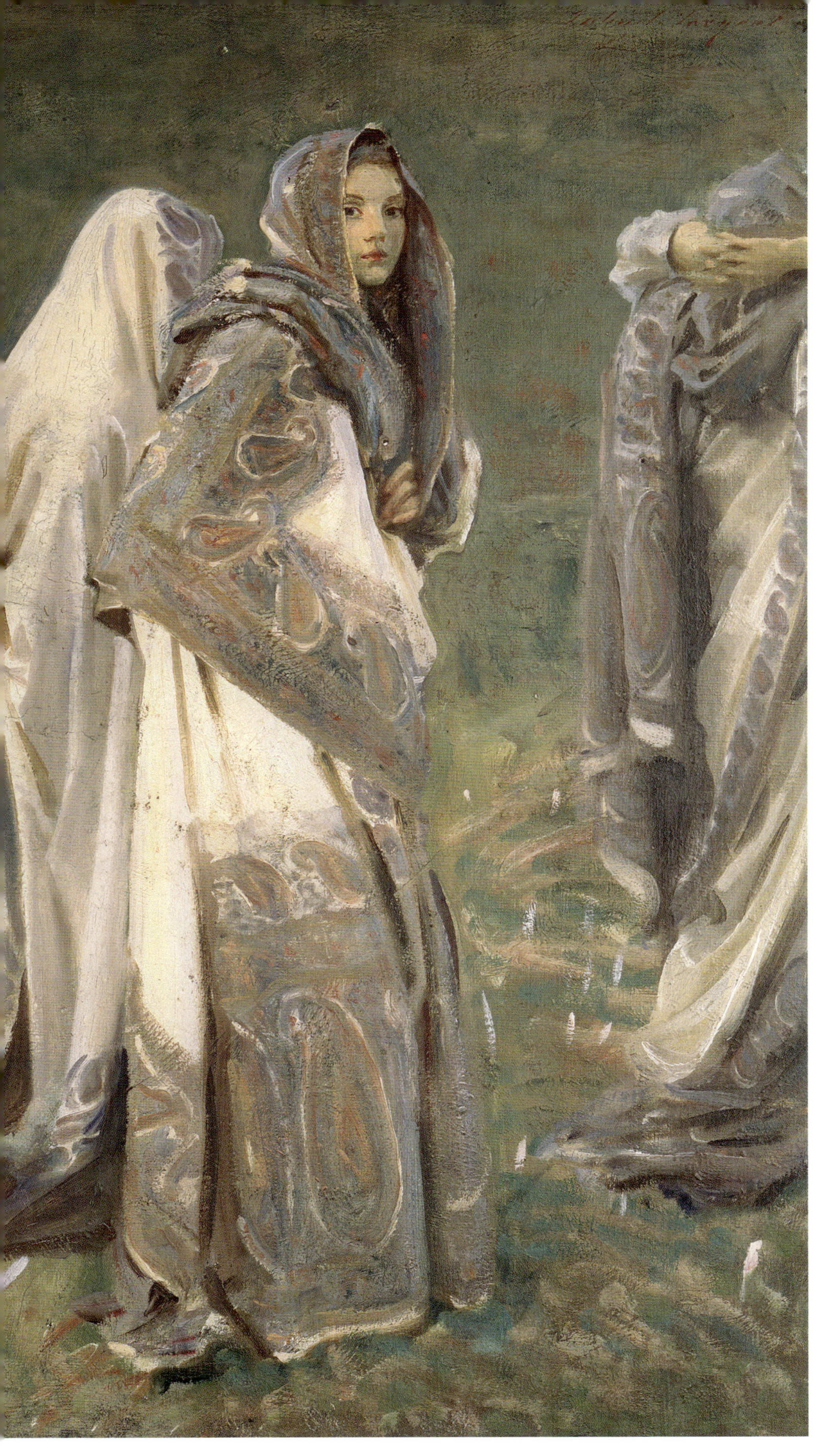

83

Cashmere

ca. 1908
Oil on canvas, 28 × 43 in.
(71.1 × 109.2 cm)
Signed: "John S. Sargent"
Private collection

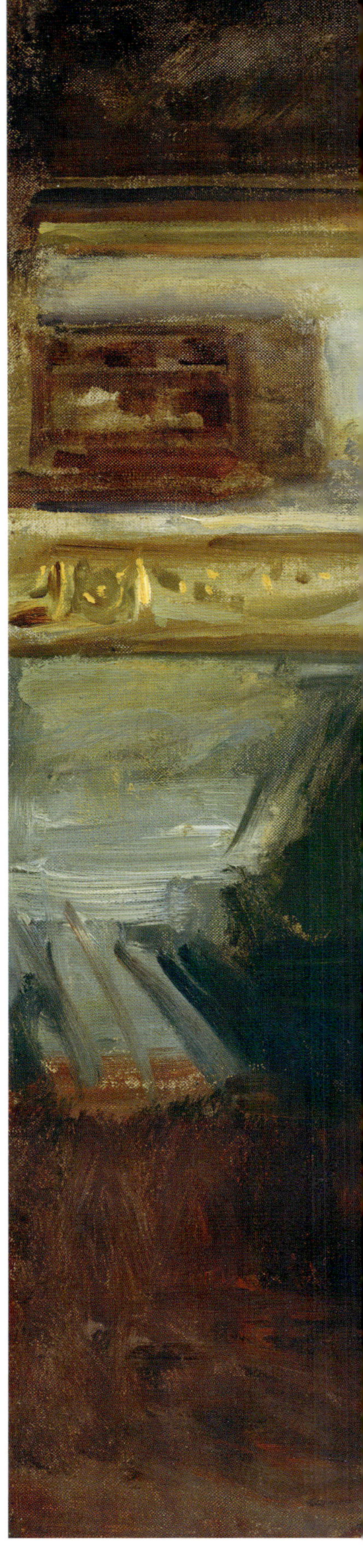

84

Nonchaloir (*Repose*)

1911
Oil on canvas, 25⅛ × 30 in. (63.8 × 76.2 cm)
Signed: "John S. Sargent 1911"
Washington, D.C., National Gallery of Art,
Gift of Curt H. Reisinger [1948.16.1]

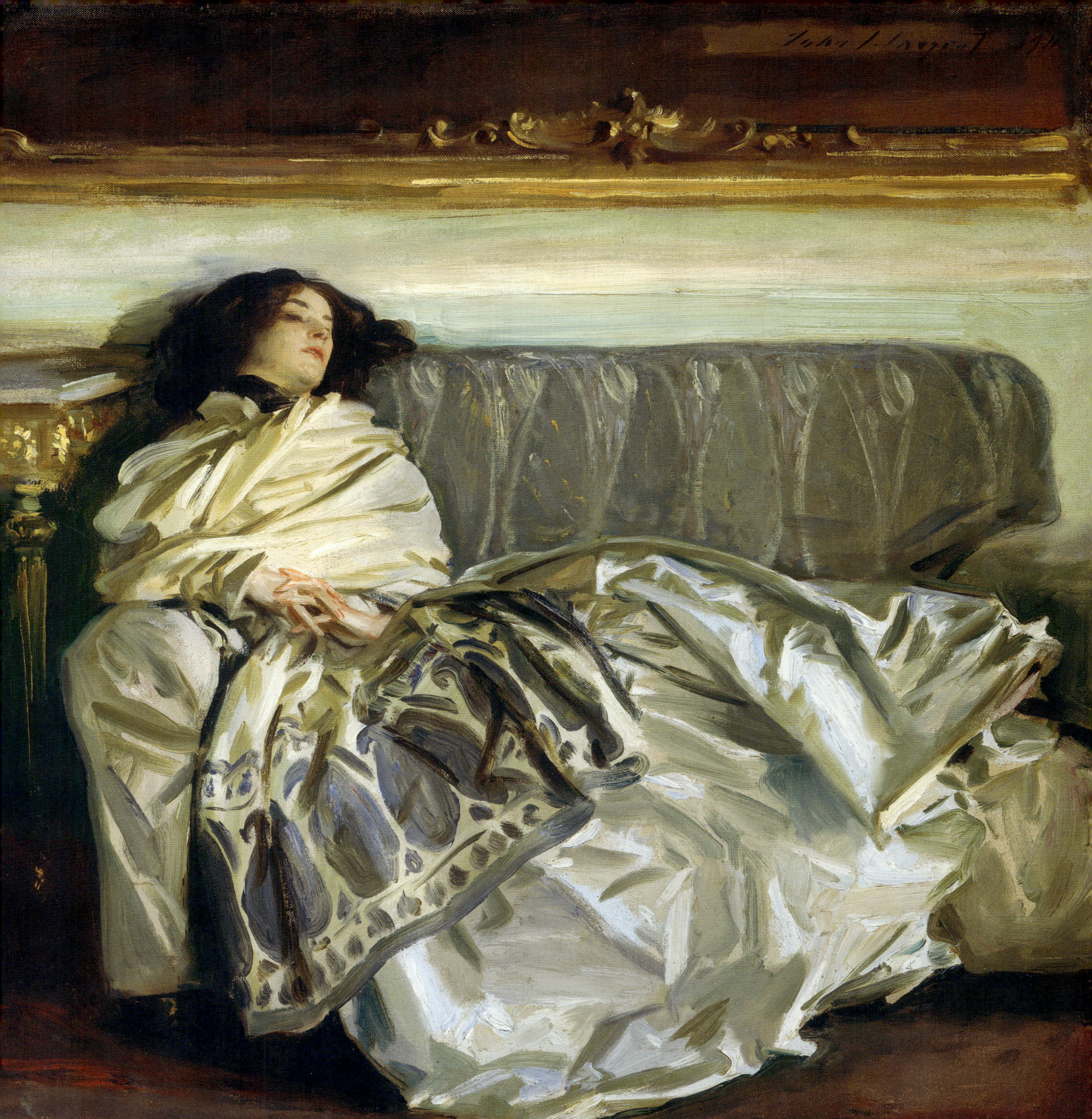

85

The Fountain, Villa Torlonia, Frascati, Italy

1907

Oil on canvas, 28⅛ × 22¼ in. (71.4 × 56.5 cm)

Signed: "John S. Sargent"

Chicago, Illinois, Art Institute of Chicago, Friends of American Art Collection [1914.57]

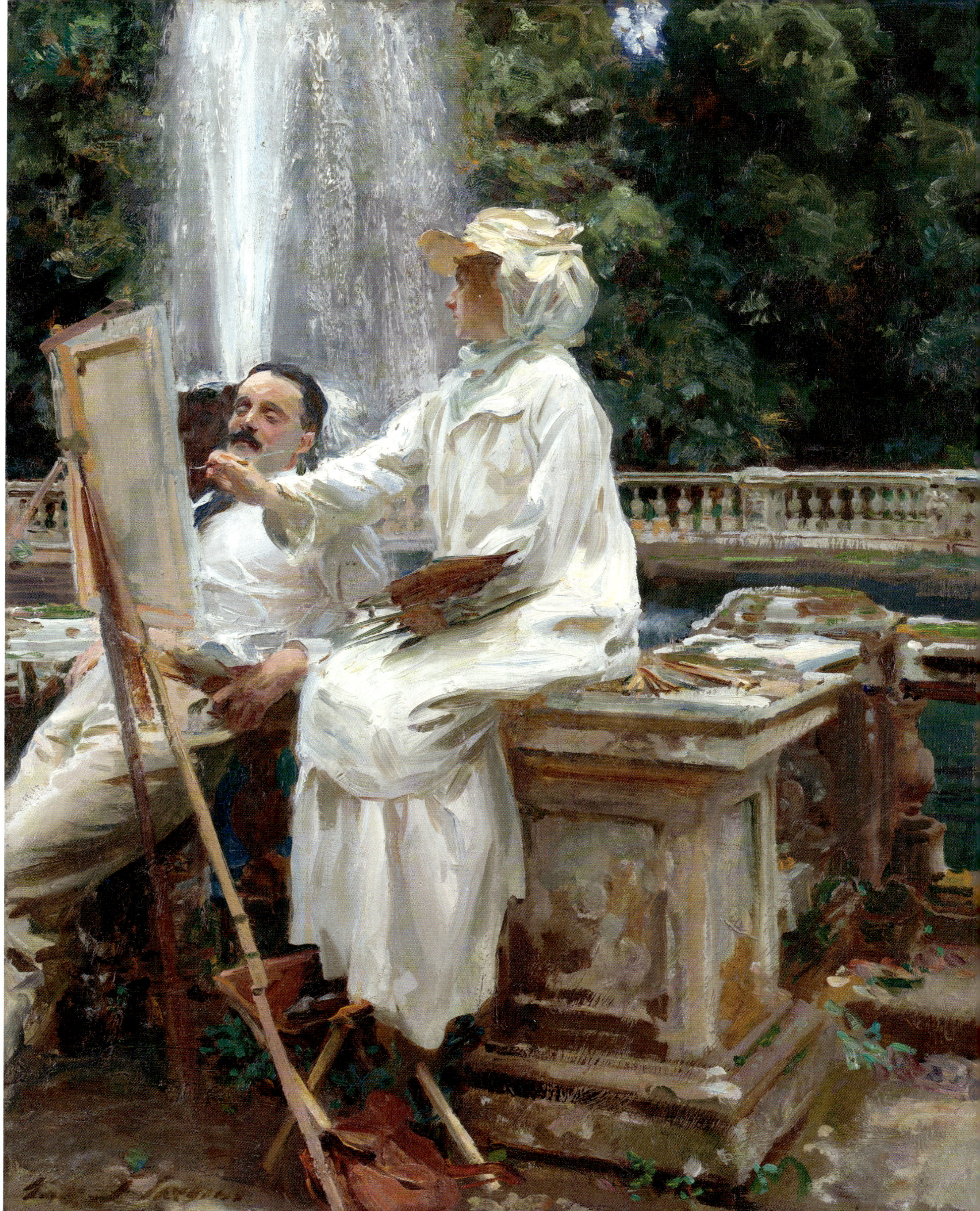

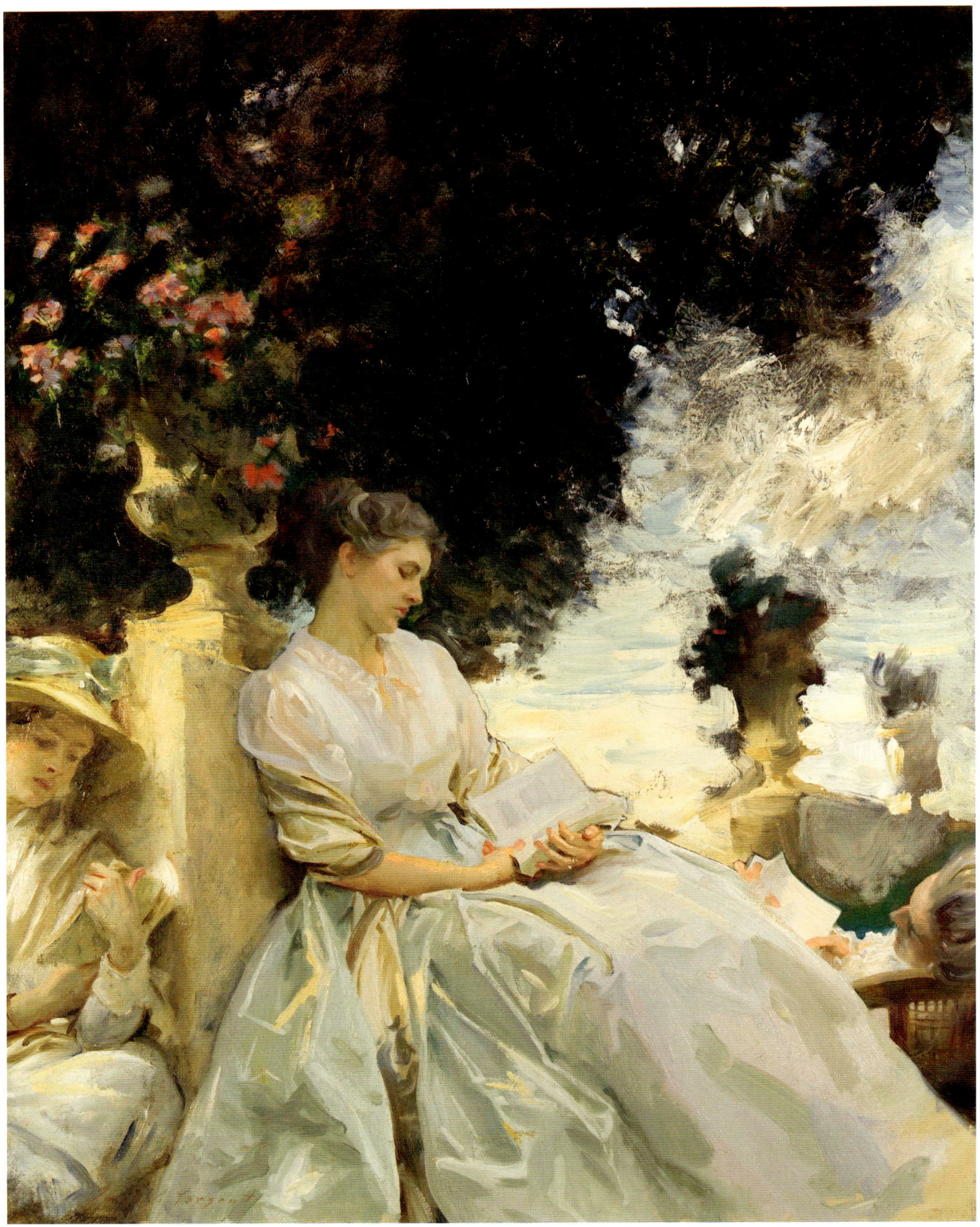

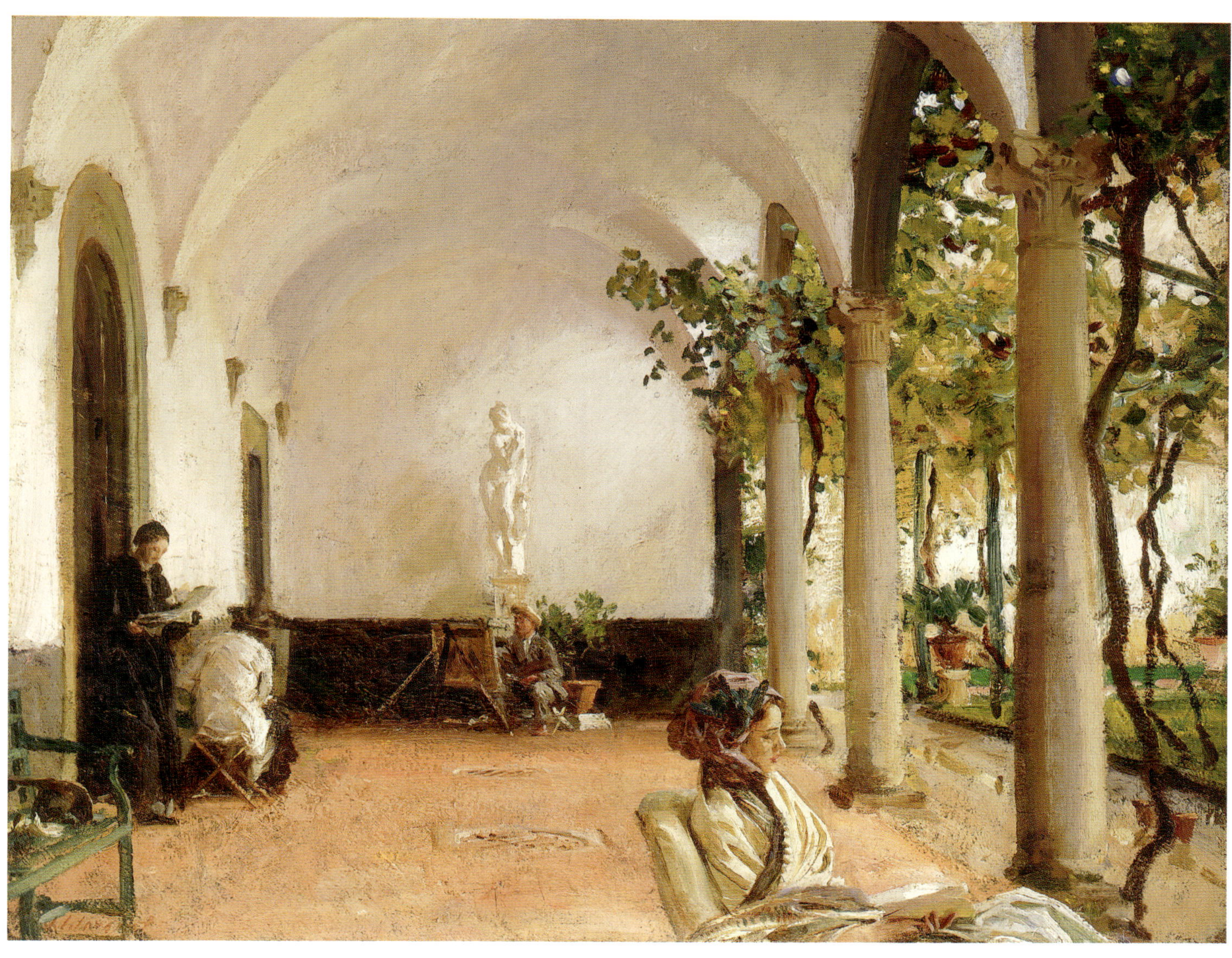

86

A Garden at Corfu

1909
Oil on canvas, 36 × 28 ⅛ in.
(91.4 × 71.4 cm)
Signed: "John S. Sargent"
Private collection

87

Villa Torre Galli: The Loggia

1910
Oil on canvas, 22 × 28 in. (55.9 × 71.1 cm)
Signed: "J. S. Sargent"
Private collection

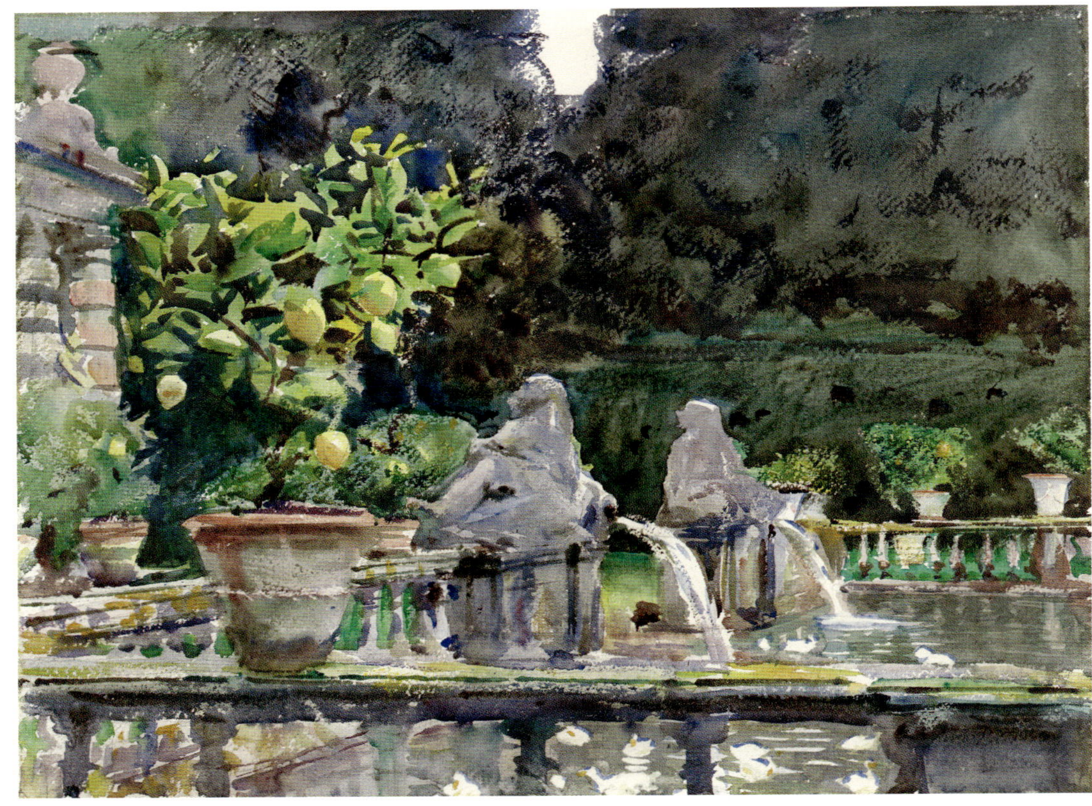

88

Villa di Marlia, Lucca: A Fountain

1910
Watercolor, gouache, graphite, and wax resist on paper, 15⅞ × 20⅞ in. (40.4 × 53.1 cm)
Boston, Museum of Fine Arts, The Hayden Collection–Charles Henry Hayden Fund [12.233]

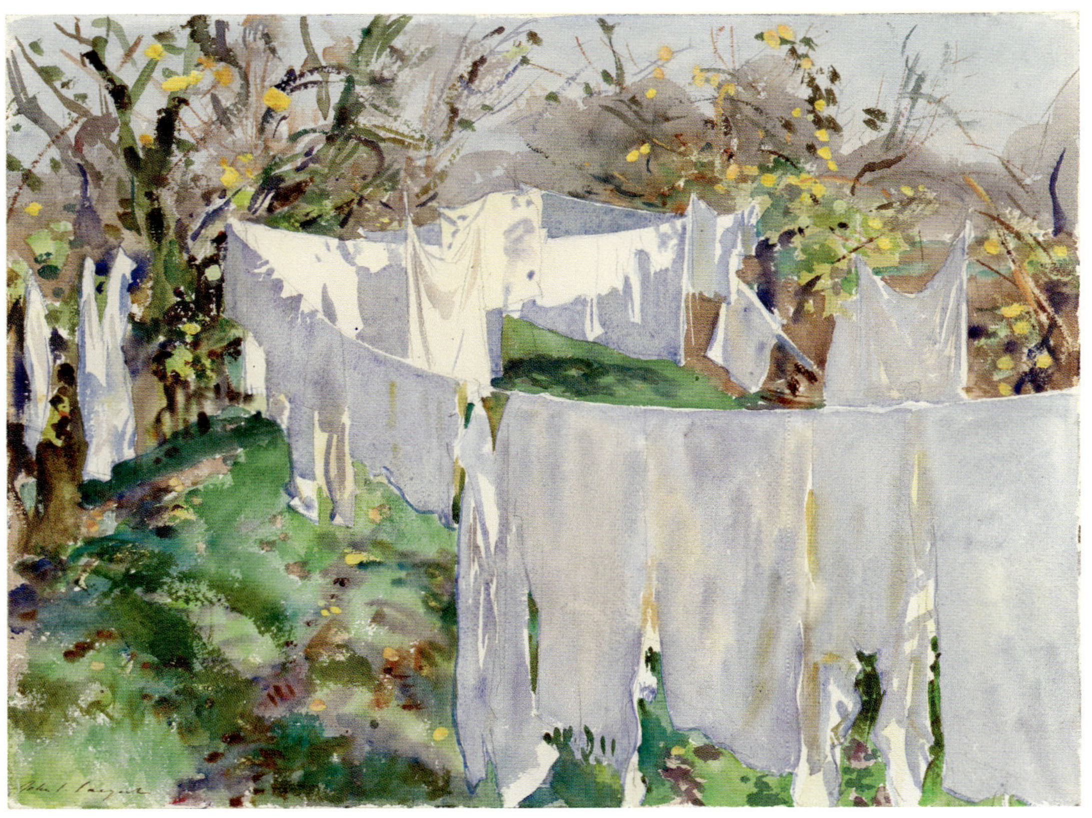

89

La Biancheria

1910
Watercolor, gouache, graphite, and wax resist on paper, 15⅞ × 20⅞ in. (40.4 × 53.1 cm)
Signed: "John S. Sargent"
Boston, Museum of Fine Arts, The Hayden Collection–Charles Henry Hayden Fund [12.229]

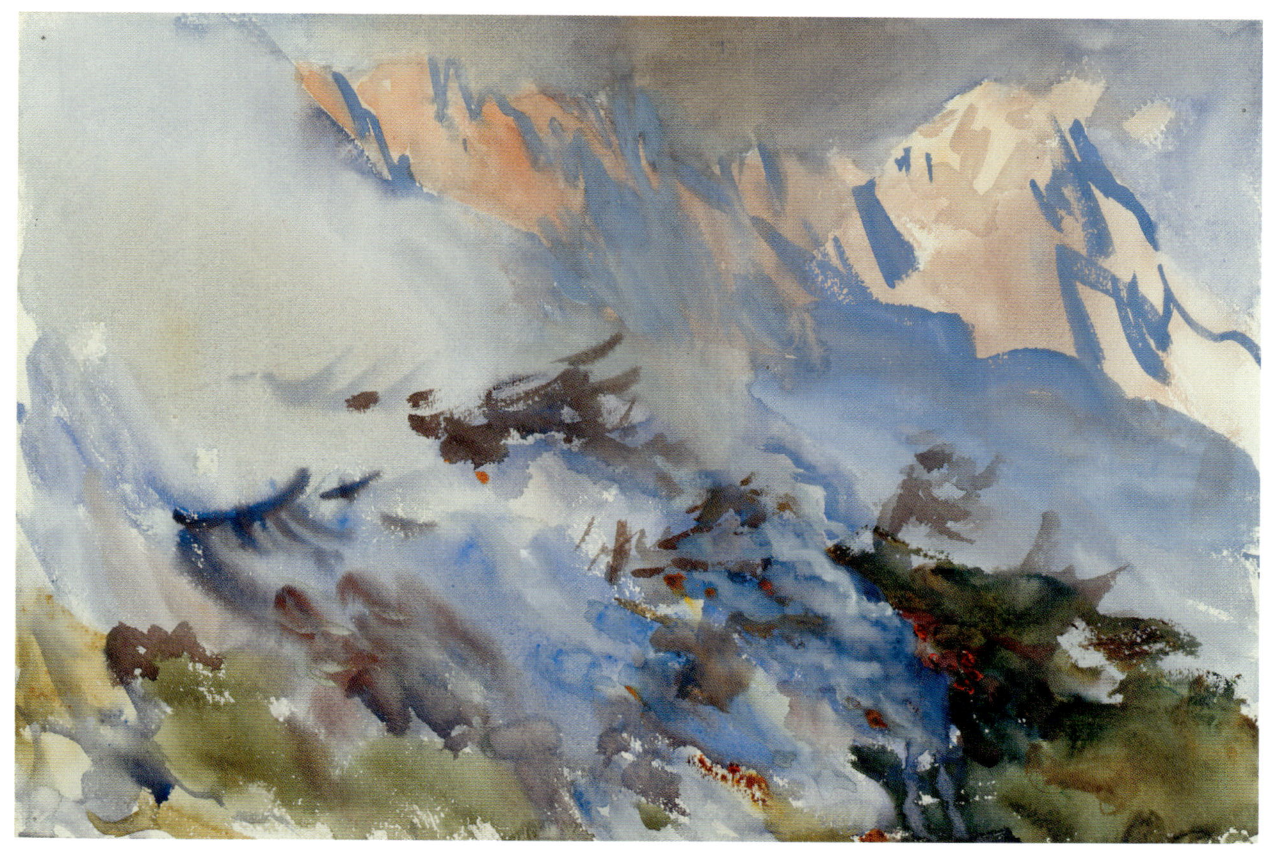

90

Mountain Fire

ca. 1907
Watercolor and gouache on paper,
$14\frac{1}{16} \times 20$ in. (35.7×50.8 cm)
New York, Brooklyn Museum,
Purchased by Special Subscription
[09.831]

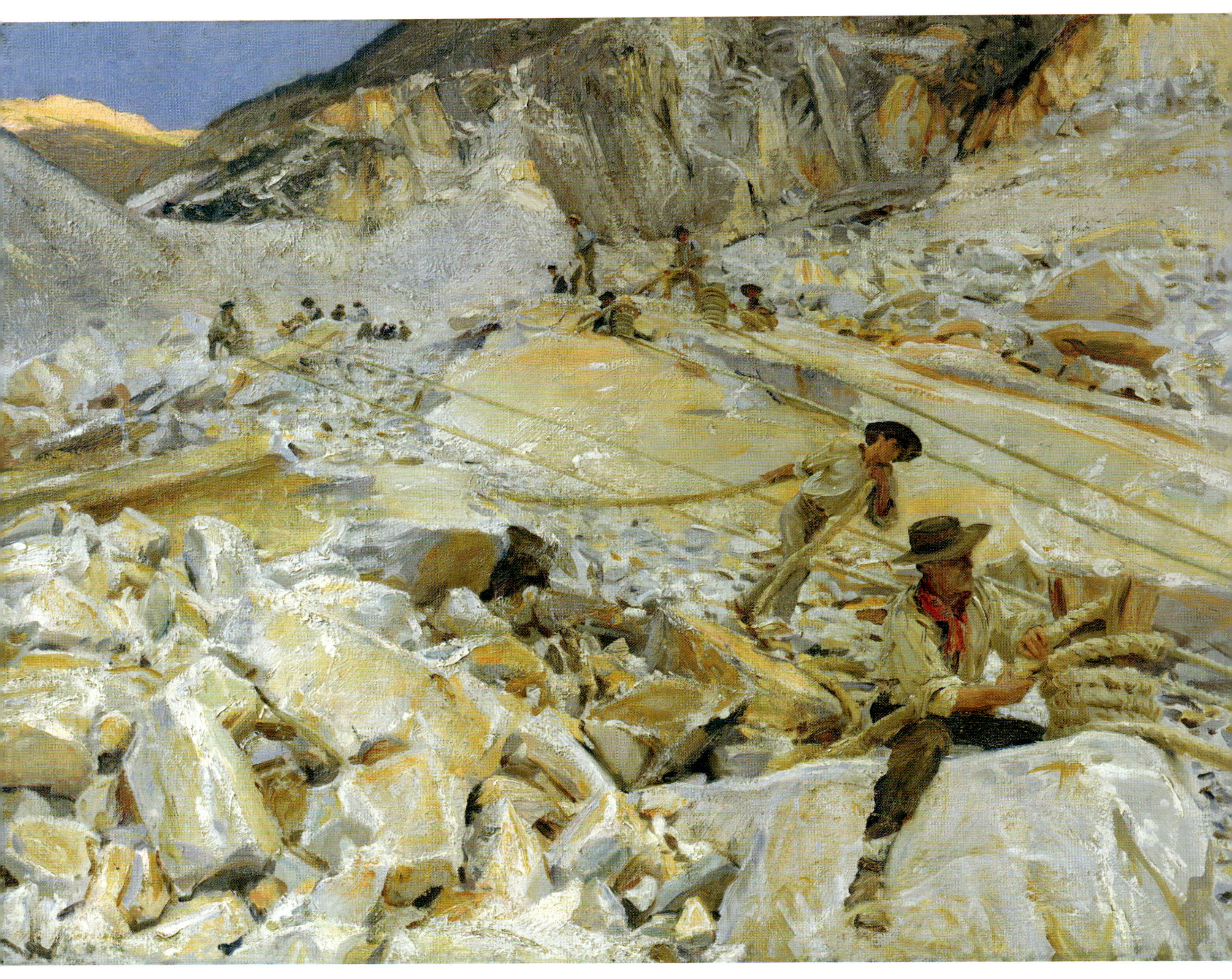

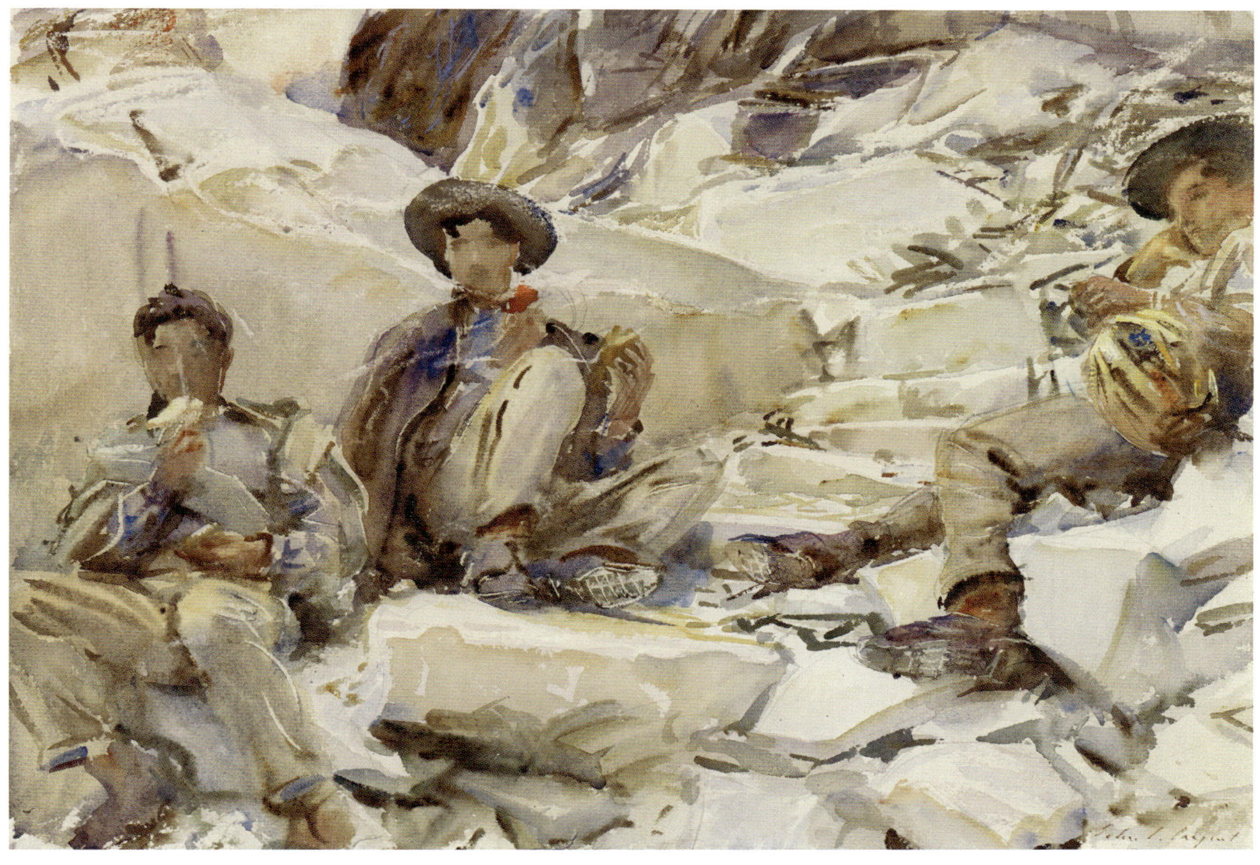

92

Carrara: Workmen

1911
Watercolor, gouache, graphite, and wax resist on paper, 14 × 20 in. (35.6 × 50.8 cm)
Signed: "John S. Sargent"
Boston, Museum of Fine Arts, The Hayden Collection–Charles Henry Hayden Fund [12.235]

91

Bringing Down Marble from the Quarries to Carrara

1911
Oil on canvas, 28 1/8 × 36 1/8 in. (71.4 × 91.8 cm)
Signed: "John S. Sargent"
New York, The Metropolitan Museum of Art, Harris Brisbane Dick Fund, 1917 [17.97.1]

93

Melon Boats

ca. 1908
Watercolor, gouache, graphite on paper,
$14 \times 19^{15}/_{16}$ in. (35.6×50.7 cm)
New York, Brooklyn Museum,
Purchased by Special Subscription
[09.829]

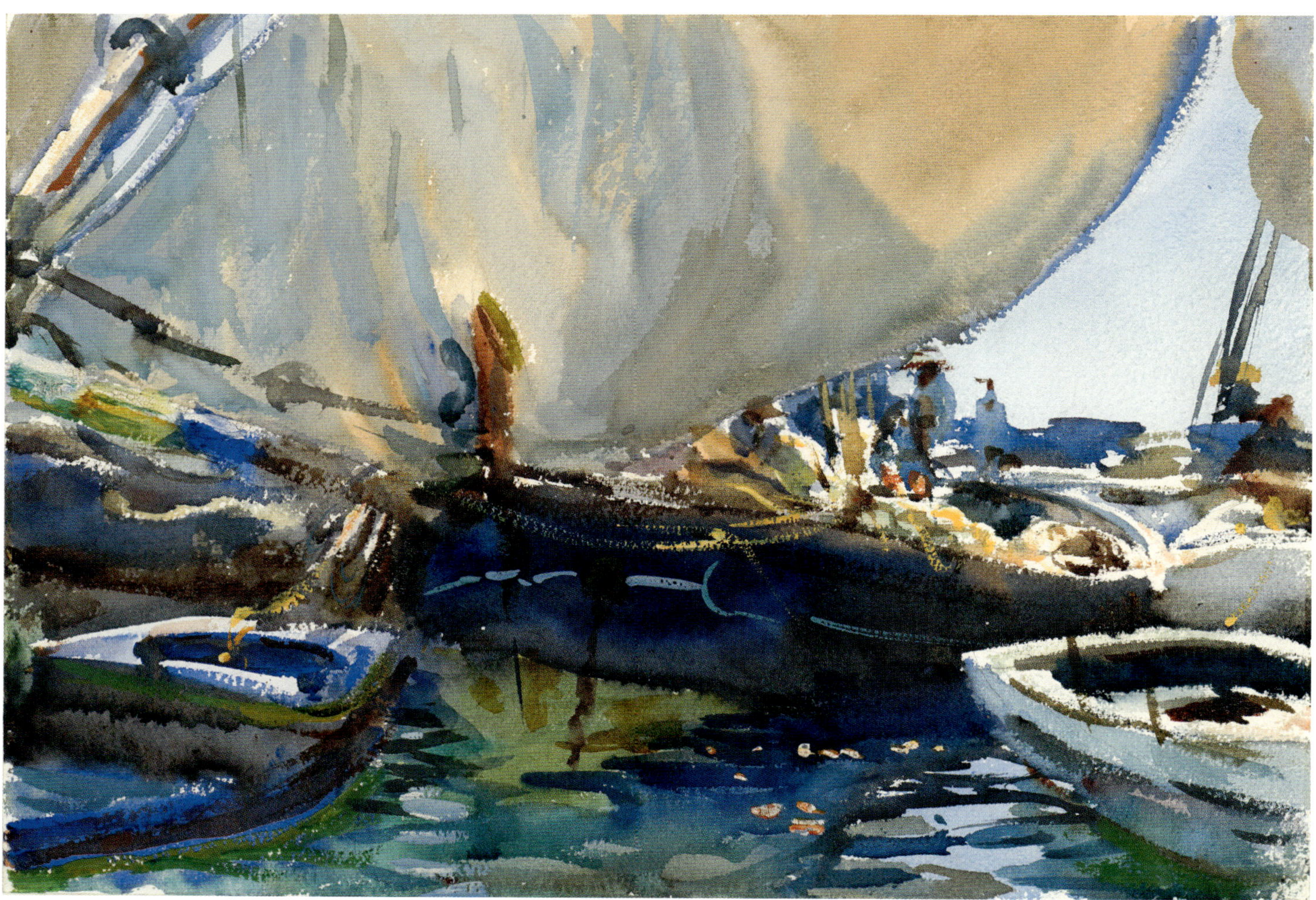

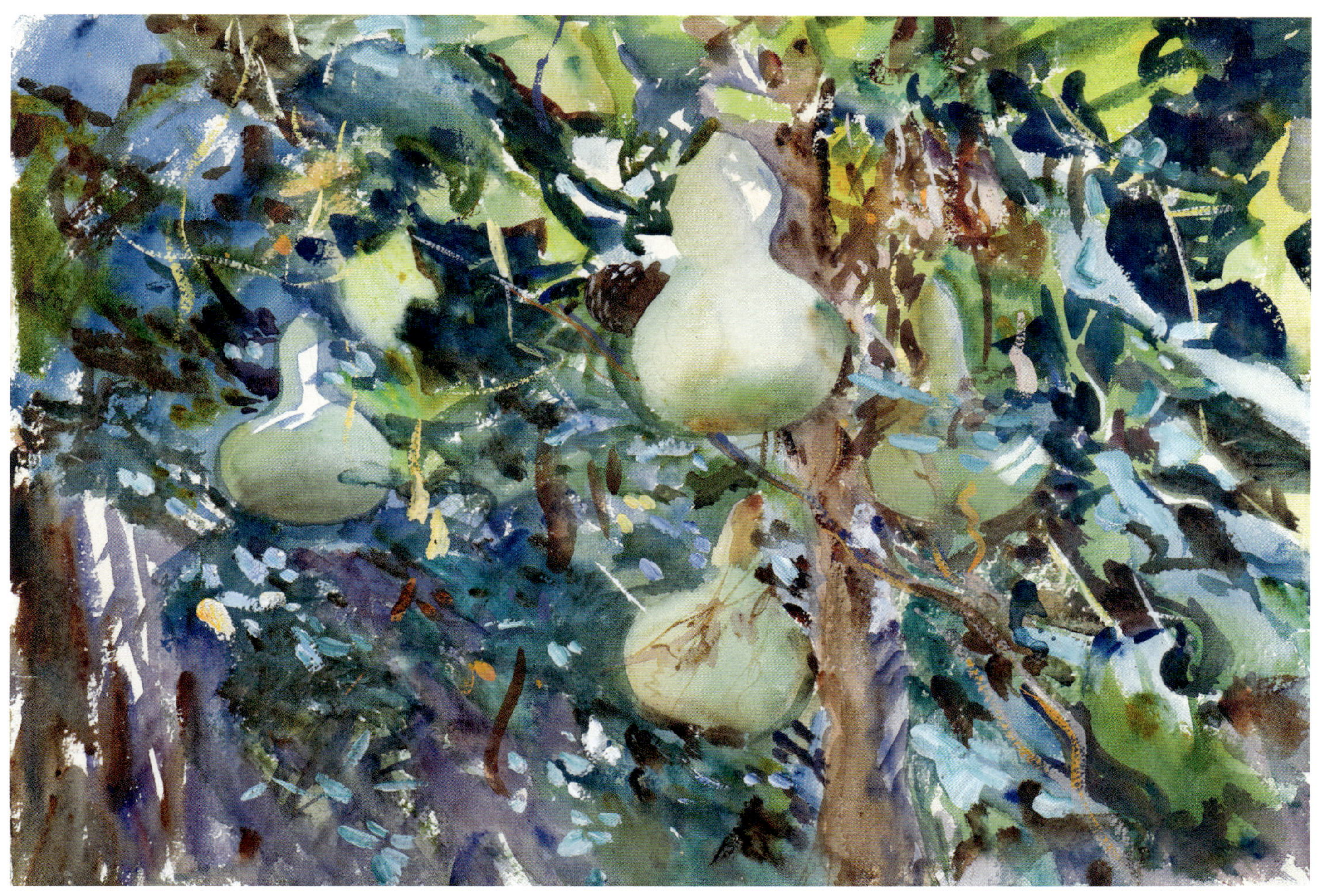

94

Gourds

1908
Watercolor, gouache, graphite on paper, $13\frac{13}{16} \times 19\frac{11}{16}$ in. (35.1 × 50 cm)
New York, Brooklyn Museum, Purchased by Special Subscription [09.822]

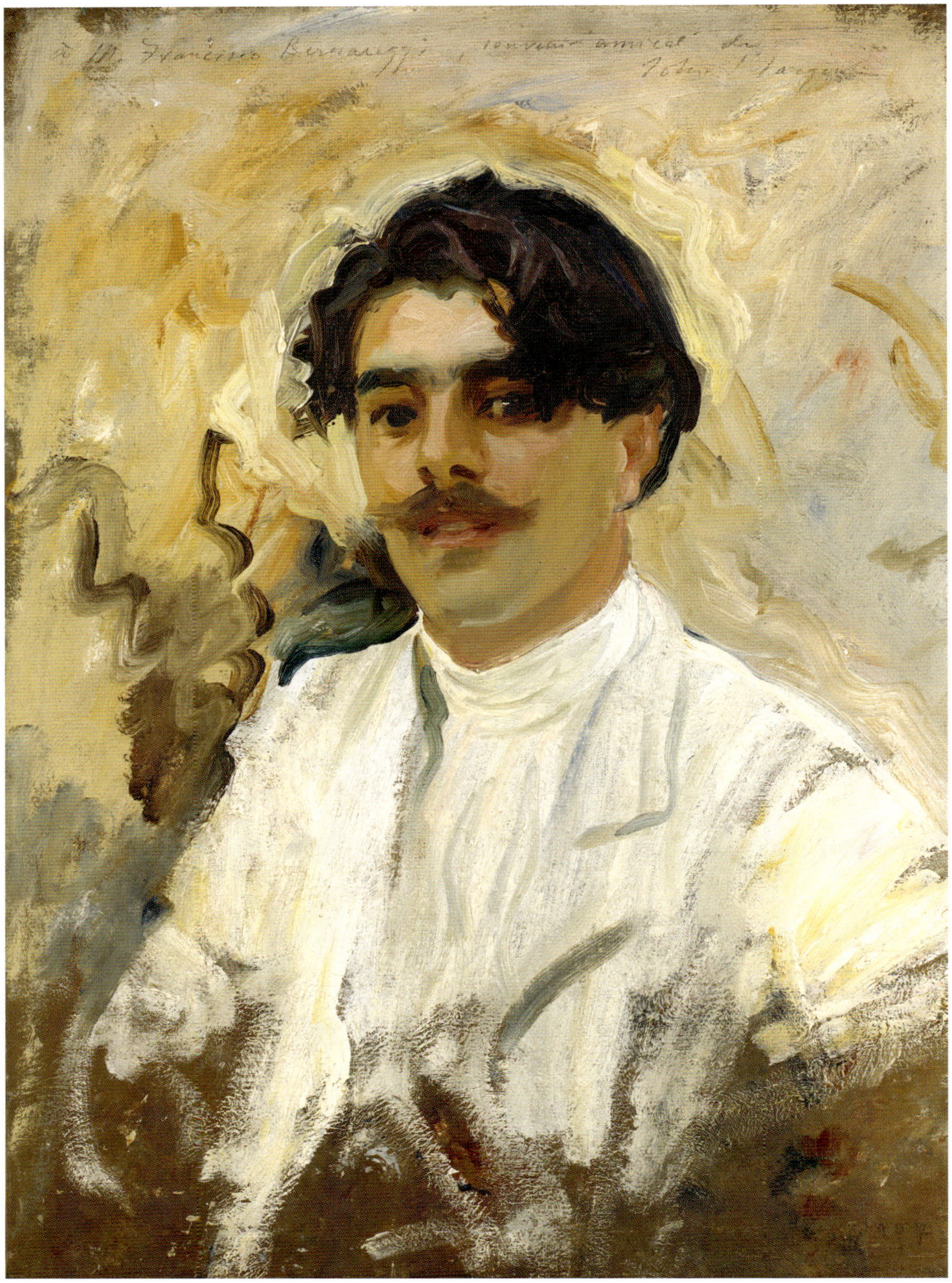

95

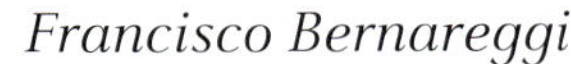

Francisco Bernareggi

ca. 1908
Oil on canvas, $26\frac{13}{16} \times 19\frac{5}{16}$ in.
(68.1 × 49 cm)
Inscription: "à M. Francisco Bernareggi, souvenir amical de / John S. Sargent"
Kansas City, Missouri, The Nelson-Atkins Museum of Art, Gift of the Enid and Crosby Kemper Foundation [F86-26]

96

In the Generalife

1912
Watercolor, wax crayon, and graphite on paper, $14\frac{3}{4} \times 17\frac{7}{8}$ in.
(37.5 × 45.4 cm)
Signed: "John S. Sargent"
Inscription: "5424" (on verso)
New York, The Metropolitan Museum of Art, Purchase, Joseph Pulitzer Bequest, 1915 [15.142.8]

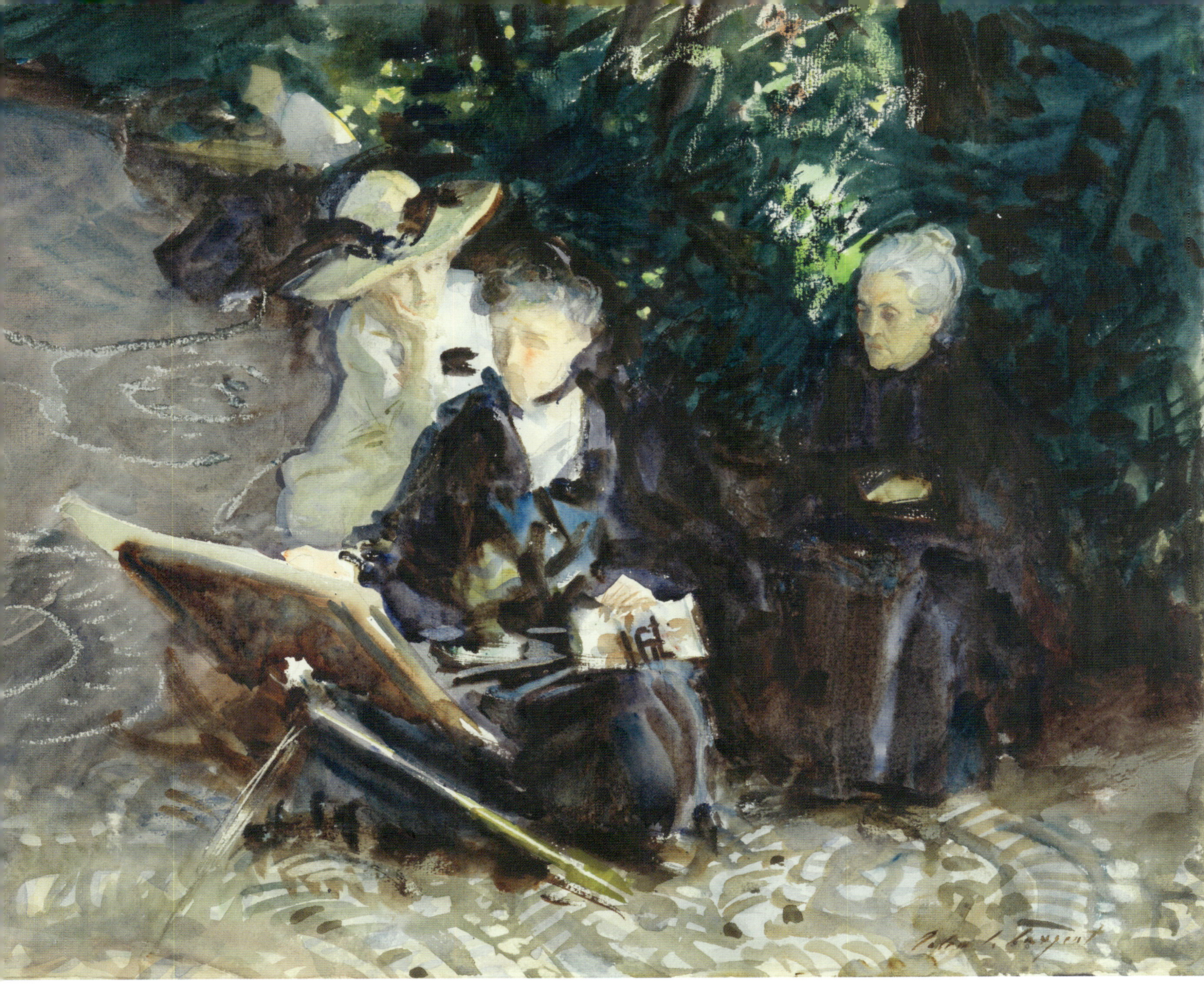

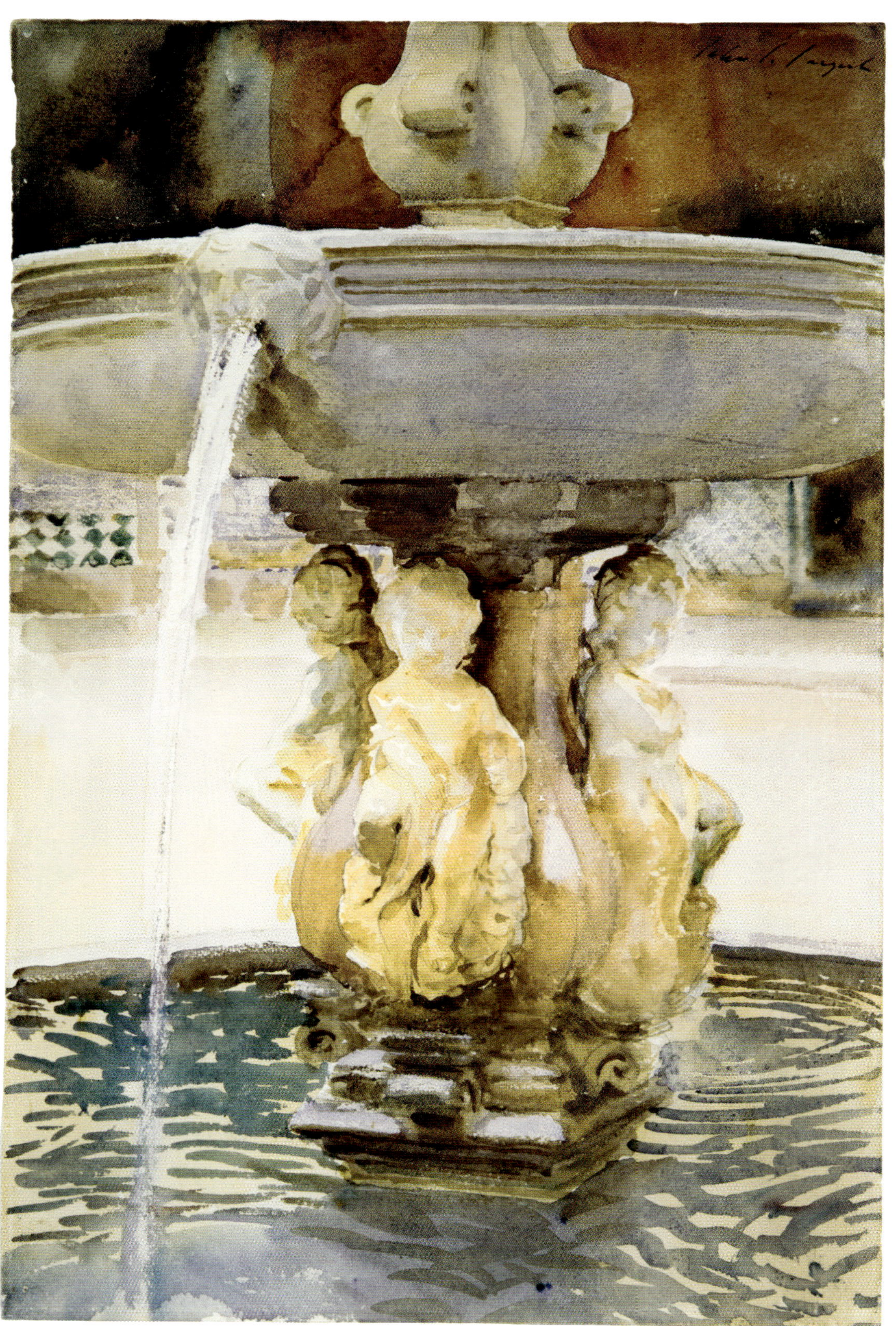

97

Spanish Fountain

1912
Watercolor and graphite on paper,
21 × $13\frac{3}{4}$ in. (53.3 × 34.9 cm)
Signed: "John S. Sargent"
Inscription: "1596" (on verso)
New York, The Metropolitan
Museum of Art, Purchase,
Joseph Pulitzer Bequest,
1915 [15.142.6]

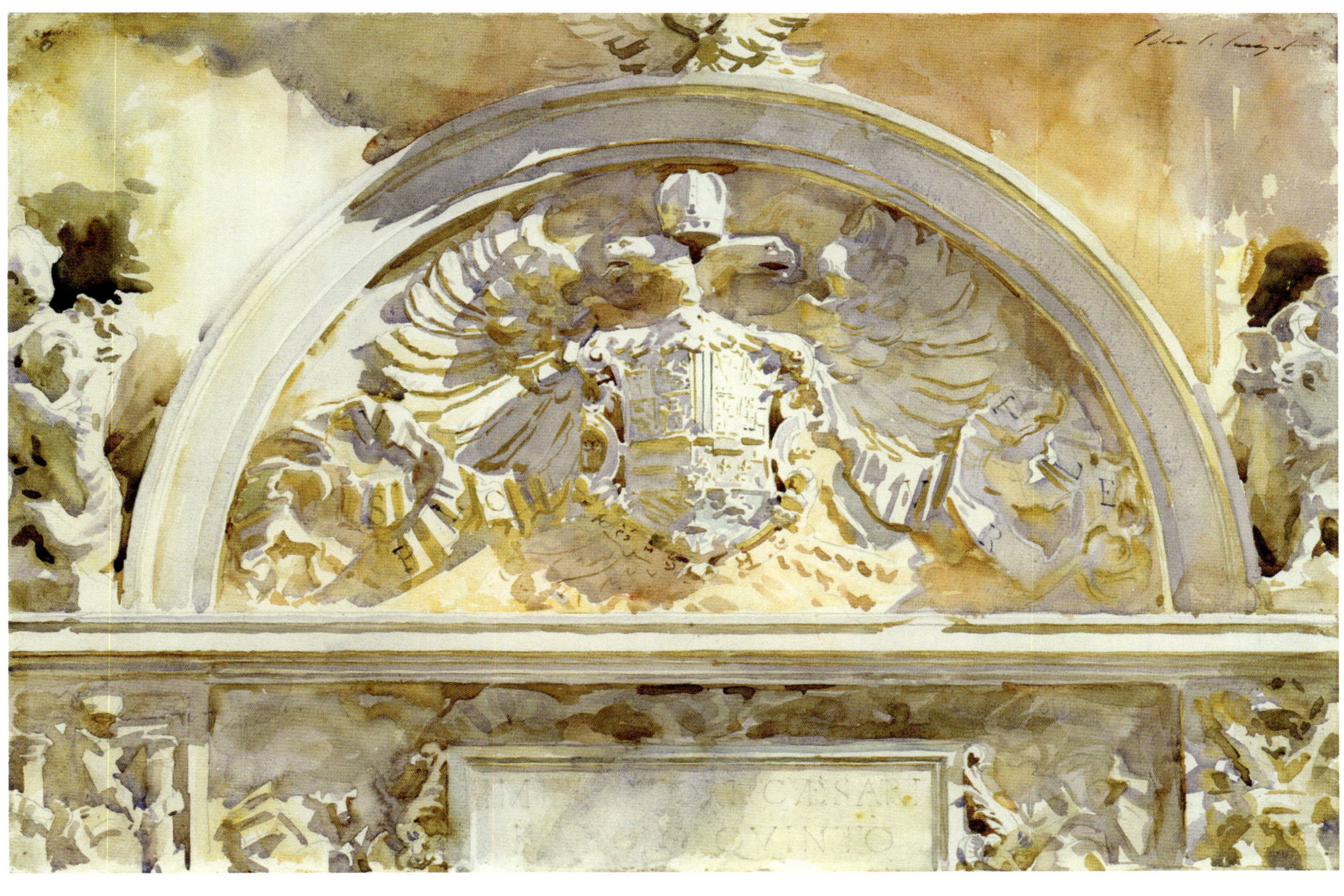

98

Escutcheon of Charles V of Spain

1912
Watercolor and graphite on paper, 12 × 18 in. (30.5 × 45.7 cm)
Signed: "John S. Sargent"
Inscription: "1577" (on verso)
New York, The Metropolitan Museum of Art, Purchase, Joseph Pulitzer Bequest, 1915 [15.142.11]

99

Graveyard in the Tyrol

1914–15
Oil on canvas, 28 × 36 in. (71.1 × 91.4 cm)
Signed: "John S. Sargent"
Dated: "1915"
Private collection

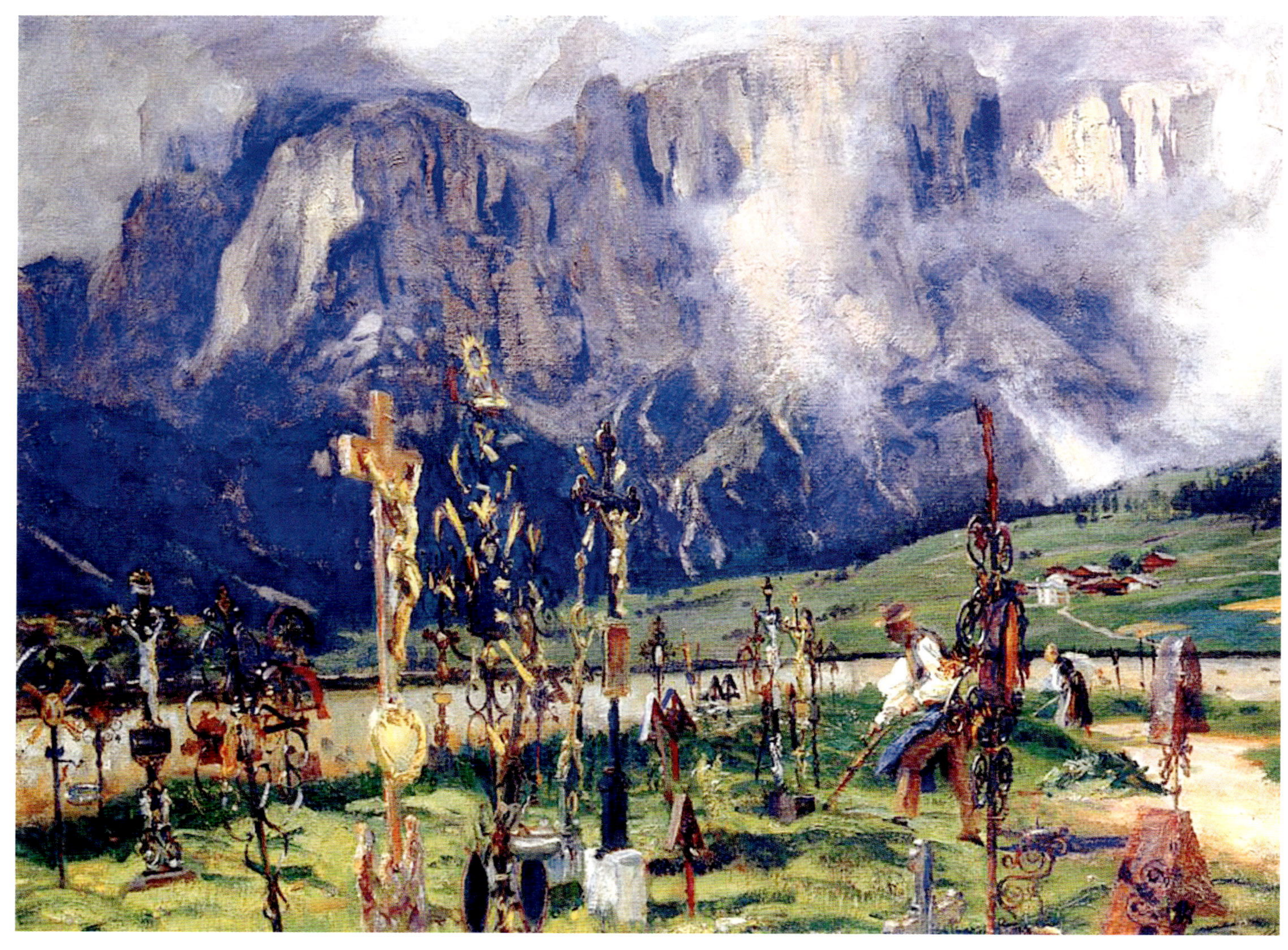

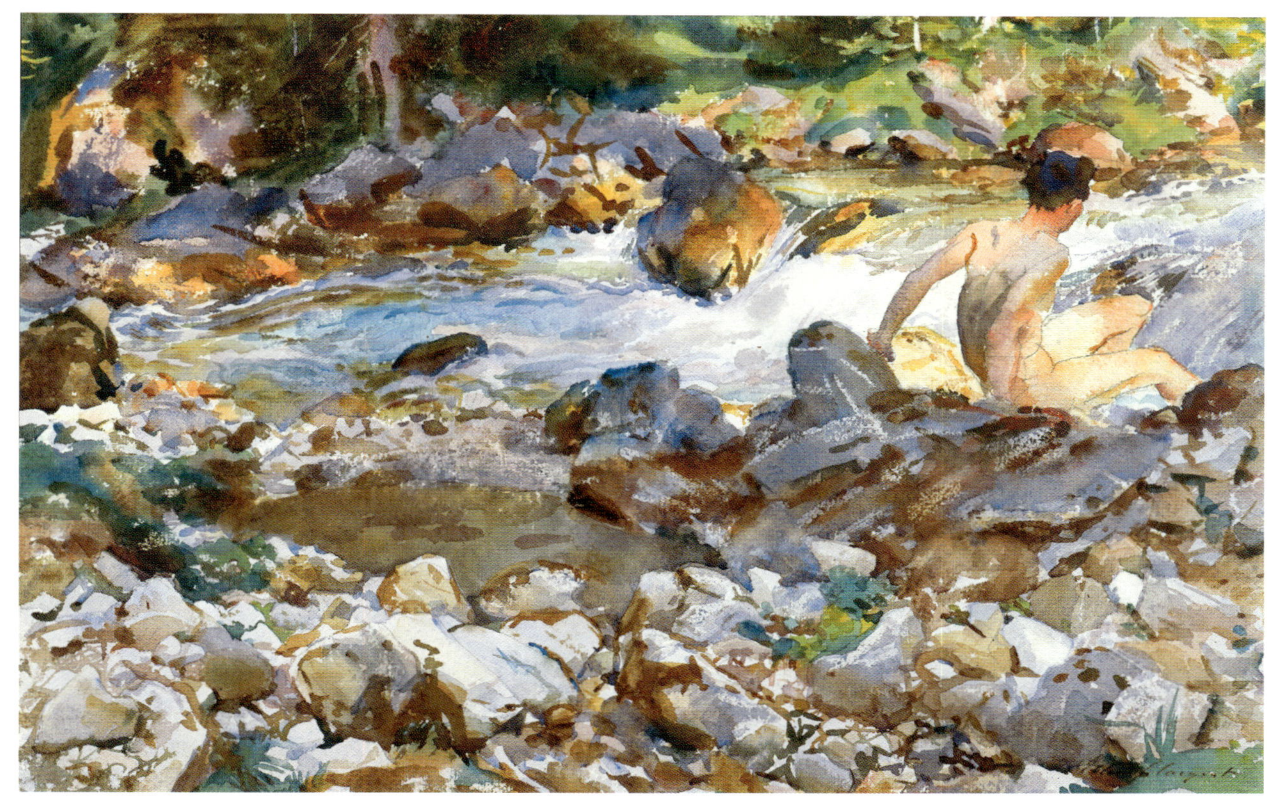

100

Mountain Stream

1914
Watercolor and graphite on paper, $13\frac{11}{16} \times 21$ in. (34.8×53.3 cm)
Signed: "John S. Sargent"
Inscription: "1004" (on verso)
New York, The Metropolitan Museum of Art, Purchase, Joseph Pulitzer Bequest, 1915 [15.142.2]

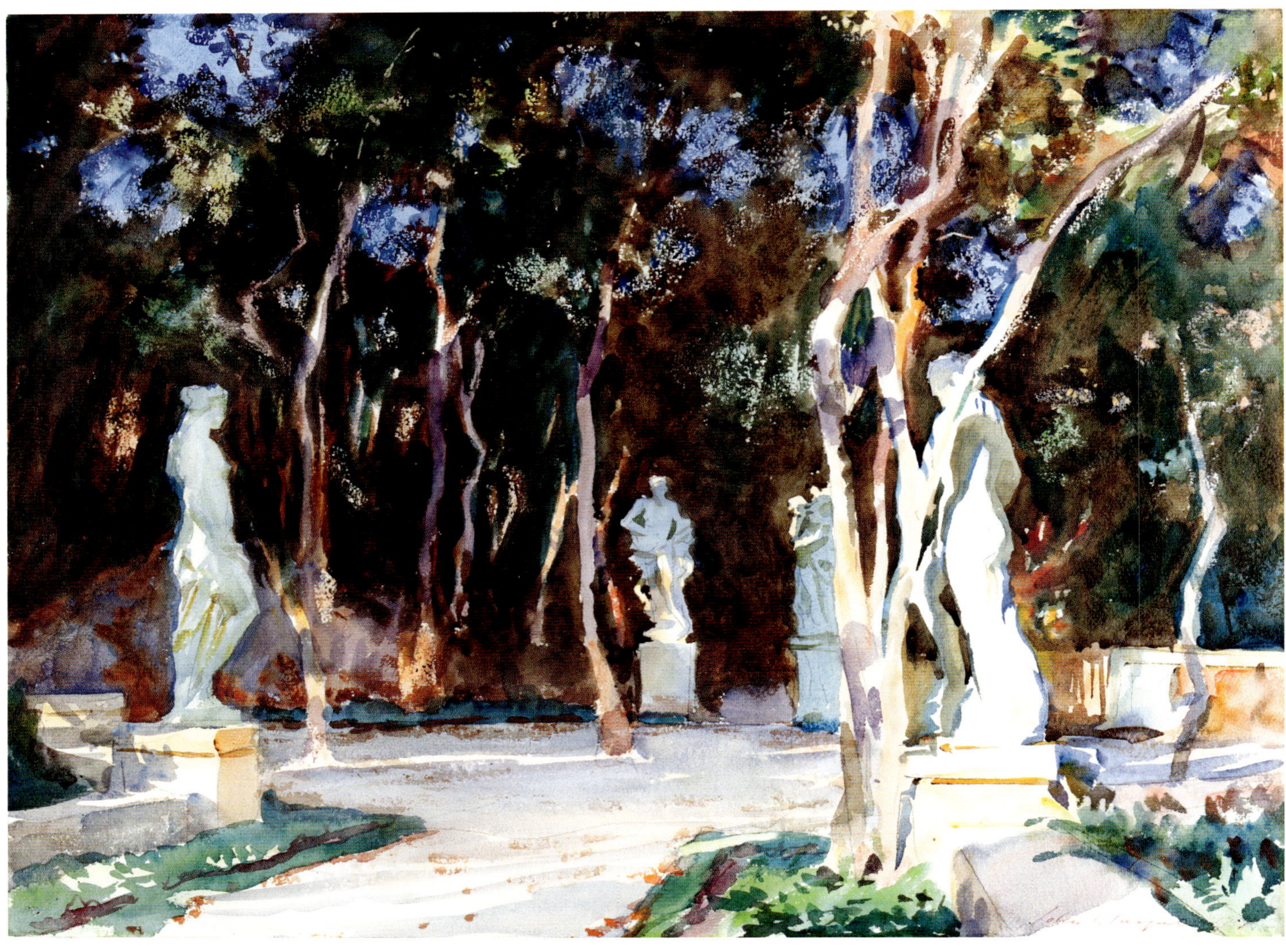

101

Shady Paths, Vizcaya

1917
Watercolor and graphite on paper, 15 5/8 × 21 in.
(39.7 × 53.3 cm)
Signed: "John S. Sargent 1917"
Worcester, Massachusetts, Worcester Art Museum,
Sustaining Membership Fund [1917.88]

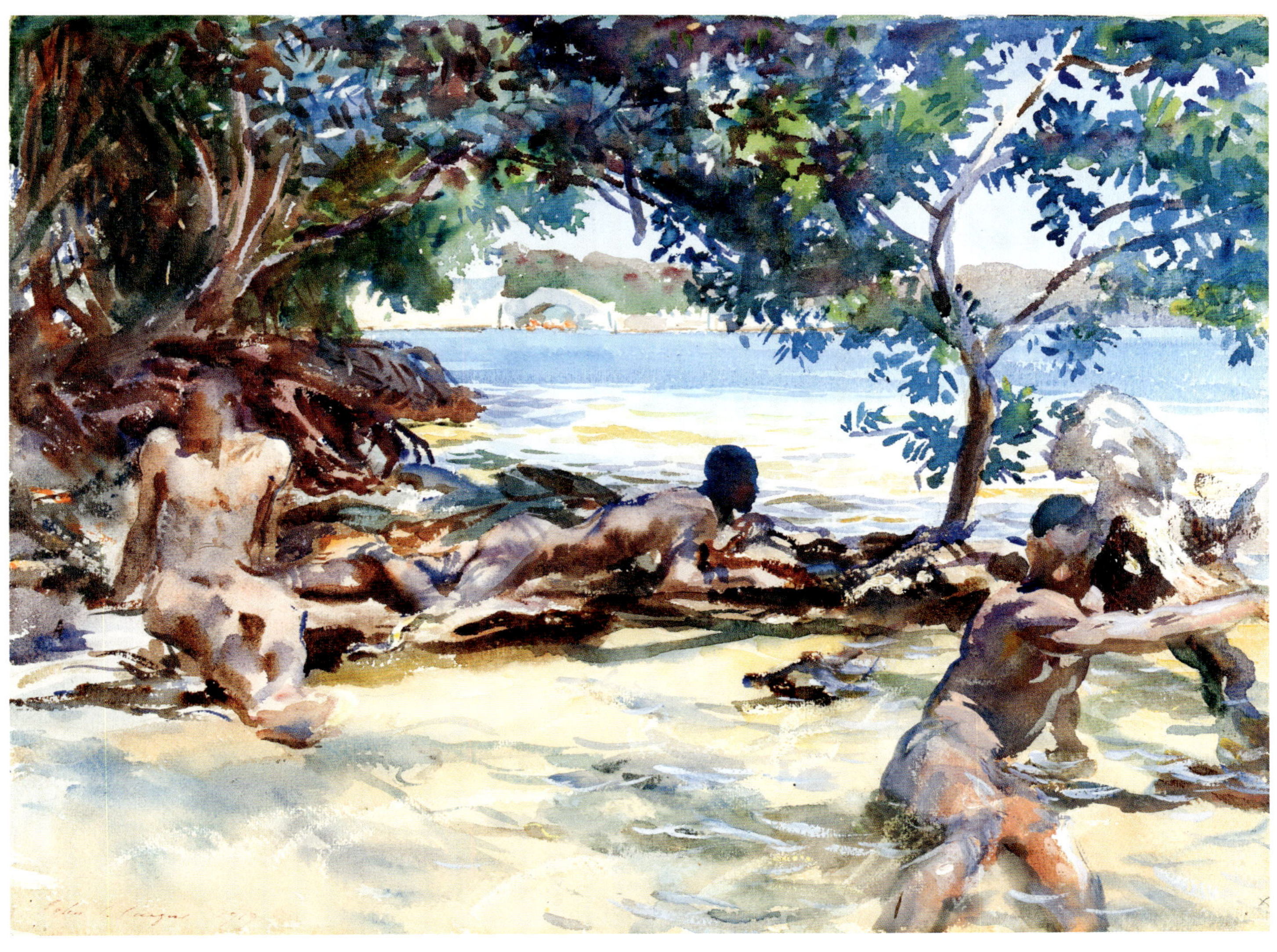

102

The Bathers

1917
Watercolor, gouache, and graphite on paper, 15 13⁄16 × 20 7⁄8 in. (40.1 × 53 cm)
Signed: "John S. Sargent 1917"
Worcester, Massachusetts, Worcester Art Museum, Sustaining Membership Fund [1917.91]

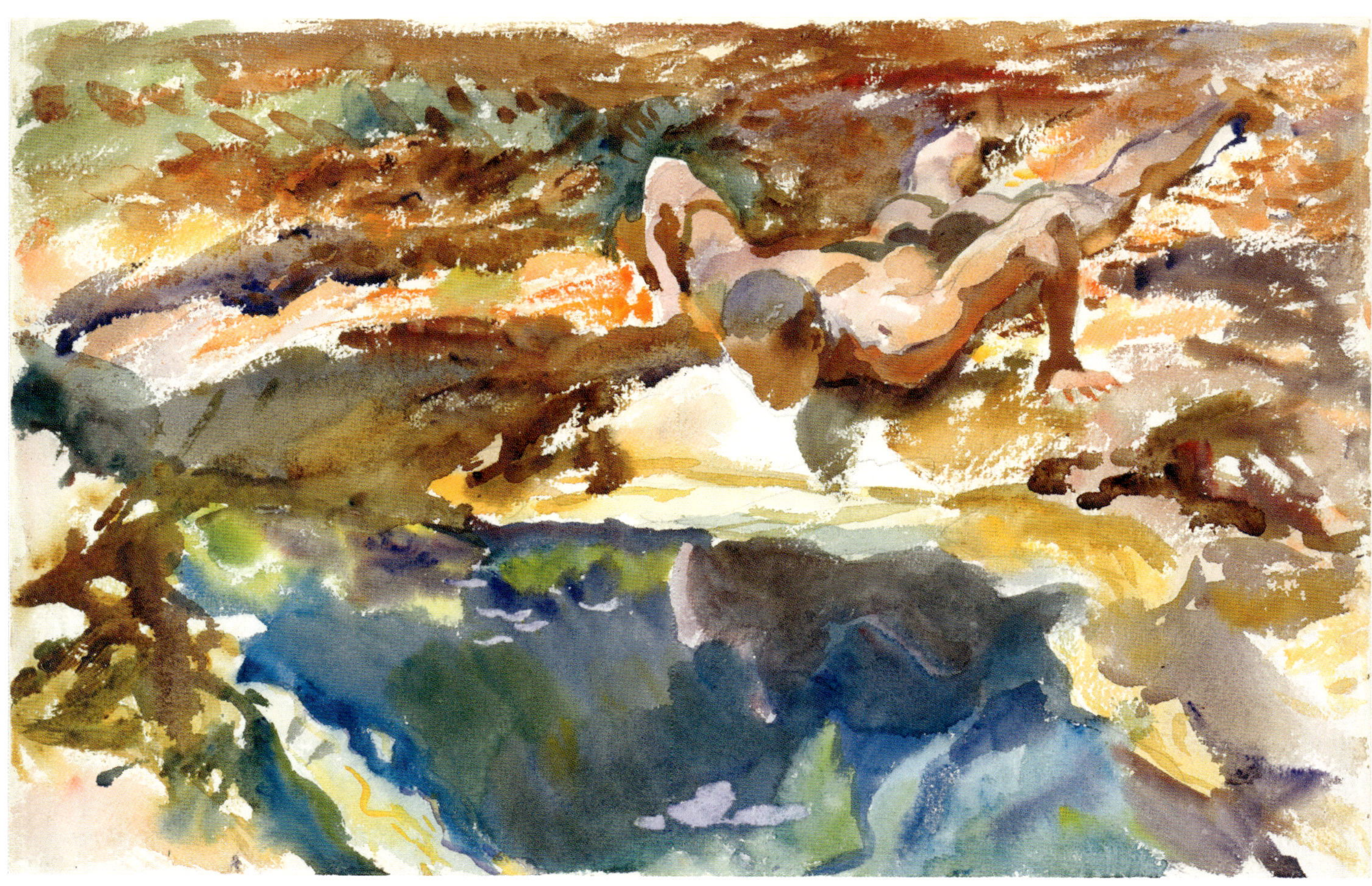

103

Man and Pool, Florida

1917
Watercolor, gouache, and graphite on paper,
$13^{11/16} \times 21$ in. (34.8 × 53.3 cm)
Inscriptions: "Met."; "F" (on verso)
New York, The Metropolitan Museum of Art,
Gift of Mrs. Francis Ormond, 1950 [50.130.62]

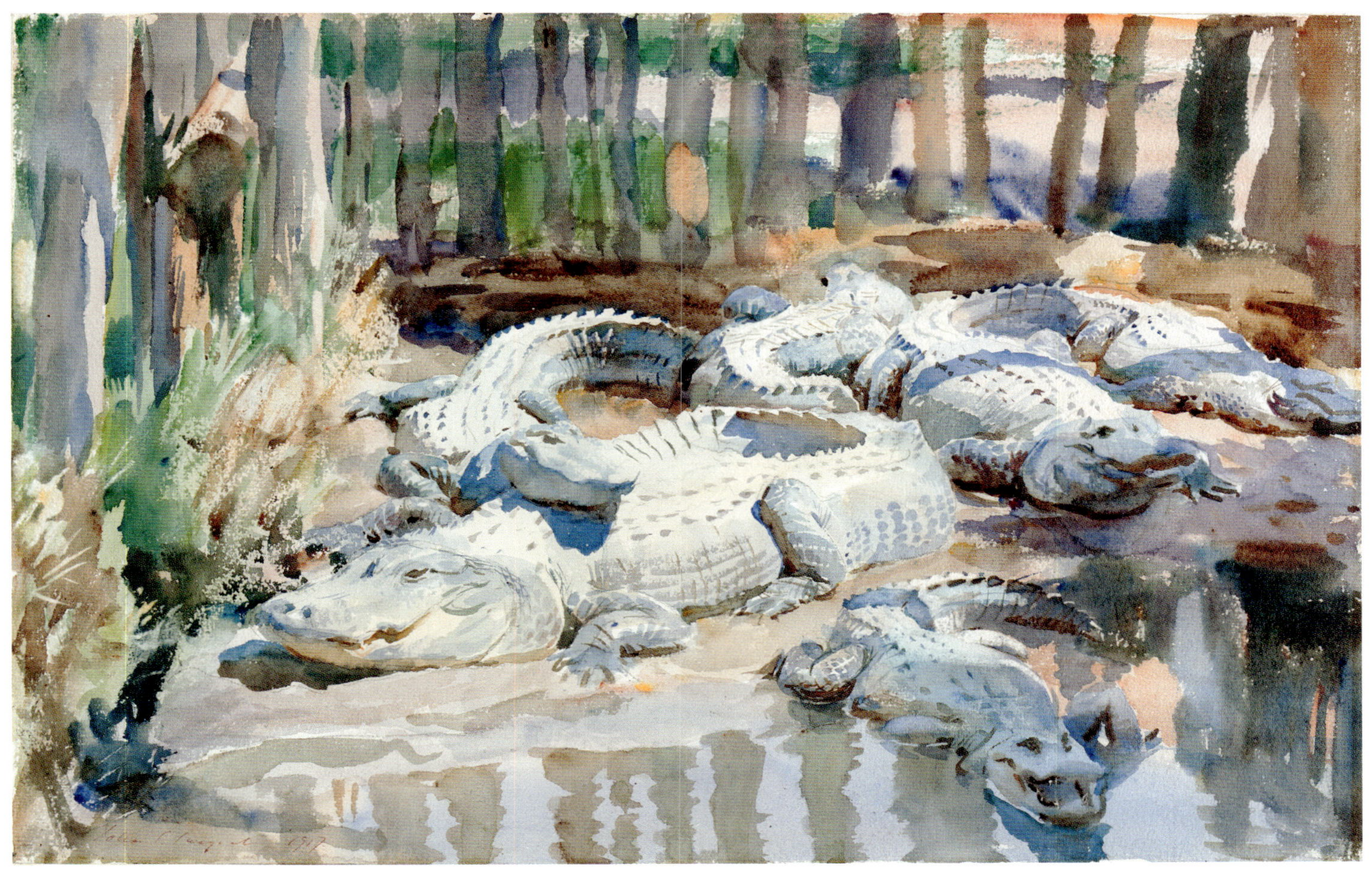

104

Muddy Alligators

1917
Watercolor and graphite on paper, 13 9/16 × 20 7/8 in.
(34.4 × 53 cm)
Signed: "John S. Sargent 1917"
Worcester, Massachusetts, Worcester Art Museum,
Sustaining Membership Fund [1917.86]

105

Charles Deering

1917
Oil on canvas, 28½ × 21 in.
(72.4 × 53.3 cm)
Signed: "John S. Sargent Miami 1917"
Inscription: "to my friend / Charles Deering"
Private collection

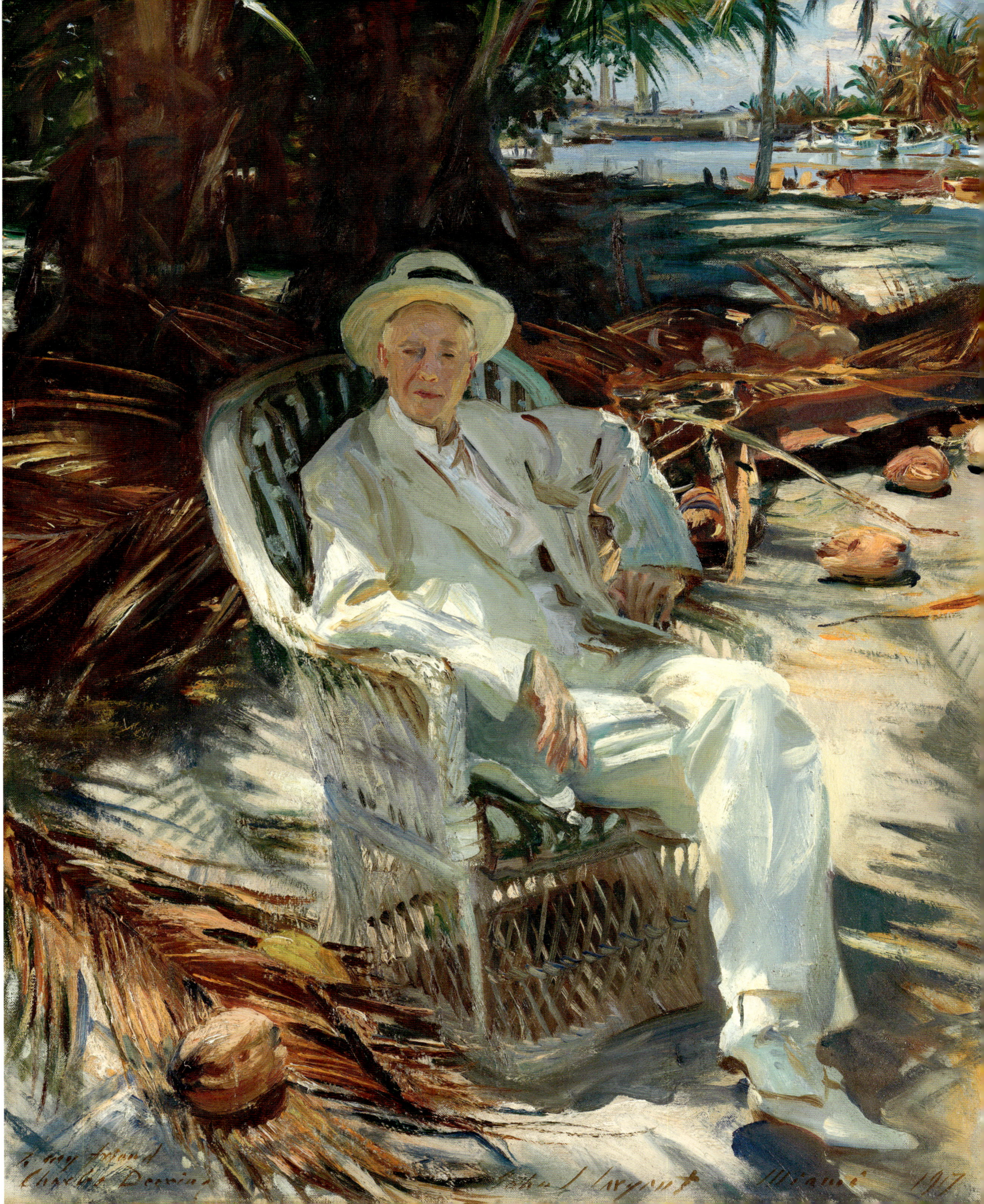
to my friend
Charles Deering
John S. Sargent
Miami
1917

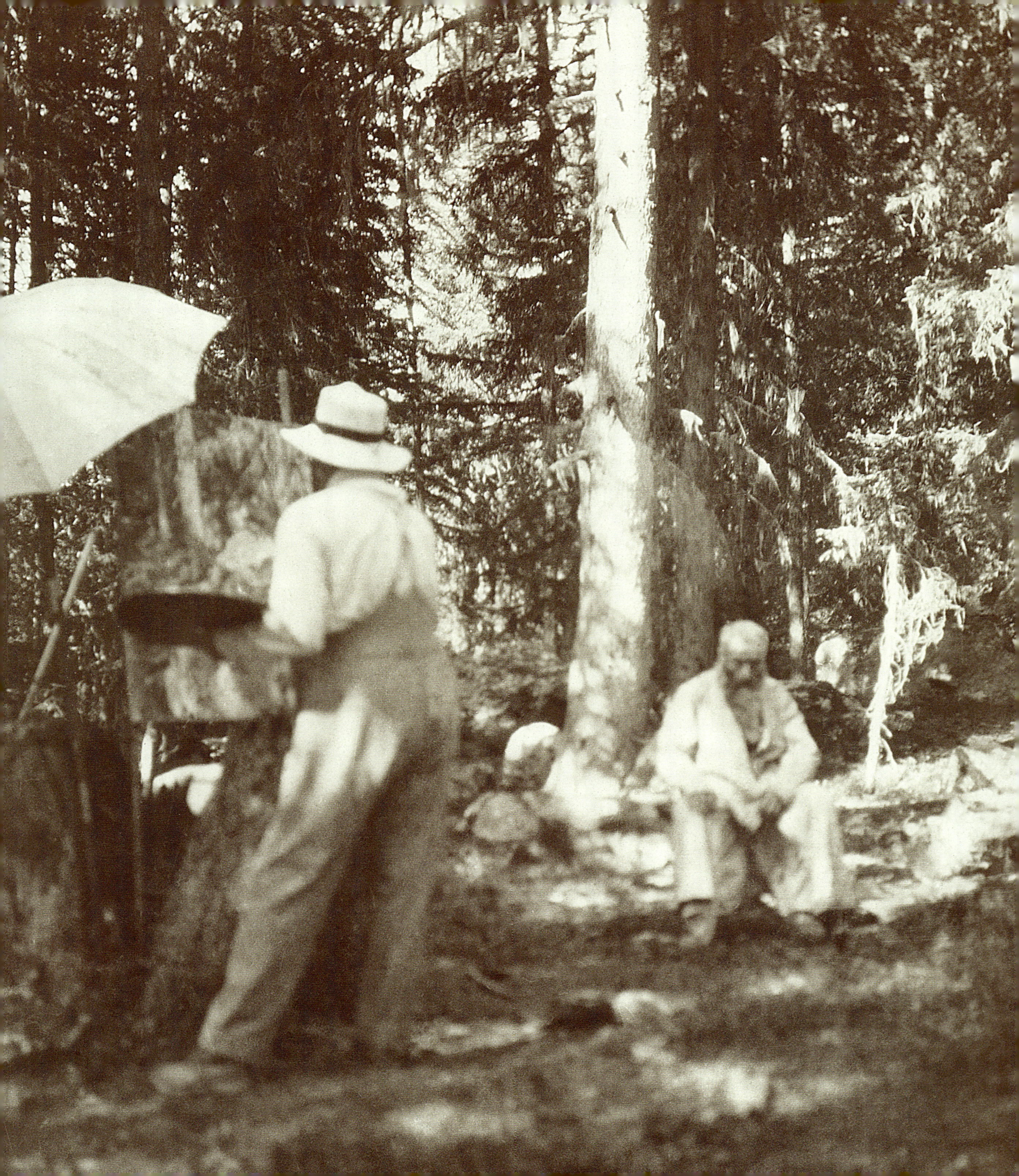

Sargent painting *The Hermit* at Purtud, ca. 1907. Museum of Fine Arts, Boston. The John Singer Sargent Archive–Gift of Richard and Leonée Ormond.

Chronology

1850–53 Sargent's parents, Fitzwilliam (1820–1889) and Mary Newbold Singer (1826–1906) marry on June 27, 1850. Their first child, Mary Newbold Sargent (1851–1853), is born less than a year later, on May 3, 1851; she dies just after her second birthday, in 1853.

1854 In September, Fitzwilliam and Mary, accompanied by her mother, Mary Newbold Singer (d. 1859), embark for Europe with the hope that a change of climate will improve the health of Mary, who is suffering after the untimely death of her firstborn. They settle in Pau, in southwestern France, for the winter.

1855 Seeking a temperate climate, the family visits several spas in the Pyrenees during the summer and moves to Florence, Italy, for the winter.

1856 John Singer Sargent is born on January 12 at the Casa Arretini in Florence. As is their habit, the family heads north for the summer, staying in Geneva, Switzerland, before returning to Italy for the winter. They reside in Rome.

1857 Sargent's sister Emily (1857–1936) is born in Rome on January 29. The family summers in Vienna and returns to Rome in the fall. Fitzwilliam resigns from his position as attending surgeon at Wills Hospital, Philadelphia.

1858 Mrs. Singer is too ill to travel north for the summer and the family remains in Rome.

1859 After a summer excursion to Switzerland, the Sargents rent an apartment at 13 Piazza di Spagna, Rome, where Mrs. Singer dies in November.

1860 The family spends at least part of the year in Rome, where Emily suffers a serious back injury resulting in permanent spinal deformity. By the fall, she is well enough to travel, and the family settles in Nice for the winter.

1861 On February 1, Mary Winthrop Sargent (1861–1865) is born in Nice.

1861–67 Constantly in search of a mild climate, the family continues their pattern of moving seasonally. During these years, they spend the winters in Nice and their summers in Switzerland. In April 1865, the family departs from Nice for the summer. En route to Switzerland, Mary Winthrop, weakened by pleurisy and a bronchial infection, dies in Pau, France, on April 18. After resting in Biarritz, they continue on to Switzerland and make a short trip to London and Paris before returning to Nice for the winter.

1867 Fitzwilliam Winthrop Sargent (1867–1869) is born in Nice on March 7.
Over the summer, the family attends the Exposition Universelle in Paris before heading to Hamburg for a month. From there, they travel along the Rhine by steamer before returning for another winter in Nice.

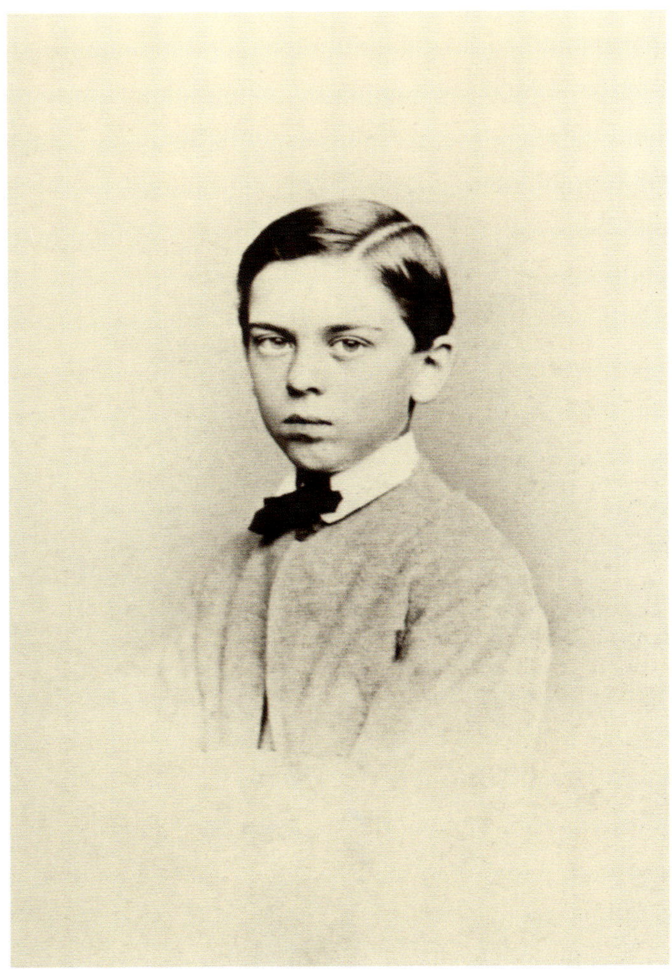

Portrait of Sargent as a boy, ca. 1867. Photograph by Franz Hanfstaendl, Munich. Museum of Fine Arts, Boston. The John Singer Sargent Archive–Gift of Richard and Leonée Ormond.

1868 After a spring sojourn to Spain, they visit spas in the Pyrenees (Biarritz and Bagnères-de-Bigorre). Concerned about the health of baby Fitzwilliam, they move to Rome for the winter and take an apartment above the Piazza di Spagna at 17 Trinità dei Monti.

Winter 1868–69 Sargent meets Violet Paget (later Vernon Lee) and German landscape painter Karl Welsch. He spends his mornings copying Welsch's watercolors and fetching beer for the studio. Members of the expatriate artistic community in Rome gather at the Sargents' apartment. Fitzwilliam acknowledges that his son will not have a career in the navy and determines to help him pursue a career as an artist.

1869 After a late spring trip to southern Italy, the family heads north for the summer. In late June, baby Fitzwilliam dies in Kissingen, Germany. After traveling in Switzerland in July, they visit Lake Como before settling in Florence for the winter. Sargent is enrolled at a day school run by a French political refugee, Joseph Domengé, in the former convent I Servi di Maria.

1870 Violet Sargent (1870–1955) is born in Florence on February 9. By early May, the family departs for the summer, spending two weeks in Venice before heading to Lake Maggiore and then Switzerland. Sargent and his father take a three-week walking tour of the Alps. The aspiring artist sketches and paints in watercolor throughout the trip. They join the rest of the family in Interlaken and continue to tour the Alps together. They return to Florence for the winter and Sargent re-enrolls at the same school.

1871 The family spends the summer in the Alps before moving to Dresden for the schools. Sargent begins to prepare for school entrance exams.

1872 During the winter, Emily becomes seriously ill, and the Sargents decide that they cannot stay in Dresden. They travel to Berlin and Leipzig. In Munich, Sargent contracts typhoid fever, and they are forced to remain there for three weeks while he recovers. After exploring the Tyrol during the summer, they return to Florence for the winter.

1873 In late spring, Dr. Sargent travels to the United States to visit relatives. Sargent, his mother, and his sisters travel to Venice and then to Switzerland where Dr. Sargent joins the family upon his return. After a visit to Bologna in September, they return to Florence for the winter. Sargent enrolls for his first formal art training at the Accademia di Belle Arti. Shortly thereafter the Accademia is closed for two months while curriculum reform is discussed. Sargent works on his own—drawing and studying art in and around Florence. Once again members of the expatriate community congregate at the Sargent household. The Sargent family considers options for John's training.

1874 In May, Sargent arrives in Paris with his family. He visits the studio of Carolus-Duran (1837–1917) on the boulevard Montparnasse. Carolus-Duran reviews Sargent's portfolio and accepts him as a student shortly before the summer break. Sargent spends his holiday with his family in Beuzeval on the Calvados Coast of Normandy. At the end of summer, he returns to Paris and prepares to take the rigorous entrance exams for the École des Beaux-Arts. He passes and matriculates at the École where he receives lessons from Adolphe Yvon (1817–1893) and possibly Léon Bonnat (1833–1922) while continuing his studies with Carolus-Duran.

1875 In January, Sargent takes a short trip to Nice with Carolus-Duran (and two other students).
Throughout the spring and fall, he maintains his matriculation at the École des Beaux-Arts and continues to work in the studio of Carolus-Duran. He spends his summer holiday with his family in Saint-Enogat, on the Brittany coast. In the fall, he shares a studio with American James Carroll Beckwith (1852–1917) at 73, rue Notre-Dame-des-Champs.

1876 In April, Sargent probably meets Claude Monet (1840–1926) for the first time while visiting the second Impressionist exhibition at Durand-Ruel Gallery in Paris.
In May, he embarks for his first visit to the United States. (He is accompanied by his mother and sister Emily.) In addition to meeting many members of his extended family for the first time, he visits the Centennial Exhibition in Philadelphia; travels to Newport, Rhode Island; takes a journey up the Hudson River and to Montreal via Lake George and Lake Champlain; he also travels to Niagara Falls. Sargent makes a brief trip to Chicago before returning to Paris in October.
He resumes his studies at the École des Beaux-Arts and with Carolus-Duran. During this period in Paris, he may have met Auguste Rodin (1840–1917), Paul-Albert Besnard (1849–1934), Albert Belleroche (1864–1944), and Paul-César Helleu (1859–1927).

1877 Sargent matriculates at the École des Beaux-Arts for the last time. He makes his public exhibition debut when he sends *Portrait of Frances Sherborne Ridley Watts* (Philadelphia Museum of Art), his first formal portrait of a nonfamily member, to the Paris Salon.
In June, the Society of American Artists is founded and Sargent is appointed juror. Around this time, he probably meets Augustus Saint-Gaudens (1848–1907).
He spends the summer on the coast of Brittany and makes sketches that become *En route pour la pêche* [fig. 4].
Later in the summer, he travels to Bex, Switzerland, to visit his family; together they go to Genoa, Italy.
Sargent and James Carroll Beckwith assist Carolus-Duran in painting a mural, depicting *The Triumph of Marie de Médici*, for the ceiling of the Palais du Luxembourg. Sargent and Carolus-Duran each incorporate a portrait of the other into the murals.

1878 Sargent visits Venice (early in the year), Naples and Capri (summer), and Nice to see his family (October–November).
At the Paris Salon, Sargent exhibits *En route pour la pêche* and receives an honorable mention. He begins the portrait of Carolus-Duran and attends the studio less often.

1879 Sargent sends two paintings to the Paris Salon: the portrait of Carolus-Duran [fig. 7] and *Dans les oliviers, à Capri* (private collection) and receives another honorable mention. He completes a portrait of writer Édouard Pailleron [fig. 8], who is pleased and commissions a portrait of his wife [fig. 9]. Sargent travels to their home in Ronjoux, France, for sittings. (In 1880, he will complete a double portrait of the Pailleron children [fig. 10].)
At the end of summer, he visits Madrid where he copies several paintings by Diego Velázquez (1599–1660) at the Prado before traveling south to Ronda, Granada, Seville, and Gibraltar. In Seville, he makes studies that will become *El Jaleo* [fig. 16].

1880 Around the New Year, Sargent crosses into Morocco and rents a house in Tangier where he paints architectural vignettes [fig. 14] and begins *Fumée d'Ambre Gris* [fig. 15]. He visits Tetuan and Tunis before returning to Paris by late February.
Sargent sends the portrait of Madame Pailleron and *Fumée d'Ambre Gris* to the Paris Salon. *Fumée* is sold for 2,000 francs.
In August, Sargent and American artists Ralph W. Curtis (1854–1922) and Francis Brooks Chadwick (1850–1943) travel to Holland to study works by Frans Hals (1582/83–1666), Hans Memling (ca. 1434–1494), Peter Paul Rubens (1577–1640), Rembrandt (1606–1669), and other northern painters.
He arrives in Venice in September and takes a studio in the Palazzo Rezzonico, where he remains into the New Year, possibly meeting James McNeill Whistler (1834–1903).

1881 In March, he departs Venice and travels to Nice to visit his family.

At the Paris Salon, he is awarded a second-class medal for his portrait of Madame Ramón Subercaseaux (private collection) and is hors concours, which means he is no longer required to submit his paintings to the jury for review.

In the spring, he meets Edward Burne-Jones (1833–1898) in London and connects with his old friend Vernon Lee, painting a brilliant portrait sketch of her in one sitting [fig. 22].

Sometime during the year, Sargent first meets Virginie Avegno Gautreau (Madame Pierre Gautreau) and begins to think about painting her portrait.

Throughout the year, he paints significant compositions in his Paris studio including *Dr. Pozzi* [fig. 19], *Lady with the Rose* (*Charlotte Louise Burckhardt*) [fig. 20], and *El Jaleo* [fig. 16].

1882 Sargent finishes his ambitious *El Jaleo* in time for the Paris Salon, where it is purchased by an American collector. He begins painting *The Daughters of Edward Darley Boit* [fig. 21]. He returns to Venice and stays with the Curtis family at the Palazzo Barbaro and then travels to Rome, Siena, and Florence.

1883 After a visit with his family in Nice early in the year, Sargent begins painting the portrait of Virginie Avegno Gautreau [fig. 25], following her to her summer home in Brittany to continue the sittings.

In the autumn, he visits Florence, Siena, and possibly Rome.

1884 In February, Sargent meets Henry James, who encourages him to move to London. In March, he visits James in London and encounters several artists, including Edward Burne-Jones, Edwin Austin Abbey (1852–1911), Frederic Leighton (1830–1896), and John Everett Millais (1829–1896). Together James and Sargent visit an exhibition of works of Sir Joshua Reynolds (1723–1792) at the Royal Academy and attend a party in Edwin Austin Abbey's studio in honor of the actor Lawrence Barrett.

Sargent returns to Paris in time for opening day of the annual exhibition at the Salon, where the portrait of Madame Gautreau is poorly received. Gautreau and her mother beg Sargent to remove the painting from the Salon; he refuses.

Sargent flees to England for the rest of the year where he already has a portrait commission from Albert Vickers. In October, he stays at Petworth, Sussex, with the Vickers family for sittings.

In November, he travels to Bournemouth to paint the first of three portraits of writer Robert Louis Stevenson (location unknown).

1885 Sargent spends the first half of the year in Paris working on portraits.

During the summer, he paints alongside Claude Monet at Giverny before returning to England for the rest of the year. At Bournemouth, he paints a portrait of Robert Louis Stevenson and his wife [fig. 32].

While boating on the Thames with Abbey late that summer, Sargent hurts his head and is taken to the home of Francis Davis Millet (1846–1912) and his family at Farnham House in Broadway, Worcestershire, to recover. He witnesses the scene that inspires the painting *Carnation, Lily, Lily, Rose* [fig. 29]. Visitors at Broadway include many writers and painters: Edmund Gosse, Frederick Barnard (1846–1896), Alfred Parsons (1847–1920), Sir Lawrence Alma-Tadema (1836–1912), and Henry James.

1886 Sargent settles in England for the rest of his life. He takes a studio at Broadway in the countryside, but while in London he resides at Bailey's hotel and moves between several studios. He is elected a member of the selection committee for the Society of American Artists and accepts membership in the New English Art Club. After packing his Paris studio, he returns to London in early May.

He spends the summer at Russell House, Broadway, where he works on *Carnation, Lily, Lily, Rose*. During the summer he travels to Paris, Switzerland (where he visits with his family), southern England, and Bayreuth for the Wagner festival. Later in the year, he rents Whistler's former studio at 31 (later 33) Tite Street, London, where, in October, Ralph Curtis, Henry James, and Isabella Stewart Gardner see *Madame X*.

1887 In the spring, after painting a third portrait of Robert Louis Stevenson at Bournemouth (Taft Museum), he travels to Paris and Nice to visit his family. *Carnation, Lily, Lily, Rose* is shown to acclaim at the Royal Academy and is purchased for the British nation.

During the summer, he signs a three-year lease on his Tite Street studio, paints at Henley-on-Thames, and visits Monet at Giverny.

In the fall, Sargent sails to the United States for his first professional visit. He goes first to Newport, Rhode Island, to paint a commissioned portrait of Elizabeth Allen Marquand (Princeton University Art Museum). By late October, he has taken a studio on Washington Square in New York City, where he paints several portraits and architect Stanford White (1853–1906) hosts a dinner in his honor. Sargent

Sargent painting *Carnation, Lily, Lily, Rose* at Broadway, 1885–86. Harvard Art Museums/Fogg Museum, Cambridge, Mass., Gift of Mrs. Francis Ormond [1937.7.27.1.A].

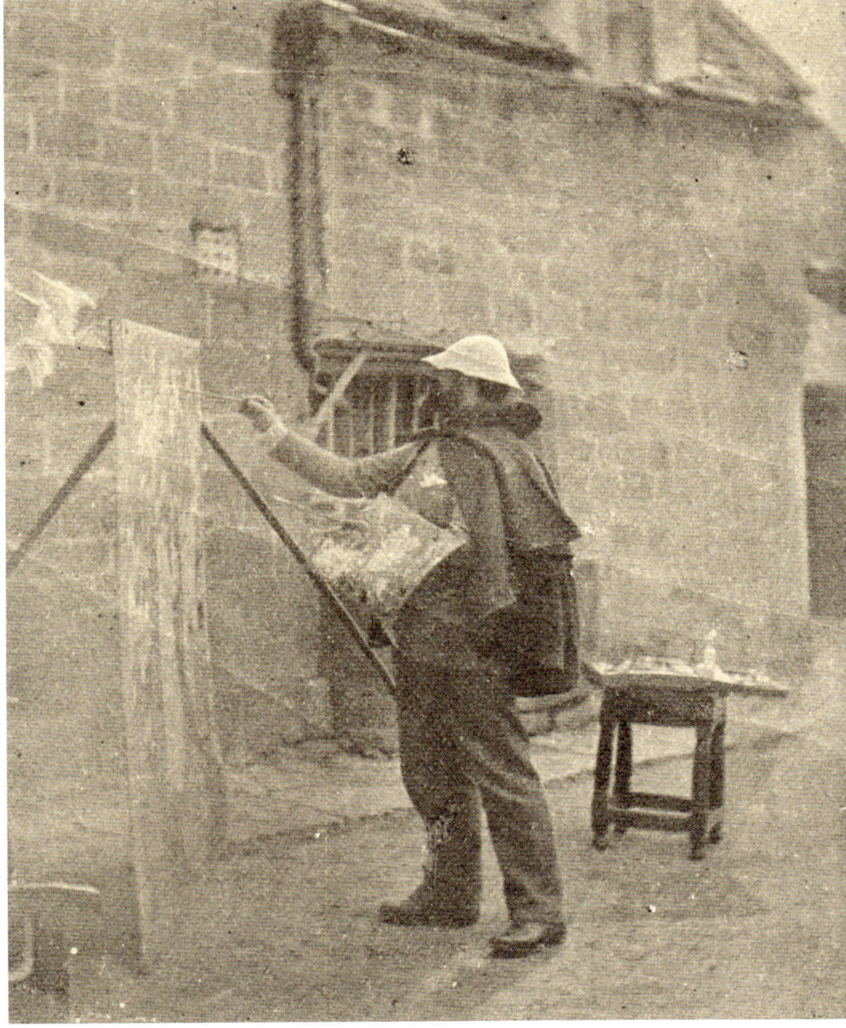

arrives in Boston in November and stays with the Edward Darley Boit family, his friends since Paris. He paints a portrait of Mrs. Boit (Museum of Fine Arts, Boston) and receives several additional commissions, including the portrait of Isabella Stewart Gardner [fig. 33].

1888 In January, Sargent's father has a stroke in Florence. His first solo exhibition opens on January 28 at the St. Botolph Club, Boston. He returns to New York, missing the opening and paints several portraits in a studio on Washington Square.
He arrives in London in May and spends the summer with his family at Calcot Mill, outside Reading on a branch of the Thames. Sargent paints river scenes and experiments in plein air painting and visits his friends at nearby Broadway.
Throughout the fall and winter, he works in London, where Claude Monet visits him. In late December, Sargent attends the opening night performance of *Macbeth* at the Lyceum Theater and is captivated by actor Ellen Terry as Lady Macbeth and determines to paint her portrait in costume.

1889 In January, Sargent begins the portrait *Ellen Terry as Lady Macbeth* [fig. 36]. He sends six paintings for display at the Exposition Universelle in Paris and wins a prize. He travels to Paris for the Exposition and makes a series of sketches and paintings of the Javanese dancers who were performing at the Dutch exhibition.
After his father dies on April 25, he spends the summer at Fladbury Rectory, Pershore (near Broadway), with his mother and sisters.
In December, he returns to the United States for his second professional visit, accompanied by his sister Violet.
During the year, he is made Chevalier of the Legion of Honor by France.

1890 In New York, Sargent uses Dora Wheeler Keith's (1856–1940) studio on Twenty-Third Street to paint several portraits, including Homer Saint-Gaudens [fig. 38], the son of friend Augustus Saint-Gaudens, the American sculptor. He attends a performance by the Spanish dancer La Carmencita at Koster and Bial, a dance hall on Thirty-Fourth Street. He hosts a party at the studio of William Merritt Chase (1849–1916) and invites Carmencita to perform for his friends (including Isabella Stewart Gardner). He convinces Carmencita to pose for him [fig. 37].
In May, Sargent meets with Charles Follen McKim (1847–1909), Stanford White, Edwin Austin Abbey, and Augustus Saint-Gaudens at the Players, a club in New York, to discuss a possible mural commission for the Boston Public Library, then under construction. Later in the month, he visits Boston to continue the conversation, and see the library. He accepts the assignment to paint murals for the Special Collections Hall.
He spends the summer in Worcester, Massachusetts, and travels along the coast of New England.
He returns to England in November but shortly thereafter sails for Egypt with his mother and sister.

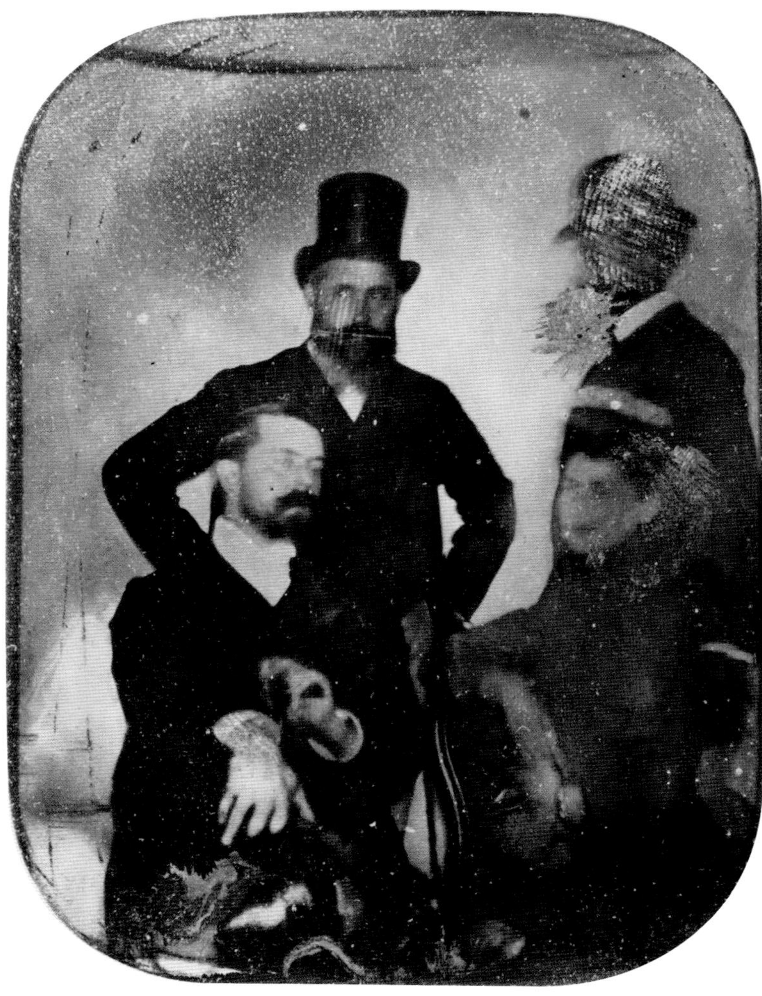

Claude Monet, during his wedding day with a top hat, Paul-César Helleu by his side, with Sargent and Ms. Helleu seated, Paris, 1892. Private collection.

1891 After spending several weeks in Cairo, he travels up the Nile on a steamer. From there, he explores sites around the Aegean: Olympia, Delphi, Epidaurus, and Constantinople [fig. 40].
He returns to Europe with his mother and sister early in the summer to attend his sister Violet's wedding in Paris. He vacations in the Alps with his mother and Emily at the end of the summer.
He returns to London in September but spends most of the winter working on his murals for the Boston Public Library at Morgan Hall, Fairford.
During the year, he is elected Associate of the National Academy of Design. He raises his portrait fees to: 200 guineas for a head, 400 guineas for a three-quarter-length portrait, and 500 for a full-length portrait.

1892 Between January and June, Sargent divides his time between London (working on portraits) and Fairford (working on murals). In May–June, he is painting Mrs. Hugh Hammersley [fig. 49] in London.
Late in the summer he visits Spain and Amsterdam.
In autumn, he has returned to Morgan Hall to work on his murals.
During the year, the French government purchases *La Carmencita* and hangs it in the Palais du Luxembourg.

1893 Sargent officially signs the contract for $15,000 to decorate the north and south ends of the Special Collections Hall of the Boston Public Library. He exhibits several paintings at the World's Columbian Exposition in Chicago and wins a medal.
In May, he has great success at the spring exhibitions in London, when he sends the portrait *Lady Agnew of Lochnaw* [fig. 48] to the Royal Academy and the portraits of Mrs. Hugh Hammersley and Mrs. George Lewis (private collection) to the New Gallery.
In the autumn, he returns to his mural work at his studio in the countryside.

1894 In January, Sargent is elected Associate of the Royal Academy.
In May, he exhibits sections of his library murals at the Royal Academy before sending them to the United States for installation.
During the late autumn and winter, he continues working on the murals at Morgan Hall. He paints the portrait of W. Graham Robertson [fig. 1], among others.

1895 In April, Sargent arrives in Boston to install the first section of the library murals. The murals are unveiled, and Sargent is invited to paint another sequence for $15,000. In May, he travels to Asheville, North Carolina, to paint portraits of Richard Morris Hunt (Biltmore) and Frederick Law Olmsted [fig. 55] at George Vanderbilt's mansion, Biltmore.
In June, he visits Emily and their mother in Gibraltar and then travels to Tangier and Madrid before returning to London.

Throughout the fall, he is occupied with portrait work in London. He gives up his share of the lease at Morgan Hall and signs a twenty-one-year lease on two studios on Fulham Road, London.
In October, he begins as Visitor at the Royal Academy Schools, London (a one-month stint almost every year until his death).
In December, he signs the second Boston Public Library contract.

1896 Sargent spends most of the year in London painting portraits, including *Mrs. Carl Meyer and Her Children* [fig. 50].

1897 In January and February, Sargent is in Italy conducting research for his library murals. He studies mosaic and mural decorations in Palermo, Rome, and Florence.
Important portraits painted in 1897 include *Mr. and Mrs. I. N. Phelps Stokes* [fig. 56] and *Asher Wertheimer* [fig. 53] (the first of a series of twelve portraits of members of the family). He continues to work on his library murals at his London studio.
During the year, he is elected to full membership at the British Royal Academy, made an Officer of the French Legion of Honor, and is elected to the National Academy of Design in the United States.

1898 He spends the beginning of the year occupied with portraits and mural work in London.
In May, he visits Venice, staying at the Palazzo Barbaro where he begins painting *An Interior in Venice* [fig. 67].
He travels on to Ravenna, Bologna, Milan, and Bergamo for mural research. He increases his fee to 1,000 guineas for a full-length portrait. Throughout the fall, he continues his mural work.

1899 In February, Sargent begins painting *The Wyndham Sisters: Lady Elcho, Mrs. Adeane, and Mrs. Tennant* [fig. 51] at the family's home in London.
A large, comprehensive exhibition of his works opens at Copley Hall, Boston (February 20–March 13). When Sargent's death is mistakenly reported in British and American newspapers, he sends a telegram to Isabella Stewart Gardner in Boston: "Alive and Kicking, Sargent." After Mrs. Daniel Curtis refuses *An Interior in Venice* as a gift, Sargent submits it to the Royal Academy as his official diploma picture.

1900 In February, Sargent hosts Claude Monet in London. In late April, he sees Monet in Paris, where he also visits with Giovanni Boldini (1842–1931) and Augustus Saint-Gaudens.
He sends six paintings to the annual exhibition of the Royal Academy in London (including *An Interior in Venice*) and three paintings to the Exposition Universelle in Paris, where he receives a medal of honor. Sargent leases the house adjacent to his Tite Street studio and embarks on a large renovation to join the two buildings. During the construction, he travels in Switzerland and Italy, stopping in Genoa, Milan, Bologna, and Florence.

1901 After visiting Fairford, Gloucestershire, Sargent returns to London and receives a visit from Monet.
During the spring, he paints the portrait of Ena and Betty Wertheimer [fig. 54] and refuses a commission to paint the coronation of Edward VII. (His friend Edwin Austin Abbey paints it instead.)
Late in the summer, he travels to Norway with George McCulloch and his family and paints *On His Holidays* [fig. 68], an outdoor portrait of his host's son.
He spends October and November traveling through southern Italy, including Sicily.

1902 After fulfilling several portrait commissions during the first half of the year, he vacations in Saas Fee, Switzerland, with Peter Harrison, Polly Barnard, and Alma Strettell. He passes through the Italian lakes en route to Venice, where he arrives in mid-September. He stays at the Palazzo Barbaro until sometime in October. From there, he heads south to Naples and Rome.
During the year, Auguste Rodin calls Sargent "Le Van Dyke [*sic*] de l'époque."

1903 Sargent arrives in New York in mid-January and travels to Boston to install the decorations at the south end of the Special Collections Hall of the Boston Public Library. In February, he goes to Washington to paint a three-quarter-length portrait of President Theodore Roosevelt and stays at the White House. Back in Boston, he is the guest of Isabella Stewart Gardner at Fenway Court, her recently completed Italian Renaissance–style palazzo. He sets up a temporary studio in the Gothic Room, where he paints the double portrait of Mrs. Fiske Warren and her daughter, Rachel [fig. 57].
In May, he receives an Honorary Degree from the University of Pennsylvania and his first solo exhibition in London opens at the

Carfax Gallery: "Loan Exhibition of Sketches and Studies by J. S. Sargent, R.A."
During the summer, he travels through Spain and Portugal, visiting Madrid (at the Prado, he signs the Libro de Copistas on June 12), Santiago de Compostela, La Coruña, Toledo, Ávila, Aranjuez, and possibly León.
During September and October, he's painting in Venice. In November, he returns to London where he works on portraits throughout the winter.

1904 In June, he receives an honorary degree from Oxford University. During the summer, he exhibits for the first time with the Royal Society of Painters in Water-Colours (now the Royal Watercolour Society) and is elected an associate member.
In August, he takes his summer painting holiday at Purtud, Val d'Aosta, Italy, with artists Alberto Falchetti (1878–1951), Ambrogio Raffele (1845–1928), and Carlo Pollonera (1849–1923). He also visits Switzerland before heading to Venice where he stays at the Palazzo Barbaro until late October. He paints a watercolor of his friends Jane (1873–1961) and Wilfrid (1870–1951) de Glehn who are visiting Venice on their honeymoon [fig. 76]. He returns to London for the winter.

1905 He begins to complain more frequently about painting portraits on commission. In May, he is elected to the American Academy of Arts and Letters in New York. The Museum of Fine Arts, Boston, buys *An Artist in His Studio* [fig. 3] for $1,000. It is his first nonportrait work to be purchased by an American museum.
He returns to Purtud and the Val d'Aosta for his holiday with Peter Harrison, Dorothy Palmer, Violet, Reine (Violet's daughter), and Rose-Marie Ormond. He paints *Group with Parasols* [fig. 77] and *Group* [fig. 78]. At nearby Giomein, he paints *Padre Sebastiano* [fig. 80].
In October, he departs for Syria and Palestine to conduct mural research. He visits Baalbek in Lebanon, Lake Tiberias, and the Jordan Valley, and travels into the desert to see a Bedouin tribe. He paints more than forty watercolors [figs. 69 and 70].

1906 On January 21, Sargent's mother dies in London. He receives the news via telegram in Jordan the following day. He arrives back in London on February 2 and attends her memorial service at St. Paul's Westminster on February 5.
He spends August and September in Purtud and then travels with Emily to Turin, Bologna, and Venice, where he stays at the Palazzo Barbaro.
In October, he meets his friend Mrs. Charles Hunter in Rome. Sargent paints a series of watercolors and oils at several villas around Rome: Torlonia, Falconieri, and Lante.
In mid-November, he returns to London via Milan, Lyon, and Paris. By the end of the year, Sargent is declining most portrait commissions.

1907 Sargent declares he will no longer paint portraits on commission. King Edward VII recommends Sargent and Edwin Austin Abbey for knighthood; they both decline rather than relinquish their American citizenship.
Sargent returns to Purtud with Violet and her family, Emily, Jane and Wilfrid de Glehn, Polly Barnard, Ambrogio Raffele, and others in August for his annual holiday. He paints a series of images, including *The Brook* [fig. 82], depicting his nieces in exotic clothing that he brought with him from London.
In September, he's at the Palazzo Barbaro, in Venice, with Emily and Eliza Wedgwood. They travel to Perugia, Narni, and through Frascati. Throughout September and October, he is painting at Tivoli, Villa Falconieri, Villa d'Este, and Villa Torlonia.

1908 In June, Sargent has a solo exhibition at Carfax Gallery in London; it includes forty-eight watercolors and two oils. He visits Majorca for six weeks and returns to London.
He spends August in the Val d'Aosta with Ambrogio Raffele. He probably paints *Cashmere* [fig. 83] during this summer.
He returns to Majorca with Emily and Eliza Wedgwood for September and October.
He is elected a full member of the Royal Watercolour Society.

1909 Sargent shows eighty-six watercolors at Knoedler Gallery in New York in the exhibition "Water Color Drawings by John Singer Sargent and Edward Darley Boit." The Brooklyn Museum agrees to purchase eighty-three of the watercolors for $20,000. Sargent is in London working on the vaults and lunettes for the Boston Public Library and does not attend the show.
In August, Sargent again returns to the Val d'Aosta and the Simplon Pass, Switzerland, with Emily, Dorothy Palmer, Polly Barnard, and the Harrison brothers (Peter and Ginx).
In September, he travels to Venice with Emily, the de Glehns, and Eliza Wedgwood. He stays at the Hotel Luna and the Palazzo Barbaro. From there, they travel to Corfu until November.
During the year, he is awarded the Order of Merit from France and the Order of Leopold from Belgium.

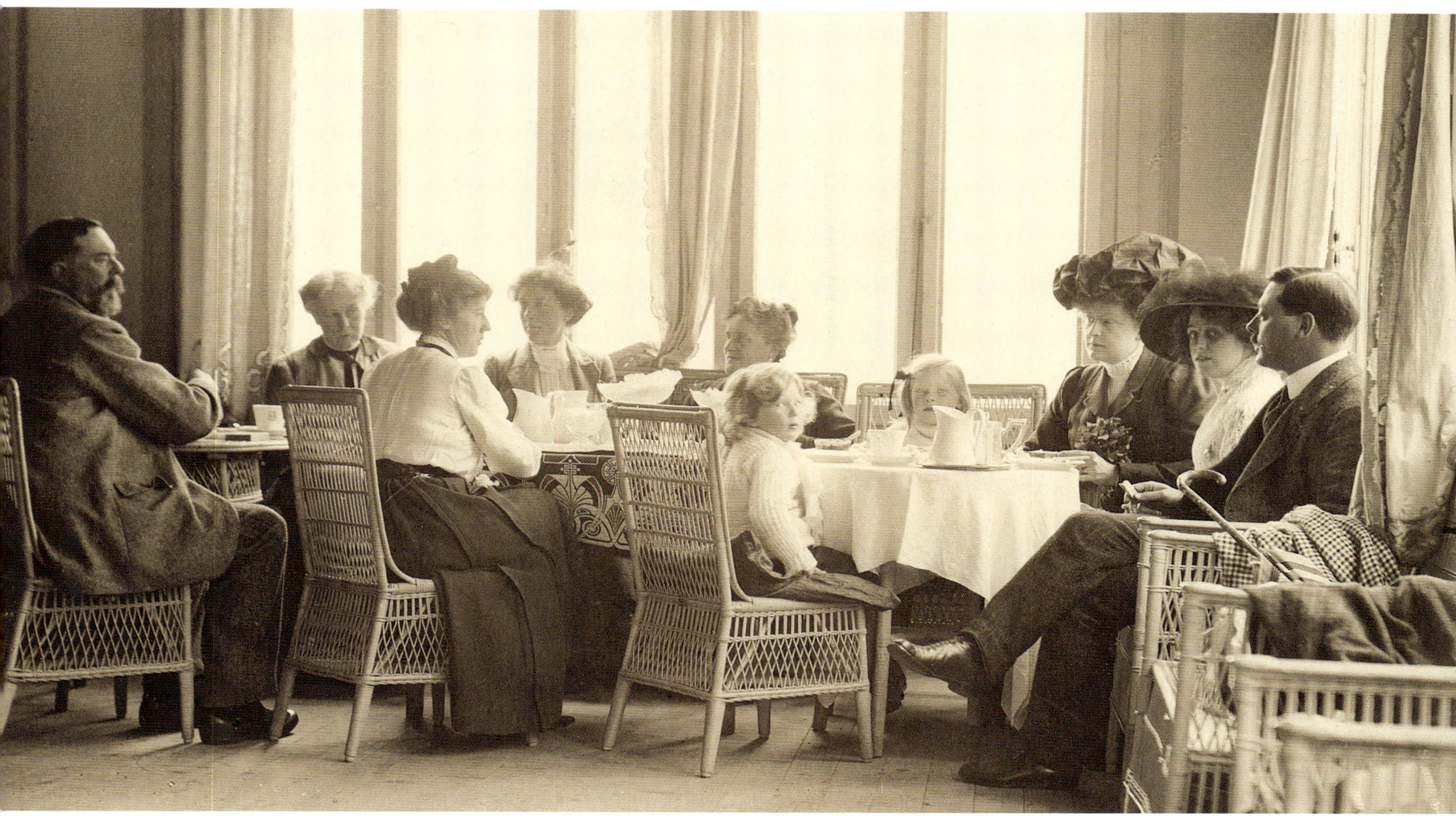

Sargent and friends, Hotel Bellevue, Simplon Pass, Switzerland, September, 1909. (From left: Sargent, Alice Barnard, Dorothy Barnard, Polly Barnard, Emily Sargent, Tommasini daughters, Gladys Tommasini, unknown, and Hugo Tommasini.) Museum of Fine Arts, Boston. The John Singer Sargent Archive–Gift of Richard and Leonée Ormond.

1910 In February, Sargent travels to Holland to recover from the flu.

He spends his summer holiday near the Simplon Pass with several friends including painter Ambrogio Raffele.

In September, he travels to Siena, Bologna, and Florence with painter Henry Tonks (1862–1937).

He spends October at the Villa Torre Galli, near Florence, with Emily, the artist Sir William Blake Richmond (1842–1921) and his wife, and paints a series of images of the villa, its loggia, and the gardens [fig. 87]. He visits Varramista and Lucca and paints in the gardens of the nearby villas Collodi and the Reale (Marlia) [fig. 88].

Back in London, he is working on the lunettes for the Boston Public Library, including *Hell* [fig. 42]. He increasingly begins offering patrons charcoal portrait sketches (as a substitute for oils).

1911 The Metropolitan Museum of Art purchases *Padre Sebastiano* [fig. 80] and *The Hermit* [fig. 81] directly from Sargent.

In the spring, he travels to Paris and Munich.

In July, Sargent returns to London to help Edwin Austin Abbey, who is near death, complete his murals for the rotunda of the state capitol of Harrisburg, Pennsylvania.

Sargent travels to the Tyrol and Simplon Pass with Charles Gere (1869–1957), Emily, the Barnards, and the Ormonds. Visitors include Ginx Harrison, and Adrian and Marianne Stokes, among others. Abbey dies in August, and Sargent helps plan his memorial exhibition at the Royal Academy.

He spends September at the Palazzo Barbaro in Venice and October sketching and painting at the marble quarries of Carrara [figs. 91 and 92].

1912 The exhibition "Water Colors by John S. Sargent and Edward D. Boit" is held at Knoedler, New York, March 16–30. The Museum of Fine Arts, Boston, buys Sargent's forty-five watercolors from that exhibition. Friends of Henry James commission Sargent to paint a portrait of the writer for his seventieth birthday.

Sargent spends his summer holiday in the French Alps with his sister Violet and the Ormond family.

From September to November, Sargent is in Spain with Emily and the de Glehns. He visits Granada (and paints at the Alhambra) [figs. 96–98] and Seville.

1913 Throughout May and June, Henry James sits for his portrait [fig. 62].

After attending the wedding of his niece Rose-Marie Ormond in Paris in August, Sargent travels to Venice (his last visit to the Palazzo Barbaro), the Dolomites, and San Vigilio on Lake Garda.

During the year, receives an honorary degree from Cambridge University.

1914 The Trustees of the Boston Public Library inquire about the status of Sargent's murals. He tells them that "the time specified was inadequate." Sargent is enjoying his annual summer holiday in the Tyrol with Nicola d'Inverno and several friends when Britain and France declare war on Germany on August 4 (and on August 10, when Britain and France declare war on Austria). Sargent is detained in Austria, unable to obtain the travel documents necessary to return to England. He continues to paint while he waits [figs. 99 and 100]. He receives the sad news that Robert André-Michel, the husband of his beloved niece Rose-Marie Ormond, has died at the western front.

In November, Sargent travels to Vienna and obtains a passport from the American embassy. He is back in London by the end of the month.

During the year, Sargent serves on the Selection Committee of the Royal Academy, is awarded a gold medal by the National Institute of Arts and Letters, New York, and is appointed chairman of the London Committee of the Panama-Pacific International Exposition in San Francisco.

1915 For an auction to benefit the British Red Cross, Sargent agrees to execute two charcoal portraits, which sell for 500 guineas and 650 guineas. Around this time Sir Hugh Lane agrees to donate £10,000 to the Red Cross in exchange for a portrait by Sargent. Sargent agrees. (Lane dies on the *RMS Lusitania* on May 7; his money goes to the Red Cross: they eventually decide that Sargent should paint President Woodrow Wilson instead.)

Sargent sends thirteen paintings, including *Madame X*, to the Panama–Pacific International Exhibition in San Francisco. Late in the year, Sargent sells *Tyrolese Interior* and ten watercolors to The Metropolitan Museum of Art.

1916 The Metropolitan Museum of Art buys *Madame X*. The library murals are rolled and packed for shipment to Boston. Sargent arrives in New York on April 4 and immediately heads to Boston. He stays at the Hotel Vendôme and rents a studio on Newbury Street before moving to the Pope Building at 221 Columbus Street.

Sargent receives honorary degrees from Yale and Harvard.

In July, he travels west to the Rockies and visits Glacier National Park in Montana with Nicola d'Inverno. They head north to British Columbia before returning to Boston in October. He paints a series of watercolors and oils, which he exhibits that fall at the Copley Society.

He completes the installation of a third section of the Boston Public Library murals in November and accepts a commission to decorate the rotunda of the Museum of Fine Arts, Boston.

1917 In February, Sargent travels to Ormond Beach, Florida, to paint a portrait of John D. Rockefeller Sr. (private collection). He visits his longtime friend Charles Deering at Brickell Point, Miami. He paints a number of watercolors at Villa Vizcaya, the unfinished estate belonging to Deering's brother, James [figs. 101–4].

America enters the war on April 6, and Sargent cannot leave the United States.

He spends most of the summer in Boston working on the murals. In June, he paints a second portrait of John D. Rockefeller Sr. at the Rockefeller estate at Pocantico Hills in Tarrytown, New York.

In October, he paints President Woodrow Wilson's portrait for the Red Cross in Washington, D.C.

1918 On March 29, Sargent's twenty-four-year-old niece, Rose-Marie, is killed in the German bombardment of the Church of St. Gervais, Paris.

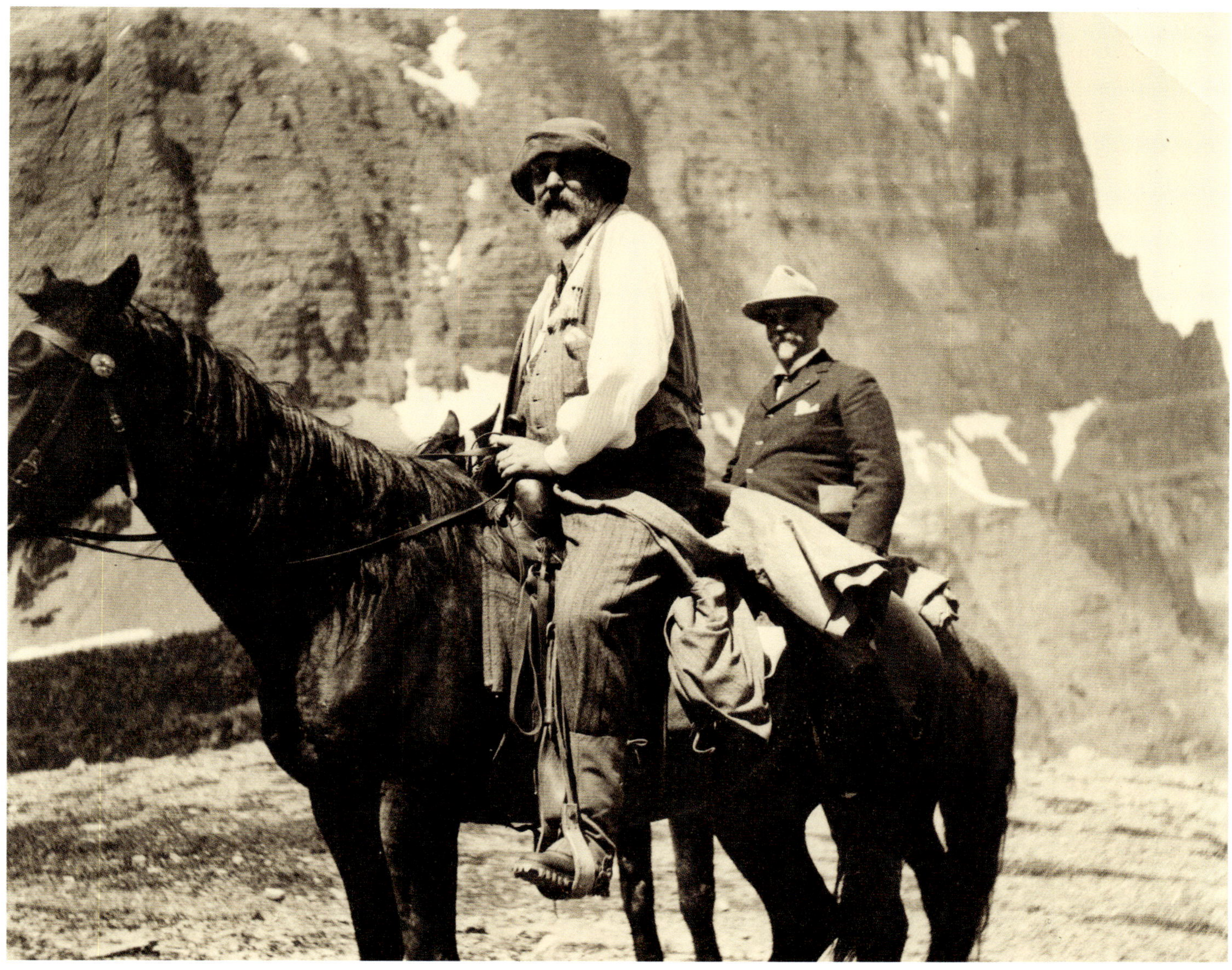

Sargent and Colonel Leonard Livermore, Glacier Park, Montana, 1916. Museum of Fine Arts, Boston. The John Singer Sargent Archive–Gift of Richard and Leonée Ormond.

Before sailing for London in May, he writes his will.

In June, he accepts a commission as an official war artist. His assigned theme is "British and American troops working together."

On July 2, he departs for the French front with Henry Tonks. Sargent is in France from July to October under the supervision of Major Philip Sassoon (secretary to Douglas Haig, the commander-in-chief of the British armies in France). He is at Berles-au-Bois, Ypres (with an American division), Peronne, Roisel, and Arras.

In September, he sees a group of soldiers waiting for treatment after being blinded by mustard gas and makes that the subject of his commission.

He is back at the Tite Street studio, London, in October.

In December, Sargent refuses to be nominated as president of the Royal Academy.

1919 Sargent accepts a commission to paint a group portrait of war officers. He completes his monumental composition *Gassed* [fig. 63] and delivers it to the Imperial War Commission. *Gassed* is shown at the Royal Academy and voted picture of the year.
He returns to Boston with Emily and Reine and installs the final panels for the Boston Public Library program: *The Synagogue* and *The Church*. He continues to work on the decorations for the rotunda of the Museum of Fine Arts.

1920 In June, he installs the decorations in the Museum of Fine Arts rotunda. After spending fourteen months in the United States, he returns to his Tite Street studio.
In September, he begins painting *Some General Officers of the Great War* (National Portrait Gallery, London).

1921 He returns to Boston, via New York, to continue his work on the rotunda of the Museum of Fine Arts.
During the summer, he visits Montreal and Schooner Head, Maine.
In October, he completes and installs the murals and bas-reliefs for the rotunda of the Museum of Fine Arts and agrees to continue the program above the staircase [fig. 44].
After returning to England, he accepts a commission to paint a pair of mural panels for the Harry Elkins Widener Memorial Library at Harvard University, commemorating alumni who died in the war.
Sargent accepts chairmanship of the British School in Rome.

1922 He returns to Boston in March and spends the summer working on the panels for Widener Memorial Library at Harvard University. They are completed and installed in October.
He escapes the summer heat in Boston with a visit to Monadnock, New Hampshire, and returns to London for Christmas

1923 In January, nine of the Wertheimer portraits are installed in the National Gallery, London. Sargent continues to work on the Museum of Fine Arts staircase panels at his Fulham Road studio in London.
On July 16, Sargent delivers a speech at the Royal Academy in honor of the bicentennial of Sir Joshua Reynolds's birth. In October, he sails for Boston with Emily.

1924 He declines to paint President Calvin Coolidge's portrait.
On February 23, a retrospective exhibition opens at Grand Central Art Galleries in New York. The show includes sixty oils and twelve watercolors. Sargent assists in the planning but does not attend.
He sails for England on July 14. Three days later Isabella Stewart Gardner dies. Her will names Sargent as a pallbearer for her funeral, but he is unable to attend.

1925 Sargent finishes painting the final panels for the Museum of Fine Arts, Boston, in his London studio.
On April 14, four days before he is set to sail to the United States, his sister Emily hosts a farewell party for him and some guests. Following the party, Sargent returns home to Tite Street and falls asleep while reading Voltaire's *Dictionnaire philosophique* and dies of a heart attack. He is interred at Brookwood Cemetery on April 18 in a private ceremony, and a memorial service follows at Westminster Abbey on April 23.

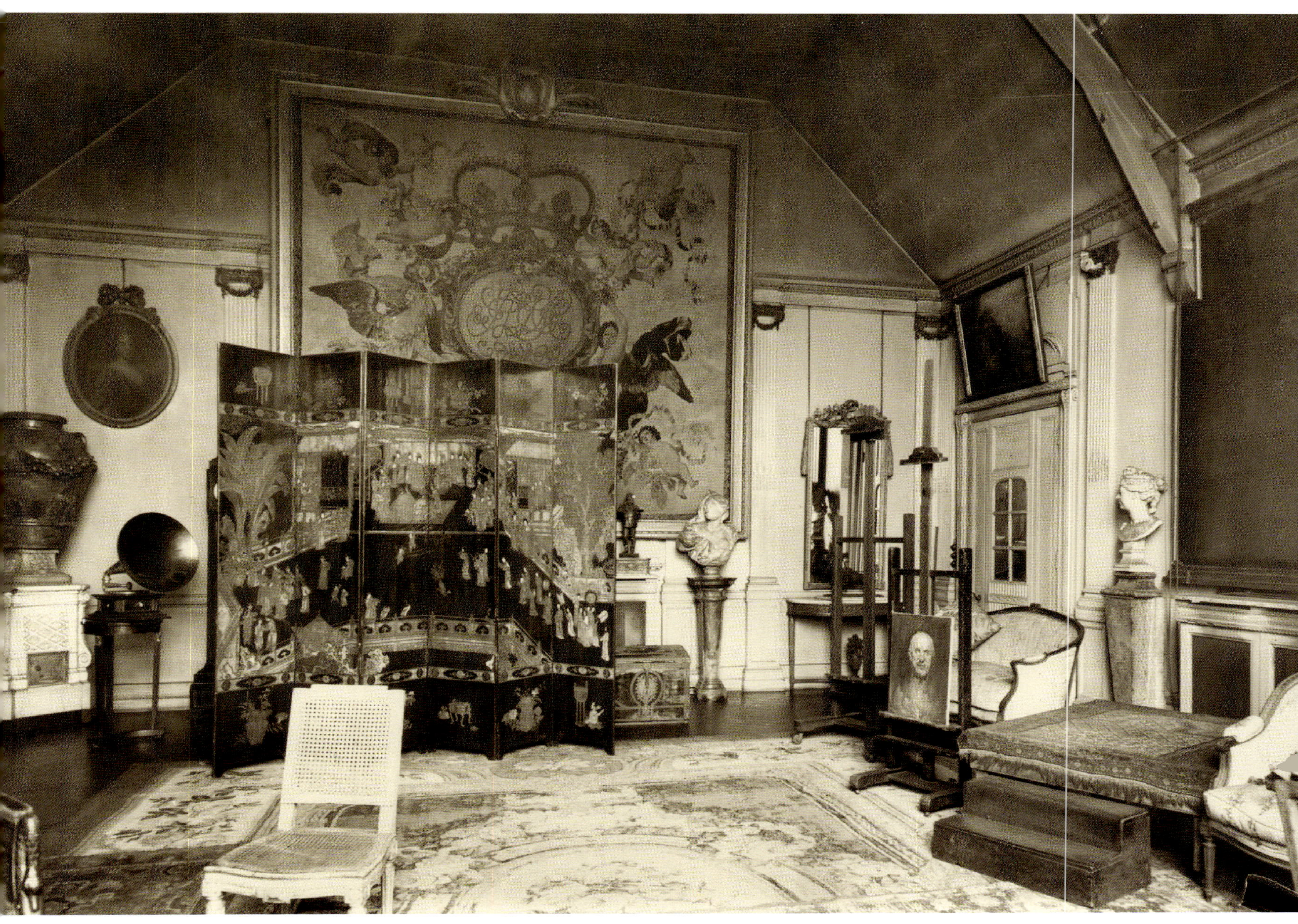

Sargent's studio at 31 Tite Street, London, ca. 1920. Museum of Fine Arts, Boston.
The John Singer Sargent Archive–Gift of Richard and Leonée Ormond

Photography credits

© Art Collection 2 / Alamy Stock Photo / Age Fotostock, Madrid: fig. 27
© Art Collection 3 / Alamy Stock Photo / Age Fotostock, Madrid: fig. 99
Barcelona, Album / Universal Images Group / Universal History Archive: fig. 34
Barcelona, Album / akg-images: fig. 74
Bakewell, © Devonshire Collection, Chatsworth / Reproduced by permission of Chatsworth Settlement Trustees / Bridgeman Images, London: fig. 52
Bentonville, Arkansas, Crystal Bridges Museum of American Art, photography by Dwight Primiano: fig. 32
Boston, Massachusetts, Isabella Stewart Gardner Museum / Bridgeman Images, London: p. 94; figs. 16, 26, 33
Boston, Massachusetts, Boston Public Library, photography by Sheryl Lancel: figs. 41, 42
Boston, Massachusetts, photographs © 2017 Museum of Fine Arts, Boston: pp. 17, 26, 28, 29, 32, 36, 82, 89, 93, 142, 149, 157, 158, 208, 210, 217, 219, 221; figs. 3, 6, 11, 21, 43, 44, 47, 57, 79, 88, 89, 92
Cambridge, Massachusetts, Photo: Imaging Department © President and Fellows of Harvard College: p. 213; figs. 24, 45
Chicago, Illinois, © 2017. The Art Institute of Chicago / Art Resource, NY / Scala, Florence: figs. 85, 105
Courtesy private collections: figs. 13, 59, 76–77, 82, 83, 86, 87
Courtesy John and Susan Klein: fig. 78
Des Moines, Iowa, photography by Rich Sanders: fig. 10
Edinburgh, National Galleries of Scotland: fig. 48
Philadelphia, Pennsylvania, © 2017. Photograph The Philadelphia Museum of Art / Art Resource, NY / Scala, Florence: fig. 12
© Fine Art Images / Age Fotostock, Madrid: fig. 71
Florence, © 2017. Photo Scala – courtesy of the Ministero Beni e Att. Culturali e del Turismo: fig. 2
Kansas City, Missouri, The Nelson-Atkins Museum of Art, photography by Jamison Miller: fig. 95
© Les Amis de Paul-César Helleu: p. 214
Lisbon, © 2017. Museu Calouste Gulbenkian / Scala, Florence: fig. 30
Liverpool, © National Museums: fig. 68
London, Private collection / Bridgeman Images: fig. 61
London, © Crown Copyright Imperial War Museum: figs. 63–65
London, © 2017. National Portrait Gallery / Scala, Florence: fig. 62
London, Royal Academy of Arts: fig. 67
London, © 2017. Tate / Photo Scala, Florence: figs. 1, 22, 28, 29, 36, 50, 53, 54
Los Angeles, California, Hammer Museum: fig. 19
Louisville, Kentucky, Speed Art Museum: fig. 40
Minneapolis, Minnesota, Minneapolis Institute of Arts / The Ethel Morrison Van Derlip Fund and the John R. Van Derlip Fund / Bridgeman Images, London: fig. 31
New York, Brooklyn Museum: figs. 35, 69, 70, 72, 90, 93, 94
New York, Courtesy The Metropolitan Museum of Art: figs. 14, 39, 46, 49, 51, 56, 66, 73, 80, 81, 91, 96–98, 100, 103
New York, © 2017 Image copyright The Metropolitan Museum of Art / Art Resource, NY / Scala, Florence: figs. 20, 25
New York, © 2017. Photo The Morgan Library & Museum / Art Resource, NY / Scala, Florence: fig. 23
Oxfordshire, Blenheim Palace / Bridgeman Images, London: fig. 58
Paris, © Petit Palais / Roger Viollet: fig. 75
Paris, Photo © RMN-Grand Palais (musée d'Orsay) / Gérard Blot: fig. 37
Paris, Photo © RMN-Grand Palais (musée d'Orsay) / Hervé Lewandowski: fig. 8
Pittsburgh, Pennsylvania, Carnegie Museum of Art: fig. 38
Private collection, Photo © Christie's Images / Bridgeman Images, London: fig. 60
© The Archives / Age Fotostock, Madrid: fig. 55
Washington, D.C., Archives of American Art, Smithsonian Institution: pp. 10–11, 39, 87
Washington, D.C., Courtesy National Gallery: figs. 4, 9, 84
Williamstown, Massachusetts, Sterling and Francine Clark Art Institute / Bridgeman Images, London: figs. 5, 7, 15, 17, 18
Worcester, Massachusetts, Image © Worcester Art Museum: figs. 101, 102, 104

The author would like to thank Richard Ormond, Elaine Kilmurray, Elizabeth Oustinoff, and Warren Adelson of the John Singer Sargent Catalogue Raisonné Project for their assistance.

Jacket front: *Carnation, Lily, Lily, Rose*, 1885–86. London, Tate (detail of fig. 29)

Jacket back: *Lady Agnew of Lochnau*, 1892. Edinburgh, National Galleries of Scotland

Page 2: *Dr. Pozzi*, 1881. Los Angeles, Hammer Museum (detail of fig. 19)

Page 3: *Madame x* (*Madame Pierre Gautreau*), 1883–84. New York, The Metropolitan Museum of Art (detail of fig. 25)

Page 4: *The Daughters of Edward Darley Boit*, 1882. Boston, Museum of Fine Arts (detail of fig. 21)

Page 5: *Cashmere*, ca. 1908. Private collection (detail of fig. 83)

Page 6: *The Brook*, 1907. Private collection (detail of fig. 82)

Page 7: *Gourds*, 1908. New York, Brooklyn Museum (detail of fig. 94)

Page 8: *Self-Portrait*, 1906. Florence, Galleria degli Uffizi (detail of fig. 2)

Edited by
Rizzoli Electa

Produced by
Ediciones El Viso

Coordination
Santiago Saavedra
Gonzalo Saavedra
Lucía Varela

Design
Subiela Bernat

Typesetting
Nicolás García Marque

Prepress
Emilio Breton

Printing and binding
Printer Trento S.r.l., Trento

For Rizzoli Electa
Charles Miers, Publisher
Margaret Rennolds Chace, Associate Publisher
Giulia Di Filippo, Editor

The authorized representative in the EU for product safety and compliance is Mondadori Libri S.p.A., via Gian Battista Vico 42, Milan, Italy, 20123, www.mondadori.it

Library of Congress Control Number: 2017964411

ISBN: 978-0-8478-6239-9

First published in the United States of America in 2018 by

Rizzoli Electa, a Division of
Rizzoli International Publications, Inc.
49 West 27th Street
New York, NY 10001
www.rizzoliusa.com

Tenth printing, 2026
2026 2027 2028 / 12 11 10

Printed in Italy

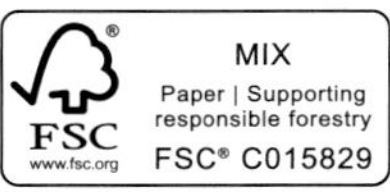

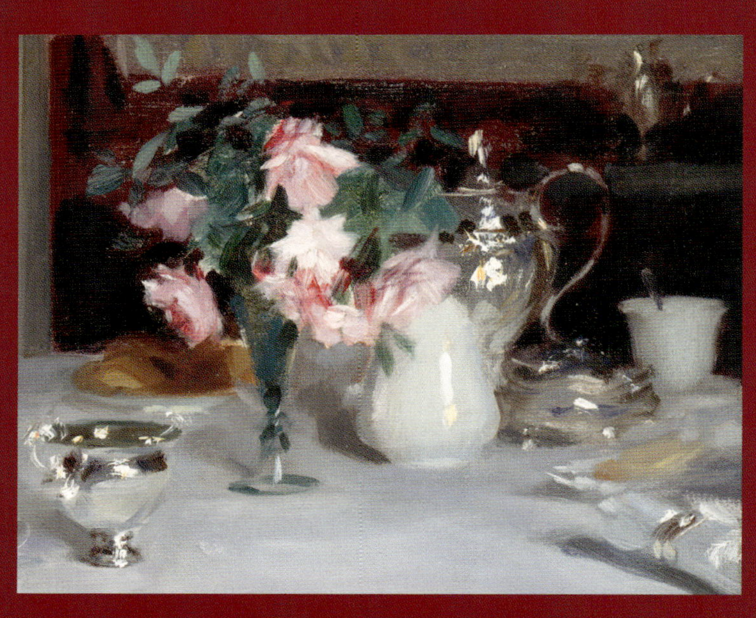